THE GREAT WAR
And the Shaping of the 20th Century

THE GREAT WAR
And the Shaping of the 20th Century

Jay Winter and Blaine Baggett

PENGUIN STUDIO

To the next generation:
Austin, Jonathan and Anna

PENGUIN STUDIO

Published by the Penguin Group

Penguin Books USA Inc., 375 Hudson Street,
New York, New York, 10014, USA

Penguin Books Ltd, 27 Wrights Lane,
London W8 5TZ, England

Penguin Books Australia Ltd, Ringwood,
Victoria, Australia

Penguin Books Canada Ltd, 10 Alcorn Avenue,
Suite 300, Toronto M4V 3B2, Canada

Penguin Books (N.Z.) Ltd, 182–90 Wairau Road,
Auckland 10, New Zealand

Penguin Books Ltd, Registered Offices:
Harmondsworth, Middlesex, England

First published by Penguin Studio, an imprint of Penguin Books USA Inc.

First printing, September 1996
10 9 8 7 6 5 4 3 2 1

Library of Congress Catalog Card Number 96–67571 96 - 67511
Printed in England

ISBN 0-670-87119-2

Contents

ACKNOWLEDGEMENTS

In some ways, we have been the most unlikely of pairings. One of us is a Cambridge historian who has devoted his academic career to the study of World War I; the other is a television documentary maker, who has turned his hand to many subjects. One of us studies what contemporaries of the time called the Great War because it is as close to the great horror of the twentieth century – the Holocaust – as he can bear to stand. The other shares his late father's sense of fascination for a war that, had he been just a year older, he would have known first-hand. For the father, the war was World War II; for the son, Vietnam. Our collaboration on the book and television series that accompanies it has been immensely satisfying, both professionally and personally. We have served alternately as tutor and student to each other. The results, we hope, are far better for our combined efforts.

The telling here of our personal journey to this project seems less important, however, than devoting this space to the odyssey required to present it in book and television form. The notion of a television series began in Los Angeles in 1990 with a casual reading (by the television producer) of Paul Fussell's acclaimed treatise on the literature of World War I, *The Great War and Modern Memory*. It was immediately apparent that here was fertile ground. Yet while the subject matter was rich, it was also immense, and translating it into television form would be an ambitious and expensive undertaking. In the United States, there is virtually only one place where critical 'first money' can be raised for major historical projects for television: the now besieged National Endowment for the Humanities. Theirs is a rigorous process, which requires the matching of academic and media expertise. It is a marriage that requires patience for both professions, but the end result can represent the best of both worlds. After three submissions over the course of two years, 'the Great War project' was awarded a substantial grant, which became a magnet for other funding: the Public Broadcasting Service (PBS), the Corporation for Public Broadcasting (CPB), the British Broadcasting Corporation (BBC) and the Arthur Vining Davis Foundations. The United States – and the world, for *The Great War* is an international project, intended for a wide public in many countries – will be far poorer in days to come if there is no longer an institution like the National Endowment for the Humanities. We especially wish to thank the Endowment's program officers, Holly Tank and Jim Dougherty. We would also like to express our appreciation for the support of Kathy Quattrone and Sandy Heberer of PBS; Don Marbury and Josh Darsa of CPB; and Dr Max King Morris and Dr Jonathan Howe of the Arthur Vining Davis Foundations.

Hugh Purcell, a consultant for the BBC, was an early advocate of the project, as was Alan Rogers. We appreciate the ongoing support of the BBC's Michael Jackson, Glenwyn Benson and, especially, Candace Carlisle, whom we often relied upon for help and advice. At BBC Books, Suzanne Webber, Martha Caute and Esther Jagger have guided the book to fruition with kindness and skill. The talents of Tim Higgins and Anne-Marie Ehrlich are evident in, respectively, the design of this book and its picture research.

The visualization of the book and the television series has come from many archives around the world. Malcolm Brown added his authoritative voice. But we owe by far our greatest thanks to the Imperial War Museum in London. Among their staff, Roger Smither, Jane Carmichael and the Museum Historian, Peter Simkins, have gone beyond the call of duty to help see this project through.

A project of this size and duration also required unflagging television production support. Bill Kobin at KCET/Los Angeles was the first to recognize its possibility. Phylis Geller and Stephen Kulczycki ably nurtured it. Jeanne Paynter and Catherine Kelly helped find funding for it.

Special thanks, of course, go to the production staff: for KCET, series producer Carl Byker; producers, writers, and directors Joseph Angier, Cynthia Crompton, Lyn Goldfarb, Margaret Koval, Isaac Mizrahi, David Mrazek and Mitch Wilson; production manager Bettina Bennewitz; associate producers Adrienne Cooksey, Theresa Fitzgerald, Alexandria Levitt-Muzquiz and Michele Morgan; editors Jim Beebe, Joe Bergen, Doug Cheek and Stosh Jarecki; graphics designer Linda Emme; location manager Jack Combs; and researchers and production assistants Laura Cinco, David Orenstein and Michael O'Toole. For legal advice, we were in the good hands of Glenn Schoeder and Linda MacCauley Mack.

For our co-producers at BBC Television, special thanks go to series producer Carol Sennett, executive producer Laurence Rees, producer Stephen Haggard, researcher and production assistant Harriet Rowe, and editor Paul Dawe.

Indispensable guidance was provided by historical advisers who gave essential help in developing the initial idea. Ron Schaffer provided strong support from the beginning. In a series of meetings in Los Angeles, the outline of the series began to take shape. Arthur Barbeau, John Bushnell, David Kennedy, Norman Saul, Peter Simkins, Louise Tilly and Robert Wohl were there at the start. Arthur Link was a warm supporter at several important moments. Over time they were joined by a number of other distinguished scholars who both commented on the screen and joined in informal discussions. Among them were Diane Atkinson, Stéphane Audoin-Rouzeau, Pat Barker, Volker Berghahn, Laura Lee Downs, Niall Ferguson, Orlando Figes, Paul Fussell, José Harris, Nicholas Hiley, Gerhard Hirschfeld, Sir Michael Howard, Bernd Huppauf, John Keegan, David Kennedy, Robert Massie, Wolfgang Mommsen, Sarah O'Brien-Twohig, Avner Offer, Norman Stone, John Terraine, Deborah Thom, A. Mete Tuncoku, Trevor Wilson and Robert Wohl. Ken Inglis, Robin Prior, Emmanuel Sivan, Diana Goodrich, Joanna Bourke, Ira Katznelson, Adrian Gregory and Volker Berghahn were kind enough to put aside their own work and comment on parts of the book. They saved us from many errors; those that remain are the authors'.

It is a pleasure to thank the many people who gave when asked and helped establish a kind of collegiality in this project which is all too rare in the academic world. If readers of this book take away some idea of the merits and pleasures of collective work, then we will have achieved one of our aims.

JAY WINTER   BLAINE BAGGETT
Cambridge, England   Los Angeles, USA

INTRODUCTION

The Shadow of the War

A few miles north of the medieval city of Ypres in Belgium is a German war cemetery. It lies in a field near the small town of Vladslo. In the cemetery are the graves of hundreds of men killed in the early days of World War 1. Among the graves is that of Peter Kollwitz, a student from Berlin who volunteered as soon as the war broke out. Two months later, in October 1914, he was killed, aged nineteen, in one of the war's first major campaigns.

Käthe Kollwitz was informed of her son's death in action on 30 October. 'Your pretty shawl will no longer be able to warm our boy,' was the touching way she broke the news to a close friend. To another friend she admitted, 'There is in our lives a wound which will never heal. Nor should it.'

By December 1914 Kollwitz, one of the foremost artists of her day, had formed the idea of creating a memorial to her son, with his body outstretched, 'the father at the head, the mother at the feet', to commemorate 'the sacrifice of all the young volunteers'. As time went on she attempted various other designs, but was dissatisfied with them all. Kollwitz put the project aside temporarily in 1919, but her commitment to see it through when it was right was unequivocal. 'I will come back, I shall do this work for you, for you and the others,' she noted in her diary in June 1919. Twelve years later, she kept her word: in April 1931 she was at last able to complete the sculpture. 'In the fall – Peter, – I shall bring it to you,' she wrote in her diary. Her work was exhibited in the National Gallery in Berlin and then transported to Belgium, where it was placed, as she had promised, adjacent to her son's grave. There it rests to this day.

Käthe Kollwitz's war memorial was an offering to a son who had offered his life for his country. That she was only able to complete it eighteen years after his death should tell us something about how unconvincing is the view that the Great

---

These two granite statues are the work of the German sculptress Käthe Kollwitz. She is on the right, her husband Karl is on the left, on their knees near their son's grave in Belgium, begging forgiveness for a war they, the older generation, could not prevent.

War ended when the textbooks tell us, on 11 November 1918. For millions of people who had to live with the human costs of the conflict the war lasted much, much longer.

It is for this reason that it makes sense to suggest that, in an important way, the contours of the history of the Great War, the history endured by millions of ordinary men and women, are visible at Vladslo.

The war opened in 1914 as a conflict which almost everyone believed would last for a few months. But the slaughter of Peter Kollwitz and the armies of 1914 did not result in a decisive victory. Instead, by the end of that year stalemate had set in: the Great War was born, a war which was to last fully 1500 days.

At the Armistice of 11 November 1918, the German Army was not far from Vladslo. It was still in occupation of large parts of Belgium. But it had been defeated. The Allies had won the war, at an unimaginable cost. In all combatant armies, over 9 million men had died in uniform; perhaps twice that number had been wounded. And an even larger number of people in every combatant country – wives and brothers, sons and daughters, mothers and fathers like Käthe and Karl Kollwitz – were in mourning. The image of Vladslo, in the midst of a Great War battlefield returned to farmland, holding together the remains of the fallen and the gestures of the survivors, suggests the dominant approach of this book.

The 'Short Twentieth Century'

We who were born long after the Armistice have also lived in the wake of war. This is true both at the intimate as well as the most general level.

The 1914–18 conflict created the fundamental elements of twentieth-century history. The clash between the Communist system and capitalism became a reality during the conflict. Reluctantly, but unavoidably, America became a world power. Britain's decline as a major power can be dated from 1917, when for the first time she became a debtor to the United States. At the peace conference of 1919, the German and Austro-Hungarian empires were divided. Germany was divided again after World War II, but most of the states created at the peace conferences of 1919–21, both in Europe and the Middle East, were still intact seventy years later.

Then came the shock waves of 1989–91, when the world was transformed. This earthquake ended what some have called the 'short twentieth century'. Communism collapsed; the Soviet empire and the Yugoslav state fragmented. Germany reunited within a robust European community. For the time being, the German problem – so central to World War I – appears to be solved. Instead, other problems have emerged, disturbingly similar to those which had plagued statesmen in 1914.

This is why the end of the twentieth century appears close to its beginnings, with the recent revival of older nationalisms, the collapse of elements of the European state system and the ideological or geo-political divide which emerged from the 1914–18 conflict. In addition, the chequered history of European integration in the 1980s and 1990s makes even clearer the need to recall the sombre history of European disintegration. If the bloody twentieth century, with its manifold disasters, is to be transcended, it is by recognizing and understanding its catastrophic character. And that means returning to the Great War. It is to inform as wide a public as possible of these issues, central to citizenship, that we have embarked on this project.

The Great War: the Cultural History of Military Conflict

Our aim is to portray the history of those who fought and of the people they left behind. It is also our objective to explore the shock waves created by this conflict – repercussions felt to this day. In short, we aim to introduce viewers to two parallel histories, inextricably intermingled: the cultural history of armed conflict, and the impact of military history on cultural life in the period of the Great War and afterwards.

To an important degree, the approach of this book is different from that of other studies and documentary accounts of World War 1. Like other studies, the narrative line is the war itself. The chronological flow of the conflict – the clash of wills, armed forces and imperial power from 1914 to 1918 – is followed throughout. But in every chapter it is the cultural context of the waging of war which is emphasized and visualized. Here cultural history means the exploration of the hopes and dreams, the ideas and aspirations, the exhilaration and the despair, both of those remote from power and of those who led them. Cultural history is the story of the way they made sense of the war and its consequences.

Until recent years military history and cultural history have lived in majestic isolation, each on its separate peak. But the work of a new generation of scholars, in Europe and North America, as well as the collection and exploitation of new archival and film sources, enables us to break new ground. The 1914–18 war was the Great War in large part because of its cultural consequences. Whereas diplomacy, political conflict and military events have long been a staple of historical presentations of the war, they have never been presented to the general public as cultural phenomena, encoded with rich and complex images, languages and cultural forms.

This is an international story with unprecedented sweep. The war touched people's lives in a multitude of ways throughout the world. It brought Australians to Turkey, the Japanese Navy to the Mediterranean, Czech soldiers to Siberia and American 'doughboys' to places they had never dreamed of seeing.

Sixty years earlier, American soldiers had started on the road to industrial warfare. Between 1914 and 1918 Europeans went through their own 'civil war', which was worldwide by virtue of the imperial possessions of the chief combatants. Europe's conflagration was bloodier than any earlier war – bloodier than the American Civil War, but the two conflicts were as filled with compassion and degradation, as dominated by industry and agriculture, as alive with racism and humanitarianism, and as evocative of the centuries in which they took place.

The links between the American and European history of warfare go further still. One of the most powerful stimuli to a new generation of historical thinking on World War 1 has been the Vietnam War. In large part as an echo of that conflict, there appeared a rich historical literature which enables us to inform this project with new interpretations.

The dimension specifically governing this literature, and through it in this book, is the sense of the war as a cultural phenomenon, for soldiers and statesmen as much as for artists and audiences. Scholars such as Paul Fussell in *The Great War and Modern Memory*, John Keegan in *The Face of Battle* and Eric Leed in *No Man's Land*, all three writing in the 1970s, have altered the historical landscape of the war. They have redefined the Great War as an event which transformed language, radically shifted the boundaries between the public and private realms, obliterated the distinction between civilian and military targets, occasioned witch-hunts for internal enemies, challenged gender divisions and opened a new phase in the history of race and empire. In more recent years, Modris Eksteins in *Rites of Spring* and Samuel Hynes in *A War Imagined* have explored the shadow of the war in astonishing and seminal works of art, as well as in more mundane features of cultural life.

Europe has produced a similarly rich literature of the cultural history of the war. Jean-Jacques Becker and Marc Ferro have opened new avenues of research on popular opinion in France and Russia, and George Mosse and Stéphane Audoin-Rouzeau have explored the war's brutalizing effects on civilians and soldiers alike. Antoine Prost has enriched our understanding both of veterans' movements and of commemorative events.

The work of these people, among others, has opened the way to a new cultural history of the war. It is based on the assumption that to understand the Great War, and its enduring repercussions, we must jettison outworn distinctions between 'high' and 'popular' culture, and between both and the political and military history of the day. In the 1914–18 conflict, all were mobilized; all were transformed. The Great War broke down the barriers between them; this book, and the television series it accompanies, are dedicated to showing how and why this happened.

Women workers at an aeroplane factory in Birmingham, September 1918. The Great War impelled millions of people into jobs and situations remote from their pre-war lives. Women changed jobs, earned wages, and had a taste of freedom. It was short-lived, but the memories of sisterhood and sacrifice endured.

1

EXPLOSION

The catastrophe of 1914 arose from the cumulative movement of many shifting fault lines – political, economic, cultural. The instabilities of European society were many, and they were just under the surface. When they erupted they destroyed whole regimes, indeed an entire way of life.

The immediate impact of war was on private life. War is always the destroyer of families, and the Great War was to date the greatest destroyer of them all. Of the 70 million men who served in uniform in all combatant countries, over 9 million died or were killed on active service; 3 million widows and 10 million orphans owed their fate to the war of 1914–18.

We will never know what trauma on this scale meant to those who went through it. But some hints of the human story of the war remain. Waiting for news of loved ones was an agonizing and unavoidable preoccupation for millions of families during the war.

In France, conveying the bad news in towns, villages and hamlets was the mayor's responsibility. When he received a message from the Ministry of War he put down his pen, left his office and walked through the streets to seek a particular home. Children peeked over their schoolbooks to see which way he was going. Shoppers froze; conversation stopped. And then came the knock.

In rural France, the approach could be seen from afar. This is how the novelist Jean Giono pictured the scene in the Provençal countryside. The widow, Felicity, saw the postman Alberic and another neighbour Jerome, coming. She

> held up her hands to her eyes to distinguish them clearly.... There was a riot among the chickens. She ran through them to the farm. Jerome and Alberic walked on slowly. They opened the door. She had understood everything already. She was bent down across the table, her face pressed against the wood, and she banged the table with both her fists. 'No!', she cried 'No!'.

Her sister, the local schoolmistress, dismissed her class. Among them was the son of the fallen soldier. His neighbour Jerome called to him: 'Come along, give me your hand. Your mother's looking for you. You'd better throw away your flowers'.

Ludwig Meidner, *The Evening before War*, 1914. Meidner was a German artist and prophet of the apocalypse. The faces of those confronting it in this drawing made in Berlin in August 1914 show panic and fear. The war crisis elicited a range of emotions in the populace, shifting from shock and stupefaction to anger and stoical acceptance of the need to fight a defensive war.

The whole village came to the house in mourning.

> The front room was full of people. The sideboard, the cupboard and the kneading-trough had been moved away. The straight-backed chairs were lined against the walls. The visitors were sitting on the chairs around an empty room. There were no flames in the hearth. The ashes had been brushed together into a heap in the middle of the hearth, a sign that there'd be no more fire. In the middle of the room there was a bare table: a yellow wax candle was burning in each corner. Everybody from the plain was there. They had all come, the old men, the women and the little girls, and they were sitting stiffly on the stiff chairs. They sat in the depths of the shadows. They looked at the empty table and the candles, and the light from the candles mellowed their hands laid out flat on their knees....

The dead man's mother sprinkled some salt in the middle of the table: 'Let us treasure in our thoughts our friendship for one who was the salt of the earth'.

The news of soldiers' deaths came home in many ways: by telegram for British officers' families, by letter or telephone for men in the ranks. For some, loss was added to loss. The commander of the French Eighth Army, General Castelnau, lost three sons. Each time he saw a sad military face entering his office or home, he asked the simple question: 'Which one?' Second-in-command of the German Army was Erich Ludendorff. He lost two stepsons, both pilots. He personally had to identify the remains of the second, shot down in April 1918. 'The war has spared me nothing,' was his laconic reaction to the news.

The knock on the door was democratic. The prominent and the wealthy knew it, as did the ordinary citizen. The Prime Minister of England, H. H. Asquith, heard the news from his wife Margot on a weekend in 1916.

> On Sunday September the 17th, we were entertaining a week-end party.... While we were playing tennis in the afternoon ... Clouder, our servant ... came in to say I was wanted. ... I left the room, and the moment I took up the telephone I said to myself, 'Raymond is killed.'
>
> With the receiver in my hand, I asked what it was, and if the news was bad.
>
> Our secretary, Davies, answered, 'Terrible, terrible news. Raymond was shot dead on the 15th....'
>
> Leaving the children, I paused at the end of the dining-room passage; Henry opened the door and we stood facing each other. He saw my thin wet face, and while he put his arm round me I said:
>
> 'Terrible, terrible news.'
>
> At this he stopped me and said:
>
> 'I know ... I've known it ... Raymond is dead.'
>
> He put his hands over his face and we walked into an empty room and sat down in silence.

'Whatever pride I had in the past', Prime Minister Asquith wrote on 20 September, 'and whatever hope I had for the far future – by much the largest part of both was invested in him. Now all that is gone.'

In October 1914, the parents of Willi Böhne, a chemistry student at the

French orphanage. France was father to these war orphans. In 1914 alone, 400 000 French soldiers died, leaving approximately the same number of fatherless children behind. In a country obsessed by demographic decline, everything was done to help these innocent victims of war.

University of Frieburg, received a letter in two parts. The first was from their son, telling them of his life of hard work: 'We are simply nothing but moles; for we are burrowing trenches so that Herren Engländer shan't break through here.' The letter stopped abruptly, and was completed by a comrade, informing the parents that Böhne had just been killed.

Four years later, the killing was still going on. Isaac Rosenberg, one of the poets killed in the war, was a Jew from the East End of London. He died during the last great German offensive, on 1 April 1918. It was not until later that month that the news of his death reached his family, by letter. After absorbing the initial shock, Isaac Rosenberg's father wrote a poem:

> *This is the day of tears*
> *For on it, my dear son, Isaac the Levite*
> *Fell on the fields of battle. . . .*
> *If you have understanding, you will understand.*

EXPLOSION

Premonitions of disaster were commonplace. Harold Owen was a naval officer serving off the coast of West Africa in December 1918, weeks after the end of the fighting. His brother Wilfred was an officer in the Manchester Regiment, and a young poet.

We were lying off Victoria. I had gone down to my cabin thinking to write some letters. I drew aside the door curtain and stepped inside and to my amazement I saw Wilfred sitting in my chair. I felt shock run through me with appalling force and with it I could feel the blood draining away from my face. I did not rush towards him but walked jerkily into the cabin – all my limbs stiff and slow to respond. I did not sit down but looking at him I spoke quietly: 'Wilfred, how did you get here?' He did not rise and I saw that he was involuntarily immobile, but his eyes which had never left mine were alive with the familiar look of trying to make me understand; when I spoke his whole face broke into his sweetest and most endearing dark smile. I felt not

fear – I had not when I first drew my door curtain and saw him there; only exquisite mental pleasure at thus beholding him. All I was conscious of was a sensation of enormous shock and profound astonishment that he should be here in my cabin. I spoke again. 'Wilfred dear, how can you be here, it's just not possible....' But still he did not speak but only smiled his most gentle smile.... He was in uniform and I remember thinking how out of place the khaki looked amongst the cabin furnishings. With this thought I must have turned my eyes away from him; when I looked back my cabin chair was empty.

I felt the blood run slowly back to my face and looseness into my limbs and with these an overpowering sense of emptiness and absolute loss.... I wondered if I had been dreaming but looking down I saw that I was still standing. Suddenly I felt terribly tired and moving to my bunk I lay down; instantly I went into a deep oblivious sleep. When I woke up I knew with absolute certainty that Wilfred was dead.

Confirmation came Christmas week 1918, through a letter from his family. Wilfred had been killed on 4 November, but the news had only filtered through to the family a week later. 'They had received the dreaded telegram at 12 noon on 11 November, Armistice Day. The church bells were still ringing, the bands playing and the jubilant crowds surging together.' The war had officially ended just an hour before.

When we hear these words, when we see these family portraits so like our own, we face the human reality of war the destroyer. In the face of so much sadness, so much loss, we join the survivors and pose the questions: 'Why did this happen?', 'Did this war have to be?' and 'Who was to blame?'

IMAGES OF VIOLENCE

Motor car factory in Berlin *c.* 1900. Pre-war Berlin was dominated by its industrial working population and an industrial city of 100 000 people grew rapidly in the suburbs, within a few miles of the Imperial Palace in Potsdam. More than in London or Paris, heavy manufacture dominated Berlin industry.

The upheaval of 1914 was the result of choices made by identifiable people under particular circumstances. War was not built into their lives, like a recessive gene suddenly turned dominant. But those choices were made at a time of great internal conflict and profound uncertainty about the future. Clashes over power, over ideas, over art, over religion, over language itself took on new and revolutionary forms in the decades before World War I. They describe a generation conscious of instability and unsure how to master it.

The greatest changes took place in the economy. The years 1880–1914 formed one of the most explosive periods of industrial growth in world history. Backed by imperial power and the expansion of rail and steam traffic, Europeans benefited from huge imports of wheat and beef; ordinary people ate better and more than their forebears had ever done.

Populations grew with unprecedented rapidity. Cities mushroomed: Berlin turned from a sleepy provincial capital of 600 000 in 1870 to a metropolis of 2 million in 1910. Migratory currents surged west, through Europe, in the wake of persecution and in hope of a better life. These human rivers deposited millions of people throughout western Europe before arriving with another and even larger deposit of new citizens in the New World.

The Great Exhibition of
1900 in Paris celebrated the
industrial revolution just as
the Universal Exhibition of
1889 – 90 had marked the
centenary of the French
revolution. Great power
politics dominated the
proceedings of the turn-of-
the-century exhibition.
Each pavilion had its version
of national or imperial
grandeur to sell, but the
setting of this extravaganza
was peaceful.

The industrial strength of the major European countries was their sign of Great Power status. Each paraded its industrial muscle in the Paris World Exhibition of 1900. All their leaders knew that military and naval power came out of the belly of a steel furnace.

Parallel to this huge leap forward in economic power was a subterranean revolutionary current in many fields of knowledge. Virtually everywhere, someone was undermining Victorian certainties. Freud demolished established verities about childhood innocence; Einstein took time – at least in the stately Victorian sense of the term – to pieces. Relativity was no comfort to those looking for settled values. The Wright brothers realized a dream that had defied Leonardo da Vinci, and space shrank with Edison's new talking machine.

The machine age and its uncertainties dominated developments in the arts. Monet caught the distortions in light caused by the billowing smoke of locomotives in the great Paris terminus of St Lazare. More daring spirits were drawn to futurism, a celebration of machinery, power, speed – and war. Bicycles fascinated the Italian Futurist Boccioni, who saw in them symbols of the universe. During the war he first served, appropriately enough, in the Bicycle Corps, but in 1916 he was killed while riding a horse.

The Futurists loved to shock. Theirs was a philosophy of iconoclasm: the more shattered conventions and certainties the better. And if anyone got hurt by the debris, that was the price of modernity. 'We intend to sing the love of danger,' declared the *Futurist Manifesto* of 1909: 'We will glorify war – the world's only hygiene – militarism, patriotism, the destructive gesture of freedom-bringers, beautiful ideas worth dying for. . . .'

Such voices did ring out in pre-war Europe. But alongside them were other artists, equally innovative, but who expressed a more characteristic ambivalence about the destructive potential of modern industrial life. Painters, sculptors and composers announced violence, disorder and a future as ominous as one lived on the edge of a volcano. Their creations capture the mood of unease much more fully than the arrogant poseurs of the Futurist movement. Unlike the Futurists, many artists were unable simply to celebrate violence. Instead they offered a series of discordant glimpses of the potential for upheaval and disorder within contemporary society. The story of two such artists can tell us much about the unresolved tensions in European cultural life on the eve of war. They were very different men: the Russian composer Igor Stravinsky and the German painter Ludwig Meidner.

Stravinsky and Meidner

A turbulent mixture of hopes and fears dominated one of the most iconoclastic moments in pre-1914 cultural history. That moment was 29 May 1913, and it was the Paris première by Sergei Diaghilev's company of a ballet written by the twenty-five-year-old Russian composer Igor Stravinsky. The ballet was called *The Rite of Spring*.

It is, in Stravinsky's own words, 'a musical choreographic work. It represents pagan Russia and is unified by a single idea: the mystery and great surge of the creative power of Spring.' Part one is a celebration of the sanctity of the spring;

Cartoon of Stravinsky by Jean Cocteau. Cocteau was a poet, painter, and patron of iconoclasm in pre-war Paris, and the storm set off by Igor Stravinsky's *The Rite of Spring* in 1913 warmed his heart. Not so the conventional theatre-goers portrayed here, whose puzzled looks reveal their shock at Stravinsky's score and at the radical choreography of the Ballets Russes.

part two is 'the Great Sacrifice', the offering-up of a virgin 'to the old men in the great holy dance'.

The music was violent and full of dissonance. But even more profoundly new was the way its rhythms were captured by the performance of his stars, Nijinsky – who was also responsible for the choreography – and Maria Piltz, the 'chosen maiden'. This was not ballet: this was revolution. Foot stamping replaced the lyrical sweep of conventional dance; rape replaced romance; the primitive replaced the ethereal.

If this was the future, the prosperous patrons of the Théâtre des Champs Elysées wanted none of it. The auditorium erupted in a scene of whistling, shouting, howling, pushing, shoving, insults, threats; blows were exchanged; forty protesters were evicted, but the performance carried on.

No one there that evening ever forgot its electrifying effect. It was, in essence, a prelude to a transformational moment, an apocalypse, full of both potential and danger. But in Stravinsky's ballet it was one lone female who was immolated, not the whole world.

The vision of Ludwig Meidner was more comprehensive. At the same time as Stravinsky configured a primitive, rural rite in ballet, Meidner painted the apocalypse as urban collapse and conflagration. A Jew born in 1884 in Breslau – then in Germany, now in Poland – he came to Berlin in his twenties and stayed there in extreme poverty to paint astonishing images of war and urban catastrophe, all well before the war crisis of 1914.

Meidner both loved and hated the city. His subject was the dynamism of the metropolis, its shapes, its sounds, its dangers. He celebrated the muscular newness of metropolitan life, while probing the explosive potential of such vast concentrations of people. In 1914 he wrote:

> Let's paint what is close to us, our city world! The wild streets, the elegance of iron suspension bridges, gas tanks which hang in white-cloud mountains, the roaring colors of buses and express locomotives, the rushing telephone wires (aren't they like music?), the harlequinade of advertising pillars, and then night ... big city night.

This was the positive side of his outlook; he had also a darker vision. Here he tells of his strolls around Berlin during the heatwave of 1912:

Ludwig Meidner, *Bombardment of a City*, 1914. This drawing could be of Sarajevo in 1994 but is in fact Berlin before the outbreak of war. The uniforms of the men bombarding their own people are German; city dwellers the size of ants flee in all directions, doomed to their unavoidable fate.

Vasily Kandinsky, *All Souls Night I*, 1911. Born in Moscow in 1866 and resident in Munich from 1896, Kandinsky repeatedly meditated on the universal catastrophe he believed was on the way. Here we have a glimpse of the Last Judgement, with the trumpet sounding the end of time.

> Sometimes when I feel a nocturnal need I venture forth into the city ... and hustle headlong along the pavements.... The screams of clouds echo around me, burning bushes, a distant beating of wings, and people shadowy and spitting. The moon burns against my hot temples.... The city nears. My body crackles. The giggles of the city ignite against my skin. I hear eruptions at the base of my skull. The houses near. Their catastrophes explode from their windows, stairways silently collapse. People laugh beneath the ruins.

The 'ruins' are what he painted, in strokes of feverish anticipation of chaos and the triumph of evil. Cities shelled; women raped; people trapped in a world gone mad; mutilated soldiers: these are his urban citizens.

Such images were the common currency of artists and writers in pre-war Berlin. The same doomed men and women of the metropolis inhabit the verse of the poets in Meidner's Berlin circle. Georg Heym wrote in 1911:

> *The people on the streets draw up and stare,*
> *While overhead huge portents cross the sky;*
> *Round fanglike towers threatening comets flare,*
> *Death-bearing, fiery snouted where they fly.*

Jakob van Hoddis called one of his poems 'End of the World'. The apocalypse was in the air.

The Russian painter Vasily Kandinsky, a friend of Meidner also working in Germany, had similar premonitions. He believed that 'A great destruction ... is also a song of praise, complete and separate in its sound, just like a hymn to new creation which follows the destruction.' He too painted the end of the world: the Four Horsemen of the Apocalypse were only just over the horizon.

Kandinsky lived in Munich where he was joined by the Bavarian painter Franz

Birthday celebrations for the Kaiser, June 1913. A grand parade down Unter den Linden, through Berlin's Brandenburg Gate, was an annual event on the Kaiser's birthday. This demonstration of popular affection was carefully stage-managed. It revealed both real feelings of nationalist ardour among the population as well as its cynical manipulation.

Marc in creating a forum for such 'new artistic production'. They called their group 'The Blue Rider', and produced an almanac to present all the revolutionary currents of the day. It announced their mission in these terms: 'Today art is moving in a direction of which our fathers would never even have dreamed. We stand before the new pictures as in a dream and we hear the apocalyptic horsemen in the air. There is an artistic tension all over Europe.' How that tension would break, these artists could not foresee.

Sources of Instability

Why the fever? Why the fear? Part of the story of this artistic anticipation of Armageddon is pan-European, but much of it is specifically German. These men lived in the heart of the most explosive military machine in the world. The German Army was superior to any other, and the new barons of the German Empire intended to keep the upper hand. They stood at the pinnacle of power of a state both modern and archaic. They had the most productive steel mills, the best chemists, the most powerful engineering industry in the world. And yet this enormously dynamic source of economic strength was lodged in an antiquated state. The Kaiser had absolute power over the Army and the executive. The people paid the bill for power but had very little say in how it was used.

This is the source of the profound instability at the heart of German life. Germany was both modern and unmodern at the same time, and anyone walking the streets of Berlin could see it. Berlin was the site of many demonstrations in 1913, the year Meidner painted his apocalyptic sequence. First came the workers: the vanguard of the largest revolutionary party in the world – the Social Democratic Party. In the elections of 1912 they won the largest number of seats in the Reichstag, the German Parliament. Then a week later came the Kaiser's birthday, celebrated in the streets of Berlin with marches and parades by one of the most reactionary military castes in Europe.

How long could this incongruous mismatch between industrial modernity and political backwardness last? No one had the slightest idea; but the explosive material under the surface of German life gave an ominous quality to similar discussions in other European capitals. For, as we can still see today, eighty years later, an unstable Germany means an unstable Europe.

Not that German artists saw this, but their work was not a direct comment on political events. They offer us something more valuable than that: a sense of the mood of the times, the anxieties of a generation, their disorientation and their mixed hopes and fears.

And yet were not these visions very similar? In the same year, 1913, many artists celebrated the iconoclastic, spring-like dynamism of the times. But they did so with a brooding and powerful sense of the violence lying just below the surface of contemporary life. Theirs was unmistakably both a celebration and a warning; they pointed to a spring both of creativity and of cataclysmic change. They responded not to a future war they could not foresee, but to the promethean character of the world in which they lived. They told us what the rest of the century has come to understand: a revolutionary age destroys at least as much as it creates.

THE KAISER

The war which broke out in 1914 would destroy the German monarchy. Kaiser Wilhelm II of Germany lost everything: the command of the German Army and Navy, the crown of Prussia, the imperial mantle itself. When he was shuffled off to asylum in Holland in 1918, there seemed nothing more that he could lose. There are those who see him as the author of his own demise; others blame a political system which manipulated him as much as he manipulated it. But whatever one's judgement, the story of his life tells us much about the political and social context in which issues of war and peace were decided.

The last Kaiser had a fascination with the sea. 'It sprang', he wrote, 'of no small extent from my English blood.' As a child, his most pleasant memories had been those of playing at Osborne, the seaside estate of his grandmother, Queen Victoria, on the Isle of Wight. At nearby Portsmouth harbour he often saw all classes of ships. 'There awoke in me the wish to build ships of my own like these some day, and when I was grown up to possess as fine a navy as the English.'

The man who would take Germany into World War I was born to the first daughter of Queen Victoria on 27 January 1859. It was a difficult birth. The breech delivery required the use of forceps. In the event, his left arm was wrenched out of its socket, causing severe muscle and nerve damage that shrivelled the limb, making it useless. His relationship with his English mother was a deeply troubled one, and paralleled the growing antagonism between the two greatest empires in the world, Britain and Germany. When Wilhelm's mother refused to drink to his health on his birthday, he sulked for days. As one close observer, the diplomat Friedrich August von Holstein, remarked: '*Quelle famille, mon Dieu, quelle famille.*' But this could equally be said of all the monarchies of Europe, the archaic leaders of dynamic industrial nations.

In his childhood, his English mother was determined that 'Willy' should overcome his handicap. She took responsibility for his general education, hoping to instill in him 'our British feeling of independence'. She proved a hard task-master. He learned to speak fluent English, with as much ease as he spoke German. Physical accomplishments, however, came slowly. He was forced to wear painful contraptions in the hope that they would straighten his withered arm. Wilhelm's response was a very human one: 'I was worried and afraid. When there was nobody near, I wept.'

Only when Wilhelm grew to manhood did he find happiness – in the Prussian Army. 'I really found my family, my friends, my interests – everything in which I had up to that time had to do without.' Under the Army's influence Wilhelm hardened – at least superficially – and distanced himself from his parents, especially his mother, whom he began calling 'the English Princess'. By now Victoria found him insufferable, and even his father, Kaiser Friedrich III, agreed. 'Considering the unripeness and inexperience of my eldest son,' he wrote to his Chancellor, Otto von Bismarck, 'together with his leaning toward vanity and presumption, and his overweening estimate of himself, I must frankly express my opinion that it is dangerous as yet to bring him into touch with foreign affairs.'

Portrait of the Kaiser as a young man. Wilhelm suffered from a deformed left arm, which he tried to conceal in photographs. He developed a violent streak remote from the niceties of court life. His anti-Semitism and propensity to call for the execution of German strikers were both idiosyncratic and common to many of his subjects.

The system

That danger did not recede when in 1888, on the death of his father, Wilhelm was crowned Emperor of the most dynamic nation on the continent of Europe. His Empire was fashioned largely by the political genius of Bismarck and by the power of the Prussian Army, victors over the French in the Franco–Prussian War of 1870–1. Under the Reich Constitution of 16 April 1871, the Kaiser's authority was vast. He alone presided over the nation's foreign affairs; it was his decision and his alone if Germany were to go to war. He appointed the political executive, the Chancellor and the Chief of the Imperial General Staff. When Bismarck was Chancellor, there was some sense of a balance of power between monarch and executive. But after he left office in 1890 no such balance existed: the Kaiser and his court were the locus of power.

The German constitution was dazzlingly complex: no balance of power here. The Kaiser appointed the Chancellor as chief executive, but he was in no sense responsible to the nation. The Chancellor answered only to the Kaiser and not to the legislature, which was elected on a franchise weighted towards the wealthy. The catch was that the legislature held the purse-strings; but the Kaiser had the power. This led to Byzantine negotiations to provide the cash needed for affairs of state. This political system provided a recipe for political deadlock. Is it

RIGHT Bismarck in 1889.
BELOW The Kaiser and the Prince of Wales—on board the Kaiser's yacht *Hohenzollern* in 1907.

The German and British monarchs, Wilhelm II and George V, were first cousins, wearing the uniforms of Admirals of each other's navies, but family ties were no barrier to political conflict. After Otto von Bismarck was dismissed as Chancellor in 1891, lesser men tried to square German ambitions with European stability. There was no way to do so.

surprising that to many people, especially those high in the Army and Navy, one way out of the domestic deadlock was war?

In effect, the German state constituted a profoundly unstable fault line cutting right across all the political, social and economic minefields of home and international affairs. It wasn't only an artist like Meidner who sensed the precarious nature of the regime in which he lived. Given the intractable political and social problems faced by a society growing through massive and rapid industrialization, many people in positions of power were similarly gloomy about the future. Add to this unstable mixture the personality and prejudices of the Kaiser, and we can see why European politics in the decades before 1914 resembled an accident waiting to happen.

Anglo-German antagonism

Wilhelm II was a reactionary at home and a believer in the expansion of German power abroad. He was not alone; around him and his court arose a chorus of voices demanding a greater share in world affairs. They were well aware of how useful the Kaiser could be to them. After all, German industry was approaching parity with Britain's; why should not economic power translate into political power on the world stage? What better symbol of world power to go along with the might of the Imperial German Army than a world-class Navy? After Bismarck's fall from power in 1892, the path lay open for the new Kaiser and his bellicose friends. After 1900, they moved to build up German naval and land strength whatever the consequences.

Wilhelm simply could not understand why the expansion of German naval strength poisoned Anglo-German relations. His affection for things English was a matter of record. In 1889 he was made a British Admiral of the Fleet. 'Fancy wearing the same uniform as St Vincent or Nelson,' he observed. 'It is enough to make me quite giddy.' In 1906, the Kaiser noted: 'One of the best days of my life, which I shall never forget as long as I live, was the day when I inspected the Mediterranean Fleet, when I was on board the Dreadnought and *my* flag was hoisted for the first time.' He meant the flag of an admiral of the *British* Fleet. When the Kaiser landed at Portsmouth in November 1907 for a state visit, he wore the uniform of a British admiral. The Prince of Wales, who greeted him on the quay, wore the uniform of a Prussian field-marshal.

The Kaiser's attitude to the British disclosed the fundamental volatility of his mood and mind. He was capable of deep sensitivity one moment, and at the next the most outrageous, and occasionally obscene, remarks. Images of bloodshed came readily to mind. During a strike of tramworkers in 1900, Wilhelm telegraphed the commanding general: 'I expect that when the troops move in at least five hundred people should be gunned down.' Three years later General von Kessel, commanding general in Berlin, noted: 'H.M. has already ordered me *twice*, on the most flimsy of pretexts and in *open* telegrams, to fire on the people.' On a North Sea cruise in the same year Wilhelm mused that in the event of a revolution he would mow down all Social Democrats, 'but only after they had first plundered the Jews and the rich'.

His anti-semitism was common knowledge. Although, like others who shared these views, he boasted of Jewish friends, his prejudices reflected ugly currents widespread within German society. His remarks about Jews betray the sinister side of his character. When he was provoked or offended – and he always seemed in danger of being offended – Wilhelm's language was full of spleen, hatred and rhetorical violence. The British courtier Reginald, Viscount Esher recorded a conversation which captured the shocking contrast between the niceties of diplomatic exchanges and the viciousness of the Kaiser's imagination. In conversation with the British Foreign Minister, Sir Edward Grey, 'he declaimed violently against Jews: "There are far too many of them in my country. They want stamping out. If I did not restrain my people, there would be a Jew-baiting."' Grey wrote, 'The German Emperor is ageing me; he is like a battleship with steam up and screws going, but with no rudder, and he will run into something some day and cause a catastrophe.'

The Kaiser's intemperate behaviour would be the stuff of caricature, not tragedy, but for the fact that Wilhelm was an autocratic head of state with authority touching all corners of German society. He was Supreme War Lord, and the leader of the strongest army in the world. He exercised personal control over every major appointment in the state, nominating every minister, bureaucrat, judge, professor and ambassador. This was the source of his very personal politics and the court intrigue which swirled around him. A Viennese joke had it that 'The Kaiser insists on being the stag at every hunt, the bride at every wedding, and the corpse at every funeral.' To a group of his own admirals he insisted: 'All of you know nothing; I alone know something; I alone decide.'

In world politics, this was an invitation to disaster. The trouble was that Wilhelm spoke for all too many of his compatriots. In 1889, just after the accession of the Kaiser, an English friend was lunching with the great chemist R. W. von Bunsen, a man of towering eminence in scientific circles. By then Bunsen was nearly eighty, a lifelong liberal and a much-loved figure in German science. The Englishman asked: 'Isn't the young Kaiser rather war-like?' Bunsen answered: 'Why not,' and slamming his palm on the table, 'if he has the guts?'

He had the guts, and made sure that everyone could see that he was not a weak man. Similarly bellicose was the military and naval élite which surrounded him. They used the Kaiser, played him off against rivals, ignored him when they could, mobilized him when they had to. When the British built a new class of battleship, the Dreadnoughts, the Kaiser insisted that Germany have them too. The German Fleet was ordered to double its size, pleasing both prophets of naval power like Admiral Tirpitz and the industrialists who got the orders.

An arms race was now underway, revealing plainly the collision course set between Germany and Britain to determine which nation would dominate northwestern Europe. And the deepening of Anglo-German antagonism prepared the way for new understandings between France and Britain, the Entente Cordiale of 1904, which secretly committed each to military support for the other in the event of war. Wilhelm had only himself and his ministers to blame for the fact that 'The bayonets of Europe were directed at her', as he claimed (with some exaggeration) in conversation with Woodrow Wilson's adviser, Colonel E. M. House, on 1 June 1914.

König-class battleships under construction. These German battleships were the signature of a world power. They also presented Britain with the unacceptable prospect of an eventual loss of naval mastery to Germany.

OVERLEAF The Kaiser with
generals on manoeuvres
before the war. Staffed by the
finest officer corps in the
world, the German Army
believed it had the strength
to break through the 'encirclement' of its enemies to the
east and to the west.

The greatest number of bayonets were in Russia, and the speed of Russian
economic growth in the pre-war decade presented Germany with an alarming
prospect in eastern Europe. There too an ancient monarchy presided unsteadily
over a rapidly changing economic and social order. And allied with Russia was
France, whose hostility in international affairs was unavoidable, given the German
annexation of Alsace and Lorraine in 1871. Russian growth opened up the possibility of a two-front war for Germany, against two industrial powers. The clock
was ticking.

When a British message to the Kaiser – in the form of conversation between the

German Ambassador to London, Count Lichnowsky, and the British Secretary of State for War, Lord Haldane – in 1912 made it clear that Britain would not tolerate a repeat of the Franco-Prussian War, with its humiliation of France, the Kaiser was livid. Once more he took this diplomatic issue as a matter of personal honour. Who had the right to tell him what was or was not tolerable? He called together his chief military (though not his political) advisers. The Kaiser initially pushed for an immediate declaration of war, but the military and naval planners urged caution. They needed more time. The Kiel Canal linking the Baltic and the North Sea would be finished in eighteen months. Other preparations were underway to strengthen the army. Caution prevailed. Eighteen months from December 1912 was the summer of 1914.

A consideration of the Kaiser's baroque mannerisms and mercurial temperament opens the door to an understanding of the profound instabilities within European life in the years before the Great War. He did not bring about the war single-handedly; but his larger-than-life personality reflected everything that could and did go wrong with the European world order. At the end of the war one formerly loyal supporter, Admiral Hopman, stranded with his ship in Sebastopol, noted bitterly: 'What Germany has sinned in the last three decades it must now pay for. It was politically paralysed through its blind faith in, [and] its slavish submission to, the will of a puffed-up, vainglorious and self-overestimating fool.' Hopman gave the Kaiser too much credit. Turn-of-the-century German society got the leader it deserved: a hereditary monarch, proud of the robust achievements of his people, but frequently out of touch with reality.

Archaic Empires

Germany was not the only major European power whose political leaders seemed out of touch with reality. Part of the problem was the persistence of an old political order at a time of rapid economic and social change. Russia, Austria–Hungary and Germany were all ruled formally by feudal hierarchies, whose rhythms and rituals carried on despite the fact that they presided over massive industrial growth. France was a republic, and Britain had constructed a compromise form of constitutional monarchy, but in central and eastern Europe the power of the old order was both formal and real.

Both the Kaiser and Tsar Nicholas II were able to influence foreign policy in a way unavailable to George V of Britain. The personal ties of these monarchs – all related to Queen Victoria – made them believe that in an international crisis they would share common interests. Wilhelm and Nicholas could write to each other as 'Willy' and 'Nicky', and presume that their friendship or mutual respect mattered in international affairs. It didn't. Such affinities existed only in rhetoric, but that they were still in evidence tells us much about the mix of the archaic and the modern in pre-1914 European affairs.

Russia was another Great Power whose political order was under particular strain in 1914. After losing the Russo-Japanese War of 1904–5 and passing through the Revolution of 1905, which established some rudiments of parliamentary monarchy, Russia entered a spectacular period of economic growth. The social and political dangers of such rapid change were immense, especially

Surrounding Queen Victoria in 1894 were her grandson Wilhelm II (seated on the left), and her nephew Nicholas II, standing behind him and to the right, next to the Tsarina Alexandra. Dynastic ties, while visible, represented the surface of power, beneath which lay much more dynamic and destructive forces.

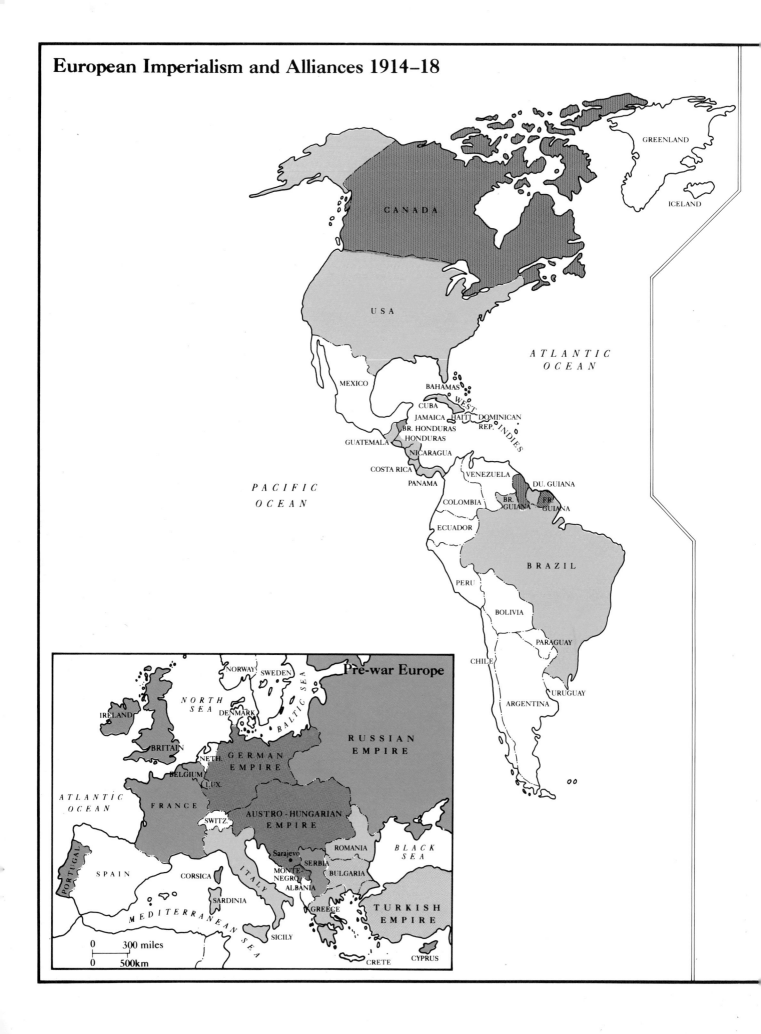

European Imperialism and Alliances 1914–18

GREENLAND

ICELAND

CANADA

USA

ATLANTIC
OCEAN

MEXICO

BAHAMAS

CUBA
JAMAICA HAITI DOMINICAN
BR. HONDURAS HONDURAS REP.
GUATEMALA
NICARAGUA
COSTA RICA
PANAMA

WEST INDIES

VENEZUELA

DU. GUIANA
BR. FR.
GUIANA GUIANA

COLOMBIA

ECUADOR

PACIFIC
OCEAN

BRAZIL

PERU

BOLIVIA

PARAGUAY

CHILE

URUGUAY

ARGENTINA

Pre-war Europe

NORWAY SWEDEN

NORTH
SEA

BALTIC SEA

DENMARK

IRELAND

BRITAIN

NETH.

GERMAN
EMPIRE

BELGIUM

LUX.

ATLANTIC
OCEAN

FRANCE

SWITZ.

RUSSIAN
EMPIRE

AUSTRO - HUNGARIAN
EMPIRE

ROMANIA

BLACK
SEA

Sarajevo

SERBIA

MONTE-
NEGRO

BULGARIA

PORTUGAL

SPAIN

CORSICA

ITALY

ALBANIA

SARDINIA

GREECE

TURKISH
EMPIRE

MEDITERRANEAN SEA

SICILY

CRETE

CYPRUS

0   300 miles
0   500km

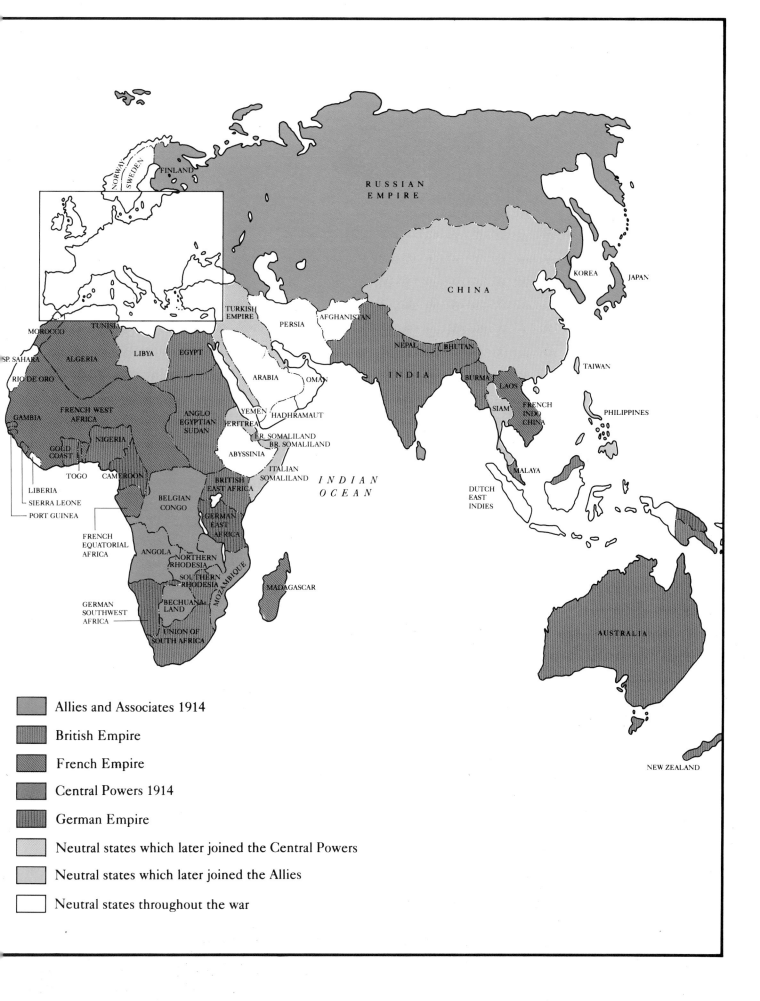

RUSSIAN EMPIRE

FINLAND
NORWAY
SWEDEN

CHINA

KOREA

JAPAN

TURKISH EMPIRE

PERSIA

AFGHANISTAN

MOROCCO
TUNISIA

SP. SAHARA

ALGERIA

LIBYA

EGYPT

RIO DE ORO

ARABIA

OMAN

NEPAL

BHUTAN

TAIWAN

GAMBIA

FRENCH WEST AFRICA

ANGLO EGYPTIAN SUDAN

YEMEN

HADHRAMAUT

INDIA

BURMA

LAOS

NIGERIA

ERITREA

FRENCH INDO CHINA

SIAM

PHILIPPINES

GOLD COAST

FR. SOMALILAND
BR. SOMALILAND

TOGO

CAMEROON

ABYSSINIA

ITALIAN SOMALILAND

INDIAN OCEAN

MALAYA

LIBERIA

SIERRA LEONE

PORT GUINEA

BELGIAN CONGO

BRITISH EAST AFRICA

DUTCH EAST INDIES

FRENCH EQUATORIAL AFRICA

GERMAN EAST AFRICA

ANGOLA

NORTHERN RHODESIA

SOUTHERN RHODESIA

MOZAMBIQUE

MADAGASCAR

GERMAN SOUTHWEST AFRICA

BECHUANA- LAND

AUSTRALIA

UNION OF SOUTH AFRICA

NEW ZEALAND

Allies and Associates 1914

British Empire

French Empire

Central Powers 1914

German Empire

Neutral states which later joined the Central Powers

Neutral states which later joined the Allies

Neutral states throughout the war

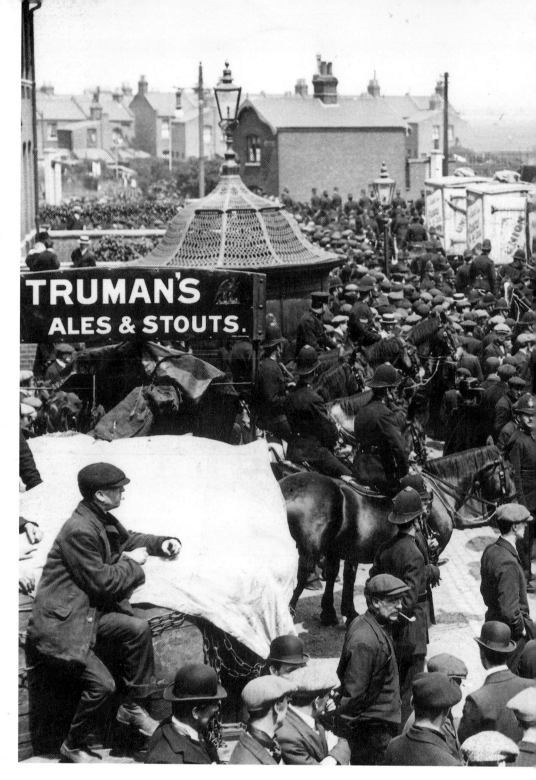

Stable Britain was rocked by a series of strikes before 1914. Many paid off: London dock workers (seen here) won better pay and recognition of their trade union in 1911; coal miners won a minimum wage the following year.

when set against the poverty of so much of the peasant population. It was from this sector that the mass of the Russian Army came. Still loyal to the Tsar and the old order in 1914, the peasantry was being squeezed by industrialization, their grievances paralleled by the protests of an increasingly vocal middle class and an organized working class.

Labour unrest was endemic throughout Europe in the decade before the war. The Austro-Hungarian monarchy faced similar strains produced by rapid economic growth. In Italy, May 1914 was a month of massive strikes. In France

militant trade unionists turned their backs entirely on parliamentary reform, trusting only in industrial action. More sedate, but threatening none the less, was British industrial unrest, which produced a dock strike in 1911, a coal strike in 1912 and a triple alliance of the largest trade unions in 1914. But industrial unrest in western or southern Europe lacked the revolutionary potential of working-class assertions in Germany, Russia or Austria-Hungary. There an archaic political order faced a new economic order in which working-class men and women clamoured for a decent life. Conflict was unavoidable.

IMPERIALISM, NATIONALISM AND REVOLUTION

One issue on which all the monarchs were agreed was the preservation of imperial power. And there was nothing aesthetic or theoretical about the violence through which empires were held together and imperial rule preserved. Each of the major European powers was an imperial power. This could have two meanings: either control over multinational populations in Europe, or control over indigenous populations outside Europe. European nationalisms were potential sources of international conflict – that was obvious. But we should not overlook the iron fist of Europe in Africa and Asia: the ruthlessness displayed by the Belgians in the Congo, the British in India and everybody in China when imperial interests were threatened by local movements towards self-rule.

Within Europe, imperial power was at its zenith in 1914, and yet the threat to that power came from all sides. Ethnic leagues challenged the right of the British to control Ireland, or the Habsburgs to control Bosnia, or the Germans and Russians to control Poland. Even more threatening at times was the linkage of nationalist groups with those preaching social revolution.

The biggest of them was the German Social Democratic Party. It was waiting for its time to come, a state within the state, hostile to the institutions of the Kaiser's regime and dedicated to its overthrow and replacement by a socialist order. In this new order, there would be no room for imperial domination.

Red Rosa

Only after revolution could the oppressed peoples of eastern Europe, and especially the Poles, lift their necks from the yoke of imperial tyranny. This was the revolutionary message preached by one of the firebrands of pre-1914 Europe, Rosa Luxemburg. Born in 1870 to a prosperous Jewish family in Warsaw, she grew up at a time when Poland was a romantic dream, drawn and quartered by imperial powers.

To escape persecution, Luxemburg left Warsaw for Switzerland at the age of nineteen. Her intellectual power was evident from her university days. In 1897 Rosa obtained a doctorate in law and political science at the University of Zurich, and the following year she moved to Germany. There she quickly emerged as one of the leading figures in the international socialist movement and the German Social Democratic Party which was at its heart.

Rosa was unique. She had a ruthless, analytical mind matched to a fiery romantic temperament. Battered in later years by repeated spells in German prisons, and by periodic setbacks to the socialist cause, she still retained her belief in love and her passion for the natural world. From one of her prison cells she affirmed:

> I feel so much more at home in a garden like this one here and still more in
> a meadow when the grass is humming with bees than at one of our party
> congresses. I can say that to you because you will not promptly suspect me of

Rosa Luxemburg making a speech in Berlin in 1907. A Marxist internationalist, she represented a powerful force within the socialist movement. Unlike Lenin, she was unprepared to accept the rule of dictatorial élites. Unlike many reformists, she was unprepared to work within the capitalist state to achieve material benefits.

betraying socialism. You know I hope to die at my post, in a street fight or in jail. But the real deep 'me' belongs more to my butterflies than it does to my comrades.

Rosa Luxemburg represented one deep current of instability in pre-war Europe: international socialism. In 1919 she would pay for her beliefs with her life, shot while in the custody of right-wing paramilitary police.

Before 1914 she was at the heart of the Socialist International, founded in 1889 as a forum for revolutionary ideas and action. Most delegates to the International were both revolutionaries and nationalists. They followed Friedrich Engels, who wrote in 1882, 'An international proletarian movement ... can only grow out of the existence of independent nations.'

But to Rosa national self-determination was not the objective. The liberation of Poland would occur not through national separation from Russia but only through socialist revolution across the entire empire. With remarkable foresight she pointed to the logical extension of nationalist movements: the fragmentation of territories into small new states, each hating the other, each persecuting the new minorities within them. This would turn the world into 'truly feudal anarchy', and create a mountain of corpses.

Nationalism, she believed, prepared the ground for another disaster: imperialist wars. 'In the era of rampaging Imperialism', she wrote, national wars were only a means of 'deception, of betraying the working masses of the people to their deadly enemy, Imperialism'.

In 1907 Rosa spent two months in a German prison for 'inciting to violence', that is for urging German workers to follow the example of the 1905 Russian Revolution. Seven years later she was back in trouble, this time for urging German workers not to take up arms against Russian workers. She was indicted for 'inciting public disobedience', was convicted and served another spell of one year in prison. The verdict was not surprising – the public prosecutor had urged that she be sent to prison, since she was likely to flee the country. Much more remarkable was her address to the court, which caused a sensation.

> Sir, if you had the slightest capacity to absorb the Social Democratic way of thought, and its noble purpose in history, I would explain to you . . . that wars can only come about so long as the working class either supports them enthusiastically, because it considers them justified and necessary, or at least accepts them passively. But once the majority of the working people comes to the conclusion . . . that wars are nothing but a barbaric, unsocial, reactionary phenomenon, entirely against the interests of the people, then wars will have become impossible even if the soldiers obey their commanders.

She suggested that both she and the public prosecutor serve a year in prison. Then they would see who would run away. 'A Social Democrat never does. A Social Democrat stands by his deeds and laughs at your judgments.'

Jean Jaurès

The socialist movement was a house of many mansions. The contrast between Rosa Luxemburg and the French socialist leader Jean Jaurès could not have been more extreme. Rosa was a minuscule Polish woman, a chain smoker, whose fiery eyes dominated those temporarily distracted by her hunched back. Jaurès, ten years her senior, was the leonine patriarch of international socialism. Orator *par excellence*, scourge of imperialism and war, he none the less captured the spirit of the republican patriotic tradition born in the French Revolution, hardened during the war of 1870, and prepared to defend the nation – as long as that word meant the people and not the oligarchy which ran it for private profit.

In 1912, when conflict in the Balkans threatened to engulf the rest of Europe, he spoke out loud and clear. A war in the twentieth century would unleash 'the most terrible holocaust since the Thirty Years' War'. The same voice carried the day in the Basle conference of the Socialist International in November that year. Jaurès introduced the key resolution calling on all affiliated parties to take whatever steps appropriate, including a general strike, to stop war.

When the moment of truth arrived eighteen months later, in the summer of 1914, Jaurès once again tried to rally the forces of international socialism. An emergency meeting of the executive of the International Socialist Bureau was held in Brussels, attended by Jaurès, Rosa Luxemburg and the leaders of all other major parties. As Rosa chain-smoked, Jaurès realized that peace was slipping through their fingers. The Germans spoke of all-out resistance, but with little

Jean Jaurès at a demonstration in Paris in May 1913. Jaurès was a democratic socialist and French nationalist who found in the French revolution a universal message. He was fervently anti-war, and was the one man in the socialist movement who could speak for European workers whatever their nationality. His oratorical power was legendary.

conviction. The aging and infirm Austrian socialist Victor Adler noted with tired resignation that war was popular in Austria, and Austrian socialists would not resist it. Events were moving too fast for even Jaurès to do anything about them.

He returned to Paris, fuming that he would write a new '*J'accuse*' (after the famous open letter from the novelist Emile Zola denouncing the cover-up in the Dreyfus affair sixteen years earlier). Now, Jaurès declared, the world must be told about the intrigues behind the war crisis. He spoke movingly at one of the last rallies against war, but two days later, at a Parisian café with most of his socialist friends, he was assassinated by a crazed nationalist, Raoul Villain, fearful of Jaurès' power to prevent France from going to war. As his body was removed, a crowd gathered. The writer Roger Martin du Gard recalled the scene:

LEFT René Villain, Jaurès' assassin.
BELOW Crowds outside the Café du Croissant after the assassination. Villain was arrested immediately, but he was tried for murder only after the Armistice. Astonishingly, he was acquitted. A French socialist in Spain in 1937 recognized him on the street and killed him on the spot.

Slowly, in a silence so deep that the footfalls of the hearers were clearly audible, the white-hung stretcher crossed the sidewalk, swayed for a moment in midair, then abruptly slipped forward into the darkness of the van. Two men sprang in after it. A police officer climbed on the seat beside the driver. The door was slammed to. Then, as the horse broke into a trot and, escorted by policemen on bicycles, the ambulance started clanging its way toward the Bourse, there rose a sudden clamour, like the roar of an angry sea that drowned the jangling bell; it was as though at last flood-gates had fallen, releasing the pent-up emotions of the crowd. 'Jaurès! Jaurès! Jaurès! Jaurès forever.'

What neither Rosa Luxemburg, with her commitment to revolution before nation, nor Jean Jaurès, with his commitment to revolution and nation, could stem was the tide of opinion unleashed by the war crisis of 1914. That conflict was understood by everyone as a defensive struggle not of their own making. That some contributed more to it than others was beside the point. In Berlin as much as in London or Paris, everyone blamed the other side for forcing the issue over the brink of war.

Another assassination triggered the declaration of war. This time it was the work of those who believed in nation, not social revolution. Within the Austro-Hungarian context, this belief was shared by dozens of tiny sects. One of them, an obscure Serbian/Bosnian radical group called the Black Hand, lit the spark that set off the conflagration we know as World War 1.

Gavrilo Princip

'Some damned foolish thing in the Balkans', Bismarck had once predicted, would ignite a major war. In 1914, as now, the Balkans were an ethnic kaleidoscope. The Austrian Empire controlled most of what between 1918 and 1989 was called Yugoslavia, or the south Slavic lands, between Austria in the north and independent Serbia in the south. This meant that an Austrian and Magyar élite controlled an ethnically diverse and increasingly hostile population. Slav nationalists of many kinds were demanding independence, and their cause was backed by important Russian elements.

Could this inherently unstable mix have continued indefinitely? Probably not. What is clear is that Austro-Hungarian hegemony was on display on 28 June 1914, when the heir to the throne, the Archduke Franz Ferdinand, and his wife Sophie visited the Bosnian capital Sarajevo, which neighboured free Serbia. The day was poorly chosen: it was the anniversary of Serbia's medieval independence.

Waiting for him were seven young Bosnian nationalists recruited by the Black Hand. While it is unlikely that this group was simply a pawn in the hands of Serbian intelligence they were not innocent bystanders.

The first would-be assassin did nothing. The second conspirator tossed a bomb at the Archduke's car. The chauffeur saw it coming and sped away. The bomb exploded in the road, wrecking the following car and wounding three aides and several spectators. The nineteen-year-old bomb thrower swallowed a cyanide pill and jumped into the nearby river to drown. Neither attempt at suicide worked, although he nearly died at the hands of the crowd that hauled him out of the river.

LEFT Archduke Franz
Ferdinand and his wife
Sophie in Sarajevo shortly
before their assassination.
BELOW The arrest of one of
the assassins. Princip himself
spent the war in Theresien
prison in Austria, later
Theresienstadt concentra-
tion camp, and died of
tuberculosis in 1918.

Franz Ferdinand insisted on maintaining the day's agenda. He spoke at the town hall. This took him near other assassins, who made no move. After his speech, he decided to alter his itinerary and visit the hospital where the injured from the earlier bomb attempt had been taken. His driver then took a wrong turn that brought them face to face with the seventh and final assassin, a young man named Gavrilo Princip. Jumping on the running board of the Archduke's car, he fired two shots at point-blank range.

From the street, Franz Ferdinand and his wife seemed to sit quietly through all the confusion and chaos that followed. Inside the car, the Archduke opened his mouth to speak. Blood spilled over his tunic. He turned to his wife, begged her not to die, and collapsed. He had been shot in the neck; she in the lower

abdomen. Within minutes, both were dead. Their bloodstained clothes can be seen today in the Austrian Historical Museum in Vienna.

The assassins were arrested. The dead couple were buried hastily, some thought shabbily. Many hoped that the resulting tensions would fade away. But this was not what the Austrian government wanted. On 5 July the Emperor Franz Josef wrote to the Kaiser, seeking his support:

> The bloody deed was not the work of a single individual but a well organized plot whose threads extend to Belgrade ... there can be no doubt that its policy of uniting all Southern Slavs under the Serbian flag encourages such crimes and the continuation of this situation is a chronic peril for my House and my territories. My efforts must be directed to isolating Serbia and reducing her size.

The Kaiser gave the Austrian ambassador, Count Szogyeny, his assessment. The risks of war were low. 'Russia is in no way prepared for war,' he told the ambassador. Austria could be assured of Germany's full backing. He next wondered aloud to his staff whether he should postpone his annual cruise to the Norwegian fjords. The German Chancellor, Bethmann-Hollweg, urged him to go ahead with his plans.

Wherever the Kaiser was, the damage had been done. Both he and his military advisers viewed with little fear an outbreak of fighting in the Balkans. Such a limited engagement could clear the air – both domestic and international – and serve as a positive stabilizing element in central European politics. One precedent was the short, decisive Austro-Prussian War of 1866, which prepared the way for the birth, five years later, of the German Empire. But in 1914 such an estimate of their capacity to control violence in the international system was wildly inaccurate.

With German support, confirmed on 6 July, Austria proceeded two weeks later, on the 23rd, to deliver an ultimatum to Serbia accusing it of responsibility and demanding Austro-Hungarian participation in a commission of inquiry into the assassination. Serbia was given forty-eight hours to reply. Despite the fact that Serbia swallowed its national pride and accepted most of these conditions, the Austrians deemed the demands to have been refused. Austria declared war on Serbia, and Austrian artillery bombarded the capital, Belgrade. 'This means a European war,' the shocked Russian Foreign Minister announced to the Austrian ambassador. 'You are setting Europe alight.' He was right.

Now the alliance system swung into action to heighten the crisis. Most allies responded: Germany to Austria's aid, Russia to Serbia's, France to Russia's and, after the German invasion of Belgium on 1 August (to swing south and attack France), Britain to Belgium's. All followed treaty obligations. As soon as armies mobilized, war was unavoidable. When both Russia and Germany mobilized (Germany slightly later, so as to appear the injured party), nothing could stop the outbreak of general hostilities. The Great War had begun.

Franz Ferdinand's bloodstained coat. His visit to Sarajevo came on the anniversary of the Battle of Kosovo, a medieval defeat of Serbs by Muslims. Militant Serbs took this as an offence to Serb nationalism. In fact Franz Ferdinand was one of the moderates in the Austrian court, and his murder tipped the balance of argument in Vienna towards war against Serbia. The extremists in both camps had won.

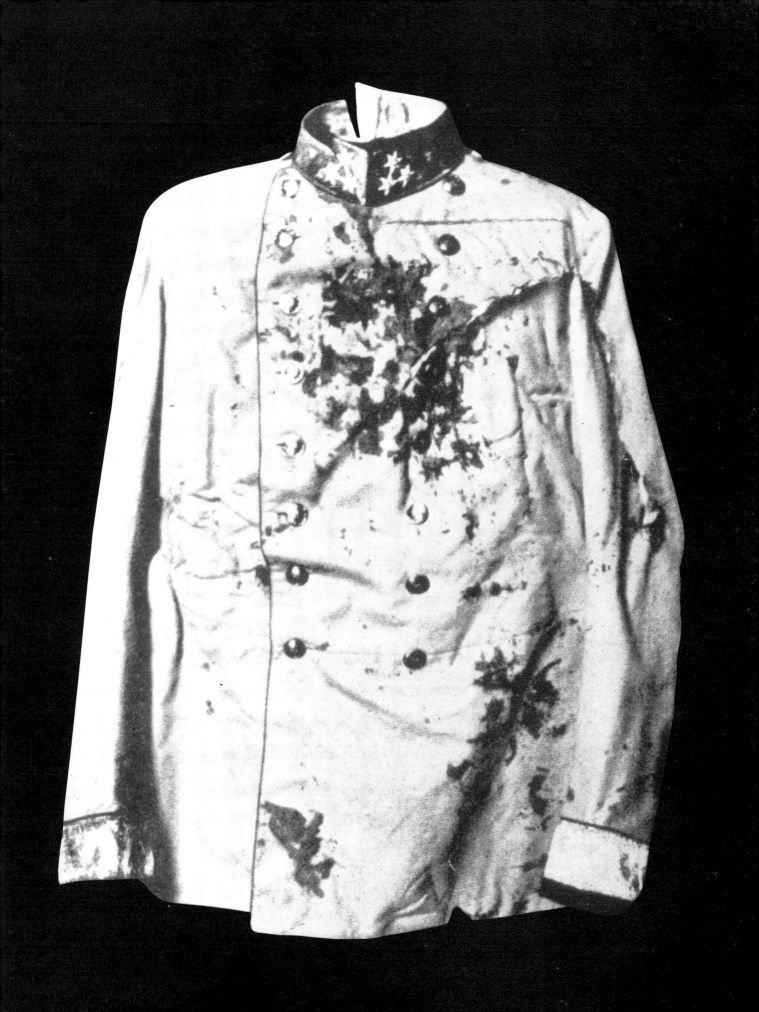

THE BEGINNING

Whenthe war finally came to Europe, ordinary people responded in many different ways. The vision of the public reaction to the outbreak of war in 1914 that is engrained in our historical imagination has cheering crowds at railway stations throughout Europe in August 1914 waving off flower-bedecked troops to Berlin or Paris. The documentary film record of such events is there, reinforced by a chorus of poets, writers and philosophers positively revelling in the moment. The Austrian writer Stefan Zweig noted that 'each individual experienced an exaltation of his ego.' The liberal philosopher Bertrand Russell walked the streets of London, discovering, as he put it, that the average man in the street positively wanted war. To the French writer Alain-Fournier, author of *Le Grand Meaulnes*, 'This war is fine and great and just.' To the German novelist Thomas Mann, the war would yield moral benefits: 'The German soul will emerge stronger, prouder, freer, happier from it.... On that never-to-be-forgotten first day ... a wave of deep moral feeling overwhelmed us.' 'Thus the August madness descended', and the twentieth century began.

But is it true? After years of research, historians have changed their minds. In all likelihood we have been misled by the intellectuals and the newsreels. They tell a part of the truth, but one which has obscured other responses to the outbreak of the war which can now be documented and illustrated.

Some people did welcome the war and, especially if they were young city dwellers, they went out in summer weather to show the flag. But within a day or two they were gone; and within a few miles, public display of wartime fervour never happened at all.

The moment when war came to the people of Europe was harvest time, and the news came to many people as they worked in the fields. Mémé Santerre and her husband Auguste were weavers from a French village near the Belgian border. In the summers, they worked as seasonal labourers in the agricultural region to the west of Paris. This year they had left their young child with his grandparents, so that, as usual, they could earn enough for the hard winter ahead. Suddenly, 'at the neighbourhood church, a furious, irregular, extraordinary bell-ringing broke out'.

A French quartermaster sergeant, decorated with the Croix de Guerre, with his family. The outbreak of war in 1914 marked the merger of family history and political history in Europe. Before 1914, the state intervened occasionally in private life; after 1914, the state was everywhere. Soldiers on active service could count on separation allowances to keep their family's budget intact. In this way the state served as a surrogate father, providing families with an income essential to the smooth mobilization of millions of married men in 1914.

> 'The tocsin!' cried someone in the field. 'There's a fire in the fields!' Then we saw men running and yelling on the road bordering the field. We couldn't hear what they were saying, but as they passed, the workers dropped their tools, running wildly, seized with some madness after a second of shock. Soon the field was swept with a wave of agitation. As the words reached them, people began running. My husband and I stared without understanding, before we heard, right in our faces, the news that a neighbour, in his turn, was yelling. 'War! It's war!'
>
> We were stunned. I remember that Auguste, turning toward me, said 'War, but what war?'
>
> Then, we dropped our tools, the little hooks that we used to pile up the sheaves, and joined the crowd, running as fast as our legs could carry us, to

Here is one view of 1914: heroic German soldiers embarking on a lightning operation against France, after which they would stroll through Paris. The faces of these men tell another story. Many of these middle-aged men were reservists, called to the colours in 1914. Their railway car is clearly marked as coming from 'Elsass-Lothringen', or Alsace-Lorraine, which they were to defend. These reservists surprised the French by putting up a very stiff fight in the east of France in August 1914. The result was a bloodbath, and the total failure of the French planned thrust eastward into Germany.

the farmhouse. Everyone was going there, in the great need that men feel to gather together when faced with a catastrophe. In the courtyard, there was more excitement than I had ever seen there before. The men usually so calm, usually so slow-moving, were seized with frenzy. Horses entered at a quick trot, whipped by their drivers, while the oxen, goaded until they bled, hurried in reluctantly. In this coming-and-going of wagons and animals, I could hear disjointed phrases: 'General mobilization. . . .' 'What a misfortune, what an awful misfortune!' 'I have to leave right away!' 'Good God, where's my bundle?' 'The Germans are attacking. . . .' 'It was all bound to come to this. . . .'

Stupefaction, not enthusiasm; shock and fear, not exhilaration and bravado also dominated the moment elsewhere in rural Europe – which is, after all, where most of the population lived.

In Brittany, a region that jealously guarded its distinctive language and culture, the invasion of France was not greeted in French. Nor was it greeted with joy. A Breton peasant, Pierre-Jakez Hélias, described the day the war came:

> At five in the afternoon the bells of the parish church were set to ringing in a mode that made one think the sexton had lost his head. Actually, the poor devil was signalling a fire that was to last for over four years throughout the world. How could he have found the right tone? He was going from one bell to another, striking them with the awkwardness of despair. But everyone clearly understood his extraordinary language.
>
> My father picked up his sickle and wielded it a few times, but more and more slowly. Then he bent one knee to the ground and lowered his head. Suddenly he stood straight up, threw his tool far into the distance, and started to walk toward the town through the fields, without ever once unclenching his jaws. My mother sat on the ground and wept into her apron.

The outbreak of war in 1914 revealed a heroism far removed from the patriotic swagger of the official press. But it was heroism none the less – made of equal parts of stoicism, determination and love of one's local landscape and community. That state of mind dominated the Great War; it was a state of mind that throughout this book is traced in the stories of individuals great and obscure throughout that dark phase of history.

Where were some of those people in August 1914? Most could not have dreamt of what was in store for them. In France, Charles de Gaulle was a twenty-five-year-old officer in the 33rd Infantry Regiment, commanded by Philippe Pétain, then aged fifty-eight.

Adolf Hitler was the same age as de Gaulle, but there the resemblance ended. Hitler lived in Munich as a failed artist. In Berlin, forty-seven-year-old sculptor and graphic artist Käthe Kollwitz had reached a level of distinction of which Hitler could only dream. Her son Karl was eighteen, a year younger than Ernst Jünger, who, much more the martial type, had just returned to Germany from a stint in the French Foreign Legion. Leon Trotsky was an obscure Menshevik revolutionary living in Vienna.

On 4 August 1914, Wilfred Owen was teaching at a school in France. Edward Thomas was a struggling writer living with his family in a cottage in Gloucester-

Marc Chagall, *Leave-taking soldiers*, 1914. After a four-year stay in Paris, Chagall returned to Russia, where he was trapped by the outbreak of war. He captured the ambivalence of the popular response to the outbreak of war. Chagall remained in Russia until 1922.

shire. Isaac Rosenberg had just arrived in Cape Town, where he planned to paint and teach.

Harry Truman, aged thirty, was a farmer in Missouri. Douglas MacArthur was a thirty-four-year-old army captain chasing Mexican bandits south of the Rio Grande. George Patton, twenty-nine, was on leave from Cavalry School in Kansas, visiting his wife's family in Massachusetts. George C. Marshall was an up-and-coming thirty-five-year-old staff officer on manoeuvres in the Philippines.

The lives of every one of these people would be transformed by the war. Most were in their prime, from between twenty-five and thirty-five, ready to begin a career, found a family, stake a claim to a future. Over the following four and a half years some died, but most survived; they were the lucky ones.

To understand their lives, and the world they passed on to us, we need to go back to that moment in 1914 when, in a sense, the twentieth century began. When we look at their faces, so hopeful, so fresh, so full of possibility, we can see some of what might have been, as well as some foreshadowing of what was to be.

The history of the Generation of 1914 is a story of decency betrayed, of the gap which separated the narrow vision of the men in power and the open hearts of millions who followed. To contrast the outlook of the leaders with the humane responses of the multitude – the people who really knew the war at its worst – is to begin to form some sense of the waste and tragedy of the Great War.

2

STALEMATE

The last 'nineteenth-century' war lasted from August to December 1914. It was a war of movement, of high drama and very high casualties. In August, the regular British Army and reserves – 120 000 strong – joined the French and Belgian forces resisting the German invasion of Belgium. All the British could do was harry the invading force, slow down its advance, and wait for help. These machine gunners in the 11th Hussars dug in near Ypres, where the British line held a salient around the town.

The German High Command, despite all that Bismarck had done in the nineteenth century to avoid fighting a war simultaneously on two fronts, now faced exactly that situation. Timing, they believed, was everything. France was to be beaten before Germany turned to Russia. The Kaiser summed up the strategy succinctly: 'Paris for lunch, dinner in St Petersburg!'

The Schlieffen Plan, named after the German general, Count Alfred von Schlieffen, who devised the scheme, was daring and years in the making. The strategy called for an intricate but massive movement of armies by rail. Consider the magnitude of the problem. It took five hundred trains, with fifty wagons each, to move four German Army corps or 180 000 men and their supplies into Belgium and France. This was just the beginning of a logistical nightmare: 1½ million men, food, arms, horses, all crossed the Rhine. Once past the German border, the means of transport for the soldiers would revert to the traditional method: their own two feet. The main thrust of the attack – involving three-quarters of the German Army – would outflank France's border fortifications by attacking through neutral Belgium. The German forces would sweep through Belgium, brushing against the English Channel, and then turn south in a huge arc to defeat the French Army and capture Paris. The loss of the capital, the German military planners believed, would cause the surrender of France. The plan required victory in the West in six weeks, time enough before the huge Russian Army, hampered by a poor rail system and far greater distances to travel, could make itself a serious threat on the Eastern Front. German soldiers departed on troop trains adorned with flowers and political graffiti, believing that they would be home before 'leaves dropped from the trees'.

The French Army had its master plan, too. 'Plan XVII' was rooted in an obsession with the Emperor Napoleon III's shameful defeat in 1871, which had cost the country two of its richest provinces, Alsace and Lorraine. In the event of war, the French generals now aimed to restore them to France. Young officers were drilled in *élan vital*, the cult of the offensive. 'In the offensive,' they were told, 'imprudence is the best of assurances.' 'Every soldier must ardently desire the assault by bayonet as the supreme means of imposing his will upon the enemy and gaining victory.' 'For the attack, only two things are necessary: to know where the enemy is and to decide what to do. What the enemy intends to do is of no consequence.' 'Success', the French Field Regulations predicted, 'comes not to him who has suffered the least but to him whose will is firmest and morale strongest.' This doctrine would cost tens of thousands of French lives in 1914.

But neither the French nor the German plan was based on sound generalship. If the French aims were little more than wishful thinking, the German strategy was a desperate gamble that pitted them not only against two armies but also against the clock. For the Schlieffen Plan to succeed, the advance would have to be rapidly prosecuted. Paris was to be taken by M-39 — thirty-nine days after mobilization. This was not the wild assumption that it seems in hindsight, as the majority of military leaders in every country believed that any modern war would be a swift affair. Recent inventions had accelerated the pace of ordinary civilian life; the same speed was expected to dominate the battlefield. Telephones would dispatch orders. Aeroplanes would conduct reconnaissance. Railways would transport troops. And new advances in weaponry — the machine gun, improved rifles and heavy cannon — would make the battlefield so violent a place that one side or the other would falter under an assault and quickly give way. In other words, what all the military strategists anticipated was a more furious replay of the Franco-Prussian War of 1870 – 1.

For a few weeks in 1914 this was exactly how events unfolded. But soon war on the Western Front began to take on a different appearance, one more akin to siege warfare. The objective, however, would be not a fortress but mere ditches. They might be taken, usually at a tremendous cost, but there would always be another one to take its place. No one had prepared for that. The German Army settled into defensive positions, leaving the Allies with the formidable task of removing an enemy entrenched on French and Belgian soil. But how? This was the war's essential question. The answers came from military leaders caught in their own culture, a culture that drew naturally on the traditions and experiences of the nineteenth century. Almost without exception, generals on both sides entered the war with a profound belief that victory lay with the offensive. That belief did not desert them later in the war.

SAYING GOODBYE

In France, news of war left people dumbfounded. 'Paris is in turmoil,' wrote Henri Desagneaux. 'The banks are besieged. Emotion is at its peak.' Desagneaux, a civilian who worked in the legal department of the French Eastern Railway Company, was a reservist in the French Army. He, like tens of thousands of his countrymen whose lives were being up-ended by the sudden news of war, was ordered to report immediately to his regiment when posters announcing the mobilization went up on 1 August. 'It's every man for himself,' he recorded in his diary, 'you scarcely have the time to shake a few hands before having to go home to make preparations for departure.' Among others, 4 million Russians, 3 million

Austro-Hungarians, 4½ million Germans and 4 million French marched off, leaving behind their jobs, their homes and their families.

At railway stations across Europe there was chaos and confusion. Regular timetables were suspended indefinitely as troop trains rushed to the frontiers. Desagneaux witnessed women and children saying farewell to their husbands and fathers at the Gare de L'Est in Paris. 'The women are crying, the men too. They have to say good-bye without knowing whether they will ever return.' They also said goodbye without really understanding why Armageddon was approaching. '*Incroyable!*' was the word that Philip Gibbs, a British journalist who had rushed to Paris in the first days of August, kept hearing over and over again in streets and cafés. '*C'est incroyable!*'

In St Petersburg – soon to be renamed as the more Russian-sounding Petrograd – the French ambassador, Maurice Paléologue, witnessed grieving women walking alongside their husbands and sons as they marched off to war. He noted one woman in particular: 'She was very young, with delicate features and a fine neck, a red and white scarf knotted around her fair hair, a blue cotton sarafan drawn in at the waist by a leather belt, and she held an infant to her breast. The couple spoke not a word, but gazed fixedly at each other with mourning, loving eyes.'

French troops departing from the Gare Montparnasse in Paris. All the railway lines in Paris in August 1914 were jammed with people on the move. Social and political differences were put aside; every able man joined his unit. Opposition to the war was non-existent; everyone felt anger against Germany and a determination to avoid the humiliation of military defeat.

It was harvest time when the war came. But instead of reapers crowding the fields of France and Belgium, soldiers trampled over them. These waves of German artillerymen in pre-war manoeuvres faced a much sterner test in 1914. They were pushed to the limits of endurance and, not surprisingly, failed to break Allied resistance.

Russian conscripts could not read. Notifying them of mobilization came not through posters or newspaper announcements, but by the posting of red cards in thousands of towns and hamlets.

Thousands of people who were living, working or on holiday in foreign countries that summer suddenly found themselves in enemy territory. Half the waiters in Paris were German: getting home was their first priority, joining up their second. Ernst Toller was a young German studying in France, who made his way back home through Switzerland:

> At last I found myself in the train, which was full of escaping Germans. Our progress was almost imperceptible. The train was always stopping, always shunting; we waited endlessly.... At midnight, only a few hours before the frontier finally closed, we arrived at Geneva, famished and tired out; but when we found ourselves on Swiss soil again we hugged one another and sang *Deutschland, Deutschland über alles*. On the other side of the platform returning Frenchmen sang the *Marseillaise*.

Soon they would be fighting, not singing.

POOR LITTLE BELGIUM

On the morning of 4 August the vanguard of the invasion, the German cavalry, crossed the border into Belgium. With their 12-foot lances they looked like invaders from another century. The Belgian Army, however, was in truth an army of the last century. It could defend, delay and harass, but could not hold out for long. What the Germans feared most was guerrilla warfare, sniper fire, sabotage of the kind they had faced in 1870; any irregular warfare of this kind, the opposition of *franc-tireurs*, would have to be stamped out swiftly and brutally so that the German timetable could be met. The Schlieffen Plan required the harsh treatment of any civilian opposition; intimidation was essential.

The German commander charged with carrying out this massive invasion was Helmut von Moltke, a sensitive and intelligent sixty-six-year-old in uncertain health. The first day of the operation gave him hope, as village after village on the frontier was quickly taken. On the second day the Germans launched a series of direct infantry assaults on the twelve forts surrounding the city of Liège. With thirty-five thousand garrison troops and four hundred retractable guns, the complex of underground fortresses, which had been discounted by the invaders, proved to be stiff opposition and cost the German infantry terrible losses. 'They made no attempt at deploying,' a Belgian officer observed, 'but came on line after line, almost shoulder to shoulder, until, as we shot them down, the fallen were heaped on top of each other in an awful barricade of dead and wounded.' The Germans, like everyone else, had their own serious lessons to learn about the stopping power of machine guns. In the midst of the battle Erich Ludendorff, a forty-nine-year-old colonel, took command of a brigade and ordered a successful attack on a vulnerable part of the Belgian defence when the commanding German general was killed. It was the first in a series of fortuitous events for a man who within two years would be running the entire German war effort.

Helmut von Moltke, who pressed for war in July and reaped defeat in September. He retired as Chief of the German General Staff two months later.

Belgian Carabiniers during the retreat to Antwerp, 20 August 1914. Holding a few key forts, the Belgian Army could do no more than offer limited resistance to the Germans. Using dogs to move machine guns, they fought a domestic war to defend their homes. Sniper fire brought heavy punishment on them and their families: the German Army responded with an iron fist.

Liège was taken, but its surrounding forts held out. Taking them required a huge siege gun, the likes of which the world had never seen. Forged in the Krupp munitions factories, it was nicknamed 'Big Bertha', a reference to the plump wife of Gustav Krupp. The gun required a crew of over two hundred, and its range was 5½ miles. Even more impressive was the size of the shells, which made short work of the concrete and steel bunkers. Soldiers inside were driven mad by the shelling. The last of the forts fell on 16 August. The Belgian commander was knocked senseless in the final bombardment and awoke a captive of the Germans. 'I was taken unconscious. Be sure to put that in your dispatches,' he demanded of his captors as he handed them his sword. It was another old response to a new and harsher age of warfare.

The old traditions also called for the end of a country's hostilities when its army was beaten on the battlefield. Belgium fought differently – and the German response was savage. 'Our advance in Belgium', Moltke wrote on 5 August, 'is certainly brutal, but we are fighting for our lives and all who get in the way must take the consequences.' On that day a number of Belgian priests had been executed for encouraging resistance to the invasion. But the Belgians needed little encouragement from their priests, as snipers shot at German soldiers laden with 25 kg packs on their backs through fields and villages. The invading forces and their commanders responded with an iron fist, burning homes, rounding up villagers – men, women and in some cases children – and shooting groups of them: six at Warsage, fifty at Seilles, nearly four hundred at Tamines and over six hundred at Dinant. The medieval town of Louvain was heavily shelled and its university's library, a treasure-house of ancient manuscripts, was torched. 'We shall wipe it out,' declared one German officer. 'Not one stone will stand upon another! We will teach them to respect Germany. For generations people will come here to see what we have done.' Louvain, like all the other atrocities committed, was to become a propaganda goldmine, and the Allies mined 'Poor Little Belgium' for all its worth, including reports of murdered children with roasted feet. The atrocities that actually occurred were terrible, and horrified German soldiers as well. Rudolf Binding, who fought from 1914 to 1918, wrote:

> When one sees the wasting, burning villages and towns, plundered cellars and attics in which the troops have pulled everything to pieces in the blind instinct of self-preservation, dead or half-starved animals, cattle bellowing in the sugar-beet fields, and then corpses, corpses, and corpses, streams of wounded one after another – then everything becomes senseless, a lunacy, a horrible bad joke of peoples and their history, an endless reproach to mankind, a negation of all civilisation, killing all belief in the capacity of mankind and men for progress, a desecration of what is holy, so that one feels that all human beings are doomed in this war.

The Belgian resistance had held up the invasion for only a few days. The real cost to Germany, however, was not the delays to a military timetable but the image of the violation of a small but brave nation fighting for its survival. The symbol of 'Poor Little Belgium' would haunt the Germans for years to come.

Schrecklichkeit, or frightfulness, was an intrinsic and inevitable part of the German war plan. Since speed was of the essence, no civilian harassment or irregular warfare would be tolerated by the Germans. They used heavy artillery, including the siege gun 'Big Bertha', a 42-cm howitzer (LEFT), on the town centre of the city of Louvain (ABOVE); they shot hostages; burnt villages; and when women were raped by German soldiers, their commanders did little about it.

DÉBÂCLE

The French commander was Joseph Jacques Césaire 'Papa' Joffre. Sixty-two years old when the war began, he was the son of a tradesman who had begun his military career as an engineer – not the usual breeding ground for army commanders. Wide in girth, laconic in demeanour and given to afternoon naps even in the midst of crisis, he was nevertheless a champion of the offensive spirit. Like his fellow officers, he saw speed and spirit as the essence of combat. Although the bayonet was the weapon of choice, the French did have a fine artillery piece, the light but quick-loading 75 mm. Heavy artillery, however, was seen as an impediment. 'Thank God we don't have any,' one staff officer declared (inaccurately). 'What gives the French army its force is the lightness of its cannon.'

German planning predicted that the French commander Joffre (ABOVE) would move his troops (RIGHT) to the east in the event of war. He obliged. French offensives were blocked with terrible casualties: 27 000 Frenchmen died on 22 August 1914, the bloodiest day in French military history. The miracle was that Joffre was still able to pull his army back towards Paris in time to meet the main German force on the Marne and defeat it.

Believing that the thrust through Belgium was a feint, most of the French Army moved north-east towards German positions in Alsace and Lorraine. Still clad in nineteenth-century uniforms of bright red trousers and blue coats, the French massed in formation, their officers carrying swords held by hands sporting white gloves. They attacked in clear view of German artillery spotters, with no thought to surprise or concealment. The outcome was a slaughter. Between 20 and 23 August 1914 over forty thousand French soldiers were killed, twenty-seven thousand alone on the 22nd. It was the bloodiest day in French military history. Their thrust was towards the Ardennes forest, but at Arlon-Virton, to the west of the River Mosel, they suffered massive casualties and retreated.

Why the defeat? The first reason was French miscalculation. They took into account only the German regular army and assumed that the reserves, deployed in occupied Lorraine, could not withstand a French assault. They were wrong.

They also underestimated the lethal abilities of machine guns and heavy artillery. It was the kind of brutal lesson, remarked one who witnessed the assault, 'by which God teaches the law to Kings'. These futile offensives were precisely what the German Army had hoped the French generals would mount. In five days the French lost 140 000 men, and while they wasted their armies in the east, the Germans swept west and south. Joffre, trying to keep in personal touch with his commanders, raced by motor car from command post to command post, driven by a three-time winner of the Grand Prix car race. It was not enough. By the time Joffre realized what was occurring, the beloved capital, indeed the republic itself, was threatened. The French Army fell back towards Paris, destroying bridges and railway lines *en route*. 'You may expect the German armies to be before the walls of Paris in twelve days,' Joffre cabled the government. 'Is Paris ready to withstand a siege?'

The Great Panic

Joffre insisted on a virtual news blackout: journalists were not allowed at the French front. The French government, too, was kept largely in the dark, but the threat of a siege sent it fleeing from the capital to the safety of Bordeaux. The following evening the British reporter Philip Gibbs, who had attempted without success to reach the front, returned to Paris to witness an extraordinary scene:

> There was a wild rush to get away from the capital, and the railway stations were great camps of fugitives, in which the richest and the poorest were mingled, with their women and children. There were many old men and women there who knew what a siege of Paris meant. To young people they told the tale of it now – the old familiar tale – with shaking heads and trembling forefingers. 'Starvation!' 'We ate rats if we were lucky.' 'They would not hesitate to smash up Notre Dame.' Most of them had a haggard look and kept repeating the stale old word, '*Incroyable!*'

Anyone with a place to go fled. Hundreds of thousands had already escaped from the fighting in Belgium into Holland, France and by sea to Britain. Now the railway and roads were flooded with French refugees. In the first three weeks of the war a British officer named what he witnessed 'The Great Panic'. The accounts of atrocities against civilians only made matters worse.

The story of Mémé Santerre and her family can stand for countless similar tales. Their reaction to the outbreak of war was amazement. As part-time agricultural labourers near Rouen in August in 1914 they found themselves right in the path of the invading force. They escaped on the local butcher's cart with a few belongings. Others around them were forced to flee with 'empty hands'. Some tried to get away with their animals: 'Cows, sheep, goats, donkeys, driven by their owners in unbelievable disorder,' she later wrote. Then their entourage collided with the French Army. 'At first, it was infantry, and that wasn't so bad. But then, the artillery rolled up, and the mess was really scary: the huge agricultural wagons got tangled with the heavy harnesses of the caissons and military wagons in an awful jumble.'

Similar scenes were encountered by Philip Gibbs, following the battle north of Paris:

When the German Army approached Paris, the prosperous fled; the old, the young and the women who remained faced shortages: the banks had no money, the workshops were closed, unemployment rose. Into the city streamed thousands of families fleeing from the German invasion.

Afterwards I became so used to it all that I came to think the world must always have been like this, with people always in flight, families and crowds of families drifting about aimlessly, from town to town, getting into trains just because they started somewhere for somewhere else, sitting for hours on bundles which contained all their worldly goods, saved from the wreckage of ancient homes, losing their children on the roadside, and not fretting very much, and finding other children, whom they adopted as their own; never washing on that wandering, so that delicate women who had once been perfumed with fine scents were dirty as gypsies and unashamed of draggled dresses and dirty hands; eating when they found a meal of charity, sleeping in railway sidings, coalsheds, and derelict trains shunted on to grass-covered lines; careless as pariah dogs of what the future held in store now that they had lost all things in the past.

What has become a characteristic twentieth-century figure was born: the refugee, fleeing from the face of war.

'The Emperor trusted me'

Refugees began appearing in Germany as well – they were fleeing from the Russian Army. What good was victory in France, an enraged Kaiser demanded of his officers, if Berlin was soon to be in the hands of the Cossacks? However slow, the Russian Army was a force to be reckoned with. Its standing army numbered nearly a million and a half; mobilization brought its size to a breathtaking 4½ million, with another 2 million soldiers in reserve. If only because of their country's size, many in Russia were convinced that Germany could be quickly defeated. And the invasion of East Prussia would force Germany to weaken her armies invading France. In the early weeks of the war such forecasts did not seem unreasonable: the Russian Army was already on the move, and moving faster than Germany had planned.

Two Russian armies, comprising some 370 000 troops, were moving into East Prussia – what is eastern Poland today. Like the Germans in Belgium, the Russians were burning villages as they advanced. The commander of the German forces in the East was sacked and replaced by Paul von Hindenburg, who at sixty-seven was brought out of retirement. The news came so suddenly that Hindenburg, who left for the front at three in the morning, was unable to have a proper field-grey uniform made for him. He departed dressed in his old Prussian blue. Appointed as his chief of staff was the hero of Liège, Erich Ludendorff. Only four days after their arrival, the German and Russian forces were joined in battle.

German refugees fled west, ahead of the invading Russian armies. Their presence in Berlin was a worrying sign, but unlike in Paris, daily life was less disrupted by the outbreak of war. Families were aided by church and voluntary organizations, which cushioned the shock of refugee life.

These Cossacks formed part of a two-pronged invasion of East Prussia. Numerically superior, but inferior to the German Army in every other respect, the Russian Army bought time for their allies, the French, and stripped the German invading force in France of divisions pulled back to defend Germany in the east.

OVERLEAF Russian troops heading for the front line. In the summer of 1914, the Russian armies in East Prussia fell into a brilliantly constructed trap. Secretly moving virtually all the German defenders in the north by rail and foot to face half the Russian force in the southern sector gave the Germans a momentary and decisive numerical advantage. The Russians were taken by surprise: by 28 August 1914 the Russian Second Army under Samsonov had been destroyed at Tannenberg.

Commanding the two Russian armies were General Pavel Rennenkampf and General Alexander Samsonov. Their differences went back years, and on the eve of the battle they were not even on speaking terms. The plan for the advance required them to split their armies in two in order to bypass the 50-mile chain of the Masurian Lakes. Once past the lakes they intended to attack the German Army, which they heavily outnumbered, from two sides, crushing it, and then racing on to Berlin. But the Russians carelessly broadcast their intentions in radio communiqués that were picked up by the Germans. This knowledge suggested to one German staff officer, Lieutenant Colonel Max Hoffmann, a bold but risky idea. If the Germans could marshal their smaller numbers against the first of the two Russian armies to arrive, they could destroy it before the other force turned up in support. In piecemeal fashion both sets of invading Russians, at the end of long supply lines, would be destroyed. That was essentially what happened.

Whatever the circumstances, the Russian troops would have been no match for their German opponents. In terms of sheer numbers the Russian Army was enormous, but its soldiers were poorly trained, incompetently led and inadequately equipped. Russian commanders were selected more for their understanding of court intrigue than for their knowledge of military doctrine. Drunkenness among the officers was rife. Artillery shells were in such short supply that they had to be rationed. In battle, many Russian soldiers had to wait until a comrade fell before they could have a rifle to shoot. At one point they were offered a bounty of six roubles for every Russian rifle picked up off the battlefield; Austrian rifles went for five roubles. The troops were, as Colonel Knox, a British military attaché, described them, 'just great big-hearted children who had thought out nothing and had stumbled half-asleep into a wasp's nest'. Samsonov's army was surrounded and quickly disintegrated; thirty thousand

Russians were dead, over one hundred thousand were taken prisoner, and the rest were running for their lives. 'The Emperor trusted me,' a shocked Samsonov muttered to one of his staff officers. 'How can I face him after such a disaster?' In the end he chose not to – he wandered into the woods and shot himself. Rennenkampf's army escaped by retreating across the border into Russia.

This battle was Germany's greatest victory in the entire war. Hindenburg's and Ludendorff's stars were now in dual ascendance, even though Ludendorff's nerve had wavered during the battle. At a critical juncture he had urged that the battle be called off, but Hindenburg chose to ignore him. Hoffmann, who had devised the plan, afterwards suggested that the battle should be called Tannenberg, in careful recollection of another battle fought nearby in 1410 at which Teutonic Knights, including an ancestor of Hindenburg's, lost against a Slavic army. The Kaiser celebrated, while France was thankful for Russia's effort. Win or lose, the brief penetration of Prussia had had its desired effect of taking pressure off the French Army, as two German Army corps and a cavalry division destined for the final push to take Paris were diverted to the Eastern Front.

Unlike the Western Front, the Eastern Front never bogged down into a continuous stalemate. There was too much terrain, and there were too few railway lines. The battles fought here more closely resembled those of Napoleon; the immense distances were partly responsible. A line connecting Britain and Morocco would approximate its staggering dimensions. The Eastern Front was, in spite of the victory at Tannenberg, far from secure for Germany and her allies. One of Russia's more competent generals, Alexei Brusilov, was making headway into Galicia in southern Poland. It was one of many places where Russia would continue to make itself felt; by the end of the year these operations would have cost over 1½ million casualties. Austria's invasion of Serbia, a 'punitive expedition', was a brutal affair. Here too there were atrocities carried out against civilians, but the Austrian Army suffered heavy losses, perhaps as many as two hundred thousand casualties, and was eventually forced to withdraw. 'The Austro-Hungarian army would have to be supported', Ludendorff concluded, 'if it were not to be annihilated.' The attempt to punish Serbia for the event which had set the entire war in motion was soon a forgotten sideshow.

RETREAT

The French had long understood the importance of enlisting Britain as a fighting ally. Before the war, a British general had visited France to discuss potential joint military plans. 'What is the smallest British military force that would be of any practical assistance to you?' asked the general. 'A single soldier,' came the French reply, 'and we will see to it that he is killed.' Britain's Navy might have ruled the waves, but its Army was not held in high esteem. Bismarck had once bragged that if a British army set foot on German soil, he would 'leave it to the police to arrest it'. Of all the major European powers, Britain alone had abstained from universal military conscription. Its army was small – a quarter of a million men – but professional. The British Minister of War, Field Marshal

British cavalry scouts (Lancers) in Flanders. Horse power dominated military life in 1914; in this pre-mechanized phase of the war, men, food, fuel, ammunition depended on horses. They took over when the rail lines stopped, which in wartime was virtually everywhere.

Earl Kitchener, was deeply pessimistic about what lay ahead. 'I don't know Europe; I don't know England, and I don't know the British Army.' As for the French, he predicted that the Germans would march through them 'like partridges'. Kitchener had other disturbing predictions for Britain's politicians. The war, he told them, would be won on land, not at sea; victory would come neither quickly nor cheaply, as the war would probably last three years, requiring the fielding of millions of British soldiers. It was a remarkable – and accurate – forecast, in opposition to most military thinking of the day.

Kitchener was worried that his small army, experienced only in minor colonial conflicts, would be quickly consumed, leaving few veterans to train the new army that victory would require. With reluctance, he ordered an Expeditionary Force consisting of four of the six infantry divisions available and five brigades of cavalry, some 120 000 soldiers, to begin crossing the Channel on 9 August, little more than a week after Britain's declaration of war. Ninety-nine years had passed since the last British army had set foot on the shores of western Europe.

John Lucy

Men of the 4th Battalion, the Royal Fusiliers, resting in the Grand Place of the Belgian town of Mons on the day before the battle. On 23 August 1914 they suffered heavy casualties. Some of them spoke of seeing an angelic figure in the sky that night, protecting them: the legend of the Angel of Mons was born.

Among the first to cross was a twenty-year-old Roman Catholic Irishman, John Lucy. He and his brother had joined the British Army before the war out of sheer boredom. Enlisting meant swearing loyalty to the Crown, a difficult oath for an Irishman, and he quickly regretted his decision — although it had nothing to do with national allegiances. What he hated was the constant drilling, and he judged his first six months in the Army as the worst of his life. In time, however, his attitude changed. He cheered news of the conflict. 'Going to war seemed like a light-hearted business,' he said. As for the Germans, 'a dose of that rapid fire of ours, followed by an Irish bayonet charge, would soon fix things'.

On 23 August John Lucy's unit went into action near Mons. After taking up defensive positions as best they could, they were attacked by waves of German infantry advancing over open fields. German tactics were as outdated as the French, for which they paid dearly. For keeping to their timetable, German commanders were willing to pay in lives. 'Our rapid fire was appalling even to us,' wrote John Lucy. 'Such tactics amazed us, and after the first shock of seeing men slowly and helplessly falling down as they were hit, gave us a great sense of power and pleasure. It was all so easy.' But it only seemed so, for the British were too few in number to stop the onslaught. The next morning, Lucy was surprised to learn that he and the rest of his unit were being ordered to throw away their packs and begin 'this retirement business'. What Lucy did not know was that most of the small British army was being badly mauled and in danger of encirclement. On 26 August at Le Cateau the retreat was in danger of becoming a rout. 'It was every man for himself,' artillery sergeant Albert George bitterly remembered. 'The retirement was a scandalous sight in the history of Britain, but it will never be published. In our hurry to get away guns, wagons, horses, wounded men were left to the victorious Germans and even our British infantrymen were throwing their rifles, ammunition, equipment and running like hell for their lives.'

John Lucy witnessed similar 'disgraceful' scenes. He remembered one officer, who, after catching up with some of his fleeing men, pleaded with them, 'For God's sake men, be British soldiers!' The commander of the British Expeditionary Force, General John French, was among those who were shaken by these events. The battle had lasted only a day. His encounters with the French military staff had been volatile and full of misunderstanding and suspicion. Worried that his shattered army might be entirely destroyed, he informed London that he was considering abandoning France altogether. Kitchener was quickly dispatched to France to steel the resolve of his field commander. Leaving the line, French was told on 1 September, was not an option.

Often separated from their units, with no idea of where they were going and what they would do when they got there, the BEF marched, day and night, for thirteen days, covering 150 miles. A retreat is one of the most perilous of military manoeuvres to execute; that many panicked was not unusual under such conditions. What was remarkable was that the fatigued British army held together in the face of overwhelming numbers and relentless pursuit. 'Our minds and bodies shrieked for sleep,' recalled John Lucy. 'In a short time our singing army

August – December 1914

AUGUST *Mobilization*

A French school teacher from the village of Vatilieu, near Grenoble, describes the bell ringing announcing general mobilization.

1 August It seemed that suddenly the old feudal *tocsin* had returned to haunt us. Nobody spoke for a long while. Some were out of breath, others dumb with shock. Many still carried their pitchforks in their hands. 'What can it mean? What's going to happen to us?' asked the women. Wives, children, husbands – all were overcome by anguish and emotion. The wives clung to the arms of their husbands. The children, seeing their mothers weeping, started to cry too. All around us was alarm and consternation. What a disturbing scene.

Harvest in the south of France

AUGUST *The Battle of Tannenberg*

Russian soldiers on their way to the front

From the War Diary of Major-General Max Hoffmann, writing about the Russian Army's defeat at Tannenberg at the end of August. Hoffmann conceived the German plan of attack, and went on to become commander in all but name of the German forces on the Eastern Front.

Allenstein, 4 September We have only gradually been able to realize how great was our success at Tannenberg. 92 000 prisoners have now been sent back – it is one of the greatest victories in history, and won by an inferior force.

SEPTEMBER *The First Battle of the Marne*

Letter to his parents from Walter Limmer, student of Law at Leipzig. Born 22 August 1890; died 24 September 1914 of wounds received on 16 September, near Châlons-sur-Marne.

South of Châlons, 9 September This ghastly battle is still raging – for the fourth day! Up till now, like most battles in this war, it has consisted almost entirely of an appalling artillery duel. I am writing this letter in a sort of grave-like hole which I dug for myself in the firing-line. The shells are falling so thick today, both before and behind us, that one may regard it as only thanks to the special mercy of God if one comes out of it safe and sound.

OCTOBER *Kitchener's Army*

Letter from Frederick Keeling, who enlisted in the 6th Battalion of the Duke of York's Light Infantry in August 1914, to his friend Miss C. Townshend. He died in the Battle of the Somme on 18 August 1916.

Sergeant Frederick Keeling

Colchester, 25 October I have been having the time of my life here among old friends. There is no idea in a normal provincial town that soldiering is a whimsical or abnormal thing to go in for, and the way in which the town has pulled together and is working for the men here is splendid.

I am very glad I am not a wholly damned de-localized intellectual. I feel I belong here to Colchester more than anywhere. This is the England I am going to fight for, anyway. At least, it is more of a microcosm of the real England than any other place I know intimately.

It was satisfactory to feel so many links to one's country, a kind of ferocious love of it....

NOVEMBER
The Race to the Sea

A regular in the Royal Irish Fusiliers, John F. Lucy describes the state of his regiment when it was relieved in Flanders on 19 November, as the BEF sought to stop the German Army taking Ypres.

This time only forty men of my regiment were able to march away. The rest were killed or wounded.

Forty – forty left out of two hundred and fifty, and only about three weeks ago there were only forty-six left out of an entire battalion. I searched my mind for total figures and roughly reckoned that in three months ninety-six men out of every hundred had been killed or wounded. I was too weary to appreciate my own luck.

DECEMBER *The Christmas Truce*

Johannes Niemann, a young lieutenant in the Saxon Infantry Regiment, writing home in December 1914.

On Christmas Eve we got the order to go into the trenches. The day before we had celebrated Christmas in our rest quarters with the civilian people and children who were presented with chocolate, bonbons and cake. It was all in good humour.

Then at darkness we marched forward to the trenches like Father Christmas with parcels hanging from us. All was quiet. No shooting. Little snow. We posted a tiny Christmas tree in our dugout – the company commander, myself the lieutenant, and the two orderlies. We placed a second lighted tree on the breastwork.

Then we began to sing our old Christmas songs: *'Stille Nacht, Heilige Nacht'* and *'O du Fröhliche'* ...

British and German soldiers, Christmas 1914

Men of the 11th Hussars resting near Paris at the end of the retreat from Mons. Retreat is the most difficult military manoeuvre to execute. Falling back day after day, the British Expeditionary Force retained its coherence and *esprit de corps*, and was there on the Marne when the crucial battle took place.

BELOW A genuinely popular soldier of the Republic, Joseph Simon Galliéni was recalled from retirement at the outbreak of war, after a distinguished military career in the French colonies, and became Military Governor of Paris on 26 August 1914. He shared with Joffre the anguish and the credit for the victory on the Marne. Galliéni died in May 1916.

was stricken dumb. Every cell in our bodies craved rest, and that one thought was the most persistent in the minds of the marching men.... Men slept while they marched, and they dreamed as they walked. They talked of their homes, of their wives and mothers, of their simple ambitions, of beer in cosy pubs, and they talked of fantasies.'

One fantasy was the Angel of Mons, a legend that may have been brought on by hallucinations caused by the exhaustion and desperation of the British retreat. The story was repeatedly told of British troops seeing behind them, as they retreated, a shining white angel in the sky. Sitting upon a white horse and holding a fiery sword, the angelic figure was holding back the advance of the German troops bearing down on them. The genesis of this legend was more likely not the battlefield, but a short story published early in the war. In it the dead from the medieval Battle of Agincourt reappear in glowing form between two armies facing each other. Whatever its origins, the comforting idea of benevolent supernatural forces at work proved irresistible to soldiers and the British public alike. In the days and years of suffering to come, there would be many more supernatural manifestations that people embraced in the hope of relieving anxiety and pain.

The Battle of the Marne

Like the retreating British army, the German army too was exhausted. By early September it had outmarched its supply lines. The German right flank, under General Alexander von Kluck, was covering 20 – 25 miles a day. The deeper his army drove, the more exposed its position. Rather than attempting to encircle and capture Paris, von Kluck pulled up short when the German forces were only 25 miles from the capital. Joffre now faced a momentous decision. He could continue with the planned retreat from Paris to save his army, or once again take the offensive and strike the Germans' exposed flank. To fail again could mean losing not only Paris but the entire war. Helped by the encouragement of the military governor of Paris, General Joseph Simon Galliéni, Joffre chose the offensive. Every available French soldier was rushed into the battle, including some six thousand who arrived on the battlefield in Parisian taxicabs. What followed was the Battle of the Marne, fought by perhaps 2 million soldiers. Between 5 and 10 September, the Allies stopped the German advance. Paris was saved; the Schlieffen Plan was in ruins; and the German commander, von Moltke, became a broken man, unfit for further duty.

How did the French and British manage to stop the German advance? One answer is by accepting appalling casualties. Like the Russians in World War II, the French made the invaders pay, but they did so at a catastrophic loss of life in their own ranks. The British Expeditionary Force took heavy casualties too, but the French bled the most in 1914.

The failure of the Schlieffen Plan was a product both of French sacrifice and of German miscalculation. It had simply stretched the German army too far. By the time the troops reached the River Marne, they were totally exhausted. It is doubtful whether they would have been able to take Paris even if it had been open to them to do so.

The Schlieffen Plan was also flawed for another essential reason. It was an idea

of genius and, like many such ideas, hovered between the brilliant and the insane. What it required was clockwork execution, but given the confused conditions of the battlefield, no such coordination was possible. At critical moments the very position of the German advance guard was a mystery to the High Command, ensconced in Luxembourg, 175 miles away. To find out what was happening von Moltke sent a relatively junior staff officer, Lieutenant Colonel Hentsch, to survey the position. It was he who effectively made the key decisions. The German army turned to the north-east of Paris, and not to the west as originally planned. A gap of between 20 and 25 miles appeared between the left flank of the German force, under General von Kluck, and the German Second Army under von Bülow. Hentsch, speaking for von Moltke, saw the danger of the German forces being

Every kind of transport was requisitioned to supply the French on the Marne. Parisian taxis joined anything with four wheels and a motor in a long supply line soon clogged with vehicles, horses and men. These men carry the essentials of combat: water, petrol and guns.

divided, and ordered a retreat from the Marne to the River Aisne, 12 miles to the north. Thus ended the dream of a repetition of the crushing military victory that Prussia had inflicted on France forty-four years before.

It was a bitter harvest that Philip Gibbs saw, resting on the fields of the Marne.

> I have been for many strange walks in my life with strange companions, up and down the world, but never have I gone for such a tramp with such a guide as on this Sunday in September within the sounds of guns. My comrade of this day was a grave-digger. Dig as hard as he could, my friendly grave-digger had been unable to cover up all those brothers-in-arms who lay out in the wind and the rain. I walked among the fields where they lay, and among their roughly piled graves, and not far from the heaps of the enemy's dead who were awaiting their funeral pyres. 'See there,' he said, 'they take some time to burn.' He spoke in a matter of fact way, like a gardener pointing to a bonfire of autumn leaves. But there, in line with his forefinger, rose a heavy, rolling smoke, slugging in the rain under a leaden sky, and I knew that those leaves had fallen from the great tree of human life, and this bonfire was made from an unnatural harvesting.

RIGHT General Alexander von Kluck. His First Army, on the right flank of the German invasion, had to march 15 miles a day; its 84 000 horses required 2 million tons of fodder per day. By 1 September, they were totally exhausted. They turned east of Paris and were defeated on the Marne.

The bitter harvest on the battlefield after the German retreat from the Marne. The Allied victory on the Marne was not the end of the war of movement. After blocking the German advance, the French and British moved north, but found the Germans dug in on the River Aisne. Attempts by each side to outflank the other to the north failed: instead, a continuous line from Belgium to Switzerland described the stalemate. Both sides measured the cost in hundreds of thousands of lives. But the worst of the war had not even begun.

ENTRENCHMENT

A false hope was briefly entertained by Britain and France that the German Army might be pushed back inside its own borders and the war ended by Christmas. But stopping the German advance was not the same as stopping the fighting, and soon both sides realized that they would not survive in the open field. They began to dig into the earth.

The spade, hated during peacetime training as a tool of drudgery, became as valued as the rifle. 'Lord, how we appreciated those entrenching tools,' Lucy noted early on in the war. Unable to move forward, both sides began moving

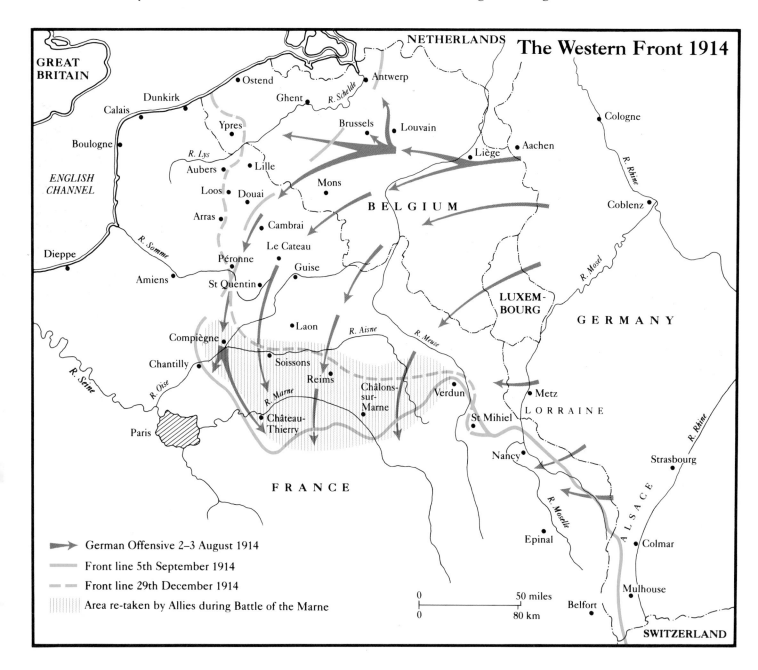

The Western Front 1914

German Offensive 2–3 August 1914

Front line 5th September 1914

Front line 29th December 1914

Area re-taken by Allies during Battle of the Marne

0   50 miles

0   80 km

French troops going through a village after the Battle of the Marne. By September 1914, one-tenth of the French population was cut off behind enemy lines. The Germans held the heartland of French industry in the north, and were still within shelling distance of Paris. Parish priests, like the one seen here, wholeheartedly supported the struggle against Germany.

laterally. The attempts by both armies to outflank each other in northern France and Flanders became known as the Race to the Sea.

John Lucy's battalion had been in reserve through most of the Battle of the Marne; now he was back in action. On 13 September a British pilot landed his plane near Lucy's unit to warn them of the disposition of the Germans. 'There they are,' the pilot pointed, 'waiting for you up there, thousands of them.' They had dug in. The next morning Lucy's unit attacked, taking a plateau. The offensive continued the next day; this time they were met by a 'murderous hail of missiles from an invisible enemy'. 'We had all thought we were pretty well invincible in attack, but we did not know what to think now.' Machine guns raked the charging British lines, killing or wounding all Lucy's officers. The swords they had been waving to direct the attack had singled them out as targets. 'From this date swords went out of fashion,' Lucy recalled. Among the dead lying on the field was his younger brother, Denis. 'I was beside myself with grief. I dreamed of him at night, and once he appeared to visit me, laying a hand on each of my shoulders and telling me he was all right.'

Lucy's grieving would come later, for the British were still on the move, not forward, but laterally towards the west and north. The trenches began to spread mile after mile, from the English Channel to the Alps, and in November Lucy found himself in one outside Ypres in Belgium. It was a town the Germans were determined to take. The heavy guns that had destroyed Belgium's forts were now trained against what was left of Lucy's battalion. 'Dumbly we suffered it. We seemed born for nothing else.' But the Germans dumbly suffered too. 'Six German army corps were marshaled in the open, advancing like a parade on the weak British Army. The magnificent Prussian Guards made a review of it. They executed their famous goose-step in the sight of their foe, and the field-grey waves came on.'

The outnumbered Allied troops fought for a month to hold back a series of German attacks aimed at capturing ports on the English Channel. At a critical point in the battle one British general, Douglas Haig, mounted his horse and rode out to bolster the confidence of his men. The gesture worked. At Ypres the war of movement ended. The trench warfare of the Western Front was born.

Victims and survivors

Reaching stalemate had been an extremely bloody affair. The French Army alone suffered a million casualties in the first five months of war. Never before had there been a bloodbath like it. The German casualty figures were also staggering, and what did they have to show for it? True, they had blunted the Russian advance into East Prussia and had conquered most of Belgium and ten departments of France, but they faced the prospect of the two-front war that decades of military and political planning had tried to avoid. The nightmare of German strategic thinking had come true. Though no one knew it at the time, the war was already lost. Four years and 9 million deaths later, that verdict would be ratified, but it had been sealed long before in the failed plans of the men who had launched the war in the first place.

By the end of November John Lucy's battalion had been virtually wiped out: only 44 of the original 250 men remained. Like Gibbs, that autumn Lucy looked out on stilled fields of dead soldiers. 'They looked calm, and even handsome, in death.' Nearby a dead sentry leaned against a tree. In another spot he envied a group of bandaged wounded who were sitting in a hollow and would soon be back home. Then came the screaming sound of an incoming artillery shell. It landed in the middle of the wounded, killing them all. 'I was too weary to appreciate my own luck.' 'My dead chums' was all he could think of to say about what had happened.

There were other survivors of 1914 who would later play larger roles in an even bigger war. One was a young French lieutenant who was hit in the knee while leading a charge near Dinant in the first days of August. 'I fell and Sgt Debout fell on top of me, killed outright. There then was an appalling hail of bullets around me. How it came about that I was not riddled like a sieve will always be one of the great problems of my life,' Charles de Gaulle wrote later. Lieutenant Bernard Montgomery was so badly wounded in the chest that he was at first left for dead by stretcher-bearers. Adolf Hitler, a young German private, underwent

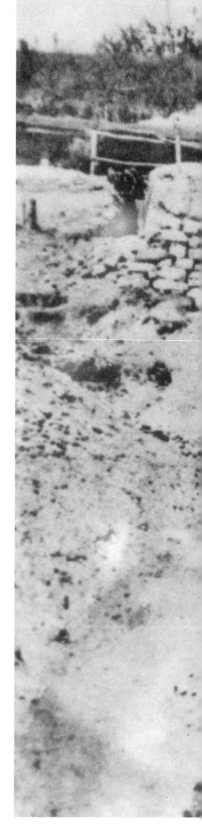

German trench systems were deeper, better equipped,
and better protected than were those of the Allies.
The Germans held the upper hand: they were on
the defensive, protecting their homes, as they put it, by
fighting on (and under) the soil of the enemy.

his baptism of fire that year. 'An iron greeting came whizzing at us,' he wrote of his first battle. 'From two hundred throats the first hurrah rose to meet the first messenger of death. The enthusiasm gradually cooled and the exuberant joy was stifled by mortal fear.' Hitler's unit was badly shot up, but he came away without a scratch and with an Iron Cross, Second Class. Winston Churchill was busy deploying the British Navy, at the age of thirty-nine the youngest ever First Lord of the Admiralty. Somehow he found time to muse in a letter to his wife, 'What would happen, I wonder, if the armies suddenly and simultaneously went on strike and said some other method must be found of settling the dispute!' Franklin D. Roosevelt was another politician who found himself attending to naval matters as US Assistant Secretary of the Navy. Dwight Eisenhower was at West Point military academy. Benito Mussolini was not on a battlefield, but he was waging political warfare. Italy's leaders were still on the sidelines, having not made up their minds which side to support. Mussolini, at the time a socialist, had no doubt. He advocated joining the Allied cause, the quicker to bring about the downfall of the government and revolution. 'Neutrals never dominate events,' he urged. 'Blood alone moves the wheels of history.'

German soldiers, winter 1914–15. The elder Moltke, architect of victory in 1870 and uncle of the Chief of Staff in 1914, had warned his successors 'Woe betide him who sets Europe ablaze.' By the new year, the younger Moltke had broken down and been replaced. These men, cold and homesick, had to carry on.

Winter of 1914

Stalemate was a condition that no one had wanted. It happened for a multitude of reasons, including failures in command. The French strategy, Plan XVII, built around so much wishful thinking, never had a chance of success. As for the Schlieffen Plan, there are many reasons for its failure. The German commander, von Moltke, had a nervous breakdown during the campaign and withdrew from his post. He was replaced by a man of tougher disposition, Erich von Falkenhayn. Others point an accusing finger at von Kluck. His decision not to expose his flanks further may have cost the chance to take Paris and gave the Allies the opportunity they needed to take the offensive. But ultimately it was not personalities that doomed the Schlieffen Plan, but an entire attitude to warfare.

The attitude was one in which a methodical, indeed a mechanical, plan had given the greatest army of its day an impossible task. The limits of human endurance were ignored by generals on both sides. We have already noted that the confusion, the chaos and the general fog of war were not even elements of the strategic vision of the generals of 1914. This criticism applies as much to Joffre and Plan XVII as it does to von Moltke and the Schlieffen Plan. Both sides failed to see that battle on this scale is not subject to rigid control. In 1914 the unexpected happened, as it always does. 'Friction' dictated the shape of the campaigns in a way that made shambles of rigid timetables with their sequence of objectives. Most military planners had failed to imagine the impact of advanced weaponry. The machine gun and modern artillery had given the advantage to the defence, especially when confronted with nineteenth-century offensive tactics. Railways, which were vital to military plans for a rapid victory, also proved invaluable for pouring defensive troops into areas to plug holes in the line. Then there were more rudimentary impediments to offensive drives, like shell holes and barbed wire. The British commander Sir John French could not believe his own naiveté about all of this. 'It is easy to be wise after the event,' he wrote candidly after the war, 'but I cannot help wondering why none of us realized what the modern rifle, the machine gun, motor traction, the aeroplane and wireless telegraph would bring about. It seems so simple when judged by actual results.'

These explanations may demonstrate why the French and German plans failed. But why was the result stalemate? There had been hints of stalemate warfare in both the American Civil War of 1861–5 and the Russo-Japanese War of 1905, but the warnings were mostly ignored. At the end of the nineteenth century, a Polish banker, Ivan Bloch, predicted with remarkable accuracy the nature of World War I in a six-volume study published in St Petersburg. His thesis was that the modernization of weaponry, coupled with the state's increased abilities to mobilize industrial resources, would naturally conclude in stalemate. The undesired outcome would be the collapse of social organization, not conquest. In the end it would be hard to distinguish the victor from the vanquished.

Nearly every weapon developed since 1870 aided defenders sheltered in tren-ches. Generals on both sides realized this fact, yet they stubbornly held to the view that staggering casualties were an 'acceptable' price if the outcome would lead to breakthrough and eventual victory. That would take years to happen. When the enemy's lines were not pierced, and no war of movement occurred,

frontal assaults, they believed, would eventually 'wear down' the other side. The inevitable outcome was attrition: whoever was still alive at the end of the war would be judged the victor.

Yet if a general could not mount an offensive, what was he to do? How long would he retain command if he did nothing? The Germans, holding enemy territory, could afford to bide their time for a while. The French and British were faced with a different set of circumstances. They were determined to throw the enemy off Allied territory, and that meant taking up the attack – whatever the cost.

Another solution to ending the war was diplomacy, but that was no longer considered an option. Diplomacy had not averted the war, and the longer the war went on – with its mounting cost in lives – the harder it became for either side to accept anything short of military victory.

The first Christmas

The war of 1914 was the last nineteenth-century war. What lay ahead as Ivan Block had predicted was a war of attrition between industrial alliances, a fight which would be more widespread, harsher and more lethal than any previous conflict in history. The war of 1914 was full of brutality, to be sure, but it had not yet hardened into what the German soldier-writer Ernst Jünger called the *Materialschlacht*, the war of steel.

But signs of the changing nature of war were everywhere. The atrocities gave hint of it, and the outrage which followed made it easier to demonize the enemy. Allied newspapers printed lurid cartoons of the enemy as a blood-soaked monster, incapable of human sentiment. Clergymen spoke of the conflict as a war of the sons of light against the sons of darkness. Schoolteachers rallied the youth of the land behind a flag raised in defence of civilization, be it German, French or British.

Soldiers at the front read the home press when they could, and frequently

LEFT This war of empires brought men from all parts of the world together. The Indian Army and Senegalese troops discovered what European winters were like. So did this elephant. Effective in hauling guns, even in freezing rain, pack animals of all kinds were mobilized.
ABOVE These men, of the 2nd Battalion, the Royal Scots Fusiliers, made the best of the wet chill of trench life. Informal understandings with the men on the other side of the trenches, limited the inevitable discomforts of living in a ditch.

laughed at its absurdities. As early as August 1914 French newspapers printed stories about the cowardice of the Germans, the ineptitude of their artillery and the bravado of French soldiers, who kissed their bayonets before charging into battle for their beloved country. Whatever the effect of these fantasies on the families of the men in the field, soldiers were irritated rather than moved by such reports. They knew how hard the struggle was, and how quickly terror replaced composure when shells began to rain down. They also knew that the men opposite them were as brave and determined as they were, and, like them, suffered from hunger, cold, lice and mean-spirited officers. This shared knowledge was leading ordinary soldiers, even in 1914, to think differently about how the war should be fought.

Charles Hamilton Sorley was a nineteen-year-old volunteer from Cambridge who saw the Western Front as it really was. He wrote home that his platoon were perfectly prepared to 'refrain from interfering with brother Bosch seventy yards away, as long as he is kind to us'. Night patrols had informal but well-established rules:

> Our chief enemy is nettles and mosquitoes. All patrols – English and German – are much averse to the death and glory principle; so, on running up against one another ... both pretend that they are Levites and the other is a good Samaritan – and pass by on the other side, no word spoken. For either to bomb the other would be a useless violation of the unwritten laws that govern the relations of combatants permanently within hundred yards of distance of each other, who have found out that to provide discomfort to the other is but a roundabout way of providing it for themselves.

Sorley, a fine poet, was killed in 1915, but others survived by following his rule. The most extraordinary instance occurred at Christmas 1914.

On Christmas Eve temperatures all along the Western Front dropped below freezing, and in some places snow fell. 'We were all moved and felt quite melancholy,' wrote German soldier Herbert Sulzbach, 'each of us taken up with his own thoughts of home.' Christmas Eve is the time when families in Germany present each other with gifts. Not surprisingly, the German soldiers drank, smoked and offered good cheer to their enemies often less than a hundred yards away. The same spirit moved some of the men on the other side of the line. One German soldier near Ypres heard 'a Frenchman singing a Christmas carol with a marvellous tenor voice. Everyone lay still in the quiet of the night. . . . We all kept our guard, only our thoughts flew home to our wives and children.'

Along some portions of the German lines, unusual lights began to appear. The British thought the enemy was preparing to attack, but then quickly realized that the Germans were placing Christmas trees adorned with candles on the parapets. Instead of rifle fire came shouts from the Germans. 'English soldiers, English soldiers, Happy Christmas! Where are your Christmas trees?' Then sounds of singing began drifting across No Man's Land – '*Stille Nacht, Heilige Nacht*'. In another part of the line, a German soldier played Handel's 'Largo' on a violin. Opposite the 1st Somerset Light Infantry, a German band performed the national anthems of Germany and Britain. The British responded with applause, cheers

Two German soldiers with Private Turner of the London Rifle Brigade posing together during the unofficial truce at Christmas 1914. Fraternization brought home to everyone the incongruity of the occasion. The war was still young, and even the bloodshed of 1914 had not drowned the sense that the men on both sides were just that – men longing for home and their families.

and their own hymns. Rifleman Graham Williams of the London Rifle Brigade recalled:

> They finished their carol and we thought that we ought to retaliate in some way, so we sang 'The First Noël', and when we finished that they all began clapping; and then they struck up another favourite of theirs, 'O Tannenbaum'. And so it went on. First the Germans would sing one of their carols and then we would sing one of ours, until when we started up 'O Come All Ye Faithful' the Germans immediately joined in singing the same hymn to the Latin words 'Adeste Fidèles'. And I thought, well, this was really a most extraordinary thing – two nations both singing the same carol in the middle of a war.

Soldiers everywhere did what they could to celebrate Christmas. Captain Rimbault saw his French soldiers celebrating mass at a 'makeshift altar' 50 yards from the German lines. 'Throughout the whole ceremony, the Boches – Bavarian Catholics – did not fire a single shot.' Robert de Wilde, a Belgian artillery captain, joined in an improvised mass at Pervyse in Belgium:

It was freezing.... The floor of a barn, with its huge double doors, was background, straw on every side, draughts everywhere – that was the chapel. A wooden table and two candles stuck in bottles – that was the altar.

The soldiers were singing. It was unreal, sublime. They were singing: '*Minuit Chrétiens*', '*Adeste Fidèles*', '*Les anges de nos campagnes*', all the songs we used to sing when we were little. The Christmases of long ago were coming to life again, all the things we had known in our childhood, the family, the countryside, the fireside, our eyes dazzled by the tree with its sparkling candles, all the things we now relive in our children.

The next morning de Wilde saw German troops at Dixmuide in Flanders leave their trenches, sing carols and heave in the direction of the Belgian lines religious objects from the church of Dixmuide, which was on their side of the line.

The unofficial truce, which probably was observed by two-thirds of the British – German lines, was also a chance to collect and bury the dead. At one funeral in No Man's Land soldiers from both sides gathered to honour the fallen by reading the 23rd Psalm, once in English and once in German. The Lord's Prayer followed. Captain Edward Hulse of the 2nd Scots Guards was there: 'They protested that they had no feeling of enmity towards us at all, but that everything lay with their authorities, and that being soldiers they had to obey. I believe that they were speaking the truth when they said this, and that they never wished to fire a shot again. They said that unless directly ordered, they were not going to shoot again until we did.'

Commanding officers, hearing of the fraternizations, ordered an immediate end to them. In other places, the fraternizations came to a natural end. Soldiers simply said goodbye and returned to their trenches. Some hoped that the comradeship would extend to the New Year and beyond. Others saw it for what it was: a reassertion of decency by men who, as 1915 dawned, persisted in the belief that, while their enemies were misguided and dangerous, they were still men like themselves.

How men endured

British generals were appalled at the news of the Christmas truce. Explicit orders threatened serious punishment should any similar incident ever happen again. But there were always, somewhere in the front lines, places where troops facing one another adopted unofficial 'live and let live' policies to reduce the lethal nature of trench life. The conditions of these 'truces' varied. One section of the line might agree not to shell each other's trenches during breakfast, latrines could be designated as off limits for shelling, while messages sent across No Man's Land could warn of an upcoming artillery attack ordered by headquarters. 'Live and let live' was just one way in which soldiers coped with life in the trenches.

Trench stalemate created a disturbingly new battlefield condition: it closely resembled siege warfare, but this time under industrial conditions. Stalemate offered armies no opportunities for withdrawal or pause. Soldiers lived in fortified ditches, often within shouting distance of their enemy: both sides could see the smoke of ordinary cooking and observe the comings and goings of daily life. There were front line trenches, support trenches, reserve trenches and connecting trenches that stretched from Switzerland to the Channel Coast. On both sides life meant, as the French poet and veteran of the Foreign Legion Blaise Cendrars put it, a 'troglodyte' or underground existence.

A short period of rain could turn the trenches into a sea of mud, glutinous, putrid and imprisoning. The possibility of death by shelling or sniper fire always lurked. So did the sense of disorientation and confusion. Life under these conditions was like being stuck in a noisy, filthy maze. The German Expressionist painter Otto Dix found the trenches a diabolical landscape beyond his worst imaginings, and summed up his experiences of life there in these words: 'Lice,

British and German soldiers meeting in No Man's Land during the unofficial truce, Christmas 1914.

rats, barbed wire, fleas, shells, bombs, underground caves, corpses, blood, liquor, mice, cats, artillery, filth, bullets, mortars, fire, steel: that is what war is. It is the work of the devil.'

Trench warfare meant living with the dead. So many bodies were dismembered or unreachable that No Man's Land became a vast necropolis. Even in 'quiet' times, men saw things in the trenches that people shouldn't see: bodies stacked and rigid like firewood, others no more than bits of human beings, scattered in the most incongruous places.

How did soldiers cope with such conditions? The deep loyalties they formed and the love they shared were the main sources of endurance. Superstition was a constant companion, and so was religious observance, conventional or otherwise. A sense of gallows humour helped, too. 'One can joke with a badly-wounded man and congratulate him on being out of it. One can disregard a dead man,' wrote the poet Robert Graves, 'but even a miner can't make a joke that sounds like a joke over a man who takes three hours to die, after the top part of his head has been taken off by a bullet fired at twenty yards' range.'

It is a misconception to think that soldiers were in the front line all the time, or that while there they were under constant attack. Time spent in the trenches could be boring, in spite of the nearly constant danger. Most of the day was spent cleaning rifles, writing letters and trying to stay out of the way of artillery shells and sniper fire. Only at night did No Man's Land come alive with activity. Protected by darkness, soldiers were able to venture, usually on their bellies, out in front of their trenches to repair barbed wire, conduct reconnaissance and carry out raids on enemy positions.

The average stay for a soldier in the front line was at most a week – men could not normally stand much longer. After a tour in the front line soldiers were rotated to the second support line, then the third reserve trench, then to the relative quiet of base camps in the rear. Until recently, what soldiers did behind the lines has not been a subject for historical scrutiny, but that has changed. An array of evidence shows how soldiers occupied themselves when they were not under fire. Life in the rear was hardly a time of rest and recreation, given the enormous manual labour requirements in support of massive armies. But there were times when men could put aside the war and try to become what they had previously been.

Military life was, by definition, not a replica of civilian life. There were no children, no old people and, above all, no women. But the echoes of civilian life were not difficult to retrieve. Behind the lines, in base camps and depots, a complex social network eventually arose among men determined to create a world resembling, though not identical to, the one they had left behind. The longer the war went on, the more sophisticated the effort became. This attempt to restore links with the communities for which they were fighting was a cultural achievement of their own making; it was not directed from above by generals and politicians. The men created their own newspapers, which bore no resemblance to the patriotic reporting by the press at home. Their language was ambivalent, mixing nostalgia, homesickness and love with exasperation at the failure of people not in the line to appreciate what it was like. They held sports events. Cavalry regiments organized jumping competitions and races. The infantry formed football leagues and held boxing tournaments. The Canadians – and later the Americans – played baseball. More solitary endeavours included fishing, with rifles doubling as fishing rods. The South African Labour Corps, made up of Zulu tribesmen, entertained their comrades-in-arms with war dances, complete with drums and grass skirts.

Like people everywhere, soldiers were enthralled by motion pictures; and so they organized film societies. Later in the war outdoor cinemas set up from the back of trucks brought films to soldiers. Charlie Chaplin was their favourite star.

The traditions of music hall decamped and came to the trenches. Men in uniform played all the parts, raising the tradition of drag entertainment to new highs. The French Army were well-versed in this recreation of femininity for fun, which also filled the time in prisoner-of-war camps on both sides.

Soldiers printed their own newspapers, including all kinds of comic fare. Some had a bite, such as this French journal of May 1917, at a time of strikes and mutiny, showing a soldier on leave gazing at a group of fat civilians decrying meat shortages at home. These newspapers were full of ambivalence towards civilians: love and longing for their families, annoyance and anger at the supposed insouciance of civilians and their enjoyment of luxuries while men suffered at the front.

Soldiers also formed dramatic troupes with names like 'The Duds' and 'The Shrapnels', and staged vaudeville shows. Lacking women, they created their own, sometimes convincingly so. One British regiment presented *Thumbs*, a revue in three scenes. The printed programme expressly notified all ranks that the leading lady, Kitty O'Hara, was 'out of bounds'. Kitty was, as an officer who enjoyed the show wrote, an ordinary, simple Canadian lad who had been over the top nine times.

With the exception of nurses, women were barred from the front lines. Drag performances were as close as the British could come to bringing 'decent' women into their lives at the front. The French authorities took a slightly different line. Even though venereal disease could be as disabling as a bullet, they considered licensed prostitution an outlet that would keep soldiers' minds away from thoughts of women at home.

Stephen Westman, who served in the German Army as a junior medical officer, observed that the German brothels 'were few and far between and too far behind the actual battle zone'. Instead, local prostitutes serviced soldiers nearer the front. One of Westman's jobs was to inspect prostitutes. Every woman picked up by the military police in the act of soliciting was put into an official brothel. Twice weekly they were examined for venereal diseases. Men on leave were given 'love parcels', which contained different kinds of antiseptics. Those who contracted VD anyway were sent to 'Knight's Castles', where they were treated and given a spartan diet to encourage them to use more caution in future. Such hopes were usually futile. The resort to prostitution was endemic, despite the fact that soldiers who entered brothels 'found ugly, dirty, worn-out middle-aged whores, who in no way resembled the pictures of the pin-up girls in the trenches. The oldest prostitute I came across', wrote Stephen Westman, 'was a woman over seventy, with lice in her hair.'

More licit entertainment was also provided. For the French there was the elderly Sarah Bernhardt, who had to be transported to the front on a settee to hide her amputated leg. For the British there was Harry Lauder, the most famous entertainer in the English-speaking world. Lauder, whose stage persona was a dancing, singing, bekilted Scot, lost his son in the war. After his death Lauder himself tried to enlist, at the age of forty-six, but was turned down. Determined to do something, he organized a concert tour on the Western Front, where he got a small taste of being under fire:

> I got through just the first verse of one of my songs all right and was just swinging into the chorus when, without the least warning, hell popped open on that trench. A missile came in that some officer at once hailed as a whizz bang. I had known, before I had left Britain, that I would come under fire. I had wondered what it would be like. I had expected to be afraid, nervous. But that day one overpowering emotion mastered every other. It was a desire for vengeance. Yon were the Huns, the men who had killed my boy.

Visits by celebrities like Harry Lauder were rare events that came later in the war. More often it was left to the common civilian-soldier's own making to join together the best of the world he had left behind with the dangerous one that now confronted him. These attempts were a way of recapturing his dignity in the face of the worst that the war could offer. That was no easy task, for this war, even as early as 1915, was evolving in new directions which no one had foreseen. The Great War was to be an entirely different kind of war: Total War.

Otto Dix, *Visit to Madame Germain's in Méricourt*, 1924. Dix recalled this brothel scene in Belgium as not untypical. The pleasures of the flesh were reduced to this grotesquerie in all armies. Whatever military authorities did to try to prevent the spread of venereal disease, they still turned a blind eye to prostitution.

3

TOTAL WAR

The Great War was total war, and the first of its kind. It spread throughout the world, and across the social spectrum of every combatant country. By late 1915, nearly every family was in mourning for a father, a husband, a son, a brother, a cousin, a friend, a companion. Total war meant universal anxiety and universal bereavement.

The Great War destroyed boundaries as easily as it destroyed lives: boundaries between continents and peoples; between classes and social groups; between the state and civil society; between the private and public realms. In the post-war years many of these demarcation lines were restored, but never precisely in the same way. As a result of the war, lives and ideas, aspirations and hopes were redrawn and rearranged in new and sometimes revolutionary ways.

A war on this scale deserves the word 'total' because of its industrial character. This was the first massive military conflict between industrialized nations, and its outcome depended on the willingness of military leaders to see armies as only the cutting edge of the nation at war. Civilians mattered in war because it was their weapons which were wielded by the men at the front, and it was their well-being for which the soldiers were fighting in the first place. Morale – the determination to go on – mattered in this war in a way that it never had before. To this end massive efforts were made to mobilize the imagination, linking artists, writers, clergymen, film stars and vaudeville artists in the production and maintenance of consent.

Consent was essential because the war was so costly; and, however powerful the instruments of propaganda and censorship, consent was never produced by force or manipulation. It came from the core of civil society itself. Consent was confirmed by propaganda only when it coincided with what civilians saw and felt: that their cause was just and that they had a chance to win. But the need to see the conflict through to victory also depended on the vilification of the enemy as the incarnation of evil. The cultural politics of hatred flourished in total war, creating the conditions for atrocity and genocide.

Total war was industrialized slaughter, drawing into the cauldron of armed conflict more people than ever before. The casualty lists dwarfed those of earlier

Industrial warfare was an experience that combined many familiar features of armed conflict in a way that produced a new kind of conflict: total war. The transformation of the gender of the labour force, as in this French factory, was one such change, as were the unprecedented casualties and the spread of the state into matters of everyday life. War seeped into every corner of society: no one was free of it; no one was safe. Everyone was a combatant; everyone at risk.

conflicts: the 'lost generation' of men who died in uniform totalled 9 million: one in eight of those who served. Another 18 million were wounded. Nothing like this had ever happened before.

But it was the universalization of hostilities, the spread of danger to everyone, which marked a new stage in military history. In total war, nobody was safe; striking at civilians who supplied arms or food was just as important as demolishing the enemy's front lines. If the enemy were women and children as well as men in uniform, and if their existence threatened the survival of the wartime state, then non-combatants had to be broken before they would accept defeat. And what of the enemy within, ethnic groups whose adherence to the war effort was suspect? Could their presence – their very existence – be tolerated? Atrocities were inevitable in a war of this scale, but in 1915, in Turkish Armenia, they too took on the imprint of total war, the signature of genocide.

Many of these things were not at all new: the ugliness of war is timeless. But taken together, the scale and spread of the brutality of armed conflict among industrialized nations produced the phenomenon of total war. In the Great War, the whole was more terrible than the sum of its parts.

Australian and New Zealand troops on their way to Gallipoli. The Gallipoli landing was a disaster caused by inadequate intelligence, insufficient attention to the terrain, an underestimate of the enemy's strength and resilience in defence of their native soil.

Gallipoli

Total war was world war, because the combatants were imperial powers with colonies and dependencies all over the globe. This immediately put Germany and Austria-Hungary at a disadvantage. Only Bulgaria and Turkey were persuaded that their national interest lay in joining the Central Powers. Italy, previously aligned with Germany and Austria, joined the war on the Allied side in 1915, convinced that a suitable reward would follow victory. They were wrong, but no one knew it at the time.

Joining the three great Allied powers were their smaller allies Belgium and Serbia, as well as Portugal, Greece, Romania and Montenegro. Japan too was on the Allied side, despite concerns about what the United States Navy would be up to while the Japanese Navy was dispatched to the Mediterranean, with troops from Australia and New Zealand. Even though not a colony, Australia went to war simply because Britain did; any other course of action was unthinkable. Imperial power was there for the Allies to deploy; its absence was a shortcoming of great consequences for the defeat of the Central Powers.

The Great War was indeed like a vortex, drawing into it men, women and arms from all over the world. No campaign illustrates this better than that of Gallipoli, a disastrous Allied operation which lasted from March 1915 until January 1916.

The idea of opening a new front in Turkey had a champion: the First Lord of the Admiralty, Winston Churchill, who, aged thirty-nine in 1914, was the youngest man ever to hold the post. Churchill was by his own admission a man of action and ideas, the brilliant champion of Liberal social reform. 'We are all worms,' he once intoned at a dinner party, 'but I do believe that I am a glow-worm.' Churchill was convinced that trench warfare had a future of only more stalemate and more blood. Germany, he argued, could be hurt by striking at her weaker allies.

The Dardanelles, the narrow stretch of water separating the Aegean, at the eastern end of the Mediterranean, from the Sea of Marmara were to be forced by naval action. In 1915 the Turkish peninsula of Gallipoli, which formed the northern border of the Straits and was said to be near the site of ancient Troy, was only lightly defended. The naval attack by British and French ships began with a bombardment on 19 February. Minesweeping followed along the 35-mile length of the straits, which narrowed from about 2 miles to 1000 yards. Bad weather, Allied inefficiency and a newly laid minefield disrupted these plans. An attempt to force the Straits on 18 March was a disaster: three battleships were sunk and three were severely damaged, all by mines. The naval force withdrew, not knowing that the Turkish forts, with most of their guns half buried in debris, were in a precarious state.

Instead, a third phase of operations, not part of the original plan, was launched five weeks later. It was to be a combined sea and land action. By then, with the help of German advisers, the Turkish defences had been strengthened. A combined force of British, Australian, French and New Zealand troops went ashore, but was quickly pinned down on the beaches. The men were trapped between the sea and the hills, ably defended by Turkish soldiers, and the bloody beachhead was as far as they got.

A fourth phase of operations beginning in August brought fresh troops to new points on the Gallipoli peninsula. They met the same fate as previous landings, this time suffering from appalling conditions at the height of summer. Everyone had dysentery. It 'fills me', wrote the commander of the operation, Sir Ian Hamilton, 'with desperate longing to lie down and do nothing but rest.... No wonder the Greeks were ten long years in taking Troy.'

With the assault force unable to move inland, the campaign was doomed to failure. Gallipoli became a charnel house; the stench of rotting flesh reached ships 3 miles out at sea. Once, early in the summer, a truce was called to allow the dead to be buried. Aubrey Herbert recalled how Muslim imams and Christian clergy conducted their services around mass trenches: 'I talked to the Turks, one of whom pointed to the graves. "That's politics," he said. Then he pointed to the dead bodies and said: "That's diplomacy. God pity all of us poor soldiers."'

It took months for the Allies to reach the inevitable conclusion that the campaign had failed and the expeditionary force would have to be withdrawn – but even then the unpalatable truth had to be thrust under their noses by a member of the press. Winter had already arrived and the ill-supplied Allied troops on the peninsula were by now enduring freezing conditions. The evacuation was carried out stealthily, with all kinds of ingenious contraptions to make it appear that the trenches were still occupied. A kerosene can, for instance, was set up so that it leaked water into a lower can; its weight eventually caused it to fall,

RIGHT By the time these Australian soldiers had secured Steele's Post at Gallipoli on 3 May 1915, their chances of realizing their objective had already vanished. Turkish reinforcements held the high ground, and would not relinquish it throughout the battle.

LEFT Australian and British troops, using periscopes, sharing a trench at Gallipoli. Churchill had hoped that the Gallipoli landing would be an alternative to trench warfare, a way to stop British soldiers from 'chewing barbed wire in Flanders'. Instead it was just another form of static warfare, an endurance contest, where sniper fire and artillery made it necessary for Allied soldiers to seek cover in even worse conditions than their comrades on the Western Front were facing.

pulling a string rigged to the trigger of a gun. The retreat was covered, and the Allies left in December 1915 and January 1916.

Gallipoli was more than a defeat; it was a débâcle, but one with unanticipated echoes. Whatever the outcome, it left an indelible mark on those who fought. It was the moment when Australian national identity was born, created by an entirely volunteer force. The anniversary of the first landing, 25 April, is Anzac Day, the Australian equivalent of the 4th of July. 'Anzac' is an acronym for the Australian and New Zealand Army Corps, chosen as the name of the beach of the initial landing. On the other side, the defence of Gallipoli contributed substantially to the creation of the new Turkey after the war. The mobilization of empire led to the unravelling of empire. No one could have foreseen the repercussions of the unlikely meeting of Turk and 'Aussie' on the rough slopes of Gallipoli.

RIGHT Mustafa Kemal, later known as Ataturk. BELOW Turkish troops. Had Kemal not rallied his forces at Gallipoli, the Allied landing would still have been a failure. But the myth of Turkish nationhood would have lost its symbol: a man of the people able to take on the West and defeat it through courage and defiance.

Kemal Ataturk

At Gallipoli, national myths were born. The first was that of Mustafa Kemal, who was given the name Ataturk (Father of Turks) after the war. The commander of the Turkish 19th Division, whose headquarters were on the Gallipoli peninsula, he led the resistance on 25 April. While organizing his troops after the initial Allied landings, Mustafa Kemal faced a company of Turkish soldiers who, having used up their ammunition, were in full flight from the invaders.

> 'Why are you running away'? I said. 'The enemy, sir,' they said. 'Where?' 'There,' they said indicating the hill altitude 261. Actually, a skirmishing part of the enemy had approached Hill 261 and was advancing freely. Imagine the situation now. I had left my troops, to let the men have ten minutes' rest.... The enemy had reached this hill.... This meant that the enemy was nearer to me than my own men, and if the enemy should come where I was, my forces would be faced with a very bad situation. Then, whether by logic or instinct I do not know, I turned to the soldiers who were running away, 'You cannot run away from the enemy,' I said.... If you have no ammunition, you have your bayonets.' And I shouted the command to fix bayonets. I made them lie on the ground. At the same time I sent an officer hurriedly back to tell the infantry regiment that was marching toward Conkbayiri ... to come to the place where I was, on the double.

The reinforcements arrived, and an all-night battle pushed the Allied advanced troops back towards the initial beach-head.

This act of leadership symbolized a new force in the war: a non-European, non-white soldier with the love of nation and pride in arms that were supposedly the monopoly of Europeans and those of European origin. Of course there were exceptions: the Indian and Japanese armies were powerful forces, but no one had anticipated that a Turkish army, trained though it was by German staff officers, could be a match for the Allies. They were more than a match. Much of the cultural material out of which modern Turkey was formed after the war can be traced here to the barren slopes of Gallipoli.

Keith Murdoch

At virtually the same moment, and in the same place, another myth was formed. It was the myth of the 'Digger', the swashbuckling, independent, irreverent Australian soldier of the Great War. British and Australian troops fought together and died together, but their identities were transformed in the process. The symbol of that transformation was Gallipoli.

News of the battle was a state secret. British and Australian journalists assigned to cover the campaign were under strict orders to show the censor all dispatches, which effectively kept the lid on the story for months. All they could do was store up the details of incompetence and disorganization for the time when the truth could be told. Finally Ellis Ashmead-Bartlett, who was covering the campaign for the London press, asked a young Australian journalist, Keith Murdoch, to take a letter to London. The letter was addressed to Asquith, the British Prime Minister, and it denounced the incompetence of Sir Ian Hamilton.

Both journalists knew they were breaking the censorship rules, but took the risk anyway.

When Murdoch got to Marseilles he was intercepted by a British army officer and asked if he was carrying any letters. The authorities had been tipped off by Henry Nevinson, who was also covering Gallipoli but was irked that someone else was going to break the story, and as a result the Asquith letter was confiscated.

Unable now to reach official circles in London, Murdoch had the ingenious idea of turning to the Australian Prime Minister, Andrew Fisher. Surely it was not disloyal to correspond with his own Prime Minister? Murdoch arrived in London on 21 September 1915. In two days, he had composed a savage 8000 word letter which blew the lid off the Gallipoli story. Gallipoli 'is undoubtedly one of the most terrible chapters in our history'. He wrote:

> I visited most parts of Anzac and Suvla Bay positions, walked many miles through the trenches, conversed with the leaders and what senior and junior officers I could reach, and was favoured in all parts with full and frank confidence.... This was always a hopeless scheme, after early May, and no one can understand why Hamilton persisted with it.... A strong advance inland from Anzac has never been attempted. It is broken, rough, scrubby country, full of gullies and sharp ridges, and it is all within easy range of the guns of the Turkish forts at the Narrows.... No serious advance could be made direct inland from this quarter.

The August landing was totally bungled. Murdoch had been on the troop ship and had seen the state of the British contingent:

> I do not say that better arrangements could have been made. But I do say that in the first place to send raw, young recruits on this perilous enterprise was to court disaster, and Hamilton would have some reasonableness behind his complaints that his men let him down, if he and his staff had not at the same time let the men down with greater wrong-doings.... I am informed by many officers that one division went ashore without any orders whatsoever. Another division to which had been allotted the essential work of occupying the Anafarta Hills were marched far to the left before the mistake in direction was noticed. It was then recalled and reformed, and sent off towards the ridge. As a practical man how much water do you think would be left in these thirsty English boys' bottles by this time – after the night on the seas, and the hot march out, march back, and advance? Of course, not a drop.

He underlined the central point by stating that: 'the work of the general staff in Gallipoli has been deplorable', and in doing so resorted to a theme which became a byword of Australian nationalism. The British were different because they were imprisoned in a class system of deference and dilettantism. Their staff officers were the worst of all: 'The conceit and complacency of the red feather men are equalled only by their incapacity . . . What can you expect of men who have never worked seriously, who have lived for their appearance and for social distinction and self satisfaction, and who are now called on to conduct a gigantic war?'

After the failed advance came the impossible conditions of beach-head life in the Turkish summer.

Keith Murdoch during a visit to Anzac Cove, August 1915. The news of the failure of the Allies to break out of their beach-head at Gallipoli was top secret. Journalists promised to obey the rules of military censorship, but this was a story which wouldn't be suppressed. Keith Murdoch got it out by writing a long letter to the Australian Prime Minister, who returned the information to the British Cabinet in London, who released it to the public. It was one of the most spectacular official leaks of the Great War.

We have to face ... the frightful weakening effect of sickness. Already the flies are spreading dysentery to an alarming extent, and the sick rate would astonish you.... When the autumn rains come and unbury our dead, now lying under a light soil in the trenches, sickness must increase. Even now the stench in many of our trenches is sickening. Alas, the good human stuff that there lies buried, the brave hearts still, the sorrow in our hard-hit Australian households.

To Murdoch the men who had borne this ordeal were transformed by it.

... anxious though they are to leave the dreary and sombre scene of their wreckage, the Australian divisions would strongly resent the confession of failure that a withdrawal would entail. They are dispirited, they have been through such warfare as no army has seen in any part of the world, but they are game to the end.

You would have wept ... if you had gone with us over the ground where two of our finest Light Horse regiments were wiped out in ten minutes in a brave effort to advance a few yards to Dead Man's Ridge. We lost five hundred men, squatters' sons and farmers' sons, on that terrible spot.

But I could pour into your ears so much truth about the grandeur of our

Frost-bitten soldiers, Suvla Bay, November 1915. As if the heat of the Turkish summer were not bad enough, British, French and Anzac troops had to endure the harshness of the winter on Gallipoli.

Australian army, and the wonderful affection of these fine young soldiers for each other and their homeland, that your Australianism would become a more powerful sentiment than before. It is stirring to see them, magnificent manhood, swinging their fine limbs as they walk about Anzac. They have the noble faces of men who have endured. Or, if you could picture Anzac as I have seen it, you would find that to be an Australian is the greatest privilege the world has to offer.

After completing the letter, Murdoch lunched with the editor of *The Times*, Geoffrey Dawson. Dawson was shocked by the story and ensured that the 'news' was forwarded to the War Cabinet. Churchill thought the letter 'lurid', but agreed that it had to be taken seriously. A copy was sent to Hamilton, who took it 'like a hit below the belt'. He replied that Murdoch's depression over Australian losses 'allowed him to belittle and to criticize us all so that their virtues might be thrown into even bolder relief'. As soon as he had replied, he received a message relieving him of his command.

The operation at Gallipoli cost 265 000 Allied casualties, of whom 46 000 died. It also left many imperial illusions and political careers in ruins. Winston Churchill was pushed out of the British Cabinet. He resigned as First Lord of the Admiralty and sought a battlefield posting on the Western Front. His war, like that of so many millions of people, was far from over.

PALESTINE

The imperial character of the war spread it throughout the globe. Precedents existed, as in seventeenth-century naval wars involving the Dutch, the French and the British, but in 1915 imperial war was total war between industrial powers. The gigantic requirements of combat led both to the mobilization of empires and to their disintegration. These pressures were plainly on display in the Middle East. Here new nationalist movements helped subvert the Ottoman Empire, with profound repercussions for the rest of the twentieth century.

One such movement was Zionism, which in the early 1900s had attracted a small but talented number of idealistic young Jews in Poland and Russia. World War I created the conditions which turned Jewish nationalism, in 1914 a tiny sect, a movement no more powerful than any of a dozen other contemporary creeds, into a plausible political programme. The war created at the same time the conditions for the emergence of modern Arab nationalism, with a powerful claim to the same land. The collision between the two – so bloodily persistent over the last eighty years – was not apparent during the war, but the boundaries of Middle Eastern politics today arose directly out of this conflict.

The subversion of empires was a common policy in the 1914–18 war. The Germans tried it in Ireland; the British in the Austrian and Ottoman Empires. The British approach to the Zionists served many purposes: to curry favour with Jews in Allied lands, and to undermine the Turks. The British approach to the Arabs was linked to the newly-found strategic importance of oil.

January – September 1915

APRIL *First use of poison gas*

Testimony by Lieutenant Jules-Henri Guntzberger to the French Commission on German Violations of the Rights of Man in May 1915.

> On 22 April towards 5.00, about 70–80 metres from the German front lines ... my attention was drawn by one of my men to clouds rising from the trenches. I saw an opaque green cloud, about 10 metres high, thick near the ground. This cloud moved towards us, pushed by the wind. Almost immediately, we were suffocated.... We were forced to flee before the cloud. I saw several of our men fall, get up again, fall once more, reach the second line behind the canal and collapse. Until three in the morning, they continued to cough and vomit.

French soldiers wearing gas masks

APRIL–MAY *Allied landings and stalemate at Gallipoli*

The French writer Jean Giraudoux serving with the French forces at Gallipoli.

> Midnight. The frogs from a Turkish stream respond to our frogs in their usual language.... An Asiatic cannon, heavier by a millimetre than ours, fires away, then calms down. Everyone, certain he will die, in effect composes in his mind a farewell letter to his neighbour on his right, who he believes will have the luck to survive.

MAY *The sinking of the* Lusitania

Evelyn, Princess Blücher, the English wife of a German count in Berlin, writing the day after the *Lusitania* went down, with the loss of 1198 lives, among them 128 American citizens.

Evelyn, Princess Blücher

> *8 May* 'Sinking of the *Lusitania* by a German submarine' was the headline in our German paper that morning, without any details of importance. A great loss of life had been the just punishment for that liner that was carrying munitions to the enemy of Germany....
>
> The Americans here in the hotel, and those of the Embassy staff, had always professed to be neutral. They had been cordial and friendly towards the Germans.... But a sudden change now took place.... Their rage and horror at the idea that Americans had been killed knew no bounds, and they gave vent to their views in unguarded terms.

MAY – SEPTEMBER *Russian retreat through Poland*

A Russian medical orderly, Konstantin Parstovsky, recalls the Russian retreat through Poland. Warsaw was abandoned on 4 August 1915.

Russian prisoners, June 1915

The summer of 1915 was hot and dry. Curtains of dust hung over the fields of Poland. The army was falling back.

The dust of defeat, with its smell of burning houses, was everywhere – it lay on the faces of our wounded, the corn in the fields, the guns and the train. Our scarlet painted goods wagons were grey with it....

Once, I remember, we were picking up casualties in a suburb of Warsaw, called Praga, on the right bank of the Vistula. The fighting was in the part of the city along the Mokotov barrier. The river reflected the low-burning fires. The houses were cloaked in smoke and darkness. Gunshots crackled on the other bank as if someone was tearing strips of linen.

JUNE *Armenian genocide*

Letter from Leslie A. Davies, American Consul at Harput in Eastern Turkey, to the US Ambassador to Turkey.

30 June Sir: I have the honor to report to the Embassy about one of the severest measures ever taken by any government and one of the greatest tragedies in all history.... Practically every male Armenian of any consequence at all here has been arrested and put in prison. A great many of them were subjected to the most cruel tortures under which some of them died....

Another method was found, however, to destroy the Armenian race. This is no less than the deportation of the entire Armenian population, not only from this province, but, I understand, from all six provinces comprising Armenia.... For people travelling as these Armenians who are going into exile will be obliged to travel it is certain death for by far the greater part of them....

During the last three days crowds of people have visited the Consulate and the American Mission for help of some kind.... All feel they are going to certain death....

Armenian refugees

Chaim Weizmann

The Zionists had one major advantage over the Arab nationalists. Among the Zionist leaders was a man who solved one of Britain's most serious munitions problems in World War 1. Chaim Weizmann was a research chemist in Manchester, and president of the English Zionist Federation. In August 1914 he went on holiday to Switzerland. Returning through France, he and his family saw horrifying sights, the wounded, prisoners, refugees. In Paris he met the banker and philanthropist, Baron Edmond de Rothschild, who told him that now was the time to act for Zionism, since 'the war would spread to the Middle East, and there things of great significance to us would happen'.

Rothschild was right. Weizmann acted, but not perhaps in a way that either had foreseen. Back in Manchester, he responded to a request for scientific help to the war effort. He had pioneered a new method of creating acetone – essential for explosives – through fermentation, a procedure ten times more efficient than

Chaim Weizmann in Palestine in April 1918. A pioneering chemist and Zionist, he found a way to increase ten-fold the production of acetone, an essential component of explosives. His reward was the Balfour Declaration pledging British support for a Jewish homeland.

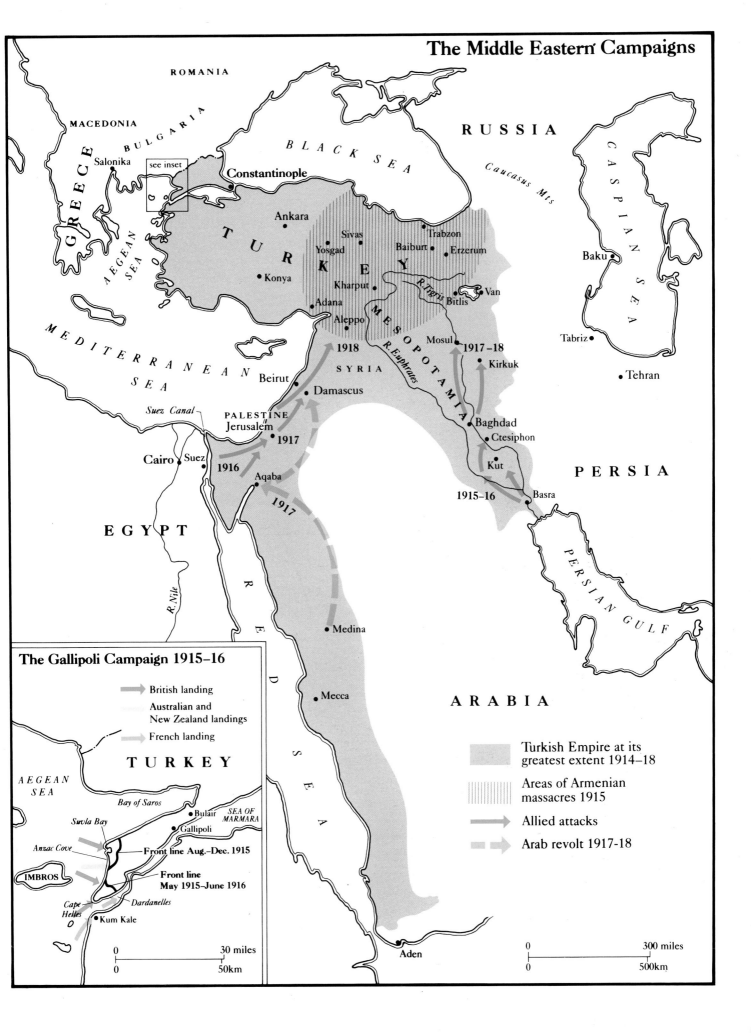

The Middle Eastern Campaigns

ROMANIA

MACEDONIA

GREECE

BULGARIA

Salonika

see inset

Constantinople

BLACK SEA

RUSSIA

Caucasus Mts

CASPIAN SEA

T U R K E Y

Ankara

Sivas

Yosgad

Trabzon

Baiburt

Erzerum

Baku

AEGEAN SEA

Konya

Kharput

R.Tigris

Van

Bitlis

Adana

Tabriz

MEDITERRANEAN SEA

Aleppo

1918

SYRIA

MESOPOTAMIA

Mosul

1917–18

Kirkuk

Tehran

R.Euphrates

Beirut

Damascus

Suez Canal

PALESTINE

Jerusalem

1917

Baghdad

Ctesiphon

Cairo

Suez

1916

Aqaba

Kut

PERSIA

1917

1915–16

Basra

EGYPT

R.Nile

R E D   S E A

Medina

Mecca

A R A B I A

PERSIAN GULF

Turkish Empire at its greatest extent 1914–18

Areas of Armenian massacres 1915

Allied attacks

Arab revolt 1917-18

The Gallipoli Campaign 1915–16

→ British landing

Australian and New Zealand landings

→ French landing

T U R K E Y

AEGEAN SEA

Bay of Saros

Suvla Bay

Bulair

SEA OF MARMARA

Gallipoli

Anzac Cove

Front line Aug.–Dec. 1915

IMBROS

Front line May 1915–June 1916

Cape Helles

Dardanelles

Kum Kale

| 0 | 30 miles |

| 0 | 50km |

Aden

| 0 | 300 miles |

| 0 | 500km |

the one then in use. One day Weizmann received a visit from a Dr Rintoul, the chief research chemist at Nobel's explosives factory in Scotland. Rintoul made an offer to buy the process – an offer which Weizmann would have been happy to accept. But before the deal was completed, Nobel's Scottish factory was destroyed in an explosion. They could not proceed. But the British government did.

Sir Frederick Nathan, head of the powder department at the Ministry of Munitions, took a look at Weizmann's methods. The research chemist was summoned to meet Winston Churchill, by then Minister of Munitions. 'Well, Dr Weizmann,' demanded Churchill, 'we need thirty thousand tons of acetone. Can you make it?' The answer was yes. A factory was built in Dorset, and Weizmann trained chemists in the task. Production began, limited only by shortages of grain required for fermentation; chemists in Canada, where there was no such supply problem, continued the effort. It was a success. In order to direct the operation, Weizmann had left his university job at Manchester and moved to London, where he promoted the other passion of his life, Zionism. His skills as a chemist were not solely responsible for the commitment of the British government in 1917 to support the creation of a Jewish homeland in Palestine; British policy aimed at using Zionism and other national movements to perpetuate their imperial control. The efforts of thousands made Zionism a reality, but Weizmann's scientific work was an essential ingredient in the mix of pressures that produced the Balfour Declaration of 2 November 1917. This was a formal statement by the British Foreign Secretary, A. J. Balfour, that 'His Majesty's government view with favour the establishment in Palestine of a National Home for the Jewish people' without prejudice to 'the civil and religious rights of the existing non-Jewish communities'.

T. E. Lawrence

Without prejudice? The Arabs did not have a chemist promoting their cause; they had a magician. His name was T. E. Lawrence, known to us as Lawrence of Arabia. His wartime history shows another way in which the Great War set in motion other forces which dominated the twentieth century: the clash between the West and Arab nationalism.

Lawrence came to Cairo in 1915 as a young and unconventional second lieutenant in the British Army's Department of Intelligence. Two of his brothers had already died in the war. Already an authority on Crusader castles, and fresh from an expedition to unearth Hittite settlements on the Euphrates, he conjured up the idea of enlisting Arabs in Mesopotamia (now Iraq) to undermine Turkish authority in the Damascus region, and broadcast such ideas in the newly-formed Arab Bureau. This group was dedicated to working with Arabs resisting Turkish rule. If these rudimentary activities could be coordinated, he wrote to his mother, the ensuing Arab revolt would be 'the biggest thing in the Near East since 1550'.

The leader of one of the Arab insurgent groups was Sherif Hussein of Mecca. Lawrence and several other Englishmen met his second son Abdullah, who was deeply impressed with Lawrence's knowledge of Arab affairs and customs. 'Is this man God', Abdullah remarked, 'to know everything?' What Lawrence knew was how to leap from a conventional English upbringing into an entirely different

T. E. Lawrence in the Arabian desert. The fascination of British intellectuals with Arab civilization had no better embodiment than in Lawrence, who went from a job as intelligence officer in Cairo to rally Arab armies against the Turks.

Emir Feisal, second son of Sherif Hussein of Mecca and T. E. Lawrence's ally and friend. Feisal led the Arab Revolt from 1916–18, and suffered the frustrations of a former ally no longer needed at Versailles. He still managed to occupy the Syrian throne from 8 March to 25 July 1920. From 1921–33, he served as king of Iraq.

world. He became British liaison officer to these Arab tribesmen. One of their leaders, Emir Feisal, asked him to wear Arab clothes: that is the image of him with which we are familiar, with the sweeping robes and hidden facial expression of an Arab.

The new Lawrence soon joined in the raising of an army of Arab tribesmen to harass the Turks and force a passage to Aqaba and the Red Sea. Aqaba became Feisal's base for further pressure on the Turks. Lawrence later served as an aide to General Allenby in his attacks on Turkish supply lines and railway links, and in 1918 entered Damascus before the rest of British forces arrived. By then his identity was neither Arab nor British, but an amalgam of the two.

His career as a master of guerrilla warfare made Lawrence a legend. But the cold logic of imperial power ultimately frustrated his dreams of using the war to help the Arabs realize their national aspirations. Like Weizmann, he saw a national future for an oppressed people in the Middle East. Like Weizmann, he knew that British support for these aspirations was essential for their fulfilment. And Britain had given similar assurances that, after the war, Arab views would be respected. But Lawrence's rhetoric was greater than his political influence. He couldn't cross the boundary between romanticism and *realpolitik*. In the post-war realignment of imperial power, the British abandoned their commitment to their Arab allies. It was far more important to them and the French to consolidate imperial power, drained as it had been by the war, than to act honourably to those who had fought by their side. National interest came before honour when subordinates were involved.

ONE FAMILY'S WAR

Wedding photo of the Goodyear family taken in 1913. The family inhabited an Anglo-centric world, dominated by the timber industry servicing the London press and its insatiable demand for wood pulp.

World history became family history in World War 1, and the story of one North American family is an intrinsic part of this vast war. From the Americas, Asia and Africa the Empire brought forth a second, third and fourth line of defence of the 'mother country'. Not all subject peoples were committed to the cause; but one family's story helps us feel what the war meant for many non-Europeans, who lived thousands of miles from the Western Front. Total war brought them to Europe. The Goodyears were Newfoundlanders; not Canadians. In 1914, union with Canada was still thirty-five years away. When war was declared, Newfoundland was a British colony, and as such, naturally went to war.

The Goodyears were among the staunchest British patriots in the colony. They lived in the town of Grand Falls, founded in 1906 to service the timber industry and in particular the demand for pulp and newsprint needed by Lord Northcliffe, the proprietor of two national newspapers in Britain, the popular *Daily Mail* and

ABOVE Raymond
Goodyear.
LEFT Kate Goodyear in her
nurse's uniform.

Newfoundland was a British
colony in 1914. The response
of the sparse population of
this fishing and timber-
farming region to the call to
arms was overwhelming. The
Goodyears were typical; they
provided five men for the
army and one woman for the
nursing corps. Kate
Goodyear survived; three of
her brothers did not, and in
later years their birthdays
were bitter moments,
etching in time what had
been lost in the war and what
would never be.

The Times, the paper of the élite. Louisa and Josiah Goodyear had seven children: six boys and a girl. Five joined up, and the youngest, Kate, became a nurse.

Raymond Goodyear was seventeen at the outbreak of war. Twice he ran away to enlist, twice he was retrieved by his father. Then he went to a recruiting meeting at which his father Josiah spoke from the platform. 'Father, now can I go?' he publicly demanded, and finally got the answer he wanted. After three months' service in the Newfoundland Regiment, he was killed by shrapnel near Ypres in October 1916.

A year later his brother Stan was killed by a shell while transporting munitions to his unit near Langemarck in Belgium. The third to die was their elder brother Hedley, who had enlisted while attending the University of Toronto. He joined the Canadian 102nd Battalion, and served on the Somme in August 1918. On 7 August, he wrote to his mother: 'My eye is fixed on tomorrow with hope for mankind and with visions of a new world. . . . I shall strike a blow for freedom, along with thousands of others who count personal safety as nothing when freedom is at stake.' The following day his unit did indeed take part in a major battle. In official accounts, Hedley was among the 110 men of his unit to die in the encounter. The truth is otherwise. He survived for another week, only to make one critical mistake. He shared a match with two Australians at night in the trenches near Chaulnes. That light was the last thing he saw: a sniper shot him through the head.

Two other brothers survived. Joe Goodyear suffered a severe thigh wound and was invalided back to Newfoundland. So was his brother Ken, also wounded. They both later re-enlisted and served in Scotland in the Newfoundland Forestry Corps. All five Goodyear boys in uniform were casualties of war.

Kate Goodyear, also in uniform, attended to wounded men at St Luke's Hospital in Ottawa. Before she knew the fate of her brothers, she nursed a nineteen-year-old private who had lost a leg. There was no room for him in the ward, so he was placed in the corridor. Unable to sleep, he asked Kate for help. The only place of respite was a private ward, off limits to the soldier. Kate decided otherwise, and then had to face the wrath of the matron and superintendent. After the inevitable dressing down, this is the explanation that she offered:

> I have brothers. . . . I have brothers overseas. I don't know where or how they are, and I can't do much to help them. But I'll do what I can wherever I am, and I'd like to think that someone might do the same for them. So let me tell you. As long as I am in this hospital, and so long as there's an empty bed, no soldier will ever spend a night in a hallway. I. Will. Not. Have. It. I shall move them to the private rooms if I have to carry them up the stairs myself.

For once, regulations gave way to compassion.

For Kate Goodyear, and for the surviving members of the family, the war didn't end in 1918. For seventy years, tears welled up in her eyes at unexpected moments. To her and millions like her, her family was defined by those absent from it. As her great-nephew put it, on three birthdays a year, as well as on public days, what was remembered was

> nothing . . . what was never to be, after the war was over. The best were gone by 1917 or doomed, and what the world would have been like had they not

died is anybody's guess. The war left their things unfinished: enterprises conceived, projects initiated, routes surveyed, engagements announced. And that's where it ended.

The three Goodyears left behind their photographs, one or two letters, a few often-repeated stories, and an emptiness that steadily compounded itself over the years. It was a different family after the war. Something was gone from the heart of it.... Somehow the wrong combination survived.... A balance was never regained.

WAR BY MACHINE

A balance never regained: this was the ultimate legacy of total war. It appeared in ways much more anonymous than the story of Lawrence and Weizmann or of the Goodyear family. And yet the story is the same. The war first transformed the structure of daily life and then frustrated the hopes and aspirations of millions of ordinary people.

What made the Great War so omnivorous was its character as a vast industrial operation. It was as if someone was pouring every industrial asset in Europe into a vast funnel for processing into weapons, uniforms, food, shells and a million other items for the front.

The effect was gigantic and it was worldwide. The Allies had one major advantage: the fruits of nineteenth-century imperial expansion. Newfoundland was but one small part of it: the British Empire was indeed ubiquitous. The Germans launched the war to gain an empire and the political power within Europe that they felt was their due. But they needed an empire and its material resources to win the war. Without one, they had to draw deeply on the reserves of human and material capital at home. These were formidable resources, but they were ultimately no match for those which the Allies could command.

This is what made the naval blockade of Germany – in place from early 1915 – so crucial. It exposed the economic vulnerability of the Central Powers. For years, German ingenuity and energy at home effectively made up the difference, but they could not do so forever. This is why they launched submarine warfare against Allied and neutral shipping: to lessen the economic odds in the Allies' favour.

To run this industrial machine, there emerged in each combatant country a new power élite of politicians, industrialists, bureaucrats and scientists. The encounter between Chaim Weizmann and Winston Churchill symbolized the novelty. So did the work of the chairman of AEG (the German General Electric Company), Walter Rathenau, whose cooperation with the military helped give Germany at least parity in munitions in the early phase of the war – a contribution which did not prevent his assassination in 1922, after he had entered politics, by anti-semitic nationalist fanatics. But later events were remote from the period when Jews were useful in Germany in 1914. Men like Rathenau were far from power at the outset of the war. Within months they were crucial partners in the war effort, and fashioned the first military-industrial complex in history.

Walter Rathenau. In 1914 he headed the giant General Electric Company (AEG) in Germany. His knowledge of industrial processes put him in a unique position to help with the initial phase of German mobilization, through his work at the War Raw Materials Office. His services to the German state did not prevent his assassination by anti-semitic thugs in 1922.

Mass mobilization on the home front

This gigantic effort presented the general population with material hardship – not comparable to that faced by the men at the front, but difficult enough. This kind of war was fabulously expensive. There was no choice for states but to pay whatever it cost to field their armies. Prices soared. For those with war contracts, so did profits, while inflation hurt ordinary people. Wages lagged behind prices, and for the most vulnerable, like the elderly, war was a very hard time. The resentment of the 'profiteer' was an inevitable outcome of the military-industrial alliances of World War I.

For the first time, working-class organizations were drawn into the central apparatus of the state. Their cooperation was essential to get war industries going and to maintain production levels. In Germany, this was a stunning change. The Social Democratic Party was a revolutionary party which had held in contempt the regime it now helped to defend. In France class enemies shared wartime responsibilities, and, in characteristically more muted tones, the same picture emerged in Britain. Class collaboration was a wartime reality. Its origins lay in the presence of millions of working-class men in uniform and hundreds of trade

Women workers trucking clay for brick making in Wales. The Great War did not bring women into heavy industry; they were already there. What changed after 1914 were the kinds of jobs they did.

The dangers of munitions work were serious. These women were attending a funeral for fifteen women workers killed in an explosion in an armaments factory in Swansea in Wales in 1915.

union officials in managerial positions in war industry. National sentiment and class consciousness were expressions of overlapping, not incompatible, loyalties.

Temporarily, though strikingly, the war altered relations not only between classes but between genders. The imperatives of war production meant that women became an essential component of the labour force. Military call-up left gaps in the workplace; these were filled by the under-aged, the elderly, immigrants and, in particular, women. It is untrue to say that women came into full-time industrial work for the first time in World War I; they were already there. What the war did was to expand the range of jobs that women could do and had to do.

These workers had to be housed and fed, which, under conditions of spiralling prices, was an increasingly difficult task. The result was the expansion of welfare provision in every major combatant country. Rents were controlled; so were the prices of some essential foods. The wives of soldiers received separation allowances. The consumption of alcohol was regulated, in Britain, through the imposition of closing hours for pubs. To keep war production going, the state acted quickly and in areas previously outside its jurisdiction. The outcome was to defend living standards, minimally though unevenly, but at the cost of extending even further the bureaucratic control of everyday life.

New rules of engagement

After 1914, war was indeed part of everyday life. On 30 August that year, the residents of Paris looked up at the sky and traced the flight of a new weapon of war. Above them was a huge but silent German Zeppelin (named after Count Zeppelin who pioneered hydrogen-powered travel) whose bombs fell on the city, killing one person. The event foretold a new kind of warfare – air war against civilian targets. This development arose directly out of mass mobilization for war production: millions of people out of uniform became legitimate targets of enemy action. Later in 1914 the first Zeppelins appeared over England. One dropped a

Zeppelin over the Campanile of St Mark's Cathedral, Venice.
In Britain in 1916, Bernard Shaw saw one go by: 'the sound
of the Zepp's engines was so fine, and its voyage through the
stars so enchanting, that I positively caught myself
hoping next night that there would be another raid.'

bomb on the East End of London which landed on a kindergarten in Shoreditch, killing twenty children. Inaccuracy rather than intention was the cause of the disaster.

The most spectacular episode in the air war against civilians was the German raid on England on the night of 2–3 September 1916. This attack by Zeppelins, which dropped five hundred bombs, half of them incendiaries, in a wide arc from Gravesend, east of London, north to Peterborough and the North Sea. Amazingly, only four civilians were killed and twelve wounded. What made the event linger in the popular mind was rather the destruction of a German airship, the *Schutte-Lanz S.L. 11*. This airship was 571 feet long and 81 feet high, and carried a crew of sixteen. It was shot down over London by a British biplane piloted by W. Leefe Robinson, who won the Victoria Cross for his achievement. The flaming wreck of the wooden *Schutte-Lanz S.L. 11* fell to earth within sight of hundreds of thousands of Londoners. To some the experience seemed to confirm the prophetic character of science fiction. Only eight years before, H. G. Wells had imagined this kind of attack in his fictional *The War in the Air*.

The commander of the Zeppelins, Peter Strasser, was bothered by the moral implications of raids that struck 'the enemy where his heart beats', but was resigned to them. It was all part of the total war between industrialized nations.

LEFT Peter Strasser, the legendary head of the Zeppelin fleet, died in March 1917 when his ship was hit and crashed over London.

ABOVE A French firing squad dispatches a German spy caught behind French lines in 1916. The danger of espionage was a constantly repeated theme of wartime propaganda. The enemy might be everywhere and anywhere.

Siege warfare was as old as the Bible, but in 1914–18 a boundary was crossed: the boundary between war on fixed sites and units – cities, armed camps, strongpoints, depots – and war on entire populations. After 1914, when an infant died, or a mother in childbirth, or an elderly man fell victim to hypothermia in a city under blockade, they were casualties of war, and meant to be so.

The new rules of engagement took many forms. The city of Paris was shelled by long-range German artillery throughout the war. About 100 yards from the Paris City Hall is the ancient Church of St Gervais. During Mass on Good Friday in 1918, a shell destroyed the nave. Scores were killed.

Sometimes the killing of civilians followed a trial. Sister Edith Cavell helped wounded British soldiers on the run in Belgium in 1915. For her efforts, she was sentenced to death by the Germans in Brussels. The sentence was carried out on

12 October 1915, despite diplomatic efforts to stop the firing squad from killing a nurse.

The German occupiers of Belgium and northern France – much like any other occupying power – shot civilians convicted of harassing their advance in 1914 or engaging later in sabotage or espionage. The Allies deemed these acts 'German atrocities', meaning not just atrocities committed by Germans: their 'Germanness' was what made them atrocious. Leaving propaganda aside, there is evidence that some German commanders believed in an iron fist in controlling occupied populations. While they did not order brutality, some effectively condoned it.

Naval blockade, too, was warfare against civilians. To deny a whole population foodstuffs was a political measure, aimed at forcing governments to capitulate. Both sides employed this strategy, but the Allies were better at it.

The war at sea also produced some spectacular catastrophes. The sinking of the liner the *Lusitania* was only the most prominent of hundreds of encounters between U-boats and Allied and neutral shipping. The *Lusitania* went down on 7 May 1915 in the Irish Sea; among the 1200 civilians drowned were 128 Americans.

U-boat warfare inevitably created these disasters. Martin Niemöller was one of the élite corps of German U-boat commanders, and he learned the truth about

The German Navy struck a medal to honour the men who sank the *Lusitania* in May 1915. Allied propaganda dwelled on both the event and its brutal commemoration by the Germans. To sail the seas in wartime was to risk death, and those on board the *Lusitania* were casualties of a new kind of war.

LEST WE FORGET

FAC-SIMILE OF MEDAL STRUCK BY GERMANY
TO COMMEMORATE THE EVENT
Translation of wording on Medal

The Sinking of the Lusitania.
May 7th 1915.

this kind of war. The son of a Lutheran pastor, and a dedicated German patriot, Martin grew up in an intensely nationalist environment. He developed a conservative outlook as a matter of course. In 1910 at the age of eighteen he became a naval cadet, then graduated to the Fleet as a torpedo officer on the *Thüringen*. It was on this ship that he learned of the outbreak of war in 1914.

To his delight, he was chosen for further training as a U-boat officer. He served as navigation officer on one patched-up U-boat, *U-73*, so damaged that it was called the 'floating coffin'. It was during this posting that he sank his first merchant vessel. He moved on to *U-39*, then to the Admiralty, and afterwards to his longest period of service, 114 days on *U-151*. He ended the war on a fourth submarine, *U-67*, which sank one enemy warship and three merchant vessels.

This harrowing war was just what Niemöller wanted. He was an impudent, daring and totally committed man of war. On 9 August 1917, an enemy destroyer passed within half a mile of his submarine, which was cruising on the surface at the time. *U-73* dived just in time to avoid being rammed. The next night an Italian schooner, the *Lorenzo Donato*, was sunk. 'Revenge is sweet,' was Niemöller's reaction. His ship not only sank a French destroyer, but also harassed a second ship sent to pick up survivors. This was not the last time Niemöller watched men drown who could have been saved.

While *U-73* was in dry dock for multiple repairs, he volunteered for service as navigator on a more battle-hardened ship, commanded by one of the most successful and daring men in the German Navy, Lieutenant Commander Förstmann. He was a man decorated with Germany's highest military honour, *Pour le mérite*. Niemöller idolized him:

> Standing alongside him in the cramped conning-tower, noting every word and movement, one realized that this officer ... will carry out his duty with complete confidence and an inflexible will. Everything goes off as per drill book, but it is in deadly earnest. After numerous alterations of course and speed we approach. The destroyer on the flank we are on passes within 60 yards of us. 'Slow ahead both!' A look at the torpedo sight on the periscope. Four more degrees till we can fire. 'A troopship! Lots of soldiers on the poop!' the captain whispers. 'Up periscope!' – 'No. 1 tube, ready!' The periscope rises and the captain looks into it, with his cap pushed back on his head.... 'Fire!' – 'Dive to 100 feet! – Down periscope!' Then comes the pause, while the torpedo speeds on its way. Twenty seconds: a hit! ... The ship is sinking by the stern and one destroyer is standing by picking up survivors.

Here is the moment of truth for Niemöller. A destroyer approaches to pick up the survivors:

> What should we do? We have no wish to interrupt the destroyer's work of saving lives. Neither do we envy her, as she cannot save many of the men! But war is war and the people being picked up out of the water are soldiers bound for the front; soldiers who are to shoot at our German brothers. War is war! And we try to get a second torpedo off at the destroyer. But she spots us and lets fly a hail of shells.
>
> They do not hit us, because a periscope is too small a target, but we cannot attack. All we can do is to put up our periscope here and there, to prevent the destroyer from picking up too many survivors.

RIGHT Torpedo sinking a ship.
LEFT Martin Niemöller in 1917.

The élite of the German Navy was in its U-boat fleet. One of their commanders was Martin Niemöller. A staunch German patriot, he accepted that torpedoing ships and sending the survivors to the bottom of the sea raised moral problems, but war came first. He changed his mind twenty years later, when, as a pastor, he faced Hitler. Then morality resurfaced in his life, and he became a symbol of the German conscience.

In a flash, Niemöller sees the moral dilemma of total war. Why not permit 'the destroyer to carry out her "life saving" unmolested'? Because the lives being saved were in the business of taking the lives of German soldiers in other military sectors. But just to let enemy survivors drown? 'Suddenly' at that moment,

> the whole complex problem of 'war' presented itself to us and we realized, from this single experience of ours, something of the tragedy which it involved and which no single man could, of his own volition, avert or contend against.... We junior officers knew nothing and cared less about theological problems. But we did see that situations involving spiritual bankruptcy did arise in which it was utterly impossible to preserve a clear conscience.

'This 25th January', Niemöller later noted, 'was the turning point of my life, because it opened my eyes to the utter impossibility of a moral universe.' What was his response? Did he call for an end to the war? Not at all: he reached the same decision as the Zeppelin commander, Peter Strasser. Stoically, he accepted responsibility for these immoral acts, necessary (he believed) for victory, and went on. On 27 January 1917, two days after this incident, Niemöller was decorated with the Iron Cross, First Class. He wore it 'with a feeling that I had earned it, by something more than the prescribed number of operations I had "assisted in"'. He had earned it in part by helping to ensure that drowning men went to the bottom of the sea.

Niemöller prevented Allied soldiers from getting back to their units; they had to drown so that German soldiers should not be endangered. The same logic lay behind the executions in Belgium. Both pointed to the brutalizing effects of total war.

THE MOBILIZATION OF THE IMAGINATION

Alongside the mobilization of men, munitions and labour, alongside war against civilians, came the mobilization of minds. Here the boundaries between the private and the public realms, between individual expression and thought control, were redrawn or obliterated.

Hindenburg: „Majestät, das Volk ist gedrückt und murrt unaufhörlich."

Majestät: „Weshalb murren sie? Wir spüren keine Last."

State propaganda in wartime is only part of the story. The propaganda efforts of both sides stretched from atrocity stories to barbaric caricatures to children's tales and outright lies. The most powerful propaganda, however, came not from the centres of power but from within these populations. The politics of hate was mass politics; it was as much visual as verbal, and it was effective. It worked because it drew on images and notions created from below, through commercial advertising, cartoons, posters and postcards, sermons, religious imagery, sentimental songs and the bad poetry which flourished in wartime. And above all, it worked through cinema.

By the middle of the war, the film industry had emerged as the most important vehicle for projecting the meaning of the war as the struggle of Good against Evil. This cinematic effort took many forms, from comedy through melodrama to tragedy. Much of this film output was neither inspired nor organized by the government, though state funding was frequently involved. To be sure, the censor was active; but the private sector took the lead. On the screen, kitsch and popular entertainment came into their own, broadcasting messages with evident mass appeal about the virtues of one side and the villainy of the other. Music hall, melodrama and the gramophone industry all chipped in, selling (at a profit) anodyne or uplifting images and songs to increasingly fatigued, anxious and irritable populations.

No wonder film was so popular during the war. It satisfied longings for the mundane at an extraordinary moment; it lampooned the dreariness of military life; and it added a large dose of outrage at the source of all the troubles – the enemy.

Chaplin at war

The cinema was at work for the cause from the first days of the conflict, but this effort took on added momentum with US entry into the war in 1917. Many war films were made in mid- to late 1918, in the expectation that the war would go on for years. One of the most popular was *Shoulder Arms*, which appeared late in the war and reflected and refined much earlier war cinema.

Its hero was Charlie Chaplin. This British-born music hall performer had gone to America and joined Mack Sennett's Keystone Company in December 1913. He was already a celebrity in 1914, and contributed to the war not by joining up but by staying put in California. A soldiers' song had it that his turn would come.

> *The moon shines bright on Charlie Chaplin,*
> *His boots are cracking,*
> *For want of blacking,*
> *And his little baggy trousers*
> *They want mending*
> *Before we send him*
> *To the Dardanelles.*

According to Alistair Cooke, Chaplin took fright at the song: 'I really thought they were coming to get me. It scared the daylights out of me.' He needn't have worried. Chaplin's on-screen service to the war far outweighed the advantages of putting him in uniform.

OPPOSITE In the first two years of the war, most propaganda was produced by the private sector, and most was written for domestic consumption. From 1917, propaganda took centre stage. Soldiers were showered with crude messages denouncing the delusions of the enemy. (LEFT) British claims to defending the honour of the weak are lampooned by a German cartoonist as imperialist hypocrisy; (RIGHT) German soldiers are reminded by a British artist that their rulers were perched on their backs.

September – December 1915

SEPTEMBER *Zeppelin raid on London*

The London journalist H. M. Tomlinson recalls the
effects of a Zeppelin raid on London.

17 September A slender finger of brilliant light
moved slowly across the sky, checked, and
remained pointing, firmly accusatory, at
something it had found in the heavens. A
Zeppelin! There it was, at first a wraith, a
suggestion on the point of vanishing, and then
illuminated and embodied, a celestial maggot
stuck to the cloud like a caterpillar to the
edge of a leaf. We gazed at it silently, I
cannot say for how long. The beam of light
might have pinned the bright larva to
the sky for the inspection of interested
Londoners, then somebody spoke. 'I think
it is coming our way.'

After a Zeppelin raid

OCTOBER *Edith Cavell shot*

Hugh Gibson, an American diplomat in Brussels, shortly after Nurse
Edith Cavell was shot for helping British soldiers evade capture in
occupied Brussels.

12 October Last night Mr Gahar got a pass and was admitted
to see Miss Cavell shortly before she was taken out and
shot. He said she was calm and prepared and faced the
ordeal without a tremor. She was a tiny thing that looked
as though she could be blown away with a breath, but she
had a great spirit. She told Mr Gahar that soldiers came
to her and asked to be helped to the frontier; that knowing
the risks they ran and the risks she took, she had helped
them. She said she had nothing to regret, no complaint to
make and that if she had to do it all over again she would
change nothing.

Nurse Edith Cavell

OCTOBER *French offensive in Artois*

Letter from Father Pierre Teilhard de Chardin, stretcher-bearer, to Sgt Jean Broussac, Professor of Geology at the Catholic Institute of Paris. Broussac was killed 22 August 1916; Teilhard de Chardin survived to become one of the most prominent Catholic theologians of the century.

Near Arras The days are terrible; the only relief from these sad memories of a time when many friends have died is the feeling of acceptance and renunciation – full of faith and thanks to the Grace of God – with which I faced the eve of battle.... This war is a terrible crisis, with its mysterious, but inevitable, train of suffering ... but it is still the most active and striking time to be alive. Compared to war, all our other preoccupations seem like child's play.

Teilhard de Chardin

NOVEMBER *Serbian retreat*

Testimony by a missionary, Mr Smith, after the Serbian retreat in the winter of 1915. The Serbian army crossed the mountains of Montenegro and Albania to be evacuated by sea by the Allied forces on the Adriatic.

It is impossible to think of the Great Retreat without calling to memory the 23 000 Serbian boys who met their fate on that cruel march. To save them from being captured by the enemy 30 000 of the boys of Serbia were ordered out of the country. They made part of the great exodus of the nation. They were young boys of twelve to eighteen years old and they were unable to stand the cold, the hunger and the physical misery of the march. Fifteen thousand died in the mountains, and those who saw the ships and the sea had nothing human left in their eyes.

The Italians at Avalona had no hospital accommodation for 15 000.... They had the boys encamped in the open country close to a river, and gave them all the food they could spare – army biscuits and bully beef. By the time that the ships to convey them to Corfu arrived the 15 000 had been reduced to 9000. About 2000 more boys died in the twenty-four hours journey between Avalona and Vido.

Serbian refugees

He was an iconic figure, a little man who was terribly vulnerable and somehow able (sooner or later) to sink his boot into the seat of authority. He was the great survivor, 'the tramp' – the title of one of his most successful films, made in 1915 – whose decency almost gets trampled, but whose resilience is indomitable. No wonder one British Highland Light Infantryman stole a cardboard figure of Chaplin and took it over with him to the Western Front.

More unexpected was the effect of Chaplin's photograph on shell-shocked soldiers. A doctor serving with the US Army said that an autographed photo of him did wonders for the men in his care. 'Please write your name on the photos', Dr Lewis Coleman Hall wrote to Chaplin, 'the idea being that nearly everyone has seen you in pictures. I will show your picture to a poor fellow and it may arrest his mind for a second. He may say "Do you know Charlie?" and then begins the first ray of hope that the boy's mind can be saved.'

Some of Chaplin's films were explicit propaganda. He used film to promote Liberty Bonds, followed up with public appeals. On 8 April 1918, his appearance with Mary Pickford and Douglas Fairbanks on Wall Street in New York drew an estimated thirty thousand people. After clowning with Fairbanks and standing on his shoulders, he told the crowds that 'This very minute the Germans occupy a position of advantage, and we have to get the dollars. We ought to go over so

Everyone's hero, Charlie Chaplin, seen here in *Shoulder Arms* (1918). Film entered the propaganda war with full force only in 1916, when *The Battle of the Somme* was seen by approximately 20 million people in Britain. This viewership has never been matched.

that we can drive that old devil, the Kaiser, out of France.' In Washington, he repeated the same pitch: 'The Germans are at your door! We've got to stop them! And we *will* stop them if you buy Liberty Bonds! Remember, each bond you buy will save a soldier's life – a mother's son! – will bring this war to an early victory!' Then he fell off the platform and (in his words) 'grabbed Marie Dressler and fell with her on top of my handsome young friend, who happened to be then the Assistant Secretary of the Navy, Franklin D. Roosevelt'. He met President Wilson and, for his British audiences, appeared with the Scottish music hall star Harry Lauder, whose son had been killed in 1916.

Shoulder Arms was first shown on 20 October 1918, and received instant acclaim. Drawing on a tour of US Army training camps, the story lampoons their rigours. After a hopeless spell of drill, the exhausted Chaplin falls asleep and wakes up on the Western Front. He captures a German unit by single-handedly surrounding them, masters the arts of camouflage by turning into a tree, and manages to capture the Kaiser himself (played by his brother Sydney).

Chaplin's original idea was to have an ending where he is banqueted by the President of France and King George v, who cuts off one of 'Charlot's' buttons for a souvenir. But in the interests of getting the film out (and preserving protocol), the film ends when Chaplin wakes up back in camp, facing the realities of military life just like millions of others.

The German side of the screen

In Germany too, film was there to spread the message. There were over two thousand cinemas in Germany in 1913, more than two hundred of them in Berlin alone. This national total was only half that of the British cinema industry, but, with Danish and American imports, on the eve of the war, German film was booming.

Initially, the film industry was ignored by the High Command, regarded as an annoyance, but with the accession to power of Erich Ludendorff in 1916, film found a champion. When, in 1917, American newsreel imports were banned, in stepped the domestic industry to produce newsreels for mass audiences with an insatiable appetite for images of the front. Alfred Hugenberg, director of the armaments firm of Krupp, took a leading part in this effort, which in late 1917 gave birth to 'Ufa' (Universum Film AG), a consortium of film companies, one-third owned by the German State Bank and under indirect military control.

Cinemas were given priority for coal and electricity in the hard months of 1917–18, and as a result attendances were consistently high throughout Germany and in occupied Belgium. In addition, the Army had its own cinema industry. There were 900 field cinemas in 1917, featuring the great stars of the German cinema, Henny Porten and Asta Nielsen. They specialized in comedies and melodrama, but were conscious of marrying profit and patriotism, thereby establishing a strong domestic film industry by the end of the war. The German film industry then came into its own both as a viable economic enterprise and as a vehicle for daring experimentation. The legacy of film propaganda in World War I was there for the Nazis to exploit *en route* to the Second.

THE CULTIVATION OF HATRED: TOTAL WAR AND GENOCIDE

In the cause of cultural mobilization, total war entailed the demonization of the other side. Some of this story is old – witness the progaganda of the Reformation and Counter-Reformation – but, aligned with the other elements of total war, the cultural history of armed conflict entered a new and strikingly original landscape. It is a space in which war crimes of a revolutionary scale and character took place. The worst was genocide.

Only one nation engaged in total war at this time committed genocide; but it was total war which created the conditions that made it possible. It entailed the brutalization of millions and thereby raised radically the tolerance of violence in some societies caught up in armed conflict. Total war has the capacity to infect everybody, but most people – through their legal systems, education, religious beliefs, military traditions or other convictions and practices – are inoculated against it. Those not so fortunate, those (so to speak) without the anti-bodies, succumb to the infection, and then the innocent suffer. Under these conditions, and in the context of total war, genocide can occur. It did during World War I.

The notion of 'total war' came out of the West. Napoleonic warfare in Spain and Russia entailed war against civilians and irregular forces. Fifty years later, the American Civil War added another dimension to the cruelty of armed conflict. It was not a Turkish tyrant but General Philip Sheridan who on 8 September 1870 told the future German Chancellor Otto von Bismarck that the 'proper strategy' in wartime 'consists in the first place in inflicting as telling blows as possible upon the enemy's army, and then causing the inhabitants so much suffering that they must long for peace, and force their Government to demand it. The people must be left nothing but their eyes to weep with over the war.' The 'people' in question were southern secessionists, it is true, but they shared the same language, many the same religion, and often came from the same families. What would wartime brutality look like when not tempered by such cultural bonds?

In the hours before dawn on 25 April 1915, the very same night that Allied troops landed at Gallipoli, the Turkish authorities began a process of repression of those whom they saw as internal enemies – the Armenian communities, numbering perhaps 2 million people, concentrated in Anatolia in the north-east, straddling the border with Russia, but also scattered throughout the Ottoman Empire. Under cover of darkness, several hundred Armenian men – intellectuals, journalists, professionals, businessmen, clergymen – were taken from their homes and shot.

That was only the beginning. Over the next two years the Armenian population of Ottoman Turkey was uprooted and expelled to the desert regions of Meso-potamia. In the process between 500 000 and one million Armenians were killed or died of exposure or disease in camps or in the Syrian desert. In the midst of

Schoolchildren at the Armenian Apostolic Church School at Mashger, a village of Arapgir in the Ottoman Empire, 1915. Only four of the children (identified by Xs) survived the genocide.

war, a substantial part of a long-established and prosperous civilian community with identifiable religious and cultural characteristics were wiped out. They were sentenced to death because of who they were and where they were; in effect, because of their ethnicity.

There had been tension between the Christian Armenians and the Muslim Turks for a long time. Armenian separatism had been suppressed, with widespread loss of life, in 1894 and 1896. After the revolution of 1908, nationalism under the 'Young Turks' changed the nature of the antagonism by projecting an even more hostile and threatening character on to the Armenians living in their midst. The outbreak of war in 1914 seemed to justify Turkish fears: Armenian units were serving alongside Russian forces in the Caucasus, and threatened fifth-column activity behind Turkish lines. On 20 April 1915, after a period of sporadic inter-communal violence, an armed attack by Turks on Armenians in the eastern city of Van was repulsed by armed Armenians; eighteen Turks were killed in the encounter. This 'uprising' provided the excuse for the nocturnal arrest and murder of prominent Armenians four days later, precisely when Turkey faced invasion from the west.

Armenian refugees.
Deportation was the first
stage of genocide. The theft
of property was followed by
a forced march to the desert,
rape and murder. These
crimes were witnessed by
diplomats and clergymen.
Their appeals reached the
American government, who
as a neutral could not act, and
the German government,
who as an ally of Turkey
would not act.

The failure of the Allied landing at Gallipoli led to a succession of repressive measures. Had the landing succeeded, resulting in a rapid advance to Constantinople, the Armenian tragedy might not have occurred. But even though the Allies had failed to break out of their beach-heads, the Turkish regime now felt itself besieged on all sides. It was in this environment of invasion and heavy loss of life among Turkish forces that the decision to expel the Armenians from their homes was taken.

It is unlikely that a precise order to exterminate every single Armenian came down from the ruling Turkish triumvirate of Tallat Bey, Minister of the Interior, Enver Pasha, Minister of War, and Djemal Pasha, Minister of the Navy. The responsibility of these men for collective deportation is clear; but deportation – a time-honoured strategy in nineteenth-century Turkey – while tantamount to death for the old, the weak and the infirm, was not genocide.

The Armenian genocide arose out of the waging of total war against an internal 'enemy' by corrupt and incompetent elements of the army. The Turkish men who fought stubbornly at Gallipoli were exceptional; they represented Turkey's future. The murderers of the Armenians highlighted unsavoury aspects of Turkey's past. For several decades steps had been taken to modernize Turkey's armed forces. As early as the 1830s Helmuth von Moltke, later chief of staff of the Prussian Army and architect of the defeat of the French Army in 1870, was dispatched to Constantinople to help reform the Turkish Army. The problem remained, though, that however wise his advice, the Turkish Army was bound to reflect the corruption of the society it served. In 1915, as when von Moltke had served with the Turkish Army in Armenia and Egypt, poorly paid soldiers and irregulars had to forage for their food. Their supplies made a grand circular tour on the black market back to the government offices which had issued them in the first place. Just to survive, Turkish units engaged in armed skirmishes or raids, which were endemic in the rough terrain of the Turkish-Russian border region.

From mid-1915 these raiding parties destroyed Armenian villages and towns; bandits in Turkish uniform, together with underpaid and undernourished soldiers, killed with impunity, harassed the deportees and herded them south, towards concentration camps or the wilds of the Mesopotamian desert.

The massacre mixed the worst of the old and the new. By 1915, the Turkish Empire was fighting for its existence, but more venal motives were also at work. Limited, though persistent, armed resistance by the Armenians provided the Turkish leaders with a pretext for getting their hands on Armenian property, land and assets. The crime they set in motion initially was theft and brutality on a grand scale, much more akin to the viciousness of the Bosnian Serbs' shelling of civilians in Sarajevo in 1995 than to the Nazis' extermination of the Jews. The Turks wanted the Armenians out of the way; they also wanted their wealth, and were prepared to kill, torture and maim to get it. Their motives were old; the means to achieve them were new and chilling. They identified an entire nation as an internal enemy and simply decided to eliminate it.

Witnesses

This crime was not done in the dark: there were numerous witnesses to the deportation and massacre of the Armenian people. One man who saw what was happening was a German missionary in Turkey, Johannes Lepsius, President of the Deutsche Orient-Mission and the Germano-Armenian Society. He prepared a detailed report to his Mission, intended for private circulation among influential people in Berlin who, he hoped, would be in a position to stop the killings; censorship prevented public discussion of a matter so potentially embarrassing to Germany's ally. Lepsius reported that three-quarters of the Armenian people had been stripped of their possessions, chased from their homes, and – if not prepared to convert to Islam – killed or deported to the desert. One-seventh had escaped the deportation. Lepsius pointed to political circles around the 'Union and Progress Committee' as being responsible for the deportations, validated though they were by government decree. Young Turk 'Clubs' recruited groups of thugs and brigands to 'convey' the deportees out of their towns, and to rob, rape and kill them when convenient.

Testimony by Armenian survivors corroborated Lepsius's account. The town of Baibourt was home to about seventeen thousand Armenians. In the first two weeks of June 1915, about seventy prominent Armenian men were imprisoned or taken into the hills, presumably to be shot. The bishop and seven other notables were hanged. Other men who refused to leave the town were killed there. Then the rest of the population and that of the surrounding villages was deported in three batches.

One widow provided a graphic description of the horror of this journey. She and her daughter were deported with four or five hundred other people on 14 June. The Turkish prefect of the town wished them 'a happy voyage'. The convoy was accompanied by fifteen gendarmes. Two hours after their departure they were set upon by armed brigands who, in league with their 'guards', stole all their

An Armenian village in Turkey, before the massacres of 1915.

Armenians massacred by
Turks in Aleppo. Some
Armenians escaped death by
conversion to Islam; others
perished through hunger,
thirst, exposure or violence.
The photographic evidence
of genocide was available at
the time. Perhaps the non-
European character of the
victims and the perpetrators
made Europeans less
sensitive to the rape of
Armenia in 1915 than to the
rape of Belgium the previous
year. But no German was
accused of a plan to wipe out
the Belgian nation; that was
an honour reserved for the
Turk's treatment of all
Armenians, victims of
total war.

possessions. Over the following week, all males over the age of fifteen were bludgeoned to death; young women and children were seized and taken away. As the refugees marched on, they saw the bodies of earlier deportees. Stripped of any possessions, sleeping without cover, they were soon reduced to near-starvation. On the road, they were passed by a convoy of cars carrying about thirty Turkish war widows, *en route* from Erzerum to Constantinople. One widow singled out an Armenian and killed him with a gendarme's revolver. Then the Armenian widow and her daughter were given the choice: stay with the column or join the Turkish convoy; the price of their salvation was their agreement to convert to Islam. When they reached the plain of Erzerum, on the banks of the River Euphrates, there were corpses everywhere. They saw children thrown into the river, to their certain death. Armenian men tried to hide by 'taking the veil' and by pretending to be Muslim women; any caught in this guise were summarily shot. After thirty-two days, the widow and her daughter reached Constantinople. What became of them is not known.

To form a sense of the enormity of the Armenian deportations, we need to multiply this middle passage thousands of times. The details of the persecution varied; its ultimate character and aim did not. These deportations were intended to rid eastern Turkey of an old and prosperous community, whose riches inspired envy and whose separate ethnic identity made them appear as potential enemies in time of war.

Lepsius was not the only Westerner to protest and beg for action to stop the killing. The American consul in the town of Harput sent horrifying and detailed reports of mass murder to the US Ambassador in Constantinople, Henry Morgenthau. At this time, the United States was neutral, but Germany too was unable to stop the slaughter.

The criminal nature of the Armenian massacres was established at post-war Turkish courts-martial held in 1919. In one such investigation, concerning killings

An Armenian mother mourning her child. Atrocities are disproportionate and violent reactions to those subdued in war, either through surrender or non-combatant status. All sides committed atrocities, but the worst record was probably that of the Turks. Some Armenians fought in the Tsarist Army against Turkey; this provided the excuse for the repression of the entire Armenian nation. The systematic extermination of the Armenian community was the first genocide of the twentieth century.

committed in the Yozgat region, three men were accused. The charges included the premeditated murder of Armenians deported from Yozgat, the pillage of the victims' property, and the abduction and rape of Armenian women. Of an Armenian population of 1800 in Yozgat in 1915, a mere 88 had survived the war. Abundant proof about these murders existed in the form of cables, coded instructions and orders signed by the defendants. The courts-martial established that there was no provocation or organized resistance to Turkish authority from the Armenians of Yozgat. The men were separated from their families, who were forcibly deported. Instructions for their murder were given to the guards who conveyed them into exile. Then the property of the victims was seized and distributed. Here is the same story reported by Lepsius in his 1916 'secret report', validated by Turkish judges themselves. Under articles 45 and 170 of the Ottoman Penal Code and Article 171 of the Military Penal Code, the most senior defendant, Mehmed Kemal, aged thirty-five was sentenced to death and executed on 10 April 1919, four years after his minor part in this bloody period of history had begun.

The Armenian genocide opened a new phase in the history of warfare. Total war provided the context and the cover for a conspiracy by Turkish nationalists and the thugs they controlled systematically to deport, degrade and murder an entire people. That children were massacred alongside their elders shows that the crime was intended to wipe out the future as much as the present Armenian population.

This genocide was a critical event in the history of twentieth-century warfare. The massacre of the Armenians was not the same as, but constituted a step on the way to, the industrialized murder of European Jewry by the Nazis. Hitler himself posed the question in 1942, 'Who today remembers the Armenians?'

Fortunately, we do. The Armenian massacres bridged the nineteenth and twentieth centuries. These crimes further lowered the obstacles to organized murder in wartime. What happened in Turkish Armenia in 1915 was indeed genocide, a terrible harbinger of worse things to come. It was in Armenia that the true meaning of total war emerged. Its consequences are with us still.

4

SLAUGHTER

There was little cheer for the Allies as 1916 began. The German Army was still firmly entrenched on the Western Front, despite every attempt by France and Britain to dislodge it. The venture to open up a new front at Gallipoli had been disastrous. Austrian troops, who throughout the war did not have much to celebrate, could savour one of their few victories when Montenegro sued for peace. News from the Russian Front was mostly of Russian defeats and massive casualties. Only in Africa was there a positive, but militarily insignificant, victory for the Allies: a French expeditionary force had taken control of Yaounde, the capital of the German Cameroons.

The United States was still at peace, but there were disturbances south of the border. In Mexico, Pancho Villa stopped a train bound for a mining camp and killed eighteen American engineers. The US government's response was to send an expedition of troops into Mexico led by Brigadier General John J. Pershing, who a year later would be leading America's Expeditionary Force in France.

The year 1916 would include the high seas battle of Jutland, the only major – but inconclusive – naval encounter of the war. Before the year ended the world would hear of the deaths of General Joseph S. Galliéni, the 'saviour of Paris', the British Minister of War, Lord Kitchener, and the Austrian Emperor Franz Josef.

These were all meaningful events, but for people everywhere the question in 1916 was: how long would the war continue? The defeat at Gallipoli and the wavering fortunes of the Russian Army in the East reinforced the strategic centrality of the Western Front. Here the war would be won or lost. But what would it take to break the deadlock? Military men on both sides believed that the answer – and eventual victory – required a massive assemblage of men and *matériel* to be hurled at the enemy. The British, who had begun the war with only a small expeditionary force, were now fielding in France and Belgium an army of a million men. France and Germany had replenished their armies. The stage was set for three massive, violent and largely futile battles.

What Gettysburg is to America, Verdun is to France and the Somme and Passchendaele are to Britain. These legendary battlefields are still today sacred

Ruined church interior, Reims. The city of Reims, where the kings of France had been crowned, was right on the front line from 1914 to 1918. Its glorious cathedral was hit repeatedly by artillery fire, directed – the Germans claimed – against artillery spotters on the roof. Other churches were razed, and in dismembered crucifixes soldiers saw an embodiment of the link between suffering and sacrifice.

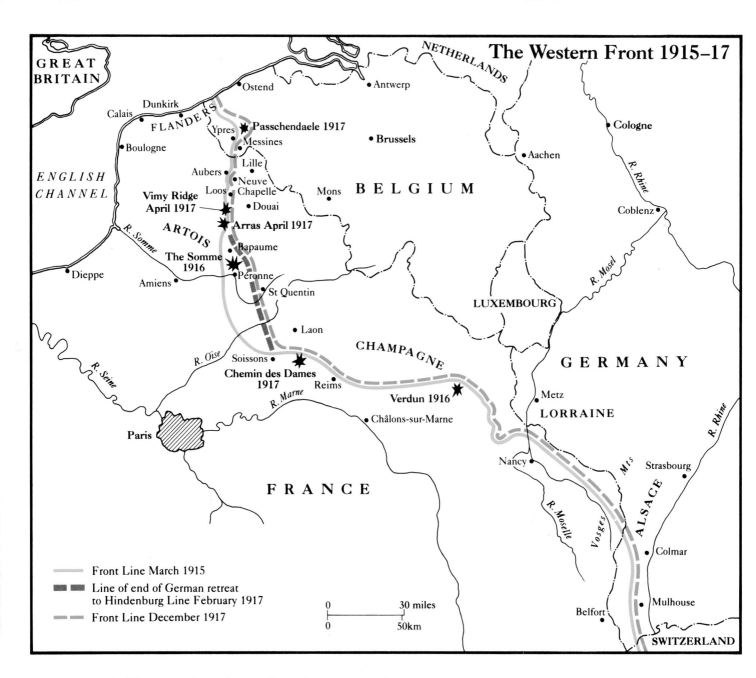

The Western Front 1915–17

Front Line March 1915

Line of end of German retreat to Hindenburg Line February 1917

Front Line December 1917

ground. They are places for sombre pilgrimages and remain in memory as the sites of the world's first global war. But they are more than places of bloodshed and memories. What happened on these battlefields gave new and terrible meanings to the notion of sacrifice – a kind of sacrifice best defined by one word: slaughter.

VERDUN

It has been called the world's 'greatest battle'. Certainly it was one of the most gruesome.

But it was more than just the killing that gives Verdun its special place in history. In a war known for 'endurance', this was the battle that changed the meaning of the word. Launched in the midst of winter in February 1916, Verdun was the longest battle of the entire war and became a symbol of the will of the French nation. On and on the killing went for ten months. Winter turned to spring and summer, then to autumn and back to winter again. Perhaps 300 000 French and German soldiers died there. Another 770 000 were wounded. Yet at the end of the encounter, the battle lines were about where they had been at the beginning.

The architect of the battle, who promised that three Frenchmen would die for every German, was General Erich von Falkenhayn, Chief of the General Staff. An aristocratic Junker who could trace his ancestry back to the Teutonic Knights of the Middle Ages, Falkenhayn had taken von Moltke's place in late 1914 following the latter's breakdown after the failure of the Schlieffen Plan. Falkenhayn was a relatively young man for his job, only fifty-three when the war began. Severe and stern, even by Prussian standards, he confided in no one but was nevertheless a favourite at the Kaiser's court. Perhaps more than any other German general, Falkenhayn was able to look beyond immediate events to the long-term perspective of the war. He was not optimistic about Germany's prospects.

At Christmas 1915 he presented the Kaiser with his assessment of Germany's best strategy for winning. This document has been lost, and is now known about only through Falkenhayn's own memoirs. There he sketched out a new kind of strategy, victory through attrition. France, he argued, was at the 'limits of endurance'. Russia was not much better off: 'Their offensive powers have been so shattered that she can never revive in anything like her old strength. ... Even if we cannot perhaps expect a revolution in the grand style, we are entitled to believe that Russia's internal troubles will compel her to give in within a relatively short period.' But an advance on the Eastern Front, Falkenhayn reasoned, 'takes us nowhere'. The real danger, he argued, was Britain, but he was hesitant to attack the enemy's strength. Yet going on the offensive was now necessary before the British naval blockade and the *matériel* and human resources of the Allies overwhelmed Germany. It was in this context that Falkenhayn favoured the launching of an offensive, one of the few on the Western Front to be precipitated by the German High Command between autumn 1914 and spring 1918. In his view, 'There remains only France. ... Within our reach behind the French sector of the Western front there are objectives for the retention of which the French General Staff would be compelled to throw in every man they have. If they do so the forces of France will bleed to death. ...'

The place of judgement

Why was Verdun so vital that France would be impelled to defend it with every man it had? Verdun was a city with no real strategic importance but a long military history. It had been a fortified camp as far back as the days of the Roman Empire, and was part of the remarkable system of fortifications created for Louis XIV by his master architect Vauban. During the Franco-Prussian War of 1870 it was the last of the French fortresses to fall. The French were determined not to see history repeat itself.

Falkenhayn gave his battle plans the codename *Gericht*, which, among other

meanings, can be translated as the 'place of judgement'. It was an appropriate choice for an operation in which the German Army secretly amassed six new infantry divisions and 1300 pieces of artillery, the largest such accumulation the war had yet seen. The arsenal included Big Berthas and their one-ton shells that had shattered the Belgian fortresses around Liège in 1914. Massive bombardment was part of Falkenhayn's plan, but not all of it. He proposed attacking on a narrow front, rendering life unsupportable in the area under bombardment. Then his infantry would occupy the devastated zone unmolested, his guns and shells would be moved forward, and the process would be resumed. In this way the French Army would be bled to death.

Among the German infantrymen massed for the attack on Verdun was Otto Heinebach, a student of philosophy from Berlin. He had no illusions about what he and his comrades faced. On the eve of the battle, he took leave of his life.

> Before Verdun, Friday evening, February 18, 1916
>
> I say good-bye to you, my dear Parents and Brothers and Sisters. Thanks, most tender thanks for all that you have done for me. If I fall, I earnestly beg of you to bear it with fortitude. Reflect that I should probably never have achieved complete happiness and contentment....
>
> Farewell. You have known and are acquainted with all the others who have been dear to me and you will say good-bye to them for me. And so, in imagination, I extinguish the lamp of my existence on the eve of this terrible battle. I cut myself out of the circle of which I have formed a beloved part. The gap which I leave must be closed; the human chain must be unbroken. I, who once formed a small link in it, bless it for all eternity. And till your last days, remember me, I beg you, with tender love. Honour my memory without gilding it, and cherish me in your loving, faithful hearts.

Then the storm struck. Heinebach died of wounds received on the first day of the battle. The French High Command were caught by surprise when the huge German attack was launched along an eight-mile front on 21 February. Nothing like it had ever happened before. One million shells were fired on the first day alone.

The heaviest bombardment was directed against a key first-line defensive position that became a zone of death, the Bois des Caures, commanded by Lieutenant-Colonel Emile Driant. Driant was a reservist who in peacetime had been a politician serving a constituency near Verdun. He was also a military writer. Ironically, eight years earlier he had written under the pseudonym 'Danrits' a novel for children describing his death on the field of battle. During the war he had been a virtual lone voice warning of a German build-up. In January 1916 he wrote, 'I await the cyclone.... Finally, if this is the hour, and I am called, I will respond: "Present," like all the others.' His admonitions about the need for reinforcements were ignored; now he and his men were bearing the brunt of the devastating artillery attack.

After two days of shelling that included poison gas, German troops probed the French lines with a new weapon, the flame thrower. The few French survivors to emerge from their holes found that the once dense forest around them had been reduced to splinters and stumps. Driant's men had held out for a day,

January – June 1916

JANUARY *Compulsory military service begins in Britain*

The First Military Service Bill, introducing conscription for single men, became law on 25 January 1916. Extract from the diary of the Rev. Andrew Clark.

1 January Mr Jas. Caldwell called – very bright and informative. It is now quite certain that compulsory military service will be adopted. The *Daily News* and the *Star*, owned by the same people, are futilely raging against it. They represent the Labour party, the members of which are not in the least concerned that the young men of the country should be exposed to the perils of war, but are terribly afraid that after the war their own power for mischief should be annulled.

It is positively disgraceful to see the crowds of men of twenty-five or so who sit all day in the cafés in London, sipping coffee, smoking cigarettes and playing dominoes. Mr Caldwell took refuge from a shower one day in 'The Mecca' Cheapside: found it full of such men and not an armlet to be seen among them....

Recruiting office in London

FEBRUARY *The Battle of Verdun begins*

The French writer Jules Romain describes the first day of the battle on 21 February.

Over the whole of the front ... to a depth of several kilometres, the same dance of dust, smoke, and debris went on, to a thunderous accompaniment of noise. Thousands of men, in groups of two, three, of ten, sometimes of twenty, bent their backs to the storm, clinging together at the bottom of holes, most of which were not better than scratches in the ground, while many scarcely deserved the name of shelter at all. To their ears came the sound of solid earth rent and disembowelled by bursting shells....

APRIL *The Easter Uprising in Ireland*

An account of the events of 24 April when armed members of the Irish Republican Brotherhood attempted to seize the Dublin post office.

At the South Dublin Union The first man to be hit was Richard O'Reilly, who had a brother, John, in the Nurses Home and two other brothers, then serving in the British Army. 'Funny', said John later, 'that day there were two of us fighting for England and two of us *against*.'

The wrecked post office in Dublin

APRIL *The Fall of Kut*

British troops at Kut in Mesopotamia were besieged by the Turkish Army from 7 December until their surrender to the Turks on 29 April. The Rev. Harold Spooner, Anglican chaplain, recalls the horrific final days. Spooner survived but spent sixteen years in a nursing home in a state of mental collapse as a result.

Monday 17 April – 23 (Easter Day) One fears to think what will happen to the Garrison if we are not soon relieved. Everyone is wasting away. Many soldiers are dying from gastro-enteritis – which is really only another name for starvation. It is all too pitiful to think about – no medical comforts or foods now – things are getting beyond endurance.

MAY *The Battle of Jutland*

The Battle of Jutland

31 May The first and last great engagement between the British and German Fleets. Although the British Fleet suffered serious losses, the German High Seas Fleet never faced them again. A German seaman saw it as a British defeat.

On 2 June news reaches us that the largest naval action ever fought took place off Horns Reef on the Skagerrak. The action concluded with an unquestionable defeat of the British fleet, which has thus been able to try conclusions with its principal adversary as to who was ruler of the seas – for the very first time since it was brought up by the *Kaiser* and *Tirpitz*. Several British battleships were destroyed....

JUNE *The Brusilov Offensive succeeds*

Alexei Brusilov, Commander of the Russian Army on the Southern Front, started his offensive on 4 June, and succeeded in pushing back the Austrian Army nearly 60 miles – the most successful Russian operation of the war. Here he recounts the battle.

I do not propose to describe step by step and in detail the engagements fought by all the armies under me during this memorable period. I will simply state that by midday on June 6 we had captured 900 officers, more than 40 000 men and taken 77 guns, 134 machine-guns, 53 trench mortars and a vast quantity of miscellaneous military booty.

Russian soldiers in Galicia

directing a withering line of machine gun fire against the advancing Germans. Driant, who at the end of the first day's bombardment had asked a priest to help him 'make his peace with God', took charge of the 59th Light Infantry Battalion and managed to reinforce some units still holding out in the Bois des Caures. Around 4 p.m. on 22 February he was hit in the head, cried 'My God' and died. He joined France's growing list of legendary heroes.

On 24 February the 37th African Division, made up of men from Morocco and Algeria with a strong reputation as combat troops, was thrown into battle. Unable to withstand the fire, they broke and ran. The following day the Germans attacked Fort Douaumont. This huge, polygon-shaped fortress, which measured nearly a quarter of a mile across, was the cornerstone of the French line of defence, yet it was inexplicably manned by only a skeleton crew of gunners. Douaumont was

ABOVE French schoolboys following the attack on Fort Douaumont.
RIGHT The ruined fort. The struggle for Fort Douaumont lasted from its capture by the Germans on 25 February to its recapture by the French on 24 October 1916.

LEFT Stephen Westman was a German physician who came to Verdun in the early stages of the battle. His memoirs tell of the terrible strain under which the ordinary soldiers lived during what some called the worst battle in history.

taken with hardly a struggle, and its capture was cause for great celebration in Germany. Church bells rang out the news and schools were let out on special holiday. But there was no joy in occupying the fort, wrote a German Army doctor, Stephen Westman.

I could feel how the whole fort shook when a particularly heavy shell, most probably with a delayed action fuse, landed and exploded.... Afterwards I strolled through the fort, with its many dug-outs and casements. The entrance to one of them was bricked up and someone had fixed a plaque, with the inscription, 'Here rest 1052 German soldiers' – a whole battalion, who were sleeping in the casemate. Apparently one of them had smoked, and barrels of fuel for flame-throwers, which were stored there, had exploded, and not a single soul had survived.

German soldiers in Fort Douaumont
which they captured with only
a handful of men. The retaking of
the fort, one French general
estimated, cost France the lives
of 100 000 men.

Dante's Hell

By now the surviving French troops in the field of fire to the north of Verdun faced an almost unbearable situation. Propaganda leaflets fell to the ground from German planes announcing that Douaumont had fallen and that the end was near. Even replacement troops entered the battle demoralized. 'We are lost!' wrote Sergeant Paul Dubrulle, a Jesuit serving in the 8th Regiment. 'They have thrown us into the furnace without rations, almost without ammunition. We were the last resources; they have sacrificed us.... Our sacrifice will be in vain.' Desperate for leadership, Joffre turned to a commander whom he personally despised: Henri Philippe Pétain.

The situation that greeted Pétain, who arrived at Verdun with double pneumonia, was critical. The icy roads leading to the city were clogged with fleeing refugees, wounded soldiers and broken regiments. Upon entering headquarters, one of his aides felt that he had 'entered a lunatic asylum.... Everybody was talking and gesticulating at the same time.' Directing the battle from his sickbed, Pétain quickly took charge. Aged sixty when called to Verdun, he was of relatively humble origins. His demeanour was noble but cold, and he remains one of the century's most intriguing – and controversial – soldiers. At a time when other French officers embraced the military philosophy of infantry attack, Pétain was a singularly outspoken advocate of firepower: 'Cannon conquers, infantry occupies.' It was his emphasis on the coordination of artillery fire that would allow Verdun to remain in French hands. Going against established French military doctrine, combined with an open contempt for politicians, had left him only a colonel when the war began, but before its end he would rise to command the entire French Army.

By the end of February the German attack had become bogged down. The reason was simple: despite the astounding size of the shells and guns, the bombardment was still short of what was needed for the task. Still Falkenhayn pushed ahead. On 1 April the Kaiser publicly proclaimed that the end of the war, like that of the Franco-Prussian War of 1870, would occur at Verdun. But while the German artillery had produced a zone of death in the area shelled, the area outside that zone bristled with French artillery. When the German infantry moved forward to occupy the territory that their shells had laid waste, they were hit by ferocious counter-fire from French gunners, regularly supplied by motorized transport along the Voie Sacrée, the 'sacred way' or life-line of supplies from Bar-le-Duc. This is what made the battle a bloodbath for the German Army too.

The area north of the city was soon a site of devastation. One pilot who flew over it thought he was peering into 'Dante's Hell'. This was an accurate description of a horrific killing ground. 'One eats, one drinks beside the dead, one sleeps in the midst of the dying, one laughs and one sings in the company of corpses,' wrote the French surgeon Georges Duhamel. To keep his sanity, he played his flute between operations.

By spring the battle had taken on a life of its own – one that had little strategic importance to either side. It is difficult to imagine a single battle that could result in total casualties – dead, wounded and missing – of nearly a million soldiers. It

General Philippe Pétain to whom the defence of Verdun was entrusted the day after Fort Douaumont fell to the Germans.

Shell cases at Verdun. Pétain used artillery so effectively at Verdun that the Germans suffered as many casualties as they inflicted on the French.

is equally hard to conceive how the French, who suffered half a million of those losses, withstood day after day of bombardment. Over the course of the struggle some 40 million artillery shells were fired by the two armies – about two hundred rounds for every soldier killed. This explains why it was the experience of bombardment that survivors such as Dubrulle returned to in their accounts of Verdun:

When one heard the whistle in the distance, one's whole body contracted to resist the too excessively potent vibrations of the explosion, and at each repetition it was a new attack, a new fatigue, a new suffering. Under this regime, the most solid nerves cannot exist for long.... Perhaps the best comparison is that of seasickness ... finally one abandons one's self to it, one has no longer even the strength to cover oneself with one's pack as protection against splinters, and one scarcely still has the strength to pray to God.

Mutilated bodies on the Western
Front. Many soldiers developed
a defensive callousness after seeing
such sights frequently, and blotted
these images out of their conscious
minds for ever.

To die from a bullet seems to be nothing; parts of our being remain intact; but to be dismembered, torn to pieces, reduced to pulp, this is a fear that flesh cannot support and which is fundamentally the great suffering of the bombardment.

Dubrulle was particularly affected by one shelling that left a headless and limbless torso stuck on a tree. 'I implored God to put an end to these indignities. Never have I prayed with so much heart.' Dubrulle survived Verdun but later began to express less orthodox sentiments for a Jesuit: 'Having despaired of living amid such horror, we begged God not to have us killed – the transition is too atrocious – but just to let us be dead. We had but one desire; the end!'

On the other side of the line, too, faith was tested. For some it was a source of strength. Johannes Haas was a twenty-four-year-old theology student from Leipzig. On 13 May 1916 he wrote to his family:

> My dear, good, old parents,
>
> Here we have war, war in its most appalling form, and in our distress we realize the nearness of God. Things are becoming very serious, but I am inwardly unalarmed and happy . . . I do not fear the Judgment. I am indeed a poor, sinful creature, but how great is God's mercy and the Saviour's love! So, without fear or dismay, I do my duty to the Fatherland and to my dear German people. I thank you, dear Parents, for having led me to the Saviour; that was the best thing you ever did. I love you tenderly. God be with you!
>
> Hans

Three weeks later, he wrote again:

> June 1, 1916
>
> Dear Parents,
>
> I am lying on the battle-field, wounded in the body. I think I am dying. I am glad to have time to prepare for the heavenly home-coming. Thank you dear Parents. God be with you.
>
> Hans

Henri Desagneaux was a survivor of Verdun who has left a record of his time there. He began the war as a reserve lieutenant in the French railway transport service, but as the supply of French officers dwindled he was transferred to the front and given command of a company. Arriving at Verdun in the middle of a rainy June night, he and his men could hear the thunder of the guns all around the citadel. He noticed with amazement the fact that there were no huts or shelters for the incoming men, even though the fighting had been going on for weeks. That was only the beginning of an experience which he described as a 'void'. 'We are no longer in a civilized world.' He was right.

> Numb and dazed, without saying a word, and with our hearts pounding, we await the shell that will destroy us. The wounded are increasing in numbers around us. These poor devils not knowing where to go come to us, believing that they will be helped. What can we do? There are clouds of smoke, the air is unbreathable. There's death everywhere. At our feet, the wounded groan in a pool of blood; two of them, more seriously hit, are breathing their last.

One, a machine gunner, has been blinded, with one eye hanging out of its socket and the other torn out: in addition he has lost a leg. The second has no face, an arm blown off, and a horrible wound in the stomach. Moaning and suffering atrociously one begs me, 'Lieutenant, don't let me die, Lieutenant, I'm suffering, help me.' The other, perhaps more gravely wounded and nearer to death, implores me to kill him with these words, 'Lieutenant, if you don't want to, give me your revolver!' Frightful, terrible moments, while the canons harry us and we are splattered with mud and earth by the shells. For hours, these groans and supplications continue until, at 6 p.m., they die before our eyes without anyone being able to help them.

Henri Desagneaux, who commanded a French company at Verdun. He spent two weeks in the front lines in June 1916, and survived unscathed. He was one of the lucky ones. To have endured Verdun, he wrote, was to have entered an entirely new world, a void churned by incessant shelling, a desert, a vast cemetery, swallowing up men who suffered from atrocious wounds without even the prospect of relief.

A Pyrrhic victory

Verdun became a French national legend even while the battle was raging. One incident bathed in myth, the 'Trench of the Bayonets', shows how this happened. The facts are undisputed. The 3rd Company of the 137th French Infantry Regiment was wiped out on 12 June 1916 in a ravine between Thiaumont and Douaumont. After this engagement, the trench they had occupied was found completely covered in. Protruding from the earth at regular intervals were a number of bayonets, beneath which were the remains of the men of this unit. Legend had it that they had stayed at their posts until buried alive; common sense suggests that they were buried by bombardment, and that their graves were marked by the German soldiers who, briefly, had occupied this sector.

The Trench of the Bayonets, like the battle itself, did not have to wait until after the war was over to become myth. A French Army commission was sent to Douaumont in 1917 to verify the incident. They found an aviator who had flown over the battlefield on 12 June and who told of seeing ground shift suddenly, thus accounting for the cave-in of the trench. What better, more moving symbol could there be of the indomitable will of the French Army not to be broken at Verdun? The commission decided that the site must be preserved. With the generosity of an American banker, George F. Rand, the site – or more likely somewhere near the site – was covered by a concrete arch. It is a place of pilgrimage to this day.

As a site of unfathomable courage, Verdun is unique. But in military terms, after ten months, when the line of February 1916 was basically restored, what had been gained? For Germany, Verdun was a failure. Wilhelm Hermanns saw that as his unit marched into the Verdun sector in the later stage of the battle.

> We saw a handful of soldiers, led by a captain, emerging slowly, one by one, between the trees. The captain asked what company we were, and then suddenly he started to weep. Was he suffering from shell shock?
>
> The captain said, 'When I saw you coming, I thought of how I came six days ago on this same road with about one hundred men. Now look at those who are left!'
>
> We look as we passed them. There were about twenty men. They walked like living plaster statues. Their faces stared at us like those of shrunken mummies, and their eyes seemed so huge that one saw nothing but eyes. Those eyes, which had not seen sleep for four days and nights, portrayed the vision of death. . . . Was this the realization of the dream of glory that I had when I volunteered to march with the Kaiser through the Arc de Triomphe?

Falkenhayn had bled the French Army white, but he was powerless to resist drawing his own forces into a cauldron that weakened Germany as much as, if not more than, France. He was replaced in August 1916 as commander-in-chief by Field Marshal von Hindenburg, who ruled the army jointly with his First Quartermaster-General, Erich Ludendorff.

For France, Verdun was at best a Pyrrhic victory. The city, with all its historical significance to the French nation, had stood fast by sending three-quarters of the French Army through the meat grinder. The Army would go on fighting, but for the rest of 1916 the burden of the Allied effort on the Western Front shifted to the British and their Dominions and the civilian armies they sent to war.

French soldiers in a shell hole near Fort Vaux. The Battle of Verdun degenerated into the desperate struggles of isolated, small groups of men, out of touch with their reserves, their supplies, and their own units.

KITCHENER'S ARMY

At the beginning, a British volunteer had to be nineteen years old and stand five feet eight inches tall. By November of the war's first year the requirements had dropped to just five feet two inches, though there was hardly a dearth of volunteers. Just two months earlier thirty thousand men had swamped the army recruitment offices in a single day. A million joined in the first five months. While height requirements were being lowered, recruiting posters were going up. Many of them featured a stern Lord Kitchener urging the male population to join up. Others conveyed more subtle yet effective messages by evoking the pressures that could be brought to bear by loved ones. 'The Women of Britain Say Go,' said one. Another enlisted the aid of children and launched a phrase that has remained a familiar question for subsequent generations by showing a worried father being asked by his children: 'Daddy, what did you do in the Great War?'

There were other social pressures, too. The writer Edward Thomas observed those brought to bear by employers. 'Wherever I went,' Thomas wrote, 'I was told that employers – "the best firms" – were dismissing men, the younger unmarried men, in order to drive them to enlist.' Young London men about town not in uniform were stopped by society women and given a white feather – a sign of cowardice. Even a night at the theatre offered no guarantee of escape. On the London stage, the lyrics to the patriotic play *England Expects* included the line: 'Oh, we don't want to lose you, but we think you ought to go.' And some 6 million in all did go – 3 million as volunteers before 1916.

One of them was Thomas. While many, thinking the war would last only a few months, rushed to join in a spirit of adventure or solidarity with mates who had enlisted, there were others, like Thomas, who went out of a sense of duty more than adolescent bravado. 'He hated the newspaper patriotism,' his wife, Helen Thomas, recalled. 'He saw through the lies and deception of the press as he had always seen through untruths.' Still, for Thomas, as for others, there was a nagging sense of obligation which eventually prevailed. He enlisted in the Artists' Rifles, a training corps for officers. When he volunteered in 1915 at the age of thirty-seven, he was just finding his voice as a poet. He could have spent his time serving as a training officer, but volunteered for front-line duty as an artillery officer. In one of the most moving personal documents of the war his wife wrote of their final night together.

Recruiting poster. One million British and Irish men joined up in 1914; another 1.5 million in 1915, but still the High Command wanted more. When sufficient numbers of volunteers failed to respond to patriotic appeals, conscription came in January 1916.

> I sit and stare stupidly at his luggage by the walls. He takes out his prismatic compass and explains it to me, but I cannot see, and when a tear drops on to it he just shuts it up and puts it away. Then he takes a book out of his pocket. 'You see, your Shakespeare's Sonnets is already where it will always be. Shall I read you some?'; He reads one or two to me. His face is grey and his mouth trembles, but his voice is quiet and steady. And soon I slip to the floor and sit between his knees, and while he reads his hand falls over my shoulder and I hold it with mine.
>
> 'Shall I undress you by this lovely fire and carry you upstairs in my khaki

Helen and her husband the poet Edward Thomas, who volunteered for active service in 1915. He was killed in action at the battle of Arras in 1917. Helen's book *World Without End* is one of the most moving personal testimonies of civilian life during the war.

overcoat?' So he undoes my things, and I slip out of them; then he takes the pins out of my hair, and we laugh at ourselves for behaving as we often do, like young lovers.

I hide my face on his knee, and all my tears so long kept back come convulsively. I cannot stop crying. My body is torn with terrible sobs. I am engulfed in this despair like a drowning man by the sea. My mind is incapable of thought. So we lay, all night, sometimes talking of our love and all that had been, and of the children, and what had been amiss and what right. We knew the best was that there had never been untruth between us. We knew all of each other, and it was right. So talking and crying and loving in each other's arms we fell asleep as the cold reflected light of the snow crept through the frost-covered windows.

For every troubled Thomas, there were hundreds who joined up and thought little about the decision. Many were happy to get away from their dreary and monotonous lives to take part in what seemed from a distance a great adventure. Some had walked twenty miles to the nearest recruiting station. Others waited hours, pleading to enlist. Units were even known to charge an entrance fee. By 1915 would-be soldiers were comforted by the knowledge that they could serve

Pals' battalion recruits. To bolster falling enlistment rolls, local notables throughout Britain sponsored detachments of neighbours and friends in their areas. Uniforms and weapons were scarce at first.

with their friends by joining a 'Pals' Battalion' made up entirely of volunteers from the same villages and towns. While this was an effective recruiting device, the British overlooked a lesson they could have learned from the American Civil War when similar groupings of men had enlisted together. Troops in heavy action could, in a matter of minutes, throw entire towns into mass mourning, which was exactly what was to occur in Britain a half-century after Gettysburg.

THE SOMME

Like Verdun, the Somme is a name which has entered the language of Western civilization. Say it today, eighty years after the battle, and the mind conjures up a disaster the magnitude of which stands alone even in the crowded history of World War 1. The Battle of the Somme lasted five months, from July to November 1916. It was contested by two million men on a 30-mile front between Amiens

and Péronne. It produced no strategic gain and over one million casualties. Like Verdun, the Somme was collective slaughter, an outcome of the terrible logic of total war.

There is great debate about the objectives of the offensive on the Somme. Was it another battle of attrition or something else? On the face of it, the plan seems clear and it did not signify attrition. This was to be the long-awaited 'big push' that would break through the German lines.

Sir Douglas Haig

The name of the British commander, Sir Douglas Haig, is forever linked to this battle. Even today controversy swirls around his name. Few generals have been so harshly judged by historians – or so fiercely defended. He is currently undergoing a rehabilitation by some military historians. His critics believe that he needlessly sent tens of thousands of soldiers to their deaths, while his defenders argue that his tactics were necessary – and ultimately victorious. What is a fair way to take the measure of this man?

Like so many generals of his day, Haig believed in the offensive. A Scotsman and old cavalry man, he was dour, headstrong and cold but socially well connected and a personal confidante of the King. Even during his time there were detractors who thought him mired in an intellectual trench of nineteenth-century tactics. He had fought in the Boer War and was later posted to India. In private, as in public life, he could make a quick decision. As a middle-aged bachelor, he proposed marriage to his future wife within seventy-two hours of meeting her. 'I have often made up my mind on more important problems,' he said, 'in much less time.' He was not heartless, as he proved after the war in his devotion to the plight of ex-servicemen in need of care and assistance.

All students of Haig agree that he was tenacious – a bulldog who stubbornly wrapped his jaws around the problem of breaking through the German lines on the Western Front and refused to let go, regardless of the cost. In the American Civil War, Abraham Lincoln had searched for years before finding just such a general – Ulysses S. Grant – whose obstinate determination to restore the Union transcended concerns about casualty lists.

By the early spring of 1916, Haig had a huge problem on his hands. The Battle of the Somme had originally been planned in 1915 as a joint Franco-British offensive. As a result of the assault against Verdun, the French ability to contribute to another theatre of operations was steadily dwindling. Yet their demands for Haig to launch a major offensive became more insistent. If the British Army did not soon go on the offensive, Joffre angrily told Haig, the French Army would 'cease to exist'. A tense meeting between the two commanders led to a decision. No later than 1 July Kitchener's armies, alongside a smaller French force, would attack on the Somme.

Kitchener himself would not live to see that day. Three weeks before the beginning of the battle, he sailed on a secret mission to Russia. On 5 June his cruiser, the *Hampshire*, struck a mine and went down in heavy seas. The whole of Britain was shocked. Some people refused to accept that he was gone, believing instead that the announcement of his death was a ruse to fool the enemy.

Sir Douglas Haig, who in 1915 became Commander-in-Chief of the British Expeditionary Force, a position he held until the end of the war. Controversy still swirls around his name. His detractors cast him as mired in outdated and murderous tactics. His supporters believe his approach was necessary to win the war.

On 23 June 1916 the British Army began shelling the German lines along the Somme. The bombardment of a million and a half shells would last a week, an artillery-pounding heavier even than at Verdun. The sound of the massive bombardment could be heard across the Channel in England. Haig reckoned that it had to be directed against a wide front. Only thus would his beloved cavalry, which were to pour through gaps in the centre, be immune from flanking fire. 'I feel that every step in my plan has been taken with the Divine help,' Haig wrote to his wife on the eve of the battle. 'The wire has never been so well cut, nor the artillery preparation so thorough.'

But Haig was merely uttering his version of Falkenhayn's delusion: that the number of shells would be sufficient for the task in hand. The one and a half million shells fired made an impressive noise and sight, but they were fired along a far wider front and at greater depth than at Verdun. There was no real chance for a breakthrough. Worse, a million of the shells were shrapnel, bombs made out of jagged pieces of metal, which could not reach the German troops who were deeply dug in. If quantity was a problem, so was quality. Poor fuses decreased the ability to cut barbed wire. As for the British high-explosive shells, these had been hastily and poorly manufactured. Many failed to explode at all. Some even blew up the guns supposed to fire them.

The week-long bombardment was doomed to failure, made only worse by another decision. The established principle of an early dawn attack, with its advantage of offering men the cover of semi-darkness, was abandoned. Instead, the British were to advance in broad daylight in hopes of catching the Germans by surprise after dawn. Cavalry units brought up to the front were to follow on the heels of the infantry and take advantage of large breaches in the enemy line. Barbed wire enclosures were built to hold thousands of prisoners. The thorough planning also required the digging of mass graves to hold the dead of both sides. Most of these, Haig believed, would be German.

The artillery, the commanders assured their troops, would cut the German wire and pulverize the German trenches. All the men had to do was advance at a steady walk with full packs across No Man's Land to those trenches, at some points a mile and a half away. It would be, the men were told, a 'walkover'. 'You will be able to go over the top with a walking stick, you will not need rifles.... You will find the Germans all dead, not even a rat will have survived.' Other units were to proceed more rapidly, or in single file, but in whatever formation they advanced, the key was the prior destruction of German defensive positions. This, the high command believed, had been done. Not everyone was so confident. Many men wrote what they feared would be their last letter home. Others made out a final will. Church services were well attended. A few soldiers disabled themselves with self-inflicted wounds.

Enthusiastic British troops on the way to the Somme in June 1916. The citizen armies raised in Britain from 1914 to 1916 were confident of victory. They were all volunteers, and made up in solidarity what they lacked in military experience.

The explosion of this giant mine under German
positions near Beaumont-Hamel in the northern
sector of the front signalled the beginning of
the Somme offensive. The attack by Newfoundlanders
which followed was one of the bloodiest failures
of the Battle of the Somme.

1 July 1916

At 7.30 on this clear, sunny and pleasant morning, the bombardment stopped. There followed a moment of silence. Then waves of British divisions went over the top. There was not a conscript among them. Every soldier was either a surviving pre-war regular or a volunteer. Over sixty thousand men, each with a 60-pound pack on his back and a bayonetted rifle in his hand, began climbing out of their trenches along a 13-mile front and walking towards the enemy line.

Difficult though the shelling had been for the Germans to endure, they had survived. Now they raced from deep bunkers to their machine guns and began mowing down the columns of men in front of them. 'For some reason nothing seemed to happen to us at first; we strolled along as though walking in a park,' wrote Private W. Slater of the 2nd Bradford Pals. 'Then, suddenly, we were in the midst of a storm of machine gun bullets and I saw men beginning to twirl round and fall in all kinds of curious ways as they were hit – quite unlike the way actors do it in films.'

Worse was to come when German artillery, largely untouched by the British bombardment, began dropping a murderous rain of shells on the slow-moving, densely packed troops. In the second assault wave was Vera Brittain's brother, Edward. 'I can't remember just how I got the men together and made them go over the parapet,' Edward Brittain later recalled to his sister. 'I only know I had to go back twice to get them. I wouldn't go through those minutes again if it meant the v.c.'

By mid-morning the outcome was clear to everyone on the front lines. Further to the rear, command received contradictory reports and pressed the offensive. More units moved out towards the German lines. One lieutenant in the 4th Tyneside Scottish reached his objective, turned around and cried out, 'Good God, where's the rest of the boys?' Only two other soldiers in his company had made it across with him. Survival was by chance. The wounded were left where they fell; those with luck found cover and prayed for help; the unlucky were raked by machine gun fire and shells for the rest of that awful day.

In the critical central sector, around the Pozières–Bapaume road, no gains were made. The London Division claimed success in a diversionary attack at Gommecourt; Ulstermen reached the Schwaben Redoubt near Thiepval; and a joint Franco-British force advanced to the south. But none of these achievements came near the breakthrough envisaged by the British High Command.

Later in the morning the attack was renewed, with the same disastrous results. Perhaps the most appalling sight was in the northern sector near Beaumont-Hamel. At 7.28, a huge mine went up under German positions at the Hawthorn Redoubt, but still the German line held. Later that morning Lieutenant Colonel Hadow, commanding the 1st Newfoundland Regiment, received a direct order to attack German positions over open ground. Units of the Essex Regiment were to attack on their right, but they were late getting through the communications trenches. By the time they arrived, the Newfoundlanders had gone over the top and been slaughtered. Of the 752 men who left their trenches, 684 (or 91 per cent) were either killed or wounded in just over half an hour. The Germans recorded no casualties in this encounter.

OVERLEAF Men of the Tyneside Irish Brigade advancing on the first day of the Battle of the Somme at La Boisselle, a few miles south of Beaumont-Hamel.

By noon on 1 July the British Army had committed to frontal assault 129 battalions of infantry, or about 100 000 men. Two-thirds had gone over the top at 7.30, the rest later that morning. Confused fighting, movement and counter-movement throughout the afternoon did not change the verdict of the day. Some objectives had been taken, mostly by the French to the south. But for the British Army it was a disaster. 'We were two years in the making,' reflected Private A. V. Pearson of the Leeds Pals, 'and ten minutes in the destroying.'

British soldiers still in the trenches were ordered not to rescue the wounded. One British general who had already ordered his last battalion into the futile attack was pressed to charge yet again. The general, in a state of near shock, told his superior, 'You seem to forget, sir, that there is now no 70th Brigade.'

Casualties on the Somme. Friedrich Georg Steinbrecher, a student of theology, wrote from the trenches in November 1916: 'The poetry of the trenches is a thing of the past.... The war which began as a fresh youth is ending as a made-up, boring, antiquated actor. Death is the only conqueror.' He was killed on 19 April 1917.

Roll-call

Sunset brought a merciful end to the slaughter. Under cover of darkness, those injured soldiers capable of doing so crawled back to their lines; but most died where they lay. By the night of 1 July the British Army had suffered 60 000 casualties, 20 000 of them dead. German losses were about 6000 killed and wounded; another 2000 Germans were taken prisoner. There were seven times as many British soldiers as Germans involved in the first day of the Somme, and the British suffered seven times the casualties they inflicted on the enemy. As the British Army regrouped, the traditional roll-call was an anguished ceremony. Only one man answered for the 14th platoon of the 1st Rifle Brigade. He had lost thirty-nine of his comrades. This was only the first day of the battle. It went on, with little gain, for nearly half a year.

The first news reaching British civilians about the battle was encouraging. Newspaper headlines declared 'Great Day on the Somme', 'Kitchener's Boys – New Armies Make Good' and 'Swift British Advance'. Journalists of the day, like Philip Gibbs, were both war correspondent and propagandist. 'On balance,' he told his readers, 'it was a good day for England and France.' Gradually the truth sank in. Within a few days the rolls of honour, the lists of deaths and casualties, began appearing in local newspapers. Citizens at home learned that in just a few minutes whole towns in Britain had been devastated. Trainloads of wounded men began arriving, and Vera Brittain was one who attended to them. Among the wounded to arrive at her hospital was her brother Edward.

Entire battalions of 'Pals' who had enlisted together, trained together and had gone to the Somme together, died together in formation. One such unit was the Glasgow Chamber of Commerce Battalion. So severe were its losses that its commander, who normally wrote individual letters of condolence, had to write an open letter back to his city.

July 6, 1916

I should like to express to all the relatives of those who have died, my sincerest sympathy with them in their present great sorrow, and to assure them that all the remaining officers, NCOs and men share their grief with them.

It may be some consolation to them to know that the battalion walked into action as steadily as if it had been on the Parade Ground, and I cannot adequately express my feeling of admiration for the spirit, gallantry, and daring with which all faced their terrible task.

Those who have, in this battle, given their all for their country, did so in a spirit worthy of Scotland's best traditions. . . .

I am, Yours very truly,

David S. Morton, Lt.-Colonel,
Commanding 17th HLI
Glasgow Chamber of Commerce Battalion

In London, within weeks of the beginning of the battle, the first-ever war film documentary was premiered. Filmed at times at great personal risk by two cameramen, G. H. Malins and J. B. McDowell, *The Battle of the Somme* gave home audiences an unprecedented chance to see their troops in action. Intended as a morale-booster, this pioneering film was a mixture of actual and re-created events. Perhaps the most famous image of the war, that of soldiers going over the top and then disappearing into the fog of war, can be found in this film. It was staged.

Not that filmgoers knew – or cared – at the time. In London alone it was shown in thirty cinemas and audiences turned out by the hundreds of thousands, riveted by screen images that would be considered quite tame today. 'I really thought that some of the dead scenes would offend the British public,' confessed Malins. Exhibitors questioned whether women should be submitted to the 'actual horrors of warfare'. One cinema refused to show the film altogether, declaring that 'This is a place of amusement, not a chamber of horrors.' While the film avoided the more gruesome realities, for people with no conception of the violence and vast scale of modern war, it was as close a glimpse as they would ever get. 'It was not a cheerful sight,' one viewer wrote, 'but it does give a wonderful idea of the fighting.' In one London cinema the orchestra stopped playing when the subtitle announced 'The Attack'. One woman in the audience could not help screaming out, 'Oh God, they're dead!' In the autumn of 1916 the film ended its run, having been seen in Britain by an estimated 20 million people.

The learning curve

Meanwhile the battle was still raging. 'In another six weeks,' Haig predicted at the end of July, 'the enemy should be hard put to find men. The maintenance of a steady offensive pressure will result eventually in his complete overthrow.' Before the campaign ended in November, British and French losses numbered nearly three-quarters of a million men. There are no accurate figures on German losses. They may have been lower, but were still severe.

By early autumn Haig was placing high hopes on a new weapon. Jumping on the chance that tanks might be the answer to breaking out of the trenches, he introduced them on to the battlefield at the first opportunity. On 15 September 1916, forty-nine tanks rumbled toward the battlefield. Seventeen broke down before reaching the front lines and only eighteen entered No Man's Land – moving at a pace of half a mile per hour. Travelling more slowly even than walking men, they made inviting targets for the German artillery. It would be another year before there would be proper tactics – and enough tanks – for this new invention to make itself felt. Undaunted, Haig pushed on with the offensive. Only when weather conditions became intolerable in November did the campaign cease. When the battle finally ended the Allies had advanced 6 miles and were 4 miles from Bapaume, which Haig's cavalry had hoped to take on the opening day.

Among the dead was Henry Webber. At sixty-eight he was the oldest British soldier to be killed in action during the war. Raymond Asquith, son of the British Prime Minister, was another to die there. After his death the Prime Minister never again showed much enthusiasm for the war. A future Prime Minister, Harold Macmillan, was injured on the Somme when a grenade exploded near his face. Another of the wounded was a twenty-seven-year-old German corporal, Adolf Hitler. He served as a dispatch runner, carrying messages up and down the

This sequence of fighting from the documentary film *The Battle of the Somme* was staged. The man on the right who is sliding down the trench appeared to be dead. He was so convincing that audiences in Britain were horrified; the music ceased at this point and in the silence that followed, civilians started to imagine how awful the experience of battle could be. The reality was much, much worse.

front line through barrages and bullets. It was one of the war's most dangerous assignments. Hitler escaped while many around him died. When a British shell smashed into his dugout, killing most of the men around him, he received a shell splinter in his face. By now Hitler had received the first of two Iron Crosses for bravery. In later years he rarely spoke of these medals; they had been recommended by a Jewish lieutenant. The British writer Robert Graves also went down during an artillery barrage. Among his multiple injuries was shrapnel that entered through his back and came out through his chest. At the medical station he was given no chance of surviving and left in a corner to die. The next day, the morning of 21 July, orderlies were astonished to find when clearing away dead bodies that Graves was still alive. He would survive the war and write his classic memoir, *Goodbye to All That*.

Why did the battle go on so long? Here we set foot on a field of great controversy. Some judge Haig's plan, his vision, his compassion, and find all wanting. Others see him as a man trying to solve a new and unknown puzzle. From a sympathetic point of view it is hardly surprising that he, like all other generals of the day, failed to find a way to break through trench fortifications. Winning the war required, among other things, an accumulation of new knowledge at all levels of the army. This lengthy process is called by some a learning curve, by others a bleeding curve. On one point there is general agreement: the key to British success was artillery, and only rarely did Haig apply firepower of sufficient weight to destroy the defences facing the British infantry.

British 8-inch howitzer in action. Many veterans said that no one could capture the sound of a massive bombardment. The German poet August Stramm, in his poem 'Shells', tried:

Deafness deadens terror
  wounds
Banging tapping churning
  screeching. . . .

This was the case on the first day of the Somme. The man who commanded the British Fourth Army on that day, General Henry Rawlinson, originally intended to attack a 20 000-yard front to a depth of 1250 yards. Preceding the assault there was to be a five-day bombardment of about 1.5 million shells, or about 300 pounds per yard of trench. But Haig changed the plans to include a much deeper penetration, to about 2500 yards. Doubling the area covered without increasing the shelling halved the effect. The result was disaster.

Two weeks later, on 14 July, a front line of approximately 6000 yards – or one quarter the area attacked on 1 July – was hit by two-thirds of the guns deployed at the beginning of the battle. Not surprisingly, the outcome was favourable: the German second line in the central sector of the front was occupied. As if to drive the point home, the British failure to occupy the German third line of defence on 15 September can be traced to the identical miscalculation as had been made

Canadian bravado inscribed on shells echoed their achievements at Vimy Ridge, when in April 1917 they dislodged German troops from an escarpment dominating the northern front.

before 1 July: the weight of artillery showered on the German lines on 15 September was half that deployed on 14 July. The result was thirty thousand British casualties on that one day: half the losses of 1 July, but in proportional terms just as murderous as on the first day of the Somme. Here is the real indictment of British command: it asked the infantry to do the impossible and, when they failed, it asked and asked again.

These artillery barrages were insufficient to break the enemy's defences, but nevertheless had placed German soldiers in the trenches under severe pressure. They withstood these ferocious bombardments and gave ground grudgingly – and at tremendous cost. Whenever the Germans lost ground, their generals immediately ordered their men to retake it. There were over three hundred German attacks on British positions during the battle. The German attacks, like all attacks across No Man's Land, were costly affairs. Karl Gorzel, a law student from Breslau who served on the Somme, hinted at what he and his comrades faced day after day. On 1 October 1916 he wrote home of the 'horrible affair at Thiepval'.

> . . . the English attack began [on 12 September]. . . . At dawn I looked around me: what a ghastly picture! Not a trace of a trench left; nothing but shell-holes as far as the eye could reach – holes which had been filled by fresh explosions, blown up again and again filled. . . . The wounded lie helplessly groaning. The supply of water runs out. . . . The fire increases to such bewildering intensity that it is no longer possible to distinguish between the crashes. Our mouths and ears are full of earth; three times buried and three times dug up again, we wait – wait for night or the enemy! . . . And the bursting shells' dance-of-death becomes ever madder – one can see nothing for smoke, fire, and spurting earth. . . .
>
> Suddenly the barrage lifts . . . and there, close in front, is the first wave of the enemy! Release at least! Everyone who is not wounded, everyone who can raise an arm, is up, and like a shower of hailstones our bombs pelt upon the attacking foe! The first wave lies prone in front of our holes, and already the second is upon us, and behind the English are coming on in a dense mass. Anyone who reaches our line is at once polished off in a hand-to-hand bayonet fight, and now our bombs fly with redoubled force into the enemy's ranks. They do their gruesome work there, and like ripe ears of corn before the reaper the English attacking columns fall. Only a few escape in full flight back through the boyaux [communication trenches].
>
> We sink down, dazed, upon the tortured earth, and tie up the wounded as well as we can, while awaiting the coming of a second attack or of the night. . . . I light a cigarette and try to think – to think of our dead and wounded; of the sufferings of humanity; to think back to – home! But away with such thoughts! The present demands its rights – it requires a real man, not a dreamer. . . . Reinforcements arrive, things are cleared up and the dead buried, and a new day breaks, more horrible than the last!
>
> Such is the battle of the Somme – Germany's bloody struggle for victory.
>
> This week represents the utmost limits of human endurance – it was hell!

In time the Germans were pushed out of portions of their well constructed trenches. But this happened slowly, and only forced them back to other elevated positions. At the end of the battle there was no British breakthrough. Karl Gorzel

German dead on the Somme. Eduard Offenbächer, a student of political economy, wrote from the front line on 14 July 1916: 'One keeps cherishing the hope that it may be possible to find some way out of this miserable situation.... The nation, the great machine lubricated by filth from the Press, is beginning to think for itself. People, both here and in other countries, are crying out for the war to end, and yet it does not end. Who is responsible for this?' He was killed thirteen days later.

and the men around him had, in essence, held the line, despite six months of unrelenting Allied pressure.

Enthusiasm was another casualty on the Somme. When Private E. T. Radford of the 1/5th West Yorks was asked to recall his strongest memory, it wasn't of the battle, but of 'all those grand looking cavalrymen, ready mounted to follow the breakthrough. What a hope!' There were similar feelings on the other side of the battle line. It would be hard to find a more dedicated German soldier than Ernst Jünger, but he too realized that the Battle of the Somme had marked a change. 'Chivalry here took a final farewell,' Jünger declared. 'The Europe of today appeared here for the first time on the field of battle.... After the Battle of the Somme the war had its own peculiar impress that distinguished it from all other wars.'

What did it all add up to? For years the horror of the first day of the Somme – a day that saw the British Army lose more soldiers killed than the combined losses of the Crimean, Boer and Korean wars – overshadowed almost all other facets of this six-month battle. For the British the first day of the Somme was eight times more expensive in human life than was Waterloo. And the men who fell were the best of the volunteers who came forward in 1914 and 1915. While the first day of the Battle of the Somme was a national disaster, it was primarily an intensely local tragedy. Over 5000 Londoners died or were wounded on that day; Manchester lost 3500 men. If anything, smaller towns and mining villages suffered proportionately even heavier losses.

All these sacrifices, and still there had been no breakthrough. Nothing had really changed. But in other respects everything had changed. More than chivalry was lost on the battlefields of the Somme. The first day of July was a cultural shock from which Britain, a society nurtured on economic mastery and naval strength, has never fully recovered. The bitter disappointment of that day and of the following months marked the point at which the illusions of one century gave way to the realism of another.

PASSCHENDAELE

There is one more battle among the major encounters on the Western Front that is synonymous with slaughter: it is Passchendaele, the popular name for the Third Battle of Ypres, waged between 31 July and 10 November 1917. No British, Australian or Canadian chronicle of the war would be complete without an account of what took place there. For even more than the Somme, Passchendaele symbolizes the futility of trench warfare.

Not one but three Great War battles were fought around the town of Ypres in the south-western region of Belgium known as Flanders, a low, swampy area made inhabitable only by an elaborate network of canals and drainage ditches. In the Middle Ages Ypres had been a major cloth town, a centre of European commerce boasting a population of two hundred thousand. Ypres thrived because of its location as a gateway to the English Channel, but geography would also be the source of its downfall as it was the site of frequent combat over three centuries.

July – December 1916

July *The Battle of the Somme begins*

Burial of a French soldier

A French general, Emile-Marie Fayolle, describes the first day of the battle.

1 July First day of the Battle of the Somme. Magnificent preparation. Attack of 20th Corps at 7.30. Saw the departure of the 1st Colonial Corps at the Lapin Woods at 9.20. All German front line positions taken in one fell swoop. Curlu, Dompierre, Bequincourt, Bugny, Fay taken, with about 4500 prisoners. Saw Joffre. He is radiant. Unfortunately, in the evening we learned that the English did not succeed on the left flank. They took Montauban and Mametz in the centre, but on the left nothing.

August *The Battle of the Somme continues*

A French soldier from Savoie, Quy Delphin, writing to his parents of his experiences on the Somme. Delphin survived the war.

23 August 17.00 Dear parents our situation is very sad. We are under a rain of fire and an opaque cloud of earth and dust. Pray for us. The trenches are destroyed on both sides and shells rain down everywhere. For the moment I think I have every chance of coming out alive. We live in the open air. Don't count on my getting leave since the battalion is near the village of Monrepas near Péronne....

August *Hindenburg and Ludendorff take command*

On 28 August Paul von Hindenburg was appointed Chief of the General Staff and Erich von Ludendorff, his Chief of Staff, became First Quartermaster-General. One staff officer is commenting here to another.

Hindenburg (left) and Ludendorff

Colonel von Marschall to General Groener

He, Marschall, feared that Ludendorff in his measureless vanity and pride would conduct the war until the German people were completely exhausted and would then let the monarchy bear the damages. He had set his views down in a memorandum, since he cannot take any responsibility for the change in the Supreme Command.

SEPTEMBER *The first use of tanks*

Cecil Lewis, then a pilot with the Royal Flying Corps, was flying a patrol the first day tanks were used at the front.

Cecil Lewis

Hoppy and I were detailed for the first contact patrol with the Tanks. It was launched on the 15th September at 6.30 am.... In my log book appears the following entry:

'The Guedecourt line should have fallen at 10 am; but this failed. It will be attacked tomorrow at dawn. We are at present digging a new front line. Little is known of what happened on our flanks; but it is pretty certain that the cavalry are not through as intended. Perhaps tomorrow. Always tomorrow! A partial success.... I shall never forget the way the Tanks waltzed through Flers. There was a little white terrier, a mascot I suppose, following one of the Tanks. Apparently the little chap was not hit, for we saw him running around barking at his Tank on the afternoon patrol.'

DECEMBER *Lloyd George becomes Prime Minister*

On 7 December Lloyd George ousted Asquith and became Prime Minister. Austen Chamberlain, then a member of the War Cabinet, wrote to his wife a few days later.

14 December I profoundly distrust [Lloyd George] – no doubt a man of great energy, but quite untrustworthy; who does not run crooked because he wants to, but because he does not know how to run straight....

Lloyd George

DECEMBER *The Battle of Verdun ends*

Final casualties of the ten-month Battle of Verdun were 377 000 French dead, and 337 000 German. Prince Max of Baden became Chancellor of the parliamentary government established in Germany in October 1918 and negotiated the Armistice.

The campaign of 1916 ended in bitter disappointment all round. We and our enemies had shed our best blood in streams, and neither we nor they had come one step nearer to victory. The word 'deadlock' was on every lip.

Prince Max of Baden

The ruined centre of Ypres. German artillery turned Ypres' medieval Cloth Hall and
adjacent buildings into pillars of rubble. The Belgian town was at the base of a British salient,
pointing north-east into German lines. This salient was the site of four major battles: in
October–November 1914, in April–May 1915, and in July–November 1917, the battle known as
Passchendaele; each resulted in bloody stalemate. In 1918, the German Army pushed the British
back, but could not break the British lines.

No experience, however, was as devastating to Ypres as the battles of World War I. In 1914 the 'Race to the Sea' ended at Ypres, with the Allies in possession of the town. It formed a vulnerable salient, a British thumb pointing into German-occupied territory, exposed to fire on three sides. The town was levelled. But having fought for it, the British were loath to give it up. A second battle ensued the following spring when the German Army, experimenting with chlorine gas, launched a new offensive – Second Ypres – which was again repulsed.

In the summer of 1917 it was Haig's turn to launch an offensive in Flanders. Why? As we shall see in the next chapter, by mid-1917 the French Army was exhausted and demoralized. The condition of the Russian Army on the Eastern Front was worse. It would be a year, perhaps two, before the Americans appeared as an effective fighting force. And Haig, once again, was convinced that the Germans were wilting and might succumb after one more onslaught.

This time there was reason for Haig's optimism. He now had tanks and aircraft and light machine guns and trench mortars. Above all, the BEF had ample quantities of guns and shells, of the right sort and quality – and British gunners were in the process of learning their craft. The creeping barrage advancing one step ahead of the infantry was perfected. The importance of counter-battery tactics (attacks against opposing artillery emplacements) emerged. Aerial photography and observation were in full use. Even weather, which affects the path of shells, was now a factor that was included when working out ranging equations. In short, assault by artillery had finally become a science.

The new tactics could not take great sweeps of territory, but they did work as set-piece attacks with limited objectives, the kind of 'bite and hold' tactics that some of Haig's subordinates had advocated on the Somme. In April 1917, the use of similar tactics showed promise at Arras when the Canadians threw the German infantry off the commanding heights of Vimy Ridge and British forces opposite Arras advanced an impressive 3½ miles. The offensive was halted by the Germans only when the British infantry outran their artillery support. Ironically, as will be seen in chapter 5, Arras was essentially a diversionary battle, launched to distract the Germans from the massive French assault on Chemin des Dames by General Robert Nivelle. Among the casualties at Arras was Edward Thomas, who was killed during a German bombardment. His effects and papers, including his Shakespearean sonnets, were returned to his wife. 'They were all strangely creased,' Helen Thomas noted, 'as though subject to some terrible pressure.'

Haig's next forward move, intended as a curtain-raiser to the real 'show' – a breakthrough at Ypres – also went well. At 3.10 on the morning of 7 June 1917, Allied sappers set off a series of nineteen giant mines dug over eighteen months under the German lines south-east of Ypres under the Messines Ridge. There had never been anything like it – a gigantic explosion of nearly a million pounds of amatol was heard as far away as Paris and London. In Lille, 24 miles away, they thought it was an earthquake. Allied soldiers who witnessed the detonations were knocked off their feet by the concussion. 'Scientific warfare,' one awed British corporal called it. Together with a highly sophisticated counter-battery operation, this stroke completely disrupted and disorganized German defensive positions. Allied troops, with New Zealanders spearheading the attack, took what

OVERLEAF Soldiers in mud holes. The wettest summer in memory made Haig's hope of a breakthrough at Passchendaele a nightmare for those who endured the battle.

was left of the town of Messines, advancing on a narrow front to a relatively manageable distance from their supporting guns.

But instead of using this masterstroke to strike out immediately at German positions, British and Allied forces regrouped. King George V paid a victory visit and was treated to a re-enactment of the battle. Six weeks passed before the offensive resumed, just in time for the onset of the wettest summer in memory, which was followed by a cruelly wet autumn. In the downpour of August the Royal Flying Corps could not spot for artillery, which had to fire blind. The rain turned the ground over which the infantry were supposed to advance into a swamp. These were not the conditions for a great offensive, yet Haig persisted.

The bleeding curve

What made Third Ypres a symbol of the whole tragedy of 1916–17 was the collective memory of the churned-up quagmire in which it was endured. The battle, which began on 31 July 1917, went on and on. One of the German defenders near Ypres was Gerhard Gürtler, a student of theology in Breslau. He was killed on 14 August. Four days before his death, he wrote home about what the battle did to him and to the men around him.

Aug 10, 1917

Nothing is so trying as a continuous, terrific barrage such as we experienced in this battle, especially the intense English fire during my second night at the front.... Darkness alternates with light as bright as day. The earth trembles and shakes like a jelly.... And those men who are still in the front line hear nothing but the drum-fire, the groaning of wounded comrades, the screaming of fallen horses, the wild beating of their own hearts, hour after hour, night after night. Even during the short respite granted them their exhausted brains are haunted in the weird stillness by recollections of unlimited suffering. They have no way of escape, nothing is left them but ghastly memories and resigned anticipation.... 'Haven't you got a bullet for me, Comrades?' cried a Corporal who had one leg torn off and one arm shattered by a shell – and we could do nothing for him.... The battle-field is really nothing but one vast cemetery.

It was no better on the other side of the line. For the British, Passchendaele amounted to the horror of warfare in a morass, in a surreal world where men and animals simply vanished in pools of mud. Just getting to the front was a horrendous experience: horses and men slipped off roads and disappeared before they could be rescued.

The dead were put to use as stepping stones, only to slip out of sight. This is the landscape of Passchendaele on 27 August, as noted in the diary of one young British officer, Edward Campion Vaughan:

From the darkness on all sides came the groans and wails of wounded men; faint, long, sobbing moans of agony, and despairing shrieks. It was too horribly obvious that dozens of men with serious wounds must have crawled for safety into new shell-holes, and now the water was rising about them and, powerless to move, they were slowly drowning. Horrible visions came to me with those cries – of Woods and Kent, Edge and Taylor, lying maimed out there trusting that their pals would find them, and now dying terribly, alone amongst the

At Passchendaele, as elsewhere, animals were the
vehicles of transport for artillery and other stores.
They suffered the same fate as the men who worked
alongside them, showed the same fear in their eyes at the
terrifying bombardments, and at times vanished without
trace in the glutinous mud of the battlefield.

Tanks had first been used on
the Somme in September
1916, to little effect. Most
broke down rapidly, and a
year later, given the weather
and mire of Passchendaele,
they were at best steamrollers
or fixed artillery, at worst
death traps for their crews.

dead in the inky darkness. And we could do nothing to help them; Dunham was crying quietly beside me, and all the men were affected by the piteous cries. . . .

Later that day Vaughan noted, 'The cries of the wounded had much diminished now, and as we staggered down the road, the reason was only too apparent, for the water was right over the tops of the shell-holes.'

Haig had not fully appreciated the effects of fighting in such terrain, just as he had underestimated the enemy he confronted. Time and again he saw the Germans as on the brink of collapse; time and again he urged one more push to bring about the breakthrough that he knew somehow was just around the corner. During a period of dry weather in late September the British Army delivered three limited attacks, taking ground at Menin Road Ridge and Polygon Wood. Buoyed by these successes, Haig wrote in his diary on 28 September that 'the enemy is tottering and . . . a good vigorous blow might lead to decisive results'. Not at Passchendaele. For the rains returned, but Haig – and his commanders – pushed on as if the sun were still shining.

Stretcher bearers in the mud. Gerhard Gürtler, a student of theology, writing from Flanders on 10 August 1917: 'those men who are still in the front line hear nothing but the drum-fire, the groaning of wounded comrades, the screaming of fallen horses, the wild beating of their own hearts, hour after hour, night after night.' He was killed four days later.

'What is Passchendaele?' asked the journalist Philip Gibbs:

> As I saw it this morning through the smoke of gun-fire and a wet mist it was less than I had seen before, a week or two ago, with just one ruin there – the ruin of a church – a black mass of slaughtered masonry and nothing else, not a house left standing, not a huddle of brick on that shell-swept height.... Thousands – scores of thousands – of our own home stock and from overseas have gone through fire and water, the fire of frightful bombardments, the water of the swamps, of the beeks, and shellholes, in which they have plunged and waded and stuck and sometimes drowned.

'The enemy,' Gibbs went on to venture, 'may brush aside our capture of Passchendaele as the taking of a mud-patch.' He was right. The ruined village had no tactical, let alone strategic, value. After the rubble was taken by Canadian troops, Haig finally called a halt to the offensive in November, with little to show for the quarter of a million British casualties but the 'slaughtered masonry' of the village which had given the battle its name. Haig had not even fought to a draw in this 'breakthrough' battle turned bloodbath. Germany, while hurt badly, had lost fifty thousand fewer men than Britain.

Not all the blame goes to Haig for continuing the battle. Lloyd George, the British Prime Minister since December 1916, had voiced his misgivings before the campaign began and reserved the right to call off the battle; but like all the others in positions of authority, be offered no alternative plan. Lloyd George did nothing to stop the killing.

By the end of 1917 the resort by generals on both sides to winning the war by bloody frontal assaults was clear to every soldier in the trenches. In spite of the strong cultural bonds and private world they had formed, many of them were beginning to question why they were fighting at all. 'For the first time,' Gibbs later wrote, 'the British Army lost its spirit of optimism, and there was a deadly depression among many officers and men with whom I came in touch.'

On 3 January 1917 Douglas Haig was promoted to field marshal, the highest rank in the British Army.

Passchendaèle, like Verdun and the Somme, lives on as a byword for military futility, a symbol of the way the machinery of war outgrew the minds of the men in control of it. If this was war, why go on with it? That question, and the answers it generated, dominated the next year of the conflict.

5

MUTINY

The war hardened in 1917. The winter of 1916–17 was one of the coldest on record. Coal was scarce. Cities were dark. Shivering populations had little to cheer about. Total casualties were now being counted in the millions, and the outcome of the war was very hard to foresee. In the East, the Russian Army was a brittle entity: to some a spent force, to others an essential magnet drawing German troops away from the key confrontation on the Western Front. One German general discounted the Russian Army entirely. Having suffered losses so high that it was impossible to count them, the Russians faced an uncertain future. On the Italian Front in October and November 1917, German and Austrian units broke through at Caporetto, precipitating a mass retreat of 60 miles, threatening Venice and the heartland of Italy itself. Only the clairvoyant could foretell who would win.

Hard men came to power in 1917. Lloyd George ran the British war effort. By December, Georges Clemenceau was Prime Minister in France. His policy was clear: 'I make war, war and nothing else.' To raise the armies needed to carry on the conflict, Canada passed a conscription law; Australia rejected it twice, but still sent overseas substantial numbers of volunteers.

Peace feelers proliferated: Pope Benedict XV tried to float the idea of a peace of equals, of no annexation and no recriminations. The idea was shot out of the sky, as were all other peace initiatives, including an Austrian one and another from the German Chancellor, Bethmann-Hollweg.

Shot out of the water might be a more accurate description of the fate of the German peace initiative. In February 1917, Germany declared unrestricted submarine warfare to force the Allies to the conference table by throttling their supply lines to North America and beyond. The gamble failed. The Allies survived, joined in April by the United States. In July Bethmann-Hollweg was dismissed as Chancellor, leaving the field free for the real rulers of Germany, the joint commanders of the German General Staff, Hindenburg and Ludendorff.

By 1917, the political character of the war was transformed. In Russia, the February Revolution led to the abdication of Tsar Nicholas II; the provisional

By 1917, stalemate and ever-increasing casualties caused men throughout the ranks to challenge their superiors. A British officer recalled: 'As a Commander of one thousand men or more, I found it frequently embarrassing when in chance conversation with a subaltern or sergeant to be asked to give reasons.... "Why do we always make our attacks in winter when any fool who knows anything about the front can see that they're bound to be a failure?"'

government that came to power decided to go on with the war and thereby brought about its own demise. Lenin and the Bolsheviks succeeded it eight months later; in December they sued for peace and took Russia out of the war. But America's entry into the conflict tipped the economic and manpower balance and ensured Germany's ultimate defeat.

What is clear eighty years later was not at all visible or certain to those who had to live through it. At the end of 1917, the German Army was in its most powerful position. It had won the war on the Eastern Front and had destroyed every Allied attempt to dislodge it from France and Belgium; its troops occupied the high ground in seemingly impregnable defensive positions from the English Channel to the Swiss border. It is not surprising that contemporaries were very uncertain of the outcome of the war in the harsh winter of 1917–18. But still they held on.

On the Western Front, the end of the war was nowhere in sight. The German Army still occupied most of Belgium and stood within striking distance of Paris. In March 1917, the Germans realigned their forward positions in Picardy by a major (and secret) withdrawal to what became known as the Hindenburg Line, 20 miles to the east. When they left their headquarters in Péronne on the Somme, they razed the town. On top of the ruins of the town hall they left a calling card for the Allies. It said: 'Don't be angry, just be amazed.'

After three years of war, more and more soldiers began to express both their anger and their amazement in a number of alarming ways, from lethargy through indiscipline to outright mutiny. By 1917 it was clear that millions of men and women at war had been pushed to the limits of human endurance and beyond. What they then did is the subject of this chapter.

How do we account for the endurance of these people? One explanation lies in the survival of nineteenth-century notions – honour, camaraderie, duty, national sentiment. Pre-1914 values and forms of behaviour did not vanish in a puff of smoke at the outbreak of war. Three years later such convictions were still there, and only by recognizing the stubborn survival of older attitudes can we understand how it was that, despite millions of casualties, the war relentlessly went on.

This raises one of the key issues in the history of the war: the balance between coercion and consent in waging it. Previous interpretations have emphasized the coercive element: conscription, propaganda, the suppression of dissent, the use of police spies and so on. Recently, the balance of interpretation has swung the other way. It is much more terrifying to contemplate the possibility that the Great War went on and on because millions of people believed that it had to do so. Revolt took many forms in 1917, but it was revolt by and large within the framework of carrying on the war.

Everywhere, in this, the fourth year of the war, men and women tried to work out how to preserve their lives and their wartime commitments – to the men in uniform, to their families at home, to their sense of social justice, to their way of life, to a set of values which most saw as being under enemy threat. In 1917 that tension was unresolved, but the overwhelming majority still accepted the need to carry on with the war, until exhaustion or the promised military breakthrough would bring it to an end.

'Don't be angry, just be amazed', was the calling card left by Germans on the destroyed town hall of Péronne after their withdrawal to the Hindenberg Line. The sign is on display in Péronne today in the Historial de la grande guerre.

The crisis of that year took many forms. In this chapter the progression is outward, from the individual suffering in a hospital ward, to soldiers protesting collectively, to anti-war movements, and to revolutionary events themselves. All show the dual character of 1917, and the collision between those forces which propelled the war forward and those which ultimately ended it.

SHELL SHOCK

Going on or going home: for countless men in the front lines the tension between these two choices became unbearable in 1917, the year of no exit, no way out of the war. To that impasse there were many responses. The inner migration to madness was one.

In the Great War, psychiatric casualties were grouped loosely under the heading of 'shell shock'. The term was first coined in 1915 by a British physician, C. S. Myers. It accounted for what happened to many men in the trenches: they broke down. But it also suggested something now taken for granted: breakdown was not necessarily the fault of the man but was, as likely as not, a reflection of the intolerable stress under which he fought.

Soldiers of all ranks suffered from shell shock. Men in the ranks were usually diagnosed as 'hysterics', meaning those who converted emotional states into physical ones. This could take the form of paralysis, contorted positions, or irregularities in gait or facial expression. Before the war 'hysteria' was more frequently associated with women, but after 1914 the term described many states of shell shock in the ranks. Officers, with greater responsibilities and greater control over the conditions under which they served, were differently categorized when they became psychologically unfit. They suffered from nightmares, loss of sleep, panic attacks or other infirmities which their contemporaries called 'neurasthenia'.

Those afflicted left many accounts of their plight; their words give us just a glimpse of the complexity, duration and poignancy of their situation. The tension of trench warfare – the terror of mutilation and death, the uncanny sights and smells – could completely unhinge unquestionably sturdy soldiers. It was not only the unceasing din of artillery that produced intolerable anguish. The strain of the daily routine and the appalling hardships of living on the line; the lack of sleep; the arbitrariness of death and wounds – all were there intermittently. During offensive operations, such periods of stress could seem to last an eternity.

No one could tell where each man's breaking point was, but that such a point existed was terrifyingly clear. One unnamed twenty-one-year-old British sapper passed it. Behind the lines, he began to recall what had happened to him:

> Joe, don't go – Give me my rifle, Joe – Ten killed. Poor old Taffy – Dreamed last night – Saw Harry Edmonds with all his ribs broken – when we had the explosion – 5000 bombs or two and a half tons of explosives blew up. – Joe – Clay said he would never live three weeks, – Glasses blown in. – Taffy killed by shell in stomach – S – – – – L – – – – All privates blown off him – Just after leaving workshop.

A German soldier, who had been a 'lackey' in civilian life, was blown into the air by a shell which hit his trench. On evacuation, he became completely mute. He could hear, and he could respond by shaking his head and writing, but could not utter a word. The man expressed his fears in short, incoherent notes. While being transported, he scribbled: 'Are we going to ride farther, I have such a bad headache.

OVERLEAF The desolate landscape of war.

BELOW A German soldier killed in an attack on 3 October 1917. 'In earlier wars, certainly, towns and villages had been burned, but what was that compared with this sea of craters dug out by machines? ... it seemed that man, on this landscape he had himself created, became different, more mysterious and hard and callous than in any previous battle.' (Ernst Jünger)

The doctor must not come. The one who wanted to shoot me if I couldn't speak. They are all bad.'

A thirty-five-year-old Russian private suffered a similar loss of bearings, this time after heavy shelling in his sector. He leaped on the shoulders of his comrades crying, 'The devil is here! This is hell and murder, and here are the devil's imps.' Behind the lines he was similarly agitated: 'His talk was incoherent and pointless. After every few phrases, he would repeat. "Don't ride there. That's hell! Murder is being done. Devils and unholy powers are beating and killing people." He would tremble, stiffen, and not respond to pin-pricks. And all without a scratch on him.'

Regular soldiers suffered such symptoms as much as conscripted men or volunteers. One British officer, a professional soldier, went through three years of trench duty before suffering a nervous collapse. After dreaming that he would be buried by a shell, he was actually hit and buried. He was frightened of everything: 'Riding on trains he was terrorized in every tunnel lest he should be crushed.' To his superiors he was a 'perfect soldier', but he was one soldier who knew in his bones that 'There is no man on earth who can stick this thing forever.'

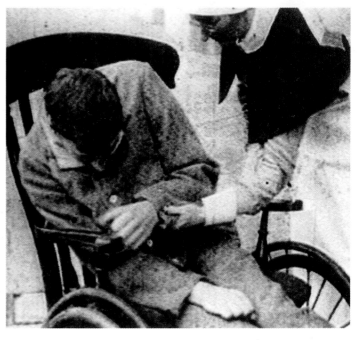

Occasionally, soldiers broke down under the strain of the anxiety associated with killing the enemy. One German private, aged twenty-two, suffered from paralysis of one leg, which remained bent at the knee, ankle and toe. He was treated by laughing gas and hypnosis and, while going under and coming out of the anaesthesia, deliriously spoke words which his doctor found 'curiously demonstrative of "sympathy with the enemy"': '"Do you see, do you see the enemy there? Has he a father and mother? Has he a wife? I'll not kill him." At the same time, he cried hard and continually made trigger-movements with his right forefinger.' This man regained the use of his leg within a few weeks. Others were not so lucky.

Yet another soldier, a Frenchman, admitted, after many months in the trenches, that 'the machine went off the track.' He suffered from trembling of the head and limbs and, even when he was evacuated to Paris, these tremors were set off by ordinary sounds.

> The subway gate noises, a flaring light, a locomotive whistle, the barking of a dog, or some boyish prank is enough to set off the trembling; ... Recently when a flag was being raised at the Invalides, I thought at first that I was going to be cured by so moving a spectacle, but then I suddenly began to tremble so violently that I had to cry out, and I had to sit down, weeping like a child. Sometimes the trembling comes on suddenly without any cause. I went to a novelty shop to do some errands with my wife. The crowd, the lights, the rustling of the silk, the colors of the goods – everything was a delight to me to look upon – a contrast to our trench misery. I was happy and chatted merrily, like a schoolboy on a vacation. All of a sudden I felt that my strength was leaving me. I stopped talking; I felt a bad sensation in my back; I felt my cheeks hollowing in. I began to stare, and the trembling came on again, together with a great feeling of discomfort....
>
> In the tramway or in the subway, I perceive that people are looking at me, and that gives me a terrible feeling. I feel that I am inspiring pity. Some excellent woman offers me her seat. I am deeply touched; but they look at me and say nothing; what are they thinking of me?

Shell-shocked soldiers in hospital during World War I; today they would be described as suffering from post traumatic stress disorder. Some men converted psychological states of terror into paralysis; others reacted to individual words. The soldier in the photograph (ABOVE LEFT) responded to nothing other than the word 'bomb'; hearing it, he immediately hid under his bed. A war of immobility trapped millions of sane men in a maze of danger and devastation; what was surprising was not the incidence of shell shock, but that many soldiers were spared it.

Healing

The treatment given to such men spanned the spectrum from indifference through hypnosis and psychotherapy to electroconvulsive shock therapy. The use of electrodes to pass an electric current through paralyzed limbs was controversial during the war. In Germany and France this practice was commonplace and, according to a number of neurophysiologists, worked wonders. Those who went through the treatment were not so certain. Some soldiers got better; others protested that they were being tortured. In France one enlisted man, Baptiste Deschamps, punched his doctor, Clovis Vincent, when he tried to apply electrodes to Deschamps' body. The soldier was tried for striking an officer, convicted, but given a suspended sentence. His case became a *cause célèbre*, and eventually discredited Vincent, whose centre at Tours had a notorious reputation for vigorous use of electrocution as a means of curing shell-shocked men. In Germany, too, some soldiers resisted this treatment, and at the end of the war sought out and settled scores with those medical experts who had – in their view – maltreated them in this way.

British doctors also occasionally tried electroconvulsive therapy, but we must bear in mind that this painful procedure was only one method of treatment. Hypnosis or drugs were more commonly employed, as were more time-consuming forms of psychotherapy.

One of the more humane men who tried to help shell-shocked soldiers by talking to them was W. H. R. Rivers. He was a man of many parts. In 1914 Rivers was fifty years old, a physician, psychologist and pioneering anthropologist. Since 1897 he had taught physiology and experimental psychology at Cambridge. From 1907 he lectured on 'the physiology of the senses', and, following outstanding work in the field of vision, became in 1908 a Fellow of the Royal Society, the scientist's ultimate accolade in Britain.

His work in experimental psychology was only one facet of Rivers' achievement. He was one of the first in Britain to explore Freudian ideas on psychopathology, and to work systematically on the study of dreams. He was also one of the founding fathers of the scientific study of anthropology, which to him was another way of studying the mind.

In October 1916 he was sent to direct the care of shell-shocked officers at Craiglockhart Hospital on the outskirts of Edinburgh. His previous work had been at a hospital for both officers and other ranks, but at Craiglockhart Rivers found an environment that perfectly suited his temperament and style. Early in the war, the British Army officer corps was selected mainly from the upper class and the prosperous urban middle class. Thus many of the inmates of Craiglockhart were of the same social stratum as the Cambridge undergraduates whom he had been teaching, and Rivers set about caring for them according to their temperaments, condition and needs.

Most of his patients were men whose trauma and later symptoms were manifest in their dreams, the content of which Rivers and his charges explored in conversation. His sympathy, compassion and impartiality were evident to all, and it was the healing power of personality – his personality – which brought his patients a degree of relief from the terrors haunting them.

W. H. R. Rivers, Cambridge physiologist, psychologist and anthropologist, who developed a humane approach to psychotherapy at Craiglockhart War Hospital. Siegfried Sassoon was one of his patients. Rivers, through his honesty and compassion, heard what Sassoon had to say, and came to rethink his own views about the war.

Siegfried Sassoon

One 'therapeutic' encounter was different from the rest. That was his relationship with Second Lieutenant Siegfried Sassoon. Sassoon was half Rivers' age. He had spent one unhappy year at Cambridge, and was the kind of undergraduate with whom Rivers was very familiar. In 1914 Sassoon enlisted in the Sussex Yeomanry, and the following year was commissioned in an élite regiment, the Royal Welch Fusiliers. In June 1916 he was awarded the Military Cross for gallantry and, after service during the Battle of the Somme, was sent home to recuperate from what he termed 'trench fever'. He was back on the Somme in the spring of 1917, and 'got a sniper's bullet through the shoulder'. 'Luckily it didn't bleed much,' is his laconic diary entry of 16 April. *En route* back to England, he noted 'My wound is hurting like hell, the tetanus injection has made me very chilly and queer, and I am half-dead for lack of sleep, sitting in a chair in my same old clothes – puttees and all – and not having been offered even a wash. Never mind. – "For I've sped through, O Life! O Sun!"' The last sentence is a joke: it quotes a line from the final verse of a poem entitled 'Escape' by a fellow officer in the Royal Welch Fusiliers, Robert Graves, who had reportedly died of wounds in August 1916. But Graves, like Sassoon, had cheated death – at least for the moment.

'At present I am still feeling warlike,' Sassoon jovially remarked on 17 April, but six days later he was in hospital in Denmark Hill, London, and his 'warlike' demeanour began to change. He wrote a poem entitled 'To the Warmongers', which marked the beginning of his shift of perspective on the war. It began:

> *I'm back again from hell*
> *With loathsome thoughts to sell;*
> *Secrets of death to tell;*
> *And horrors from the abyss.*

While wanting some relief from the nightmares, he could not escape them. 'My brain is screwed like a tight wire,' he noted in his diary on 25 April:

> All day I have to talk to people about the war, and answer the questions of friends, getting excited and overstrained and saying things I never meant to. And when the lights are out, and the ward is half shadow and half glowing firelight, and the white beds are quiet with drowsy figures, huddled outstretched, then the horrors come creeping across the floor: the floor is littered with parcels of dead flesh and bones, faces glaring at the ceiling, faces turned to the floor, hands clutching neck or belly; a livid grinning face with bristly moustache peers at me over the edge of my bed, the hands clutching my sheets.

Sassoon felt the reproach of these spectres, jealous of his light wound. They look imploringly at him, mocking his luck, and one tries to give him a letter: '... just as he reaches forward to give it me his head lolls sideways and he collapses on the floor; there is a hole in his jaw, and the blood spreads across his white face like ink spilt on blotting-paper. I wish I could sleep.' At this time, Sassoon was still committed to carrying on. On 29 April he mused, 'Things must take their course; and I know I shall be sent out again to go through it all over again

Siegfried Sassoon in 1915. His poetry expressed the anger of weary men on the front line. War poetry was a house of many mansions. His war poetry could condemn the war and its suffering; it could also search for the sacred. *'My spirit longs for prayer, And, lost to God, I seek him everywhere'*, wrote Sassoon in his poem 'The Church of St Ouen' of March 1917.

January – June 1917

JANUARY *The Turnip Winter*

Ernst Glaeser describes the 'turnip winter' of 1916–17 in Berlin.

This was a very hard winter.... Hunger demolished solidarity: children started to steal other people's rations. Soon, women in long queues outside of shops spoke more of their children's hunger than the deaths of their husbands. The war had changed things. It had created a new front. On this front, the battles were between women and police and bureaucrats. Soon enough roast lamb meant more to us than the fall of Bucharest.

German family, winter 1916–17

APRIL *The United States enters the war*

On 6 April the US declared war on Germany. Edmond Genet was a young American volunteer who served in the French Foreign Legion, and the Lafayette Escadrille in January 1917. This extract from his diary was written twelve days before his death in action.

Edmond Genet

4 April 975th day of the conflict.... President Wilson officially asked Congress today to open hostilities against the German Empire and declare war. The declaration will come today. The whole country must be upheaving with excitement.... I'm one of the few Americans who are already over here fighting tho I did desert my country's service to be here.... I tore into shreds a little American flag which I've carried since the beginning of my enlistment. Somehow it seems a mockery to rejoice over the entrance of our country into conflict with the Entente when we have been over here so long giving our all for right while our country has been holding back. She should have been here long ago.

APRIL *The Battle of Arras*

Billy Bishop, a Canadian pilot who served with the Royal Flying Corps and became one of the outstanding aces of the war, viewed the battle from above.

British troops in the centre of Arras

14 April The waves of attacking infantry as they came out of the trenches and trudged forward behind the curtain of shells laid down by the artillery were an amazing sight. They seemed to wander across No Man's Land and into the enemy trenches as if the battle was a great bore to them. From the air it looked as though they were taking it all entirely too quietly. That is the way of clockwork warfare. These troops had been drilled to advance at a given pace. They had been timed over and over again in marching a certain distance and from that timing, the 'creeping' barrage which moved in front of them had been mathematically worked out.

MAY *French mutiny and strikes*

André Kahn, a sergeant in the French Army, writing to his fiancée.

23 May I don't think there will be a revolution in the army. What [is] said is that the soldiers, as always after a failed and murderous offensive, have had enough, and have told anyone who would listen that they weren't going to go on in the same way. For three years, I have seen this low level of morale, but usually after a month or so, they go back.

Certainly the textile workers' strike – especially if it spreads – is even more serious.... But I have hope that the strike is merely a little spring effervescence.

JUNE *The mining of Messines Ridge*

On 7 June, nineteen huge mines went off under the German lines. Major-General Charles Harington, writing here, was Chief of Staff.

Mine exploding at Messines Ridge

7 June I went over to the Ridge the next morning, partly by Tank, and I shall never forget the sight. I remember so well going into a concrete dugout at Spanbrookmolen – our biggest crater – and finding four German officers sitting round a table – all dead – killed by shock. They might have been playing bridge. It was an uncanny sight – not a mark on any of them. I can see their ghastly white faces as I write. In the wallet of one of them was a copy of a message sent at 2.40 am – 30 minutes before zero – saying 'Situation comparatively quiet'.

with added refinements of torture.... But surely they'll manage to kill me next time'.

A few weeks after this, on 16 May, he wrote: 'For a while I am shaking off the furies that pursued me.' Four days later he was not so certain: hearing birdsong in the early morning, he remembered his men on the Western Front 'blundering about in a looming twilight of hell'. Someone had to speak for them; someone had to denounce the smugness and blindness that Sassoon found all around him in Britain. Someone had to speak out.

In his memoirs, Sassoon noted that it was at this point that he 'began to think' and started to question whether the war ought to go on. He reacted 'intuitively ... not unlike the young man who suddenly loses his belief in religion and stands up to tell the Universal Being that He doesn't exist, adding that if He does, He treats the world very unjustly'.

On 15 June Sassoon sent an open letter to his commanding officer, but really he intended it as a message to the nation as a whole. He sent copies to prominent writers and journalists, and to a Liberal politician who read it out in the House of Commons on 30 July. The next day *The Times* of London printed the text. On 31 July, Haig launched the bloody Third Battle of Ypres, now known as Passchendaele. This is what Sassoon had to say:

> I am making this statement as an act of wilful defiance of military authority, because I believe that the War is being deliberately prolonged by those who have the power to end it. I am a soldier, convinced that I am acting on behalf of soldiers. I believe that this War, upon which I entered as a war of defence and liberation, has now become a war of aggression and conquest. I believe that the purposes for which I and my fellow-soldiers entered upon the War should have been so clearly stated as to have made it impossible for them to be changed without our knowledge, and that, had this been done, the objects which actuated us would now be attainable by negotiation.
>
> I have seen and endured the sufferings of the troops, and I can no longer be a party to prolonging those sufferings for ends which I believe to be evil and unjust....
>
> On behalf of those who are suffering now, I make this protest against the deception which is being practised on them. Also I believe that it may help to destroy the callous complacence with which the majority of those at home regard the continuance of agonies which they do not share, and which they have not sufficient imagination to realise.

Sassoon knew he was in for trouble, but he still retained some hope that, if only soldiers 'would speak out; and throw their medals in the faces of their masters', they might puncture the self-delusions of their elders. This was a prelude to his casting into the River Mersey the Military Cross ribbon he had been awarded for bravery in action.

After writing letters and throwing away medals came blatant disobedience. Sassoon's leave expired at the end of June; he stayed put. On 4 July he received orders to rejoin his regiment immediately. Two days later he replied to his commanding officer, 'I am writing you this private letter with the greatest possible regret. I must inform you that it is my intention to refuse to perform any further military duties. . . . I am fully aware of what I am letting myself in for.' Yet on 12 July he reported to his unit. Robert Graves pulled some strings to arrange a medical board for his wayward friend. At first he refused to appear, but then Graves persuaded him to change his mind and he finally presented himself for inspection on the 20th.

Graves put on an act to convince the board that Sassoon was not traitorous but ill. He spoke tearfully, begging for understanding of his hero-friend. Then it was Sassoon's turn. While awaiting the interview, he had purchased a copy of *The Morals of Jean-Jacques Rousseau*, and got into his head a ditty by the poet Cowper which refused to go away. It went:

> *I shall not ask Jean Jacques Rousseau*
> *If birds confabulate or no.*

Sassoon had to concentrate hard during his interview not to reply with this couplet to all the inane questions. No, he had no objection to fighting. No, he was not sure he had the qualifications to decide if the war should go on. Sassoon determined to be polite, and busied himself repeating the couplet under his breath. The result: Sassoon was deemed to be suffering from shell shock, and was instructed to report to Craiglockhart War Hospital.

Craiglockhart

It was in hospital that he met Rivers. The exchange between doctor and patient, scientist and poet, teacher and student, older man and youth captured the knife edge of tension between going on with the war and going home.

Rivers heard out Sassoon in lengthy conversations; he learned of Sassoon's war service and the dreams that haunted him. They discussed the European political scene, the peace initiatives that never came off, and (of course) Sassoon's protest. 'In that Mecca of psycho-neuroses,' Sassoon later recalled,

> Three evenings a week I went along to Rivers' room to give my anti-war complex an air. I would give a lot for a few gramophone records of my talks with Rivers. All that matters is my remembrance of the great and good man who gave me his friendship and guidance. I can visualize him, sitting at this table in the late summer twilight, with his spectacles pushed up on his forehead and his hands clasped in front of one knee; always communicating his integrity of mind. . . .

This sketch is from Sassoon's fictionalized war memoirs, *Sherston's Progress*. It is striking that, while Sassoon changed the names of virtually everyone in his book, the chapter on Craiglockhart is simply called 'Rivers'. It is as if the goodness of his doctor was so palpable that in retrospect he stood just as he was, apart from the rest, as the 'real' Rivers had done during the war.

Rivers was Sassoon's 'father-confessor', to whom the younger man poured out his feelings, described his dreams and, above all, presented his dilemma about whether or not to go back to the front. All the while, Sassoon stuck stubbornly to his views on the madness of the war, reinforced by his reading of the protest of another soldier-pacifist, Henri Barbusse.

Barbusse's novel *Under Fire* had just won the coveted French literary prize, the Prix Goncourt, and had been translated into English. It was a *cri de coeur* from a serving soldier determined to expose the cruelty of civilian illusions about the war; the truth had to be told, whatever the consequences. War was an abomination, Barbusse insisted; any other view of it was an obscenity.

Like Barbusse, Sassoon was a pacifist in uniform, staying the course through an unshakable loyalty to the men at the front. He began to plot with Rivers a way out of the impasse created by his commitment to irreconcilable views: the war had to stop, and yet he had to go back to it. He feared he would be reassigned; yet the only way he would go back to the war would be if he were allowed to return to his unit, to the men he had left behind. This 'compromise' required some delicate negotiation with the War Office, which Rivers agreed to conduct.

Rivers sympathized with Sassoon's position, but he was not against the war. He knew that Sassoon was entirely sane, and that his 'anti-war complex' was no barrier to his being passed fit for front-line service. As Sassoon himself put it, he had not broken down, just broken out. If a military board passed him fit for service, Rivers reasoned, it would tacitly accept the sanity of the man who had made the embarrassing protest published in *The Times*. It would be a small victory for Sassoon, but one worth winning. So a board was set up. Much to Rivers' chagrin, Sassoon failed to turn up. Petulantly he said that he was annoyed at having to wait outside the room, and had simply left. A second board was arranged for 26 November 1917, and Sassoon managed to be there. This time he had a ditty from Tennyson in his head:

> *Comrades, leave me here a little, while as yet 'tis early morn,*
> *Leave me here, and when you want me blow upon the bugle-horn.*

They called him; he appeared, and announced that he had not changed his views on the war but would go back to it anyway. As he told Graves, his stubbornness in continuing to oppose the war caused 'surprise'. But Rivers had 'obtained, previously, an assurance from a high quarter that no obstacles would be put in the way of my going back to the sausage machine', and Sassoon was duly certified fit for active service.

That was the end of the extraordinary episode of Sassoon's stay at Craiglockhart. At the end of the day, the dilemma of 1917 – to go on or to go home – was resolved for Sassoon by his return to active service. What had incapacitated him was not shell shock, but the recognition that the war was an act of collective madness. To see this meant that he was sane. Since he was sane, he had no alternative but to return to the scene of insanity, where he would join the men in his unit whose fate he chose to share.

The poetry of compassion

This paradox was shared by other war poets, one of whom was also at Craiglockhart in the summer of 1917. Wilfred Owen, then a twenty-four-year-old second lieutenant in the 2nd Battalion, the Manchester Regiment, had had a deeply disturbing baptism of fire on the Western Front. As he wrote to his mother on 16 January 1917:

The cover of *The Hydra*, the fortnightly journal edited by Wilfred Owen at Craiglockhart Hospital for its patients. This edition contains Siegfried Sassoon's poem 'Counter-attack'. Soldiers' journalism spread throughout the British Army, but rarely produced verse powerful enough to survive the war, such as the poetry of Sassoon and Owen.

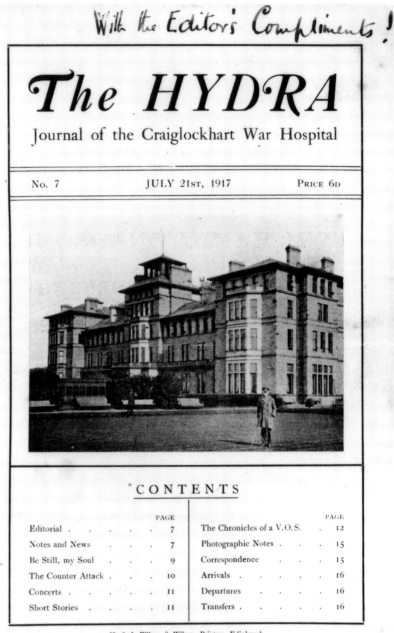

With the Editor's Compliments!

The HYDRA
Journal of the Craiglockhart War Hospital

No. 7   JULY 21ST, 1917   PRICE 6D

CONTENTS

H. & J. Pillans & Wilson, Printers, Edinburgh.

I can see no excuse for deceiving you about these last four days. . . .

I have not been at the front.

I have been in front of it.

I held an advanced post, that is, a 'dug-out' in the middle of No Man's Land . . . the ground was not mud, not sloppy mud, but an octopus of sucking clay, 3, 4, and 5 feet deep, relieved only by craters full of water. Men have been known to drown in them. . . .

The Germans knew we were staying there and decided we shouldn't.

Those fifty hours were the agony of my happy life. . . . I nearly broke down and let myself drown in the water that was now slowly rising over my knees.

In March he had suffered a concussion from falling into a cellar near Amiens, and later took part in a difficult assault on entrenched German positions on the Somme. While hiding under a railway embankment, he learned what extended exposure to close bombardment did to a man's mind. In May that year he was invalided out of the line, suffering from headaches, fever and 'neurasthenia', for which read 'shell shock'. To his sister he wrote from hospital: 'I certainly was shaky when I first arrived.... You know it was not the Bosche that worked me up, nor the explosives, but it was living so long by poor old Cock Robin (as we used to call 2/Lt. Gaukroger who lay not only nearby, but in various places around and about, if you understand. I hope you don't!' On 6 June he returned to England, and after a spell in hospital in Hampshire arrived at Craiglockhart later that month.

There is no evidence of his being treated there by Rivers; the man who mattered most to Owen was Sassoon, seven years older and already a published poet. They apparently met in mid-August 1917. Owen sought from the older man help, advice and sympathy. He got all three. As he told Sassoon, '... you have *fixed* my Life – however short. You did not light me; I was always a mad comet; but you have fixed me. I spun round you a satellite for a month, but I shall swing out soon, a dark star in the orbit where you will blaze.' Sassoon gave Owen a copy of Barbusse's *Under Fire*, 'which set him alight as no other war book had done'. Until mid-November 1917, when Owen left Craiglockhart, the two men shared literary interests and experiments, and separately created some of the finest poetry of the war.

Poetry was a concentrated way of expressing the tensions which in thousands of soldiers produced shell shock. Sassoon found one language for it: open protest. Owen found another: compassion. Their verse captured the stress that soldiers faced, and the state of mind of those broken by it. But Sassoon was, after all, only one man, and his defiance quickly disappeared in the rush of events; his poetry has lasted longer.

Shell-shocked men were imprisoned in their own worlds. Just reaching them was an Olympian task; for them to act together was impossible. That is why Owen and Sassoon spoke to them and for them in their poetry. In 'Sick Leave', Sassoon described how the war went with them, like a time-bomb that threatened to detonate every night.

When I'm asleep, dreaming and lulled and warm, –
They come, the homeless ones, the noiseless dead

and then 'the homeless ones' ask him why he does not return to his (and their) brothers at the front. Was it not better than staying with civilians and their patriotic illusions? In 'Does It Matter?' Sassoon muses that 'people won't say that you're mad' when the 'dreams from the pit' come; all that matters is that you fought for your country. In 'Survivors', men who had gone to war 'grim and glad' are reduced to 'Children with eyes that hate you, broken and mad'. With heavy irony he notes, 'No doubt they'll soon get well' and forget 'Their dreams that drip with murder'.

The title of Sassoon's poem 'Repression of War Experience', was taken from a

Wilfred Owen as a cadet in 1916, before he had seen active service on the Western Front, his dreams as yet unhaunted by the men he killed and suffering he saw.

lecture given by Rivers in 1917. It shows what the two of them faced: images of the war, moments

> *When thoughts you've gagged all day come back to scare you;*
> *And it's been proved that soldiers don't go mad*
> *Unless they lose control of ugly thoughts*
> *That drive them out to jabber among the trees.*

Owen's poetry traverses the same terrain, but with a quieter voice. In his Craiglockhart verse he created some of the most powerful and enduring images of the war. 'Dulce et Decorum Est' was written there. It recalls standing behind a wagon, where a man suffering from gas poisoning lay dying. If civilians heard the sound of blood 'Come gargling from the froth-corrupted lungs', they would not repeat the old lie that it is sweet and fitting to die for your country. Instead they would ask, in the words of 'Anthem for Doomed Youth', 'What passing-bells for those who die as cattle?'

This manuscript was a working draft of the poem 'Anthem for Doomed Youth', composed by Owen and annotated in pencil by Sassoon when both were in Craiglockhart in September 1917. The poem has endured as a timeless evocation of grief and loss in war. It was set to sacred music in Benjamin Britten's *War Requiem*, written after World War II but returning to the poetry of the 1914–18 conflict.

In 'Dead Beat' Owen presents a man whose mind has gone, and who dies without a physical wound. He surveys the same terrain of madness in 'Mental Cases', a poem written in 1918 but which still captures the shadows of Craiglockhart:

Who are these? Why sit they here in twilight?
Wherefore rock the purgatorial shadows,
Drooping tongues from jaws that slob their relish,
Baring teeth that leer like skulls' teeth wicked?

The answer has endured:

These are men whose minds the Dead have ravished.
Memory fingers in their hair of murders,
Multitudinous murders they once witnessed. . . .

By placing this verse in the context of 1917, we can see what it encapsulated: the surreal world of the trenches, the stress of combat, the breaking-point of soldiers, the prospect of years more of war. Their poetry described a ghastly landscape, in which insanity took on new and infinitely terrifying meanings.

ESCAPE

Shell-shocked men lived alone with their nightmares, imprisoned in the war. Others joined together to try to break out of the impasse of trench warfare. Some did so through mutiny. The most spectacular mass protest about the way the war on the Western Front was waged took place in France in the late spring of 1917.

The trigger was a new offensive, this time between Paris and Verdun on the Chemin des Dames, the slopes of the River Aisne, where the ladies of the court of Louis XIV had once strolled. The plan was formulated by the new commander of French forces in the north and north-east sectors, General Robert Nivelle, who had replaced Joffre. This dashing and self-confident man swept up his fellow officers in his conviction that he could end the stalemate. But his plan to break out of the trenches at last and win the war primarily with French troops was doomed. On 16 April 1917, nineteen divisions of the French Fifth and Sixth Armies moved north against formidable German positions. The next day the French Fourth Army, east of Rheims, also moved north against formidable German positions. On the third day, the French Fourth Army, east of Reims, moved north. Most of the units involved in the action had survived Verdun; they were dedicated to making this attack the prelude to the long-awaited breakthrough. It was not to be. After initial heavy losses, the attack was relaunched over the next twelve days – with further massive casualties and negligible results. By the end of April more than a quarter of a million French casualties had been suffered for a gain of some 500 yards of ground.

It was at this point that French troops decided to act *en masse* to stop the slaughter. They had had enough. Groups of men, entire units, refused to go back up the line. Their action was repeated sporadically over the next six weeks. A

Architect of the successful French counter-offensive at Verdun in 1916, Nivelle never lived down the failure of the Chemin des Dames offensive the following year.

French infantry going up the line along the Montigny Road, Marne, 7 June 1917. These were the men who bore the brunt of Nivelle's offensive in 1917. From the outset of the war, the French Army had taken almost the full weight of the German assault on the Western Front. Nivelle's strategy preserved that leading French role, but at a cost impossible for the infantry to bear. Men in sixty-eight divisions refused to continue the offensive, and made it clear to the French High Command that their loyalty was to the defence of the country and not to a failed commander.

total of sixty-eight divisions – over 500 000 men – were affected. This was a collective expression of discontent, a strike against needless suffering, not against the effort to throw the Germans off French soil. The mutineers' demands were mostly non-political. They wanted better leave arrangements, better medical care, better food. And they wanted an end to the offensive. They were prepared to stop the Germans from getting through their lines, but not to attack impregnable positions simply because staff officers could not think of anything else for them to do.

Much of the language of mutiny was stridently civilian. 'I am ready to go into the trenches,' wrote one machine gunner of the 74th Infantry Regiment, 'but we are doing like the *midinettes* [clothing workers]. We are going out on strike, everyone has really had enough.' These are men reclaiming their right as citizens to tell the army high command that enough is enough.

Louis Barthas

Barthas was one of the men who said 'enough'. In 1914 he was a thirty-five-year-old barrel-maker from a small village in the south of France. He was a *militant*, a Catholic who was active in the local socialist party and organizer of a farm workers' union. It was as a Christian socialist and patriot that he joined the army on 4 August 1914, and a Christian socialist he remained throughout four and a half years in uniform.

Barthas served in the ranks, mostly as a corporal, but sometimes demoted to a private soldier when his guerrilla war with the officers in his unit turned particularly ugly. His vision is that of the men at the bottom of the army pyramid, who shared every hardship and every night under fire. In his unit their bond was particularly strong since, unlike their officers, they all spoke not French but the language of the south of France, Occitan.

From the outset, making war was an onerous duty for Barthas, a man who believed that war was 'the worst of all plagues', 'a blot on our century'. From early in the war he came under the scrutiny of a series of petty tyrants, martinets whose pleasure was in forcing men to bend their knee to authority. Just before heading north to the battle front, Barthas asked for a day's leave to see his family one more time. 'No,' came the answer from one 'Grand Inquisitor', since requests for leave had to be deposited on Tuesdays and the request had been made on a Wednesday.

What countless soldiers in the Great War experienced is encapsulated in this tiny incident: the capacity for military life to generate what soldiers in the Second World War called 'chickenshit', the petty humiliation of enlisted men by their superiors. Barthas handled his own petty tyrant in a risky manner: he took off anyway and dared the officer to do something about it. In 1914 he got away with it.

After two months' delay, his unit embarked for the front. Six days later they arrived in the north, not (as the trains were inscribed) at 'Berlin',' but at 'Barlin' in the Pas de Calais region, 'one letter and a thousand kilometres away' from their objective. Soon enough Barthas and his platoon moved forward, and passed sights they would never forget: their first vision of dismembered bits of humanity, all mixed together in 'a lugubrious tableau'.

In this part of northern France Barthas fought two wars: one against the Germans in the trenches opposite, and one against his own officers, who treated the men in the ranks 'not as citizens but as a herd of animals'. The command, he scoffed, must have had 'the hide of a hippopotamus' to order attacks against heavily defended positions, without the slightest idea of how hard it was to achieve these objectives. What was worse, after an attack there was little medical help for the wounded. This he chalked up to a particularly callous medical officer, 'a real ass' whose inaction was scandalous.

French infantry in action. 'We fought because we could not do otherwise.... We were forced to make war and to fight by all the social ties which bind us....' (French soldier, quoted in a trench newspaper, *Le Tord-boyau*, August 1917)

Like Louis Barthas (LEFT), many French soldiers saw themselves as citizens of a republic, men with a voice as well as a gun. Barthas captured this mood of loyal indiscipline in the diary (RIGHT) he wrote in the form of a scrapbook in 1919, replete with postcards of destroyed villages in which he had served.

Barthas' grumblings were restricted to his trusted friends, muttering to each other in Occitan. A fellow soldier who spoke out clearly that in his view the Army was commanded by a bunch of asses was sentenced to two years' imprisonment and shipped out of the regiment. Other forms of insubordination were harder to quell. For example, Barthas, as a corporal, had to deal with orders for his platoon to take on onerous or dangerous jobs. Most of these they did, but in one case he refused point-blank an order to dig under fire a latrine near the bloody front lines at Lorette.

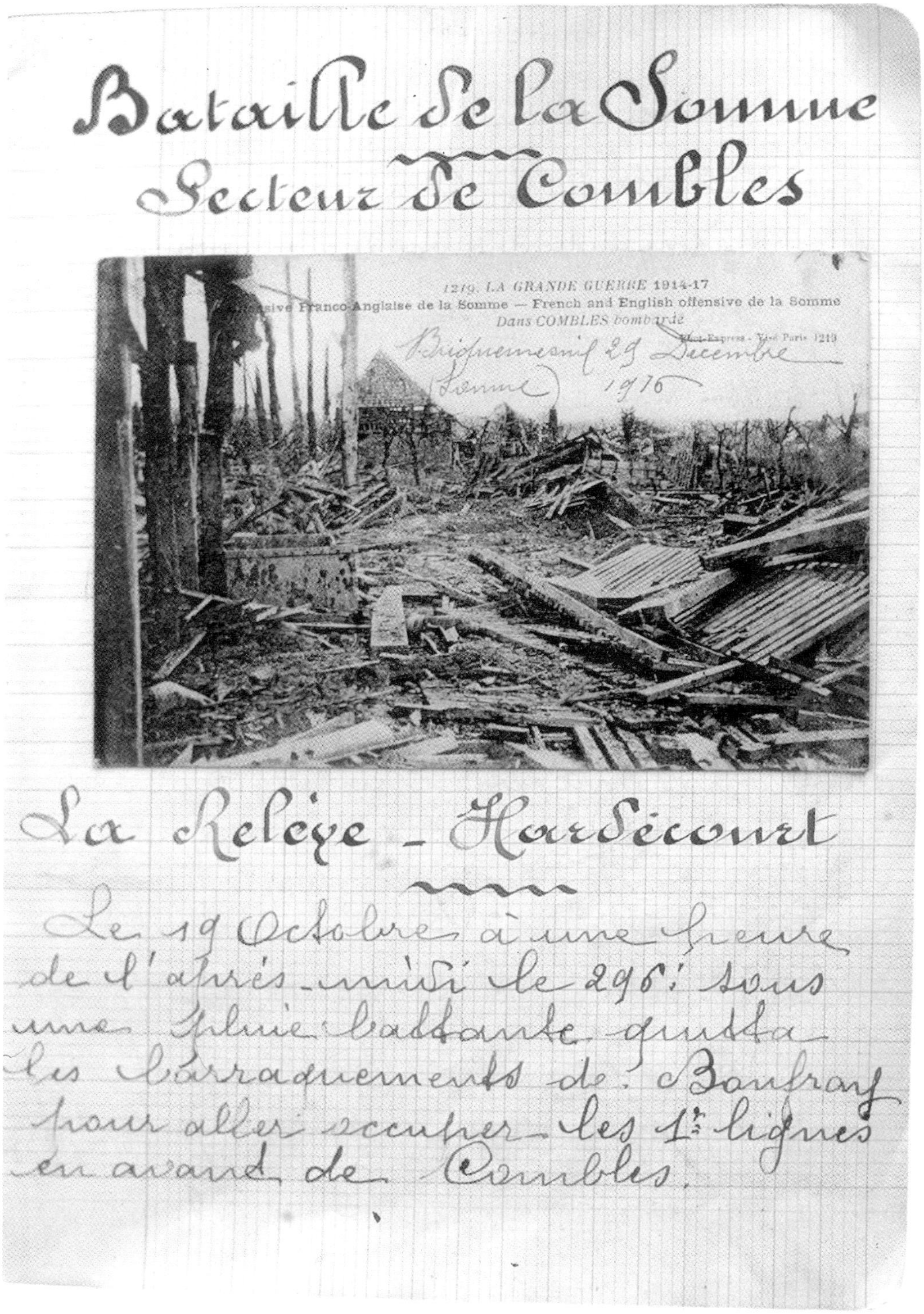

Bataille de la Somme
Secteur de Combles

1219. LA GRANDE GUERRE 1914-17
Offensive Franco-Anglaise de la Somme — French and English offensive de la Somme
Dans COMBLES bombardé

Briquemesnil 29 Décembre
(Somme) 1916

La Relève – Hardécourt

Le 19 Octobre à une heure de l'après-midi le 296e sous une pluie battante quitta les barraquements de Bonfray pour aller occuper les 1res lignes en avant de Combles.

Barthas was a spectacular grumbler. He protested about inadequate food. He griped about the constant displacement of his band of 'wandering Jews of the trenches', so often prostrate in the trenches 'like Moslems'. He raised his voice against the infestations of lice in men who never came in sight of a bath, let alone leave. In the teeth of these hardships the men eked out their miserable existence – very similar to that faced by German soldiers a few hundred yards away.

This sense of mutual misery produced clear incidents of fraternization with the enemy. To Barthas, 'the same community of suffering brought their hearts

French prisoners of war: some of the 8 million prisoners of war taken during the 1914–18 conflict. 'The *poilu* is a man.... A pro-longed sojourn in water or mud may leave him with rheumatism or frostbite; he may be prostrated with fatigue, and, since his sense of self-preservation has not been eliminated, he suffers from the weakness of wanting to save his own skin.... He may curse himself and even quarrel with his companions under arms, and everyone knows that the distribution of any extra wine in the squad is rarely a peaceable occasion. He eats his bully-beef with caution and mutters when there is a shortage of food. He does not sing as he goes into attack, preferring to not waste his breath....' (From a trench newspaper, *Le Périscope*, 1916)

together, obscured hatreds, provoked sympathy between men who were either indifferent to each other or adversaries'. One soldier from his unit, Barthas claims, even visited the German trenches. On his return, an officer told him he was under arrest. The man took off and dared the officer to come and get him: (in Occitan) '*Béni mé querré!*' The soldier continued on his way back to the enemy trench, from which he did not return.

From the northern sector, Barthas' unit followed the bulk of the French Army to Verdun. There he volunteered for a particularly dangerous reconnoitring mission, but only on condition that he would be let off three days of fatigue duty. A deal was struck, and he came back alive. After Verdun came the Somme, with all its horrors. Then it was back to Champagne, where he mused on the sight of roadside Calvaries torn to pieces, with the Virgin looking on just as she had done centuries before.

French infantry in Champagne. 'Poor happy stay-at-home, you have never been cold. You need to have been here all this winter . . . sitting tight for six days and six nights . . . you need to have felt despair that nothing in the world can warm you again. . . .'
(From a trench newspaper, *Le Crapouillot*, 1917)

It was there in the frosty April of 1917 that Barthas participated in the mutiny of the French Army. After a series of failed assaults on the German lines, as part of the Nivelle offensive, Barthas' unit was stationed about 3 miles from the front line. They were simply too cold to move. A Colonel Robert, to his credit, refused an order to throw Barthas and his men into the battle. He told his superiors that they were exhausted and could not face the inevitable gas attack which awaited them. They were spared.

Even after a respite, they were unwilling to carry on with their part in the Nivelle offensive, a campaign which, like Passchendaele, has become a synonym for failure. Barthas joined in singing a popular tune called the 'Song of Craonne', about a soldier about to 'lose his hide' on this part of the Western Front:

> *Adieu, life*
> *Adieu, love,*
> *Adieu, all the women*
> *It's all over*
> *It's for good*
> *This ghastly war.*
> *At Craonne*
> *On the plateau*
> *We had to lose our hides*
> *Because we are condemned.*
> *We are the sacrificed.*

Barthas summarized the reasons for the mutiny: the casualties in the Nivelle offensive, the prospect of months more of the same, and the long delay in getting home leave: 'this is what irritated the soldiers'; 'after having risked our lives for our country, we say that the time for leave is long overdue'. He joined in crying 'Down with the war!' and 'We want leave!', seemingly without noticing the contradiction. With the others, he resisted the urging of officers to go back to their bivouac areas.

On 30 May 1917, his unit considered forming a 'soviet' and putting him at its head. He refused on the grounds that he 'had no wish to arrive at the execution pillar simply to mimic the Russians'. Instead he urged strictly legal protests.

These protests were heard in two-thirds of the infantry units that had fought hard for three long years. Their patience had come to an end and, Barthas believed, had an attempt been made to restore order by force, there would have been a bloodbath – and not of the mutineers. Instead, a subtler restoration of discipline took place. There were courts-martial, though Barthas does not record anyone in his unit facing military justice. Instead, his battalion was sent out of the line to a distant rural area and disbanded.

But Barthas' war was not over yet. He fought again in the March 1918 offensive, and was finally invalided out of the line, due to general exhaustion, after forty-four months of continuous military service. His point of view was distinctive, but his reflections enable us to understand much of what impelled the men of 1917 to seek a way out of the dead end of offensive warfare. Above all, his writings show us that the mutineers' protests did not undermine the French Republic, but strengthened it by affirming that soldiers were citizens in uniform, and therefore retained the right both to think and to be treated like men.

'We want peace'

Once the lid was taken off, the grievances that poured out were powerful, varied and, not surprisingly, confused. Griping is a soldier's time-honoured prerogative but, aside from the inequalities of rank and the hardships of military service, the complaints of 1917 were marked by a sense of the futility of it all. That is what the word 'peace' meant: a reason for going on, an aim, a destination. On 29 May, mutineers of the 36th and 129th infantry regiments met and put their case in these words:

> We want peace ... we have had enough of the war and we want the deputies to know it.... When we go into the trenches, we will plant a white flag on the parapet. The Germans will do the same, and we will not fight until the peace is signed. We want the deputies to know about our demonstration; it is the only means we have at our disposition to make them understand that we want peace.

All this makes sense only if we jettison the absurd idea that soldiers cease to think when they put on uniforms. The French Army mutinies of 1917 brought to the surface a dialogue between rank-and-file and command which was there implicitly in every sector throughout the war. Orders were obeyed when possible, but the shape of battle was determined at its cutting edge, not in staff headquarters. This give-and-take is what fighting on the Western Front was all about. In the 1917 mutinies, this implicit pattern of order and response became explicit.

The French mutinies demonstrate that soldiers were still part of the political nation they were defending. This is the crucial difference between their state of mind in the spring of 1917 and that of Russian troops in the summer, remote from the tsarist state, or German sailors in late 1918, who had long since parted ways with the Kaiser and his court. In France the bonds between front and home front held, and the Army staff, charged with containing the mutinies, knew it.

Although it was never admitted, the mutinies were more successful than the offensive that had precipitated them. Nivelle was sacked. He was replaced by Pétain, who had the reputation of being very 'parsimonious' with the lives of his men; leave arrangements and material conditions improved. Still the disturbances continued. His appointment lanced the wound, but the fever evident in dozens of French battalions grew out of years of hardship and a sense that no one was listening. This time the Army and the nation heard.

There was, it is true, a judicial reckoning. Military tribunals found 3427 soldiers guilty of various acts of mutiny. A total of 554 men were sentenced to death. Of these, 49 were shot. Hundreds were convicted of lesser infractions, and received terms of imprisonment. Under the circumstances, in the Army as a whole – just as in Barthas' regiment – justice was lenient.

The reason was clear. The mutiny had been conducted in such a way as not to alert the Germans of the trouble in the lines facing them. Nobody marched to Paris; whatever some embarrassed generals said, no outside agitators were responsible for the mutiny. It was obvious that these angry French soldiers were still committed to the defence of the nation, although not to Nivelle's way of handling it. Going on, yes, but not blindly, madly, to certain death.

French soldier in a trench. 'He suffers from *le cafard* [depression] when he thinks of his family and his life before the war.... As for what is Right, for Civilization and Humanity, the *poilu* does not think about them much. It would be quite easy to count up the numbers of *poilus* who have a clear idea of such abstractions.' (From *Le Périscope*, 1916)

The escape artist

The tension between going on and going home took many forms in 1917. A total of 8 million prisoners were taken in the Great War; for many of them, going home meant going back to the fighting – and the sooner the better.

One such prisoner of war was Charles de Gaulle. In 1914 he was a young professional soldier, a twenty-four-year-old graduate of the élite military college of St Cyr. His first posting had been to the 33rd Infantry Regiment at Arras, the setting for the last act of the romance to match all romances, *Cyrano de Bergerac*. The regiment was commanded by Pétain, a man who believed more in the strength of artillery than in rhetoric. Unlike Pétain, the young de Gaulle was a man of the old school, a man who believed in 'the offensive spirit', and the sole idea of 'advancing, advancing to the attack, reaching the Germans so as to spit [at] them or make them run away'.

Within a year, de Gaulle had his chance to live up to his ideals. In August 1914 he was shot in the leg in Dinant in Belgium, producing paralysis of his right foot. Chastened by his baptism of fire, he still retained his bravado. He told his mother: 'Our dead must have quivered in their graves when they heard the victorious steps of our soldiers and the terrible rumbling of our guns.'

His commitment to the offensive was renewed when he returned to the front. He scoffed at those officers who wanted to operate a principle of 'live and let live' with the Germans. Such caution, he told his father, was 'lamentable'. Now a temporary captain, he commanded an infantry unit in Champagne ('an ocean of mud', he told his mother), and was wounded again. This time a shell splinter went right through his left hand. After more medical treatment he was back at the front, unmoved by shellfire which sent other officers scurrying for cover.

In March 1916 he was at Verdun, just north of Fort Douaumont, now occupied by the Germans. He stood in terrain completely devastated by artillery: 'there was no front-line trench, no communication-trench, no wire, no sketch-map,' he wrote in his regimental diary; the only certain point was that the Germans would attack. They did, surrounding de Gaulle's unit. He reacted characteristically, charged the enemy, was wounded by a bayonet thrust through his thigh and taken prisoner. Pétain, then commanding French forces in this sector, thought that he had been killed. He was saddened by the loss of 'an incomparable officer in all respects'.

The loss was real, but the officer had survived. De Gaulle was given medical care and then transported to Germany, where he began a period of servitude in a series of prison camps. Miserable at 'finishing the campaign like this', regretting his 'lamentable exile' from the Army at the front, de Gaulle's response was to scheme and plot a way out: not out of the war, but back to it.

The story of de Gaulle and his fellow officers desperately seeking a way to return to the front has been immortalized in Jean Renoir's film masterpiece *La Grande Illusion*. In the film a group of French officers try everything to get out of a series of prisons. For failed attempts the worst offenders are sent to a fortress prison, from which two men succeed in escaping while a third, a career officer of faultless manners, draws his captors' attention and gunfire. He dies nobly, and his comrades reach Switzerland.

Captain Charles de Gaulle. Captured in 1916, he spent the rest of the war as a POW. As an officer he retained certain privileges, and was held with other officers in a series of German camps where conditions were usually bleak, but better than in the typhoid-ridden camps on the Eastern Front. His *idée fixe* was to return to the front. To do so he attempted many ingenious but always futile escapes. When Jean Renoir immortalized French prisoners of war in his film *La Grande Illusion* (see p. 242), he mixed together many of de Gaulle's escapades with those of other Frenchmen facing incarceration and despair.

Stripped of its tragic ending, this justly celebrated film of 1937 is a fictionalized biography of prisoners like de Gaulle and Renoir's friend, General Pinsard, another escape artist. De Gaulle moved from one camp near Münster further east to Neisse on the Danube. A failed attempt at escape landed him in a camp for recalcitrant prisoners in Lithuania. There he met an extraordinary group of hard-core escape artists. Together with a former engineer, de Gaulle started to tunnel his way to freedom, but, as in *La Grande Illusion*, discovery led to transfer to a still more arduous prison camp, Fort IX at Ingolstadt in Bavaria.

Fort IX housed about 150 officers, Russian, French and British. Among them were the French air ace Roland Garros and a young Russian officer, Mikhail Tukachevsky, who did indeed manage to escape. He later became a Marshal of the Soviet Army at the age of forty; three years later, he was shot in one of Stalin's purges.

All these men joined in plotting escape. De Gaulle swallowed picric acid, an antiseptic, and got himself sent to the garrison hospital outside the fortress. There, with another prisoner, he obtained German uniforms and a map and simply walked out of the hospital. They got two-thirds of the way to Switzerland, when they were spotted and returned to Fort IX.

Still escape was not far from his mind. De Gaulle was transferred in July 1917 with other officers to the fortress at Rosenberg near Bayreuth. This is the prison in *La Grande Illusion*, although its commandant, General Peter, was nowhere near as dashing as the one in the film version, played by Erich von Stroheim. There plotting resumed. De Gaulle and three others plaited 90 feet of rope and on 15 October descended to the rocky base of the castle. They were on the run for ten days until some peasants alerted soldiers, who took them back to Rosenberg. A mere five days later, the would-be escapees sawed through their prison bars and, wearing false moustaches and civilian clothes, slid down the walls again and took the nearest train towards the Dutch frontier. Once again, they were quickly spotted and captured. This time it was back to Ingolstadt, despondent, imprisoned in a room with 'shuttered windows, no light, special diet, nothing to read, no

The filmic masterpiece of the war is *La Grande Illusion* directed in 1937 by Jean Renoir. In his film French officers plot their escape from a German prisoner-of-war camp. The commandant of the camp, von Rauffenstein, played by Erich von Stroheim (ABOVE), wears a metal neck brace, not because he is a stiff aristocratic German but because his back was broken in combat. De Boieldieu, played by Pierre Fresnay, during a diversionary tactic on the roof to cover two comrades' escape (RIGHT), is shot by Rauffenstein. In this film Renoir presented war as imprisonment and offered a profound statement on war without showing a single scene of combat.

writing materials, half an hour's exercise a day in a court measuring a hundred square yards'.

From here they were transferred to two other fortresses; further escape attempts followed, but all failed. For de Gaulle, this period was desperately difficult. 'I am buried alive,' he wrote to his mother, 'a ghost' of his former self, stricken by 'bitter regret at not having played a better part' in the war. There he remained until repatriated after the Armistice.

The figure of de Gaulle the prisoner of war was one facet of the story of 1917: his will to fight, to defend his country, was undiminished. His plight was precisely the opposite of that of Siegfried Sassoon, Louis Barthas and Wilfred Owen, who presented the other side of the soldiers' war: men whose imprisonment was to be in the war, in the midst of the carnage.

THE GERMAN IMPASSE

Rosa Luxemburg, prisoner of conscience

In 1917 imprisonment took many forms. In all combatant countries there were prisoners of conscience. One such was the German revolutionary leader Rosa Luxemburg, co-founder of the Spartacus League – named after the leader of the first-century BC slaves' revolt against the Romans, and a precursor of the German Communist Party. Arrested on charges of sedition on 10 July 1917, Rosa spent two weeks at the women's prison at Barnimstrasse in Berlin before flinging an inkpot at a detective, telling him to get out of the visitors' room since he was 'just a common spy and *Schweinhund*'. For her insolence she was transferred to police headquarters at Alexanderplatz, known as 'Alex' and later in the twentieth century the scene of Nazi torture chambers. Not wanting the publicity of a trial, the authorities simply held her incommunicado. After six weeks in 'Alex' she was transferred to a prison cell in an old fortress at Wronke near Posen (now Poznan), an edifice not unlike the prison, where de Gaulle was held. But Luxemburg and de Gaulle inhabited entirely different worlds. Her escape was conceived not on the level of the individual or the military unit, but rather on the level of collective revolt.

In prison Rosa was cold and hungry, plagued by sadness and stomach troubles, and yet she retained her compassion, her thirst for knowledge, her *joie de vivre*. She comforted Sonja, the wife of her fellow revolutionary and Spartacus founder Karl Liebknecht, who had also been imprisoned for opposing the war, when she received news that Sonja's brother had been killed in action. Rosa offered to send her one of the few items of colour she had in her spartan cell, a shawl. She fretted much as de Gaulle did at the same time: 'on my usual "promenade" along the wall I paced back and forth like an animal in a cage, and my heart was convulsed with grief that I could not get away from here as well.'

Rosa's hair turned white in prison, but her political vision remained intact. She believed in the masses and injected this romantic vision into the Spartacus League, which the authorities hoped to destroy along with its two leaders. The members of Spartacus were convinced that the old Social Democratic Party, to which both

The fire-brand of the left-wing of the Socialist International before 1914, Rosa Luxemburg was instrumental in keeping alive the revolutionary vision during the war. Imprisonment did not still her pen, and in a series of pamphlets and articles which she managed to smuggle out, she excoriated the patriots in the German Social Democratic Party who discovered in 1914 that they were more German than socialist.

leaders had previously belonged, was rotten to the core, and that it was time for a new movement based on the idea of the mass strike. Rosa admitted that the war had shown how the masses could be manipulated. But

> the psyche of the masses like the eternal sea always carries all the latent possibilities: the deathly calm and the roaring storm, the lowest cowardice and the wildest heroism. The mass is always that which it *must* be according to the circumstances of the time, and the mass is always at the point of becoming something entirely different than what it appears to be.

Rosa took great pleasure in birds, insects and plants, recalling the pleasures of seeing ducks flying over the Havel River in Berlin. She took walks with a small bird in the prison garden: 'There is no type of weather which we fear, and the two of us have even taken our daily walk in a snowstorm.' She savoured the idea of forgetting politics and flying to her true love, botany, which made everything else vanish.

In March 1917, before her imprisonment, she told one friend that she felt 'like a frozen bumble bee' waiting for the thaw (and freedom) to come alive again. The February Revolution in Russia brought her hope, not only for Russia but for Germany as well. She wrote in April that 'it is our own cause which is victorious there. It *must*, it *will* serve as a deliverance for the entire world, it must radiate to all of Europe.'

This internationalism separates her from most of those who were struggling with the tensions of war in 1917. To Rosa, nations and nationalism were the enemy. Her Jewish origins did not lead her to dwell on the sufferings of her own people. When a friend made a comment about anti-semitism, Rosa replied:

> What do you want with this particular suffering of the Jews? The poor victims on the rubber plantation in Putumayo, the Negroes in Africa with whose bodies the Europeans play a game of catch are just as near to me. Do you remember the words written on the work of the Great General Staff about Trotha's campaign in the Kalahari desert? 'And the death-rattles, the mad cries of those dying of thirst, faded away into the sublime silence of eternity.'
>
> Oh, this 'sublime silence of eternity' in which so many screams have faded away unheard. It rings within me so strongly that I have no special corner of my heart reserved for the ghetto: I am at home wherever in the world there are clouds, birds and human tears.

Nothing better captures her imagination and her temperament than a letter that she wrote in December 1917 to Sonja Liebknecht. By then Rosa had been moved to prison in Breslau. She told Sonja

> In the yard where I walk, military wagons often arrive, packed full with sacks, or old uniforms and shirts often spotted with blood.... They are unloaded here, passed out in the cells, mended, then reloaded, and delivered to the military. The other day, such a wagon came drawn by water buffaloes rather than horses. This was the first time that I saw these animals up close. They are built sturdier and broader than our oxen, with flat heads, their horns bent

flat, their skulls rather resembling the skulls of our own sheep; the buffaloes are completely black with large soft eyes. They come from Rumania, they are trophies of war. . . . Anyway a few days ago, a wagon loaded with sacks drove into the prison. The cargo was piled so high that the buffaloes could not make it over the threshold of the gateway. The attending soldier, a brutal character, began to beat away at the animals with the heavy end of his whip so savagely that the overseer indignantly called him to account. 'Don't you have any pity for the animals?' 'No one has any pity for us people either!' he answered with an evil laugh, and fell upon them even more forcefully. . . . Finally, the animals started up and got over the hump, but one of them was bleeding. . . . Sonitschka, buffalo hide is proverbial for its thickness and toughness, and it was lacerated. Then, during the unloading, the animals stood completely still, exhausted, and one, the one that was bleeding, all the while looked ahead with an expression on its black face and in its soft black eyes like that of a weeping child. It is exactly the expression of a child who has been severely punished and who does not know why, what for, who does not know how to escape the torment and brutality. . . . How far, how irretrievably lost, are the free, succulent, green pastures of Rumania! How different it was with the sun shining, the wind blowing; how different were the beautiful sounds of birds, the melodious calls of shepherds. And here: the strange weird city, the fusty stable, the nauseating mouldy hay mixed with putrid straw, the strange, horrible people – and the blows, blood running from the fresh wound. . . .

'We both,' Rosa added, 'stand here so powerless and spiritless and are united only in pain, in powerlessness and in longing. . . .'

Meanwhile, the prisoners bustled busily about the wagon, unloading the heavy sacks and carrying them into the building. The soldier, however, stuck both hands into his pockets, strolled across the yard with great strides, smiled and softly whistled a popular song. And the whole glorious war passed in front of my eyes. . . . Write quickly. I embrace you, Sonitschka.

Your Rosa

Sonitschka, dearest, in spite of it all, be calm and cheerful. That's life and that's how one must take it: courageously, intrepidly and smilingly – in spite of all.

The war of steel: Ernst Jünger

Courageously, intrepidly, smilingly – in spite of all: by 1917 these words informed the views of many other Germans who were embroiled in the war's tragedies, but who did not cry out for an end to the conflict. Instead they found ways and means for its even more vigorous prosecution. One such man was Ernst Jünger.

The son of an apothecary who later became a chemical factory owner in Heidelberg, in 1912, at the age of seventeen, Jünger ran off to join the French Foreign Legion. Retrieved by his father, the young adventurer escaped again, this time to the 73rd Hanoverian Fusiliers which he joined at the outbreak of war.

For the next four years he saw active service on the Western Front as a highly decorated lieutenant and then captain, and subsequently wrote one of the most

July – December 1917

JULY *The last Russian offensive*

A British nurse, Florence Farmborough, serving with a medical unit with the Russian forces, witnessed the final Russian offensive in Galicia.

Russian troops on the Galician Front

1 July All night long there was loud chaotic movement. Artillery and troops were constantly overtaking us. Now and then when soldiers saw us in our van, they called out and some of their remarks were far from agreeable. It was the first time ... that we had met rudeness from our own men; we felt dismayed and humiliated.

JULY *The Battle of Passchendaele begins*

On 31 July at 03.50 hours the offensive was launched. Guy Chapman, then a captain with the Royal Fusiliers, described the day.

31 July The battle opened in mist and rumour. The rumours proved false, and the mist turned to drizzle, to rain and then to a savage torrent, in which the sky competed with the guns and conquered.

OCTOBER–NOVEMBER *The Battle of Caporetto and the Italian retreat*

The joint German-Austrian attack started on 24 October in the Caporetto area in the Italian Alps. Erwin Rommel was serving as a lieutenant in the German Army.

25 October The fortified knobs of Kolovrat Ridge sparkled above us in the morning sun.... I reported my decision to break into the hostile Kolovrat position.... I had just put down the telephone when a brief report came from Streicher: 'Scout squad broke through, took guns and prisoners.' Silence reigned in the enemy position and not a shot had been fired. With maximum speed I proceeded with the execution of my break-through plan.... A second's delay might have snatched away the victory.

German and Austrian troops near Caporetto

NOVEMBER *The Bolshevik Revolution*

Morgan Philips Price, Russian correspondent for the *Manchester Guardian*, describes the events of 7 November (in the new calendar) when the Bolsheviks seized power.

7 November I tried to imagine a committee of common soldiers and workmen setting themselves up in London and declaring that they were the Government, and that no order from Whitehall was to be obeyed unless it was countersigned by them. I tried to imagine the British Cabinet entering into negotiations with the Committee for the settlement of the dispute, while Buckingham Palace was surrounded by troops and the Sovereign escaped from a side entrance.... And yet something of this sort in Russian surroundings had actually happened. It was almost impossible to realize that the century-old Russian Empire was actually dissolving before one's eyes.

Russian workers' detachments

NOVEMBER–DECEMBER *The Battle of Cambrai*

George Coppard, a corporal in the Machine Gun Corps, describes the devastating effect of British tanks at Cambrai.

20 November But the *pièce de résistance* was, of course, the tanks. Like all the rest I was excited at the prospect of going into battle behind these new-fangled Wellsian monsters.... Zero was at 6.30 am on that memorable day, 20 November. We heard the sound of tank engines warming up.... At last the officer began to count. He was bang on, and in a flash the black sky was ablaze with stabbing shafts of light, a vast drum of terrible thunder swept along the eight-mile front and a chorus of shells streamed over to the east.... The tanks, looking like giant toads, became visible against the skyline as they approached the top of the slope. Some of the leading tanks carried huge bundles of tightly-bound brushwood, which they dropped when a wide trench was encountered, thus providing a firm base to cross over.

British tank at Cambrai

celebrated accounts of the nature of trench warfare. He called it *Storm of Steel*, and the title conveys both the war he fought and the consistency of his mind.

Jünger's outlook was as romantic in his own fashion as Rosa Luxemburg's was in her way. That is about all they had in common. He represented the generation of austere young German patriots who had been brought up on Prussian military virtues and Nietzsche's exploration of the spiritual realm 'beyond good and evil'. His idealism, his stoicism, his bravery, and his intelligence and creativity in the arts of war tell us much about how and why, despite millions of casualties and untold suffering, the German Army faced the crisis of 1917 and still carried on the struggle.

Jünger was the poet of the machine war. The Battle of the Somme, he recalled, 'first made me aware of the overwhelming effects of the war of material'. There he encountered a 'faithful ... picture of the soul of scientific war', a juggernaut which transformed war and the warrior. In *Storm of Steel* he wrote:

> The modern battlefield is like a huge, sleeping machine with innumerable eyes and ears and arms, lying hidden and inactive, ambushed for the one moment on which all depends. Then from some hole in the ground a single red light ascends in fiery prelude. A thousand guns roar out on the instant, and at a touch, driven by innumerable levers, the work of annihilation goes pounding on its way.

What was new was the absurd, overwhelming, terrifying imbalance between men and material. The war was a giant factory of death,

> For I cannot too often repeat, a battle was no longer an episode that spent itself in blood and fire; it was a condition of things that dug itself in remorselessly week after week and even month after month.... Chivalry here took a final farewell. It had to yield to the heightened intensity of war, just as all fine and personal feeling has to yield when machinery gets the upper hand. The Europe of today appeared here for the first time on the field of battle. [It] seemed that man on this landscape he had himself created, became different, more mysterious and hardy and callous than in any previous battle.... After this battle the German soldier wore the steel helmet, and in his features there were chiselled the lines of an energy stretched to the utmost pitch, lines that future generations will perhaps find as fascinating and imposing as those of many heads of classical or Renaissance times.

Jünger's face bore the lines of this new kind of warfare. He was the 'storm-trooper' *par excellence*, one of the men who embodied the profound change in the tactics of trench warfare which took place after the Battle of the Somme and which made the war of 1917–18 fundamentally different from that of 1914–16.

After the ferocity of the British bombardment on the Somme, in August 1916 two new men came to control the German High Command: Paul von Hindenburg and Erich Ludendorff, respectively Commander-in-Chief and Quartermaster General of the German Imperial Army. The latter was the real power, and took it upon himself to conduct a review of German defensive doctrine. The result was a new system, devised by Ludendorff's operational staff, which changed the face of the battlefield.

Instead of crowding men into the front lines where they were torn to pieces by

Ernst Jünger was nineteen when the war broke out. An austere conservative, his account of the war, *Storm of Steel*, was the Bible of the political right in Germany. An intellectual, he was too much of a snob to join the Nazis. He served in the German Army in Paris during World War II, and knew many of those arrested after the July plot to kill Hitler in 1944. His Great War record probably saved his life.

Ernst Jünger (centre) and comrades at the front. 'After the battle of the Somme the war had its own peculiar impress that distinguished it from all other wars. After this battle the German soldier wore the steel helmet, and in his features there were chiselled the lines of an energy stretched to the utmost pitch, lines that future generations will perhaps find as fascinating and imposing as those of many heads of classical or Renaissance times.'

Allied artillery, the new German defensive system divided the front into three parts: an outpost zone extending about half a mile back from No Man's Land; a battle zone about a mile and a half deep; and a rear zone of even greater depth. The new disposition protected German troops from artillery: the further back you went in the defensive position, the stronger it was and the less vulnerable to enemy fire. Under attack, Jünger insisted, the line would resist, bend and snap back like steel.

This system resisted Allied pressure all along the line in 1917, and created conditions in which counter-attack predominated. From that phase of the war, the emphasis was on small groups of mobile soldiers bearing light machine guns. Their task was to infiltrate the enemy lines rather than assault them directly. The results were devastatingly effective. The Allies paid the German Army the ultimate compliment by adopting similar tactics in the last year of the conflict.

Jünger was one of the men who realized the potential of this new kind of war. Storm-troop units were formed of men like him: highly motivated soldiers whose aggressiveness and initiative were given full freedom even in trench warfare. This was the key to their tactics: to create a field of force where individualism could re-emerge from its eclipse in mechanical war.

Well aware of the starkly paradoxical character of this new kind of warfare, Jünger faced machines which dwarfed his will and yet found a way to retain that will intact. In the new system of counter-attack Jünger's courage, flair and initiative were at a premium. This is what made him such an extraordinary soldier. This is what made him see that, as he wrote in *Storm of Steel*, while the war meant the domination of machines over men, yet

OVERLEAF German troops advancing, Picardy 1917. 'For I cannot too often repeat, a battle was no longer an episode that spent itself in blood and fire; it was a condition of things that dug itself in remorselessly week after week and even month after month.'
Ernst Jünger, *Storm of Steel*

to-day more than ever it is the individual that counts. Every one knows that who has seen them in their own realm, these princes of the trenches, with their hard, set faces, brave to madness, tough and agile to leap forward or back, with keen bloodthirsty nerves, whom no despatch ever mentions. Trench warfare is the bloodiest, wildest, and most brutal of all warfare, yet it too has had its men, men whom the call of the hour has raised up, unknown

One of a cycle of fifty etchings by Otto Dix, entitled *Der Krieg*, 1924. He wrote: 'Lice, rats, barbed wire, fleas, shells, bombs, underground caves, corpses, blood, liquor, mice, cats, artillery, filth, bullets, mortars, fire, steel: that is what war is. It is the work of the devil.'

foolhardy fighters. Of all the nerve-racking moments of war none is so formidable as the meeting of two storm-troop leaders between the narrow walls of the trench. There is no retreat and no mercy then. Blood sounds in the shrill cry that is wrung like a nightmare from the breast.

Here we have an echo of the *Iliad* in a landscape of battle which Jünger himself described as profoundly modern. His vision of war captures much of the character of that war and what kept it going: it both destroyed individuals and reasserted individualism; it showed men that war was infinitely ugly and yet contained something awesome, terrifying, at times even beautiful. It drowned romanticism in an ocean of mud and recreated it in the camaraderie of arms, especially among small units of men whose endurance and courage were pressed to breaking point and beyond.

Jünger's message was that the war was an inner experience of infinite variety; one in which dignity and honour (as he understood them) could and did survive despite the domination of the machine. He escaped the passivity of siege warfare in the trenches by finding a field for individual initiative. This is why, against all the odds, his vision of war as noble did not vanish in the harsh months of 1917, when Jünger and his comrades fought in the devastated landscape of Picardy and Flanders. His vision endured through another year of combat and, for some like him, it survived long after the Armistice.

BREAK-OUT: RUSSIA 1917

The February days

Given the stalemate on the Western Front, there were two ways for Germany to win the war in 1917 and after: one by land, and one by sea. The first was to break the will of the Russian Army to carry on the war. The second was to starve Britain to the conference table through a submarine offensive. The first objective was realized, and in its wake it brought the end of the Romanov dynasty and the birth of the Bolshevik regime.

In Russia there was the same mix of war-weariness, severe shortages, industrial conflict and military disorder found in the West. What made the Russian situation worse was the greater inflexibility of the political system to adjust to the material and political pressures of a war of this scale and duration.

Part of the problem was the lottery of hereditary monarchy. The Tsar tried to rally mass support by taking personal command of the army, but had not the slightest competence in military matters. The Tsarina helped undermine the political order by protecting a group loosely associated with the monk Rasputin, a man whose vision mixed elements of fraud, the occult and debauchery.

Intrigue so displaced policy that new organizations emerged to cope with the day-to-day problems of waging war. A Pan-Russian Union, led by Prince Lvov, was set up to help wounded soldiers. A committee of war industries filled the vacuum created by the inept bureaucracy. Devolution by neglect and necessity created parallel political systems: alongside legally constituted authorities there arose informal but essential agencies which ensured that life went on.

This *ad hoc* reform of the state could not stem the tide of inflation and material hardship. By early 1917, these difficulties triggered off a series of strikes which inaugurated a new and ominous phase of mass protest. A police report noted that

> the proletariat in the capital is on the verge of despair. It is believed that the slightest disturbance, on the smallest pretext, will lead to uncontrollable riots with thousands of victims. In fact, the conditions for such an explosion already exists. The economic condition of the masses, in spite of large raises in wages, is near the point of distress.... Even if wages are doubled, the cost of living has trebled. The impossibility of obtaining goods, the loss of time spent queuing up in front of stores, the increasing mortality rate because of poor housing conditions, the cold and dampness resulting from lack of coal ... all these conditions have created such a situation that the mass of industrial workers is ready to break out in the most savage of hunger riots.

What was worse, industrial protest took political form: cries of 'Down with the war!' followed immediately from anger at the government's inability to provide food for the hungry population.

By mid-February mass protests over food shortages turned into revolution. Soldiers shared the disgust of civilians at their leaders. Some officers tried to disperse the massive crowds surging into the streets of Petrograd, now renamed from the Germanic St Petersburg. On the 26th they killed about a hundred demonstrators, alienating many soldiers who were unwilling to fire on their own people. Authority evaporated by its violent exercise, a mistake which the French Army studiously avoided in the mutinies later in the year.

Bread queues in Petrograd. Women sparked off the first Russian Revolution of 1917, their protest in part provoked by bread shortages. The city's inhabitants had to queue for hours for basic foodstuffs, and by February 1917 they had reached the limits of their endurance. International Women's Day was the occasion of a series of demonstrations led by women and joined by factory workers. Loyal troops were ordered to disperse the angry crowd, and fighting broke out.

In Petrograd, soldiers handed their weapons to demonstrators, openly defying their officers. An eye-witness, the Count de Chambrun, recorded the moment when power passed from one order to another:

> While the Palace of Justice was burning, the Pavlovsky Regiment marched from its headquarters, with its band playing. I watched these battalions pass in close order, led by non-coms [corporals and sergeants]. Instinctively, I followed them. To my surprise, they marched toward the Winter Palace, went in, saluted by the sentries, and invaded and occupied it. I waited a few moments and saw the imperial flag come down slowly, drawn by invisible hands. Soon after, alone on this snow-clad square, my heart heavy, I saw a red flag floating over the palace.

The following day, 27 February (in the old-style Russian calendar; 12 March to the rest of Europe and the world), the Tsar was obliged to appoint a provisional committee to maintain law and order. Prince Lvov was at its head. The same day Petrograd workers formed a soviet, or committee of workers' and soldiers' deputies. Three days later, the Tsar handed the provisional committee his abdication.

These two new authorities – a provisional government and the Petrograd soviet – separately filled the vacuum left by the collapse of the monarchy. Such a situation of dual sovereignty was inherently unstable, but in the short run it worked because it continued the form of government by committee which had come into being earlier in the war.

The war goes on

Crucially, the new regime decided to carry on the war, and for a time managed to restore faith in the cause. All depended on the Army, which in 1915 had gone through a terrible retreat, but recovered to register (at great cost) major gains under General Brusilov the following year. By 1917 the Army was stretched to its limits, but still contained elements prepared to go on.

One was highly unusual. It was a women's battalion, 'the battalion of death', led by Maria Botchkareva who was known to her soldiers as Yashka. Illiterate, married at the age of fifteen, abused by her first husband, exiled to Siberia with her second, she escaped from this harsh life into the Army. Her decision to join up was greeted with derision, but she sent a petition to the Tsar begging for the right to serve, and her appeal was approved.

In later years Yashka recounted her initiation – inconceivable outside of war – into this masculine world, and much of the abuse with which she had to contend to realize her dream. Some of her reminiscences were fanciful, but her career was not. She earned the respect of her comrades by sharing their hardships and by bringing wounded men back from No Man's Land. She suffered from frostbite and was wounded several times, once by shrapnel which temporarily paralyzed her.

Back at the front in 1917, she was stupefied by news of revolution. She recalled being astonished by the proclamation of 'Freedom, Equality and Brotherhood' for all, and at the prospect of land for the landless. She welcomed the chance to swear allegiance to the new government and 'drive the Germans out of Free Russia, before returning home to divide up the land'.

OVERLEAF At its peak, the Russian Army mobilized about 16 million men. Supplying and provisioning them was a massive task. Logistical problems proliferated, less because of production bottlenecks than because of organizational confusion.

Yashka believed in carrying on the war no matter what the cost. When the men in her unit decided enough was enough, Yashka went to Petrograd to find another way of fighting. Her version of events is that she approached the former President of the Duma (Parliament), Rodzianko, with the idea of forming 'a Women's Battalion of Death'. Speaking to a group of soldiers' delegates: ' "You have heard of what I have done and endured as a soldier," I said, rising to my feet and turning to the audience. "Now, how would it do to organize three hundred women like myself to serve as an example to the army and lead the men into battle?" ' And this is precisely what she did. Her hope was 'not to imitate the demoralized army', rather to restore discipline and duty. But, as she saw at the front, the rot had already set in; few units had the heart to carry on.

Yashka typified those who wanted to go on. So did Alexander Kerensky, who in June 1917 became the key figure in the Provisional Government. He ordered the Army to launch a new offensive in early July. The Germans counter-attacked. The Russian Army disintegrated.

In July 1917 Kerensky launched the last Russian offensive of the war, to demonstrate the new regime's commitment to the Allies and to rally support for his government. Yashka (LEFT) and her Battalion of Death (BELOW) were thrown into the battle, but the strategy failed completely: a German counter-offensive broke the Russian lines.

The 'Battalion of Death' – among other units – went forward, but to no avail. The Army was a broken reed. Yashka was knocked unconscious and taken to hospital with 'shell shock'. When she recovered, she found chaos in the Army. According to her memoirs, she had meetings with Kerensky and General Kornilov, Commander of the Russian Army on the Southern Front, both of whom believed in restoring order through force. Their attempt to do so only produced a further loss of support for the Provisional Government. No one could reverse the tide taking Russia out of the war.

The return of the exiles

This disastrous phase in the Russian war effort links the February and October Revolutions. Military events determined the course of the Revolution in 1917. The beneficiaries of the disaster – those who came to power later on – were not even in Russia for most of the war.

Leon Trotsky was one of them. In 1914 he was a thirty-five-year-old

revolutionary, more moderate than Lenin, a leader of the Revolution of 1905, on the Menshevik (moderate majority) wing of the Russian Social Democratic or RSD Party. He was a man of immense intellectual and oratorical power, and aware of his gifts. 'He loved the workers and loved his comrades,' wrote one colleague, 'because in them he loved himself.'

Like most other revolutionaries he was shocked at the collapse of international solidarity among workers, but he predicted correctly that in Russia the mass support for war of 1914 was merely a façade. In 1914–15 he was on the move, evading arrest as a subversive or undesirable alien agitator in a number of countries. This was the fate of most of the leaders of the Revolution of 1917. Many found a haven in Switzerland. There Lenin lived, after spending a short time in an Austrian jail in Galicia.

In September 1915, in the Swiss hamlet of Zimmerwald, Trotsky joined Lenin and Rosa Luxemburg (recently released from prison) in the first attempt to revive international socialism. At this time Trotsky was not a political ally of Lenin – he only joined the Bolsheviks, the radical minority of the RSD, two years later, in the midst of the Revolution.

In 1916 he was working as a military correspondent in Paris until in September his newspaper was banned and he was expelled from France. He crossed the Spanish border, was arrested, but after a delay was released to further exile in New York where he arrived in January 1917. There he edited another revolutionary newspaper, and according to legend worked on a film set in the Bronx.

The news of the uprising electrified him, on account of its meaning both for Russia and for the rest of the world. 'In all the belligerent countries the lack of bread is the most immediate, the most acute reason for dissatisfaction and indignation among the masses,' he wrote. 'All the insanity of the war is revealed to them from this angle; it is impossible to produce the necessities of life because one has to produce instruments of death.' Stirring words from New York, but to light the spark to set the world on fire he and all the other exiles had to return to Russia. This was no easy matter. After the February Revolution, his friends purchased a ticket to get him back to Russia. He left on 27 March, but six days later, *en route*, he was arrested by the British at Halifax, Nova Scotia – the remit of British Intelligence was broadly interpreted – and spent another period in jail. After further delay he was freed, and reached Petrograd on 17 May 1917.

Lenin had arrived at the Finland Station in Petrograd one month before. He had travelled across Germany in a sealed train generously provided by the German authorities, who were happy to help in subverting the new regime. Lenin immediately called for the overthrow of the Provisional Government and an end to the war.

Military collapse and political upheaval

Subversion was unnecessary. Lenin and Trotsky did not make the revolution; they merely presided over a set of events arising from the Provisional Government's disastrous decision to go on with the war. By the summer of 1917, the population had simply had enough. Similar tensions existed in the West, but people there accepted hardship because it followed the consent of the governed.

Alexander Kerensky suffered the fate of a moderate in a revolutionary situation. Prime Minister of the Provisional Government from August 1917, he aimed to defend the fruits of the first Russian Revolution, but by carrying on the war he ensured the victory of the second.

Stupefied by the collapse of the Socialist International, Lenin had to rework his ideas. In exile in Switzerland he saw that war could hasten revolution by breaking the capitalist network at its weakest link – Russia. On his return in April 1917, he proclaimed his programme: 'Bread, Peace and Land.'

What did consent mean in Russia? This is what Trotsky found on his return to Petrograd:

> The soldiers sang revolutionary songs as they marched and sported red ribbons in their tunics. It all seemed as incredible as a dream. The tram-cars were full of soldiers. Military training was still going on in the wider streets. Riflemen would squat to charge, run a distance in a line, and then squat again. War, the gigantic monster, was still standing behind the revolution, throwing its shadow upon it. But the masses no longer believed in the war, and it seemed as if the training was going on only because no one had thought of stopping it.

Consent was precisely what was lacking when the Kerensky government ordered a new offensive in early July 1917. Gestures, like the deployment of the Women's Battalion of Death, were futile. As Trotsky put it, the Army had voted with their feet against the war.

It was in this atmosphere that units in Petrograd, including a few members of

The war was won and lost on the Western Front, but the carnage on the Eastern Front was more widespread and more murderous. There soldiers suffered high casualty rates not only due to enemy action but also through disease. On the Eastern Front a nineteenth-century war was fought with twentieth-century weapons. Approximately 2 million Russian soldiers died, or about 10 per cent of the total mobilized.

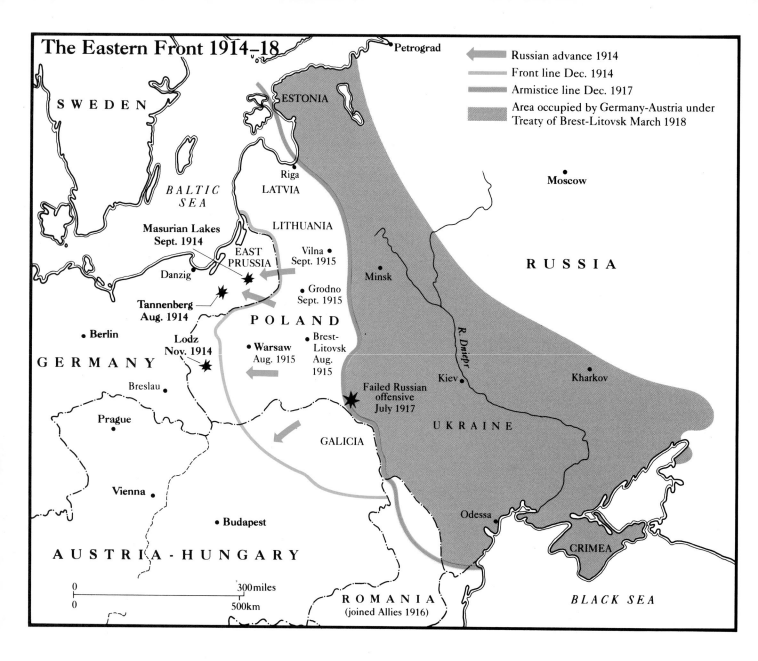

Russian advance 1914
Front line Dec. 1914
Armistice line Dec. 1917
Area occupied by Germany-Austria under Treaty of Brest-Litovsk March 1918

Petrograd

SWEDEN

ESTONIA

BALTIC SEA

Riga
LATVIA

Moscow

LITHUANIA

Masurian Lakes Sept. 1914

EAST PRUSSIA

Vilna
Sept. 1915

RUSSIA

Danzig

Grodno
Sept. 1915

Minsk

Tannenberg Aug. 1914

POLAND

Berlin

Lodz
Nov. 1914

Warsaw
Aug. 1915

Brest-Litovsk
Aug. 1915

R. Dniepr

Kiev

Kharkov

GERMANY

Breslau

Failed Russian offensive July 1917

Prague

UKRAINE

Vienna

GALICIA

Budapest

Odessa

AUSTRIA - HUNGARY

CRIMEA

0   300 miles
0   500 km

ROMANIA
(joined Allies 1916)

BLACK SEA

the Bolshevik Military Organization, were ordered to the front. Outraged, they took to the streets in armed demonstrations on 4 July to demand the overthrow of the Provisional Government. The uprising lasted two days, and was suppressed by loyal troops still backing the government.

Trotsky saw how thin was the veneer of power covering the new regime.

> The soldiers were now saying, to the last man: 'Enough of bloodshed! What good are land and freedom if we are not here?' When enlightened pacifists try to abolish war by rationalistic arguments they are merely ridiculous, but when the armed masses themselves bring weapons of reason into action against a war, that means that the war is about over.

He was right, but for the time being Kerensky held on. Lenin and other leading Bolsheviks were forced into hiding. To Trotsky, the July days were the moment when the revolutionaries flexed their muscles. They had to retreat and regroup, but only to await the right moment to seize power. He himself was arrested on

23 July, but, like a latter-day Mafioso, still directed events from his prison cell. Only then, in August 1917, did he finally join the Central Committee of the Bolshevik Party.

When counter-revolutionary troops under General Kornilov threatened to overthrow the Provisional Government, some sailors visited Trotsky in prison to ask his advice: 'Should they defend the Winter Palace or take it by assault? I advised them to put off the squaring of their account with Kerensky until they had finished Kornilov. "What's ours will not escape us."'

'What's ours will not escape us': this phrase echoed through the vast reaches of the Russian Empire. From April 1917, thousands of peasants seized land in increasing numbers. First under the cloak of legality, then by force, the face of peasant Russia was transformed. This movement was applauded by the Bolsheviks, suddenly the champions of private property. Their position was realistic to some and cynical to others: they simply cheered on what could not be turned aside. The longer the conflict dragged on, the more Bolshevik support increased. As Trotsky put it: 'Every soldier who expressed a little more boldly than the rest what they were all feeling, was so persistently shouted at from above as a Bolshevik that he was obliged in the long run to believe it. From peace and land the soldiers' thoughts began to pass over to the question of power.'

The seizure of power

The partnership of Lenin and Trotsky – two men who treated each other with both respect and suspicion – is the key to the Russian Revolution. Lenin provided the political direction; Trotsky the military force to achieve it.

By September the military situation had become critical. The German Army had seized Riga and was advancing on Petrograd. By then the Bolsheviks formed the majority of the body in which real power lay, the Petrograd soviet, which formed a military revolutionary committee to deploy Red Guards and other military units in defence of the city. The Provisional Government was becoming more and more isolated. From this base in the Petrograd soviet, the Bolsheviks armed the men who launched the insurrection on 24 October (or, in the Western calendar, 6 November). Trotsky was at their head.

The insurrection itself was Trotsky's design. He personally directed operations from the Smolny Institute. A thousand tasks needed coordination: a detachment of troops had to secure the printing presses of the Bolshevik Party, which had been shut down by the Provisional Government; another squad had to evict military academy students who were blocking the telephone exchange; and so on. On 24 October, the tension rose. This is how Trotsky remembered the day:

> October 24, a gray morning, early. I roamed about the building from one floor to another.... Along the stone floors of the interminable and still half-dark corridors of the Smolny, the soldiers were dragging their machine-guns.... There is a telephone booth in the large empty room adjoining us, and the bell rings incessantly about important things and trifles. Each ring heightens the alertness of the silence.

During those hours Red Guards, with the help of some regular army units, gained control of key factories and fortresses, effectively isolating and surrounding

In the early weeks of the Revolution, crowds on the streets of Petrograd were the daily occurrence: every colour of political opinion sought a voice in Russia's reconstruction. But first came the question of war and peace. The failure of the July offensive led to massive disturbances and arrest of those like the Bolsheviks calling for an end to the war. The Provisional Government became more and more isolated, abandoned by its foreign and domestic allies alike. Its days were numbered.

Trotsky joined the Bolshevik Party only in the summer of 1917, but nevertheless directed its seizure of power in October. He represented the new regime at the Brest-Litovsk peace conference where his oratorial and analytical genius failed to blunt the cutting edge of German power, which required Russia to cede huge parts of its European domains.

the remnants of the Provisional Government. All night reports came in to the third floor of the Smolny Institute:

> A telephone call from Pavlovsk informs me that the government is bringing up from there a detachment of artillery, a battalion of shock troops from Tsarkoye Syelo.... I order the commissaries to place dependable military defences along the approaches to Petrograd and to send agitators to meet the detachments called out by the government.... 'If you fail to stop them with words, use arms. You will answer for this with your life.'

The waiting continued. More key points were taken.

> At the railway terminals, specially appointed commissaries are watching the incoming and outgoing trains, and in particular the movement of troops. No disturbing news comes from there. All the more important points in the city are given over into our hands almost without resistance, without fighting, without casualties. The telephone alone informs us: 'We are here!'

The Bolsheviks had indeed arrived. The city was theirs, and only then did Trotsky begin to see the immensity of what had happened.

> 'Give me a cigarette,' I say to Kamenev.... I take one or two puffs, but suddenly, with the words, 'Only this was lacking!' I faint.... As I come to, I see Kamenev's frightened face bending over me.
> 'Shall I get some medicine?' he asks.
> 'It would be much better,' I answer after a moment's reflection, 'if you got something to eat.' I try to remember when I last had food, but I can't. At all events, it was not yesterday.

Kerensky fled, and the government disintegrated. His meagre attempts to rally troops failed. The Red Guard had secured the position of the new regime. This Trotsky explained to the Petrograd soviet at 1 p.m. the following day. The delegates heard his words in tense silence for a few seconds. Then applause began, a not very stormy, rather thoughtful applause. The assembly was feeling intensely and waiting.... Ahead of us there was probably the greatest resistance from the old world; there were struggles, starvation, cold, destruction, blood and death. 'Will we overcome this?' many asked themselves.

Then Lenin appeared before the soviet, coming out of hiding for the first time since the July days. He received a 'tumultuous welcome', according to Trotsky, and restored some semblance of belief in the future.

No one, including Lenin and Trotsky, was sure the insurrection would succeed. 'Later that evening,' Trotsky recalled, 'Lenin and I were resting in a room adjoining the meeting-hall, a room entirely empty except for chairs. Someone had spread a blanket on the floor for us; someone else, I think it was Lenin's sister, had brought us pillows. We were lying side by side; body and soul were relaxing like overtaut strings.... We could not sleep, so we talked in low voices.' In Petrograd – and only in Petrograd – the Bolsheviks had won. Fighting broke out in Moscow. After bloody skirmishes over the next ten days, the Kremlin was in their hands.

Lenin's initial pronouncements established his government's programme. It restated the same objectives he had proclaimed shortly after his return to the Finland Station in April: peace, bread and land. The peasants were seizing the land anyway. Bread required peace, and that was the first order of business. The Bolsheviks immediately approached the German Army with a request to negotiate a cessation of hostilities. A ceasefire was agreed on 3 December 1917.

Peace at Brest-Litovsk

Trotsky, appointed Foreign Minister of the new regime, went to the Ukrainian capital city of Brest-Litovsk to turn ceasefire into peace. But first he published the contents of the archives of the Tsar's Foreign Ministry, showing to what extent Allied post-war intentions were a cover for greed. The Tsar's pay-off was to be Constantinople. Trotsky tried to stir up feeling in Europe that the war was a bankers' ramp not worth a single additional drop of blood.

War-weariness in the West was a card Trotsky wanted to play in the negotiations. But in Western Europe there was hardly an echo to his appeal. Anti-war groups were smashed and strikes more easily contained in 1918 than in 1917. Consequently it was only military power on the Eastern Front which determined the outcome of the deliberations. Germany demanded domination of most of European Russia; this Trotsky refused to accept, and after a month he walked out of the talks.

'No peace, no war' was his slogan. The Germans knew better, and simply moved their Army further into Russia, forcing the Bolsheviks to accept even harsher terms in March 1918. By then the last and decisive phase of the war was about to begin.

6

COLLAPSE

O n New Year's Day 1918, no one could have predicted the outcome of the war. The German Army was massively entrenched in a powerful defensive position on the Western Front: Paris was still within range of German artillery, and the Allied offensive around Ypres had failed to achieve a breakthrough. On the Eastern Front, Germany had the upper hand; Russia was suing for peace. At sea, the war was inconclusive. The Allied naval blockade of Germany was hurting food production and the munitions effort, and was bringing serious deprivation to every part of the country. But the German U-boat campaign had taken its toll too, causing substantial strain and anxiety in Paris and London.

It was not a good time for the Allies. And yet, eleven months later, the Central Powers capitulated. This reversal of fortunes, leading to a comprehensive Allied victory, occurred in a relatively short period. On 21 March 1918 the Germans began a massive and initially successful onslaught on the Western Front; by July they had reached the River Marne, where in 1914 the initial German offensive of the war had been stopped. Then, slowly and bloodily, the Allies pushed the German Army back. In retreat, the Germans were unable to reform a stable defensive line, and after August they could not replace losses and supplies.

The German High Command received reports from the front that their men had given up their belief in victory. They saw that they could not win the war. What was the point, then, in going on? Tens of thousands of German troops surrendered, though the Army remained intact and continued to inflict heavy casualties on the Allies. The German Navy, penned up in their North Sea ports, was ordered to sea for one last – and hopeless – show of strength. Sailors doused their engines and refused to die for nothing.

At the same time, Germany's allies collapsed. The Turkish Front rolled up. Bulgaria collapsed. The Austrian Army disintegrated, leaving unprotected the south-eastern approaches to Germany itself. Through intermediaries, the Germans turned to President Woodrow Wilson to broker an Armistice. It was signed on 11 November 1918.

German prisoners taken in the battle of the St Quentin Canal, between 29 September and 2 October 1918. The coordination of infantry, artillery, tanks and aircraft on the Allied side in the counter-offensive of the summer and autumn of 1918 broke the German will to fight on. German units surrendered *en masse*.

Winter conditions were harsh on the Italian Front,
the terrain of which spanned steep Alpine slopes and
forests. Italian mountain troops manoeuvred and
were supplied on skis; artillery had to be hauled up
over mountain passes to rocky emplacements.

CAPORETTO

At the beginning of 1918 the war effort of the Central Powers was still in the ascendancy. To see what this meant, all you needed to do was to stand in the north-eastern Italian village of Caporetto, the site of one of the most spectacular Allied defeats of the war. In this part of Italy the Austrian and Italian armies had fought a series of inconclusive battles since 1915. Around Caporetto the balance of forces was roughly equal: about thirty-five divisions each. But giving the Central Powers additional, and decisive, weight were German reinforcements, in particular the Alpine Corps. Among them were elements of the Württemberg Mountain Battalion, led by Captain Erwin Rommel.

On 24 October 1917, German artillery laid down a massive bombardment of gas, heavy mortar and heavy shell fire. This triggered an advance by three élite Austrian divisions and the German Jäger division, commanded by the Austrian General Krauss. He told his troops: 'Let this be your motto: no ease or rest until the Italians are shattered.' And shattered they were. Much of the damage was done by units from von Stein's 12th Division, which infiltrated five miles behind two Italian divisions, then wheeled right to attack the Italians just as they were being pulverized by an Austrian frontal assault. The Italian 19th Division ceased to exist, leaving a gaping hole in the Italian lines.

At the same time the Alpine Corps, with Rommel's troops leading the way, occasionally on their own initiative, managed through stealth and with the aid of fog to penetrate a ridge to the south of Caporetto. The next day Rommel's troops went on to secure Mount Kolovrat through a daring rear attack on enemy machine gun posts, and then broke into hilly terrain behind the Italian line. Once there, Rommel's men simply waited for retreating Italian soldiers to fall into their hands. At the Lucio–Savogna road, Rommel noted

> single soldiers and vehicles came unsuspectingly toward us. They were politely received at the sharp curves of the road by a few mountain soldiers and taken prisoner. Everyone was having fun and there was no shooting. Great care was taken that the movement of the vehicles did not slacken on the curves. While a few mountain troops took care of the drivers and escorts, others seized the reins of the horses or mules and drove the teams to a previously designated parking place.... Business was booming.... The contents of the various vehicles offered us starved warriors unexpected delicacies. Chocolate, eggs, preserves, grapes, wine and white bread were unpacked and distributed.... Morale two miles behind the enemy front was wonderful!

Then Italian reinforcements arrived. Some tried to retake the road, but Rommel's men had superior position on the slopes surrounding the road and superior firepower. Whole Italian units surrendered.

Rommel's men kept up the pressure, appearing further and further behind the positions of the Italians, who were looking the wrong way. Whenever his unit was approached by larger Italian formations who were unaware of their proximity to German Alpine troops, Rommel walked calmly into the road, waved a white handkerchief and asked the Italians to surrender. In one encounter, on the south slopes of Mount Matajur, Rommel recalled,

> I came to within 150 yards of the enemy! Suddenly the mass began to move and, in the ensuing panic, swept its resisting officers along downhill. Most of the soldiers threw their weapons away and hundreds hurried to me. In an instant I was surrounded and hoisted on Italian soldiers. *'Evviva Germania!'* sounded from a thousand throats. An Italian officer who hesitated to surrender was shot down by his own troops. For the Italians on Mrzli peak the war was over. They shouted with joy.

A bare fifty-two hours after the start of the campaign Rommel's men reached the summit of Mount Matajur, having traversed a mountain range ascending to 16 000 feet, carrying with them machine guns and other weapons. It was a staggering physical ordeal, but the prize was equally remarkable: total disorganization of the Italian line and more than nine thousand prisoners, for the loss of just six men.

Once the line was broken, the move west was irresistible. The Italian command was divided. Luigi Capello, the bedridden commander of the Italian Second Army, saw the disaster for what it was and urged the High Command to organize a deep retreat. But commander-in-chief, Luigi Cadorna, forbade it. His words, however, meant nothing. Deep retreat occurred not by design but by panic and flight, first 30 miles to the Tagliamento River, then a further 30 miles west to the Piave. Along with disorganized Italian units came a flood of refugees, local inhabitants and camp followers, clogging the roads and presenting a seemingly endless chain of misery and exhaustion. Wholesale looting marked the descent into degradation and despair of the estimated 750 000 people fleeing from the front. In his war novel *A Farewell to Arms* Ernest Hemingway provided an unforgettable account of the disaster, uncannily accurate despite the fact that Hemingway arrived in Italy six months after Caporetto.

The Allies managed to stem the tide, rushing reinforcements to Italy. Now that German and Austrian units were in the heartland of the country, within shelling distance of Venice, a patriotic campaign rallied Italian support for the effort to throw the invaders out of their country. Cadorna was dismissed and his place was taken by General Armando Diaz. By the spring of 1918 the crisis had passed, but like many other events in this period it had scared the living daylights out of the Allies.

ONE SEAMAN'S WAR

However many setbacks they faced, it was not the Allies who disintegrated in 1918 but the Central Powers. Some clues to this puzzle may be found in the German North Sea ports, where much of the Imperial German Fleet was penned up by the Allied blockade. What happened to this instrument of war and to the men who served in it explains much about the difficulties that Germany faced in 1917–18 and the unravelling of that country's will to go on during the last phase of the conflict.

Seaman Richard Stumpf. Revolutionaries are made, not born; the harsh treatment by officers of men cooped up in port throughout most of the war eroded their loyalty and created a mass of unlikely rebels. Stumpf joined the sailors who broke the German Empire in November 1918 by refusing to carry on.

Seaman Richard Stumpf was a patriot. Originally he had been a tinsmith, a devout Catholic and a member of a Catholic trade union. In 1912 he enlisted in the Navy and then served on the same ship, the *Helgoland*, for six years. Twenty-two when the war broke out, he was an ordinary German sailor, a conservative and a nationalist, perhaps more widely read than many of his fellow sailors.

Throughout the war Stumpf kept a diary, in which we can see traces of the disintegration of the German Empire through the erosion of the loyalty of the men who at first had been devoted to its defence. On 2 August 1914, on receiving news of the declaration of war with England, he noted: 'All of us breathed a sigh of relief. The very thing for which we had so long waited and hoped, the thing we had yearned for and feared, had come true.' English 'envy and petty trade jealousy' had finally found a way to precipitate war: 'The pursuit of Mammon has deprived that nation of its senses. Can they actually believe that they can conquer a Germany which stands united behind its Kaiser with their soldiers who they pay ten shillings a week? Can they actually believe that?'

He and his fellow sailors stayed in port at Wilhelmshaven, following with great 'joy' the reports of German military victories in Belgium and at Tannenberg in East Prussia. He took to jotting down patriotic poems. An encounter with the British Fleet in the North Sea on 28 August further lowered his already jaundiced view of the British; only half the British shells had exploded, and one unexploded shell, when examined, was found to contain only 60 per cent of the explosive charge in German shells. This discovery was kept a secret so that the English and their 'yellow monkeys' (the Japanese) would not improve their shells. All they could offer, Stumpf wrote, was calumny, both 'abominable' and 'cowardly', about non-existent German atrocities.

Stumpf's commitment to the cause did not waver in the long months of inactivity that followed; nor did his anti-British attitude. Only his impatience for a showdown increased. Slowly, signs of friction began to appear. He felt it odd in April 1915 that on the eve of setting out to sea for a battle exercise 'none of our exalted gentleman officers deemed it necessary to provide us with any sort of explanation regarding the action which lay ahead'. But his patriotic certainties and those of his comrades were still intact. He cheered the sinking of the *Lusitania* and noted: '1300 people perished. Many among them were Americans (which makes me all the happier).' When the U-boat which had sunk the *Lusitania* returned to port, its crew was greeted with 'thundering cheers'.

But his own war contained no such exciting moments of action, and the irritation caused by inactivity was exacerbated by a widening rift between officers and men. Soon petty inspections began to bridle more than usual. Sailors were punished for 'dust or spots' on their uniforms. Stumpf grumbled in late 1915 that

> there is now a greater gulf between the officers and the men than at any previous period of my naval career. The fact that the officers have made no sacrifices at all so far contributes significantly to this painful situation. While we have to content ourselves to live on half rations of bread, in the officers' mess they hold feasts and drinking bouts at which six or seven courses are served.

January – July 1918

JANUARY *Wilson's Fourteen Points*

On 8 January, President Woodrow Wilson presented his programme for peace to the US Congress. The French Prime Minister Georges Clemenceau commented in late March.

President Woodrow Wilson

28 March I note the words and the excellent intentions of President Wilson, but unfortunately he eliminates sentiment and memory.... The history of the United States is a glorious history, but a brief one; for them, one hundred years is a very long period; for us, it is a minor matter.

MARCH *The Treaty of Brest-Litovsk*

On 3 March the Bolsheviks signed a peace treaty with Germany in which they gave up all claims to Poland, the Baltic States, the Ukraine, White Russia, Finland, and Bessarabia. General Hoffmann was the German Commander in Chief on the Eastern Front.

Trotsky with Joffre at Brest-Litovsk

25 February I am expecting the Peace delegation to come in one by one today and tomorrow. Whether Trotsky will take the road to Canossa in person or will send someone else, is not yet certain. The negotiations here will last three to four days at most, as this time the comrades must simply swallow what we put before them.

MARCH
Germany launches new offensive

The Kaiser

On 21 March, Ludendorff launched a new offensive. Wilhelm Reinhard was serving in the 109th Leib Grenadier Regiment.

During the night we had helped to push this great 28-centimetre gun into position.... We wanted to see the first shot and were only two or three metres from the gun.

Someone shouted '*Feuer frei*' and then the gun went off with a great crash. We all fell over on our backs and the gunners laughed at us. The gun settled down to fire steadily after that – about one shell a minute I would say – but we didn't stay long. We went back to our trench.

April *German offensive halted*

In Picardy, a fresh German offensive towards Amiens was halted by Australians at Villers-Bretonneux on 24 April. The commander of the Australian Corps was Lieutenant-General Sir John Monash who describes the day.

Anzac Day was celebrated yesterday.... The day was also signalized by a wonderful fight carried out by the 13th and 15th Australian Brigades (Glasgow and Elliott), both of which brigades have been under my orders for the past few weeks. My 9th Brigade had securely kept the Boche out of Villers-Bretonneux for three weeks.... On 24 April the Boche attacked (with four divisions) and took the town. Late at night we had to organize a counter-attack. This was undertaken by the 13th and 15th Brigades in the early hours of Anzac Day. They advanced 3000 yards in the dark without artillery support, completely restored the position, and captured over 1000 prisoners.

German troops in Picardy

June *American troops in action at Belleau Wood*

On 26 June the American Marine Brigade took Belleau Wood after weeks of fighting. From the diary of J. E. Redinell, who was serving with the Marines.

21 June I was equipped with rifle & heavy pack & went back to the front. Arrived battalion hdqrs 6th Marines on June 21st. They were in reserve then. Lt Marshall came over & shook hands with me & wanted to know what happened & I told him. He said 'you're just in time, we go back in again tomorrow.'

About 3 pm in the afternoon he & I went back to the front line.... What a difference there was since the last time we were there on June 3rd. Not a house left standing. Ammunition dump under a big tree in the centre of town blown to pieces.... Dead horses & cows lying out in the fields. So this was the price of war.

July *Allied counter-offensive turns the tide*

German troops, reaching the Marne, were beaten back by the French Army. Rudolf Binding was serving in the German Army.

I have lived through the most disheartening day of the entire war, though it was by no means the most dangerous.... All the telephone wires were cut, shot to pieces or broken by our own guns and transport; consequently the division received no reports from the Front.... One could feel the panic of the troops deserted by their Commanders gradually growing.... We did not see a single dead Frenchman, let alone captured gun or machine gun, and we had suffered heavy losses.... Since our experiences of July 16 I know that we are finished.

British troops attacking

Even so, as yet these complaints amounted to nothing more than the usual grumbles of naval life.

Stumpf went on leave in 1915, and was struck by the sad state of wounded French and Belgian prisoners of war. He still believed that the war would end by the spring of 1916. Friends home from the front told him that the English 'forced line after line of Negro troops to charge forward' to certain death.

Returning to his ship after his leave, he failed to report to a work fatigue fast enough and earned himself a punishment tour cleaning the gun turrets. After that he set about conscientious shirking for the next four days: 'This is how we revenge ourselves against the excesses of the Imperial Navy.' Later he griped about further harassment and petty orders: men were to wear only whites day and night; no books or newspapers were allowed in gun turrets; arrest would follow failure to wear a lifejacket; hammocks were strictly forbidden. This last order particularly irked Stumpf: 'I cannot fathom the reason behind this. Only deliberate nastiness could conceive of such a thing.' It turned the men into sworn enemies of 'the privileges of the officers' caste'. Some sailors went so far as to question whether Germany should keep occupied territory after the war; 'Who would have thought it possible that these extreme Socialist views would ever crop up among us?' Stumpf's diary records. But by June 1916 he too was accepting this point of view.

Tension was never far from the surface. When a chief petty officer punched a seaman hard enough to put him in hospital, the assailant got seven days' confinement to quarters. Stumpf wondered what would have happened if the roles had been reversed. The petty officers delighted, it seemed, in treating 'the common seamen with inconceivable cruelty'. Men had to run around with their rifles for stupid reasons, or no reason at all. 'My greatest ambition in life', Stumpf noted, 'is to get away from this stupidity and harassment!' All this was recorded alongside reactionary and occasionally anti-semitic jibes. He was furious with 'the Jew Liebknecht' and other troublemakers – but he was still more concerned about poor rations. The officers 'complain the loudest since they no longer get their fried eggs for breakfast'. They insisted on treating sailors like 'drones', and most of the officers, he felt, were superfluous anyway. But still he retained his faith in victory.

Stumpf finally got to see action at the Battle of Jutland on 1 June 1916, but the inconclusive result left him despondent. He and his mates were 'depressed' at the loss of sister ships, although after the action the Kaiser himself came to celebrate the 'victory'. But after the visit came the rumours: food riots at home, with women and children shot down by the militia in Braunschweig (Brunswick) or Leipzig or Cologne or Berlin. Always false, the rumours suggested the unrelieved anxiety of men about their families at home, an anxiety that increased the longer the war went on.

By spring 1916, Stumpf started to talk of Germany having 'to surrender all our conquests' in a war where 'there will be no victors and no vanquished'. But such large themes were at the margins of his field of vision. More directly galling were the regulations which continued to make everyday life so difficult. On 31 July he wrote that they were really 'excuses to torture and harass us. It is simply shocking and more than one can bear without striking out that we have to ask a twenty-year-old lieutenant for leave to go to the toilet. Moreover he heaps insult upon injury by asking if it is an emergency or merely a pretext for not working.' The sight of a man repeatedly kicked by an officer for not being able to swim revolted him. And all this endured for a plate of soup at lunchtime. He could not help speaking out, to which he ascribed his failure to be promoted to the rank of seaman first class.

Stumpf's patriotism was strengthened on leave when he got into a conversation with a discharged man on crutches, who said that English doctors had deliberately set his bones to make them knit crookedly. Stumpf felt compassion for workmen in dry dock who hoarded any food scraps they could find. But despite all, he vowed to go on. 'I am filled with a genuine and deep love for the Fatherland. I am utterly convinced Germany has a mission to civilize the world.' After all, he was a monarchist, though not 'a blind one'.

If only the caste system in the German Navy had been less rigid, Seaman Stumpf's innate loyalty would have endured and over-ridden the annoyances common to sailors and soldiers of every fighting force. It was the same petty kind of humiliations that infuriated Louis Barthas, then serving in the French Army near Arras, which angered Seaman Stumpf. On 16 September 1916 Stumpf noted:

The engine room on a warship. Life aboard ship for seamen of all countries was dirty, demanding and occasionally very dangerous. Casualties among officers and men were roughly equal. What they didn't share were the same material conditions.

The mutiny of German sailors at Wilhelmshaven, November 1918. This is the face of revolution: soldiers refusing orders to sail to certain defeat and death at sea by officers more interested in saving their reputations than the lives of their men.

'Since we have had such limited contact with the actual war, we wage a sort of internal war among ourselves on the ship.'

The sailors had no soap and resorted to soda and sand, but they still had to present themselves for regular fingernail inspection. What they got at mess was entirely predictable: potatoes once a week; turnips the rest. Hungry workers included crippled men invalided out of the army; when they scavenged food at the docks, they were beaten and humiliated publicly by young officers. This made Stumpf irate. In February 1917 he wrote: 'Our military system has accomplished

what no book, no newspaper and no Socialist could ever have done. I have learned to hate and despise its authority more than anything else in the world.' And in April he insisted: 'How can we perpetuate a system which deprives the working people of their rights and freedom? I would feel proud to be a German if I had been treated as a human being during my five years of service, rather than as an animal. But I see this band of thieves [the officers] carousing and loafing on their beds all day.' The establishment of a Food Inspection Committee to hear the men's grievances aboard ship did not relieve the grumbling. He penned his own

pseudo-medical 'diagnosis' of the men's morale: 'High state of excitement caused by a total lack of confidence in the officers. Persistence of the fixed notion that the war is conducted and prolonged solely in the interests of the officers. Manifestations of bitter anger due to fact that the enlisted men are starving while the officers carouse and roll in money.' In July 1917 two men on his ship were court-martialled for spreading disaffection in the Navy, while two others, serving on the *Prinzregent Luitpold*, were shot.

A year later, the trouble reached breaking-point. By then, the last gamble of the spring offensive of 1918 had failed. All of Germany, Stumpf noted in his diary, 'is dejected', and the seriousness of the situation is 'shamefully and stupidly misrepresented in the Reichstag [Parliament]'. As in the Navy, the leaders of Germany were treating ordinary people like idiotic children. Food shortages worsened by the week. By October 1918, Wilhelmshaven 'resembles a bubbling volcano. Mass refusals to obey orders have become routine; one talks about them the same way we used to discuss a horse race.'

In late October the Fleet was ordered out of port to conduct one last campaign for the glory of the German Navy, or rather for the prestige of the general staff. But the sailors refused to put to sea for one last great and futile battle; their action filled Stumpf with *Schadenfreude* – or glee at the misery of the officers. The disillusioned men, knowing that this pointless sortie would be suicide, doused their ships' boilers and refused to fight for their officers' present reputations and future standing. To Stumpf, 'Long years of accumulated injustice have been transformed into a dangerously explosive force which now erupts with great power all around.' Rallied on by revolutionary workers in the North Sea ports, they demanded peace and revolution. On 11 November they got peace; revolution was somewhat harder to achieve.

DEFEAT ON THE WESTERN FRONT

The story of Seaman Stumpf, like that of so many others who served throughout the war in the German Navy, embraces many of the sources of Germany's strength and Germany's defeat. The commitment to victory, the belief in the nobility of German destiny and the dignity of arms were all present at the outset. But then came the harshness of the war, its cruelties and material shortages; social cleavages ignored or exacerbated by autocratic and insensitive leaders; and finally military failure in 1918.

The sources of German defeat were both internal and international. As social tensions increased at home, Germany's leaders expanded their appetite for postwar annexations, from Belgium to the Baltic Sea. But whatever the delusions of its military and naval leaders, Germany was still far from victory – in part because her war aims were so extreme that the Allies could never accept them and justify such terms to their populations. But German victory was a chimera for another reason: despite increasing strains and shortages at home, those in command underestimated the significance of taking on a new and even more powerful enemy: the United States.

German troops, 1918. The achievements of the German spring offensive were formidable: the first major breakthrough on the Western Front in over three years. But a breakthrough to what? A tactical masterstroke was a strategic defeat.

The German Navy's campaign of unrestricted submarine warfare was the issue that blunted American isolationism sufficiently to enable President Wilson to lead a wide consensus in support of entry into the war in April 1917. But the logic of German naval operations was that the United States was already at war with Germany, in the sense that American bankers and industrialists were filling the coffers and stores of the Allied war effort. That logic was correct, but the cavalier attitude of the German authorities to a formal American declaration of war was a colossal mistake. The commitment of millions of American troops to combat in Europe was not a trivial matter. Furthermore, the submarine war did not bring the Allies to their knees. The actions of the German Navy, in taking civilian lives by sinking both neutral and Allied vessels without warning, did not convince the Allies that a compromise peace was desirable, but rather made it clear that Germany had to be destroyed as a military and naval power. When Germany's U-boat campaign failed, the High Command reverted to its only other option. If victory were to come for Germany, it would have to come on land, and where it had begun: on the Western Front.

American potential steeled the resolve of the Allies just as it corroded that of the Central Powers. That is why the German Army decided to risk all their reserves and their best troops, depleted though they were by years of bloody combat, to one last gamble: the Kaiser's Battle, the beginning of the end of the war.

The Kaiser's Battle and beyond

The battle began on 21 March 1918. Its purpose was a large one: in Ludendorff's words, to 'beat the British'. He calculated that if his infantry could split the Allied line south of Péronne in Picardy and drive the British back, the French would collapse and the Americans would decide not to come in force. To achieve his aims, he struck at the juncture of British and French forces on the Somme. He intended, while holding the French in place, to drive the British right across France and into the English Channel.

The new campaign was based on new tactics. In its first stages, the key lay in the integration of artillery and infantry. Instead of firing a massive preliminary bombardment going on for days and nights, Ludendorff opted for a short but highly intensive bombardment lasting no more than four hours. The tactic worked, in part because of its sheer weight, in part because of improvements in the accuracy of artillery sighting, and in part because the German war economy had provided the Army with the ordnance it needed. In 1918 German munitions production was at its peak – higher than at any time during World War II. But artillery worked, necessarily, only to the depth that shells could travel. After that the burden fell on the infantry.

Supported by a creeping barrage of artillery fire, squads of élite storm-troopers, armed with automatic rifles, light machine guns and flame-throwers, would then penetrate the shattered British front line, skirting around remaining pockets of resistance. Their first job was to overwhelm British artillery positions behind the front lines. After that they would be into open country, and could sweep forward irresistibly against a crumbling adversary.

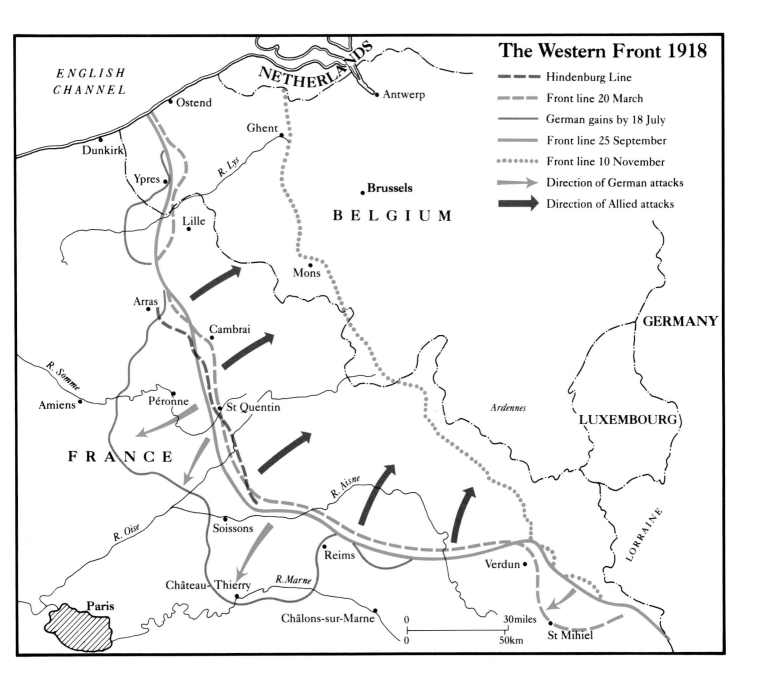

The Western Front 1918

- – – Hindenburg Line
- – – Front line 20 March
- —— German gains by 18 July
- —— Front line 25 September
- ••••• Front line 10 November
- → Direction of German attacks
- → Direction of Allied attacks

That was the plan, and initially it worked. At 4.40 on the morning of 21 March 1918, the beginning of the end of trench warfare opened with the most massive concentrated artillery barrage of the war. Seven thousand artillery pieces began firing off over one million shells; one in four was a gas shell. This is what Ernst Jünger heard and saw:

A tremendous roll of fire brought us to our feet; our uncertainty was dispersed by the instantaneous crash, the like of which has never been heard before by land or sea, from thousands upon thousands of guns roaring on a front of 30 miles, and we knew that the hurricane had broken on us at last. The noise transcended anything I had ever conceived. We were stunned by the concussions of literally thousands of bursting shells, and although the light was uncertain, for there hung a mist, we could see that all our front stood wrapped in a sea of smoke and flame, as the earth heaved and twisted under our feet.

289

Troops of the German
Eighteenth Army in the
ruined streets of St Quentin
just before the opening of the
offensive in March 1918.
The Germans attacked at
the point where the
French and British forces met
in Picardy.

Not a single artillery piece, let alone a rifle, could be heard above the roar. Conversation, even shouting, was impossible. On the British front the exploding shells sliced through telephone lines, cutting off communication with headquarters. The barbed wire was destroyed. Instead of trenches, there were only craters and a few men left to endure the shelling.

What remained of the British Fifth Army on the Somme collapsed as the storm-troops moved in, and in two days they broke through lines occupied for over three years. They had advanced 14 miles, the greatest gain of territory since the beginning of the war. The first day of the battle had been a disaster for the British Army. This is the way 2nd Lt C. C. H. Greaves of the 4th Lincolns saw it:

> Most of the brigade was killed or captured and, by nightfall, there were only several small groups gathered together and under the command of colonels and majors. We had a meeting of the remaining officers and all that the colonels and majors had to say about the day was that it had been 'a bugger'.

What seemed the end of the nightmare of trench warfare was the beginning of Haig's, who asked for urgent French aid but received only scant support. Pétain's first priority was the defence of Paris and the French forces to the north of it. The Kaiser was ecstatic. According to Admiral Georg von Müller, 'His Majesty returned from Avesnes bursting with news of our success. He shouted to the guard on the platform as the train pulled in: "The battle is won! The English have been utterly defeated." There was champagne for dinner.'

LEFT This dead soldier lay by his gun as the fighting passed him by in the last phase of the war.

German troops in action, 1918. The British Fifth Army was forced back as a result of Germany's spring offensive, but Allied reinforcements were rushed to the front lines. Further German pressure on the British around Ypres and on the French and Americans east of Paris on the River Marne frightened the Allies but did not produce any major victory for Germany. The gamble had failed.

As usual, the Kaiser's emotions clouded his vision. Within a week, the advance had ground to a halt. Much territory had been over-run, but none of it was of any strategic importance. The British had fallen back, abandoning hundreds of guns. But every gun lost was replaced from the huge stockpile produced by Allied munitions factories. And despite a massive retreat, Haig's forces were still holding an unbroken line of defence. The outcome of the March offensive was a bulge, not a breach.

The reasons for Ludendorff's failure lay in his unrealistic objectives, which required his infantry not just to over-run the British front positions but to press on far beyond them, against new positions being speedily created. As the storm-troopers advanced rapidly, they left their artillery behind them. Over time,

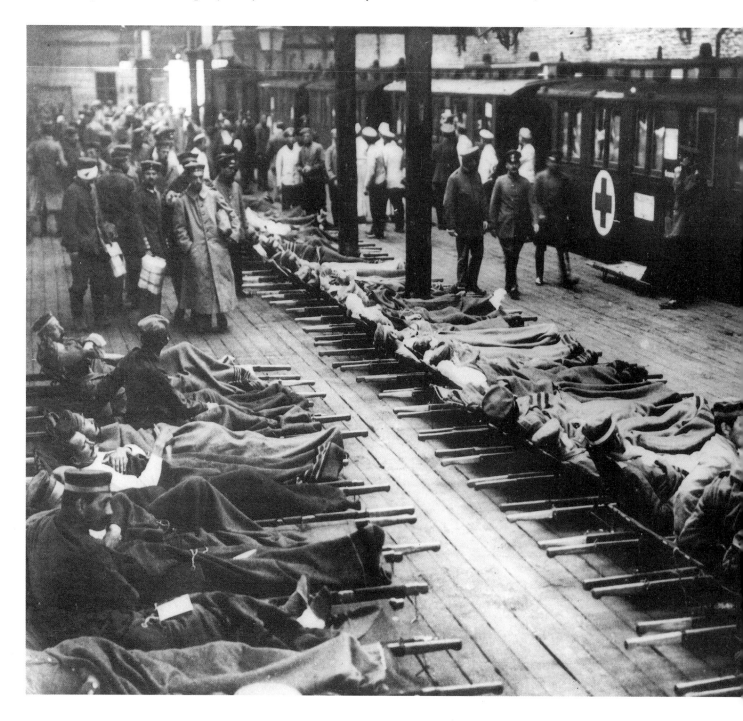

Wounded German soldiers on their way home. German casualties in the 1918 offensives totalled approximately one million men. Civilians saw the results in the continual trainloads of the wounded arriving in German towns. After the high hopes of March 1918, the bitter truth began to sink in: the war could not be won.

sequential attacks had to be made with ever-diminishing quantities of shells. And ever-increasing losses stripped the offensive of irreplaceable combat-tried troops. For a nation running short of manpower and spare parts, this was a prescription for disaster.

Since no breakthrough on the Somme had been achieved by mid-April, Ludendorff decided to try against the British in Belgium. In June and July, he attempted an assault on the French further south. But it was always the same story: a spectacular early success as his great assemblage of guns devastated the Allied front lines, and then a steady fading of achievement as his infantry tried to seep forward, either to the sea (against the British) or to Paris (against the French). By mid-July, the multiple offensive had ground to a halt. At that moment, as the German commander was readying his forces for yet another strike, first the French and then the British counter-attacked. In a few days the face of the war was transformed. It was not that Ludendorff had surrendered the initiative. Rather, it had been wrenched from him.

The changing character of the battle is visible in such actions as the Anglo-American-Australian attack at Hamel on 4 July, the strike of British, Canadian, Australian and French units at Amiens on 8 August, and above all the British victory against the supposedly impregnable Hindenburg Line of fortifications at the end of September. On 29 September, at the Bellenglise salient, the 46th (North Midland) Division was able at points literally to walk across the supposedly impassable set of waterways protecting German positions. At other places they had to cross what remained of the canal on rafts and by swimming, but cross it they did. How did they manage it? Their task had been rendered feasible by the overwhelming artillery fire already directed at the site, a bombardment which had devastated the German defenders. The commander of Fourth Army artillery, General Budworth, described the scene. A forty-eight-hour bombardment caused

> Severe damage ... to the front and support lines east of the Canal. Some of the entrances to mined dugouts were partially blocked. The walls of the Canal were hit at frequent intervals, and banks of debris formed, up which the attackers could scramble. Many of the specially defended localities were rendered mere heaps of debris. ...
>
> The great result of the bombardment was that the defenders were driven into their deep dugouts, and so demoralized that to a large extent they failed to man their defences on the day of attack.

Furthermore, artillery bombardment prior to the attack was, according to prisoners, 'extremely effective, and ... it was owing to this that the pioneers of the 2nd [German] Division were unable to blow up the bridges over the Canal at Bellenglise, as they did not receive food for two days and dared not leave their dugouts owing to the artillery fire'. This is how the Allies pushed the German Army out of some of its most powerful positions.

All these operations had one feature in common: their objectives were moderate and limited, and so they could be achieved without excessive casualties. This was essential, since the bulk of American troops being trained had not yet arrived in

France, and the Allies were running as desperately short of manpower as were the Germans.

These operations pinpointed objectives clearly within artillery range and very vulnerable to the huge amounts of weaponry which the Allies could bring to bear against them, in particular a prodigious arsenal of high explosive shells, supported by guns and mortars, poison gas, aerial bombardment and tanks. This coordination of different forms of firepower into an integrated weapons system gave the attacking infantry a degree of protection which they had lacked earlier in the war. But it was crucial that Allied infantrymen (unlike the Germans in the Ludendorff offensive) were required to advance only so far as the artillery could protect them.

The artillerymen had developed a new range of skills. Their counter-battery fire knocked out a substantial proportion of enemy guns, while their gas shells incapacitated enemy gunners. And they had perfected the firing of a creeping barrage just ahead of their attacking troops, which forced enemy machine gunners and riflemen to keep their heads down just as their trenches were being over-run.

By employing such tactics the Allies, having stemmed the German advance, now reversed it. What German field commanders saw in the slow, bloody, step-by-step Allied offensive of late summer 1918 was that Germany's cause was irretrievably lost. One indication was the propensity of German units to surrender *en masse*. Another was the failure of men on leave to return to their units.

Over there

The climactic battles of September 1918, which saw the rupture of the Hindenburg Line, were not confined to one part of the Western Front. The whole Front was ablaze, not least in the southerly part where the US Army under General John J. Pershing held the line.

The Americans played an important, but not a decisive, role in the final phase of the war. Initially what the US Armies could offer was limited. It was a newcomer to this kind of warfare, and was trying to learn the rules of engagement in a hurry. Inexperience was complicated by the inevitable collision of Americans with people who (inexplicably) did not speak the English language. There were numerous stories of bewildered US soldiers asking, 'Don't any of these people speak American?'

One collision was particularly painful, and it happened to someone who was not even a soldier. e. e. cummings was an ambulance driver with the American Red Cross in France. And he decidedly did not have a good war. He was detained in October 1917 after the French censor had read some critical letters which he had injudiciously written home from the front. He was held on suspicion of treasonous correspondence in a foul prison at La Feré Macé, and stayed there until someone from the American Embassy finally found him. He brought back from France a jaundiced view of the war and bureaucracy in general, and in his book *The enormous room*, published in 1922, expressed many of the sentiments voiced by soldiers in other armies trapped by the war.

The men of the US Expeditionary Force were hardly soldiers in a fit state to challenge the German Army. Future President Harry S. Truman, on his father's

General Pershing, Commander of the American Expeditionary Force, fought to keep
his men under American commanders. After the Germans had launched their offensive
in March 1918, independence was a luxury the Allies could no longer afford.
The Americans worked alongside British and French troops, as here in action in
the St Mihiel Salient, east of Verdun, in October 1918.

farm when the United States declared war on Germany, was one of them. Before the war he had obtained a commission to West Point, but had failed the eye test. This time, the Army was less selective. He joined the Artillery Corps as a first lieutenant, and was promoted to captain.

Men like Truman had to be deployed together, their commander General Pershing ruled, and not dispersed to fill holes in the depleted Allied armies. That was his public explanation for the retention of a separate command structure for American forces. Among the men who led these embryonic units in France was one of the Army's rising stars. As soon as the United States had entered the war, Captain George C. Marshall was entrusted with the job of opening two officer training camps in Plattsburg, New York. Chaos reigned, and Marshall made enemies as he tried to cut through the Army's red tape even to get enough blankets for the men he had to train. He was transferred to the 1st Division, made up of four infantry regiments from the south-west. Everything was done in such haste that the ship transporting them to Europe forgot the ammunition for its own gun crews.

Marshall was one of the first Americans to step ashore in France. He was struck by the number of women in mourning, and with the eerie quiet. 'Everyone seemed to be on the verge of tears,' he noted. The chaotic supply situation which had preceded embarkation to France continued after the troops had arrived. Newly formed howitzer, mortar and 37 mm cannon crews 'hadn't even heard' when their weapons would arrive. Their training area was to the east, in Lorraine, in what he told Pershing was beautiful countryside near Domrémy, the birthplace of Joan of Arc. Twenty-seven years later, during another tour of duty in France, this time as American Army Chief of Staff, he brought gifts to the family who gave him lodgings in 1917.

So did George S. Patton. He too was in France in 1917 and in 1944, and made

LEFT The identity card of Harry S. Truman of the Artillery Corps. He fired his artillery until the very last moment in November 1918. The same man, as president, fired the last shot in World War II – the atomic bomb.

ABOVE American machine guns and supply wagons in a shattered town in the St Mihiel Salient, October 1918. In action in 1918, the US Army learned what all other combatants had discovered years before. Whenever they moved forward rapidly, their advance was pulled to a halt by their supply columns, unable to move with the same speed as the infantry.

it his business to find out what had happened to the French family with whom he had lodged in World War 1. Patton had fought with Pershing in Mexico, and in 1917 took up the challenge of setting up the first American Tank Corps. The Army started with precisely two tanks, custom-built in Washington from French blueprints. When they arrived, he personally drove them off the carrier. He had no choice: he was the only man there who knew how to drive a tank. He also knew how to drive his men to distraction by his obsession with spit and polish. A smart salute was known in the American Expeditionary Force in France as a 'georgepatten'.

Commanding the 42nd 'Rainbow' Division – consisting of men from twenty-six states – was Colonel Douglas MacArthur. He too had to go through all kinds of difficulties to find equipment for his men; carefully prepared stores were raided

American coastal artillery pounding the German lines in the Argonne region, September 1918. The war was won and lost on the battlefield, and through the coordination of artillery, infantry, tanks and air power, the British, French and Americans comprehensively destroyed the German defensive line. This 340 mm gun was part of the barrage that finally broke the German will to carry on.

The extreme youth of the soldiers who fought the battles of 1918 was a result of attrition. This German prisoner found a helping hand from an unexpected quarter: an American padre.

by headquarters to supply other troops. He also had to work hard to block a move to split up his division and distribute them as replacements among other American infantry units. The Rainbow Division coalesced in time for the fighting of spring 1918, but not without a huge logistical and training effort.

There were by then over 500 000 trained US troops in France; each month brought another 250 000, swelling available manpower in late 1918 to 2 million men. This reservoir had to be tapped, despite Pershing's caution about throwing his men into action before they were ready.

At Cantigny on the Somme in May American troops helped fill the gaps

Colonel Douglas MacArthur, Commanding General of 84th Brigade, April 1918. MacArthur was one of many distinguished soldiers of World War II who made names for themselves during the 1914–18 war.

between French and British lines created by the German offensive. The action was planned by George Marshall and his staff at 1st Division Headquarters. The 2nd and 3rd Divisions helped stem the German offensive further south at Belleau Woods and Château-Thierry. Further to the east, at St Mihiel, on 12 September 500 000 American troops went into action to eliminate a German salient established four years earlier. Colonel Patton's tanks, all 174 of them, spearheaded the advance. Only about 70 made it to the German lines; the rest broke down, ran out of petrol or were knocked out. The Germans retreated, leaving over 15 000 prisoners behind.

On the first day of the battle Patton encountered Douglas MacArthur, in command of a brigade. Patton later noted: 'We stood and talked, but neither was much interested in what the other said as we could not get our minds off the shells.' George Marshall, now a colonel at General Headquarters, did the staff work. Thus it was three of the men who dominated World War II – Patton, MacArthur and Marshall – had their baptism of fire in mechanized warfare at St Mihiel in 1918.

American troops were at the heart of the Meuse–Argonne offensives that followed. On 26 September nine US divisions went into action, supported by 189 tanks and 800 aeroplanes. Over the following seven weeks over one million American soldiers were in action, and suffered approximately 120 000 casualties. Some believed that inexperience, and a willingness to take heavy losses, had increased the toll. One American commander estimated that ten of his men were killed for every German life lost. The French theologian Teilhard de Chardin, then a stretcher-bearer, told his sister: 'We had the Americans as neighbours and I had a close-up view of them. Everyone says the same: they're first-rate troops, fighting with intense *individual* passion against the enemy and wonderful courage. The only complaint one would make about them is that they don't take sufficient care. They're too apt to get themselves killed.' In fact, they were just learning what everyone else had discovered on the Western Front: movement cost lives, and the German Army was not a pushover. Whatever the price, though, it was apparent from September 1918 that Germany had lost the war. It was only a question of where and when capitulation would come.

FOOD CRISIS: 1918

What made German defeat unavoidable was the fact that military disaster coincided with a food crisis on the home front. By the summer of 1918, the people at home had little to eat and less to hope for. What was the point of sacrifice if victory was out of the question?

Shortages were not new to most German civilians, who had accepted them on the grounds that they were temporary discomforts and bore no comparison to the hardships suffered by the men at the front. Belt-tightening was not at issue; fairness was. What ordinary people – as much as serving soldiers and sailors – could not accept was the galling spectacle of the rich and the well-placed living well while others went hungry.

August – November 1918

AUGUST *The 'Black Day' of the German Army*

On 8 August, an Allied attack with more than 450 tanks near the Somme led to the surrender of thousands of German officers and men. From the diary of Colonel Albrecht Their, then on the German General Staff in Flanders.

German prisoners of war

We had expected too much from the great effort of March, perhaps even the end of the war. That is why everyone joined together and consolidated their support for the war. Now the deception is there, and it is huge. This is why our attacks, even when well prepared by artillery, are stopped.... Inferior troops panic the moment they are hit by losses.... There is insufficient artillery and in several cases I have the impression that the provision of drink comes first.

SEPTEMBER *Breaking the Hindenburg Line*

The Allied counter-offensive gathered strength as Haig and the BEF broke through the Hindenburg Line in late September. Deneys Reitz was a South African major with the First Royal Scots Fusiliers.

British troops in action near the Hindenburg Line

Graincourt being captured, I went to the right. On my way I passed enemy gun positions from which they had launched their barrage that morning, and I counted more than fifty pieces standing in their emplacements. I went no nearer the fighting line. The British had by now bitten three miles from the German defensive system since dawn and they had reached the final objective of their battle plan at practically every point.... On this day the British took ten thousand prisoners and two hundred guns. On a fourteen mile front ... they had blasted through the Hindenburg Line into the open country beyond, and from then onward the evil of the old trench warfare was a thing of the past, and a new phase had begun.

OCTOBER
Influenza

An epidemic of influenza swept across Europe and many other parts of the world in the autumn of 1918. Sergeant André Kahn wrote to his fiancée.

19 October Striking news, my love: Lille, Bruges, Ostende have fallen. When will it end? No one knows. I write every day, but the post moves inversely with victory. My flu is better. But take care. The number of cases in Paris is disastrous; the number of dead even more frightening. Don't take any risks.

US policeman with flu mask

NOVEMBER *The German revolution*

Revolutionaries in Berlin

The revolution in Germany which began with mutiny and strikes by the sailors in late October, soon spread to workers in ports and cities. Rosa Luxemburg spoke to the founding convention of the German Communist Party on 1 January 1919, two weeks before her murder.

What has the war left of bourgeois society beyond a gigantic rubbish-heap? Formally, of course, all the means of production and most of the instruments of power, practically all the decisive instruments of power, are still in the hands of the dominant classes. We are under no illusions here. But what our rulers will be able to achieve with the powers they possess, over and above frantic attempts to reestablish their system of spoliation through blood and slaughter, will be nothing more than chaos. Matters have reached such a pitch that today mankind is faced with two alternatives: it may perish amid chaos; or it may find salvation in socialism.

NOVEMBER
The Armistice

On 11 November, the Armistice was signed. From Virginia Woolf's diary.

Armistice Day in London

11 November Twenty-five minutes ago the guns went off, announcing peace. A siren hooted on the river. They are hooting still. A few people ran to look out of windows. The rooks wheeled round, & [had] for a moment, the symbolic look of creatures performing a ceremony, partly of thanksgiving, partly of valediction over the grave. A very cloudy still day, the smoke toppling heavily towards the east; & that too wearing for a moment a look of something floating, waving, drooping.

In theory, rationing provided fair shares for all, though on a reduced level. In practice, unfairness was the rule. To begin with, a huge and incomprehensible bureaucratic structure produced enormous confusion. But what made it politically dangerous was that the official system was supplemented by another, unofficial regime: the black market. During the war the most prosperous households were able to procure what they wanted *hintenherum* – 'by the back door'. Large hotels and restaurants continued to serve their prosperous clientele semi-officially with supposedly unavailable foods. In the railway depots of Berlin whole carriages full of foodstuffs went missing, only for these items to reappear on side streets a few hours later.

The authorities were well aware of such practices, but could not stamp them out. Instead, by setting rations at ridiculously low levels, officials tacitly invited ordinary people to bypass regulations. In effect, everybody in Germany had to

Searching for potato rinds in a German town. The subsistence crisis in Central Europe in the winter of 1918 forced millions of people to forage for scraps of food and fuel. This situation increased public anger at inequalities and black marketeers.

break the law in order to survive. This created a system of suspicion and bitterness not about the enemy, whose naval blockade was the root cause of the trouble, but about your neighbour with the seedy overcoat and pockets lined with scarce goods. These men thrived, while the old and the poor went hungry.

With the launching of the March 1918 offensive, the country collectively paused to see if the long-promised victory was at hand. Social solidarity had been stretched almost to breaking-point, but there was still enough patriotism and belief in the Army to reinforce the notion that maybe their sacrifices had been justified.

Nothing could have been further from the truth. In the summer of 1918 this cauldron of hopes, tensions, seething suspicions and anger all came to a boil. Berlin ran out of potatoes, while thousands of soldiers on leave told their families that the war could not be won. Their loyalty to the old regime was at an end. Many of these infantrymen never made it back to their units; they found some hospitable garret in which to live and 'unofficially' extended their leave until the Armistice. When it came, all but the most fervent patriots breathed a sigh of relief.

SURRENDER

By late September the German High Command knew that the war was lost. The Army had been outfought comprehensively that year by forces which had completed a slow and painful process of learning how to master industrial warfare on a staggering and unprecedented scale. Here leadership mattered, and the Allied commanders pressed home their advantage throughout the late summer and early autumn of 1918.

The best description of the German offensive of 1918 was that in operational terms it was a monumental failure. But with great subtlety and consummate immorality Ludendorff tried to hide this fact and to pass on blame for the defeat. Already at the end of September, in Spa in eastern Belgium, he had discussed with like-minded men the usefulness of constitutional reform – a 'revolution from above' – as a means of avoiding a 'revolution from below'. This managed revolution would also have the advantage of shifting the responsibility for working out the Armistice from the military to a civilian government, thereby implicating as many people as possible, in Ludendorff's phrase, in the defeat. Ludendorff and Admiral von Hintze, a leading right-wing politician, persuaded Hindenburg and finally the Kaiser to support this change. For the first time in German history a Chancellor, Prince Max of Baden, would be responsible not to the Kaiser alone but to the nation through the national legislature; he had the confidence of a majority, just as the Prime Minister did in Britain. But the irony was that the first use of this new constitutional power helped to discredit it: the new leaders of Germany were given power by the Army so that civilians would enter the final negotiations leading to the ceasefire of 11 November.

Civilians, Ludendorff told section chiefs of the German High Command on 1 October, would 'now eat the soup which they have served us'. The same line

may be followed in this exchange between him and German civilian ministers on 18 October:

> GENERAL LUDENDORFF: I should like to paint for you gentlemen a picture of the situation. Yesterday we had a battle at Ypres. The English and the French attacked us with very strong forces. We knew that, and we wanted to hold our own; we saw the danger approaching. It was a difficult situation to be in, to have to say we are going to be driven back, and yet to have to hold our own. We were driven back, but it came out well. It is true that gaps four kilometres wide were broken in our front, but the enemy did not push through, and we held the front. How much reinforcements from home would have meant to us then!
>
> The strain on every individual man has reached a stage that cannot any longer be overestimated. Soldier and officer have a feeling of isolation. If an officer leaves them, the men say: 'Where are you going, sir?' and then they run away. If we can fill up the gaps, we can hold our own against all inroads. If we can say to the men at the front, 'you will get reinforcements', they will gain confidence and we, too, can feel confidence.
>
> MINISTER OF WAR SCHEUCH: If I understand His Excellency Ludendorff correctly, he says that if he gets the reinforcements all at once, the situation will be materially altered.
>
> GENERAL LUDENDORFF: Yes.
>
> MINISTER OF WAR SCHEUCH: Are you still considering the fact that the Americans will right along get greater reinforcements than we?
>
> GENERAL LUDENDORFF: The Americans must not be rated too highly. They are pretty dangerous, but up to the present we have beaten them back. They make a difference to the relative number, it is true, but our men do not worry about the Americans; it is about the English. Our Army must be relieved of the feeling of isolation.

Notice the cavalier dismissal of the American Army, and Ludendorff's optimism that a defensive line could be re-established. Notice, too, the emphasis on the isolation of the German Army, on its abandonment by a civilian society unable to come to its aid at its moment of need. Both are attempts to cover his personal responsibility for the imminent defeat of the German Army on the Western Front.

Ludendorff admitted that his men were poorly supplied, and that shortages of everything undermined morale. But instead of accepting that it was his own leadership that had brought the Army to this sorry state, he skilfully found other, external explanations for the crisis that the German war effort was facing. Here is another characteristic exchange on this point:

> GENERAL LUDENDORFF: I come to another point ... the morale of the army. It is very important ... The [41st] Division absolutely refused to fight on the 8th of August; that was a black day in the history of Germany. At present that same division is battling gloriously on the eastern bank of the Meuse. That is all a matter of morale. The morale was bad at that time. The division had *grippe*; it had no potatoes. The spirit introduced by the men from home was also bad. The drafts arrived in a state that in no way correspond to order or discipline. There were gross cases of insubordination.

A British brigade on the banks of St Quentin Canal, 2 October 1918, after the assault on the Hindenburg Line. This series of linked fortified German positions was broken by British infantry and artillery in late September and October 1918. The Allied achievement was remarkable, well worth celebrating by the men who brought it about.

To this, Secretary of State Scheidemann replied that there was nothing left on the home front to give to the troops. Civilian morale was also, he said,

> a question of potatoes. We no longer have any meat. We cannot deliver potatoes because we are short 4000 cars every day. We have absolutely no fats left. The misery is so great that it is like asking a complete riddle when one asks one's self: What does North Berlin live on and on what does East Berlin exist? As long as the riddle cannot be solved, it is impossible to elevate the popular morale. It would be the height of dishonesty if we left anyone in doubt on the question.

The Kaiser in exile. At his headquarters in Belgium, the Kaiser and his military staff tried to work out what should become of him. Clinging futilely to the title of King of Prussia, he was told that he had abdicated, and spent the rest of his life in exile in Holland.

Otto Dix, *Roll Call*. Those men in German uniforms still standing at the end of the war marched home as an army. For some, that fact papered over the humiliations of defeat. Otto Dix's post-war art reminded Germans of what the war had really been like: no glory here.

Ludendorff was an expert on exploring the 'heights of dishonesty'. He insisted that 'we should not accept any conditions that would appear to make the resumption of hostilities impossible'. But how or why to go on? How to justify continuing casualties? Ludendorff never had an answer. He only found a scapegoat: civilians had lost Germany the war. The myth of the 'stab in the back' so crucial to the Nazi seizure of power in 1933 was born then, in the last days of World War I.

One week later, Ludendorff resigned. The last remaining requirement for an Armistice was the abdication of the Kaiser. Long debates took place at his headquarters at Spa in Belgium. When it was agreed that abdication was unavoidable, Hindenburg refused to be present and took a walk in the forest instead. The generals even discussed whether to use the Army to restore the Kaiser's authority; they were divided on the issue of whether the Army would respond to this order. The Kaiser agreed to abandon the imperial crown, but insisted on remaining King of Prussia. No one listened. He was informed that he had abdicated on 9 November 1918. The German Empire had collapsed; the Armistice was signed two days later.

CELEBRATION AND SADNESS: THE DEATH OF A POET

The firing stopped on 11 November, but it is an illusion to think that the war ended then. There was a peace treaty to negotiate and a reckoning to make. That is why Armistice Day was an ambiguous moment on both sides of the line. In Germany the bitterness of defeat was palpable, but at least the killing was over. On the Allied side mixed emotions prevailed as well. Sadness and relief accompanied joy even at the moment of victory. This sombre, unsettling moment in history has been lost in the shadow of documentaries showing cheering crowds and smiling politicians among the victors. Newsreels tell part of the truth. On the Allied side, many celebrated; many more mourned.

Two days after the war ended, the poet Guillaume Apollinaire was buried in Père Lachaise cemetery in Paris. He was thirty-eight years old. Born Wilhelm de Kostrowitzky in 1880, of noble Polish ancestry, Apollinaire, as he became known, was a noted avant-garde poet and art critic before 1914. He introduced Braque to Picasso in 1907, and was active in Berlin as well as in Paris in presenting the message of Cubist art. After leaving Paris for Nice at the outbreak of war, he volunteered for the Army, even though he was not yet a French citizen; his application was approved eighteen months later. As his friend André Billy observed, Apollinaire the soldier-poet was a great surprise to his friends. No one expected this 'corpulent dreamer' to put up with military discipline, but he did very well.

LEFT Armistice scene in London.
RIGHT US sailors celebrating.

Celebration took many forms after the Armistice. Victory parades matched street parties in ingenuity. The shortages, the greyness, the anxiety of 1500 days of war were over for them. Normal life could begin again.

His war poetry is patriotic and exuberant. It is also unique: his visual poems, called caligrammes, burst out of conventional line forms. Part of his poem 'The little auto' forms a car; 'Far from the pigeoner' flutters across the page; 'Here is the coffin' is precisely that, resting on its bier:

```
        H E R E
       IS THE C
       OFFIN IN
       WHICH H
         E REST
       ED   RO
         TTING
       AND P
         A L E
```

```
     LONG LIVE FRANCE!
     HE  SLEEPS IN HIS LI
     TTLE  SOLDIER'S BED
     MY RESUSCITATED
     P                    O
     E                    T
```

As remote as could be from the poetry of disenchantment of Wilfred Owen or Siegfried Sassoon, Apollinaire's verse accepts the war, in Billy's words 'laughing at its risks'. At Bois des Buttes, near Berry-au-Bac, he was hit in the head by a shell fragment on 17 March 1916. He survived trepanning, and other forms of military medicine, but while recovering from his wound was struck down by flu and died just two days before the Armistice.

What killed him was a special and virulent form of influenza, which contemporaries called 'Spanish flu'. This was a misnomer derived from the notion that the infection was brought by sailors from Asia to Spain or Portugal. No one knows its origins; no one knows why in mid-1919 it vanished. By the time it had disappeared, it had left an estimated 20 million victims in its wake, one of the worst pandemics in history.

In 1918–19 this plague killed more people than did the war, and it hit young adults, in or out of uniform, with particular ferocity. Both in its incidence and in its suddenness it was worse than the great epidemics of smallpox, cholera or typhus of the early nineteenth century. It came in two waves: the first in mid- to late 1918; the second in the spring of 1919.

More people died of the flu in India and the United States than in Europe. One estimate puts deaths in India alone at over 7 million. The disease cut a swathe through Africa, killing over a million in West Africa and, according to one medical officer, reducing Accra in the Gold Coast (now Ghana) to a ghost town, with closed markets and empty, silent streets. The flu forced Australian authorities to stop coastal traffic and close borders between states. The Pacific islands suffered worst of all: perhaps 25 per cent of their entire population was wiped out in autumn 1918. The epidemic had political overtones. Nationalists in

Drawing of Apollinaire by Pablo Picasso. Among those who survived combat and injury, but perished during the Spanish flu of 1918, was the French poet and champion of modern art, Guillaume Apollinaire. The dressing of his wound is visible in this drawing, but everyone thought he was on the road to recovery. He died on 9 November 1918.

Africa complained about the failure of British administrators to help striken people in the colonies. Some thought the epidemic helped to poison the atmosphere of the peace negotiations in Paris and to undermine President Wilson's efforts to convince the United States Senate to ratify the Peace Treaty. If ever there was a worldwide disaster, this was it.

The epidemic was not caused by the war, though wartime traffic helped spread the infection. It is debatable whether wartime conditions lowered the resistance of European populations to disease in general; but Spanish flu was no ordinary disease, and it killed as swiftly in the Middle West of the United States, where the war produced an economic boom, as it did in central Europe where hunger was the rule. Wherever it struck, 'Spanish flu' hit the rich as fiercely as the poor. It hit soldiers on both sides of the line, both wounded and healthy, at times causing a pause in military activity in order to evacuate the sick. Men and women

Apollinaire's friend, the poet Blaise Cendrars, who had lost his arm in 1915. He was among the mourners who collided with a victory parade on the way to bury Apollinaire. Cendrars went his own way, and in the November fog couldn't find the grave site. A bleak end of the war for Cendrars: cold, fog, and sadness.

were struck down rapidly with a high fever, and within a few days they were dead. Most doctors were in uniform and therefore unavailable to help, but their absence made no difference. There was no treatment for the Spanish flu. Preventive measures, such as wearing gas masks or fumigating the households of victims, were useless.

After 1500 days of fighting, after millions of men had died and millions more had been wounded, this is the way the war ended: with exhausted populations having to cope with the worst epidemic since the Black Death of the fourteenth century. The story of the death of Apollinaire reveals much about the sombre mood of the last months of the conflict, and about the strange, disease-ridden setting of the Armistice.

The Swiss-born poet and adventurer Blaise Cendrars tells us what happened. Cendrars, in the middle of filming the motion picture war classic *J'accuse* with the director Abel Gance in Nice, went to Paris to arrange for items for the set. There he bumped into Apollinaire on Sunday, 3 November. They lunched in Montparnasse and spoke of 'the subject of the day, the epidemic of Spanish flu which had more victims than did the war'. Five days later, Cendrars met the *concierge* of Apollinaire's building who told him that Apollinaire had caught the flu. Cendrars bounded up the stairs and was met by Apollinaire's wife Jacqueline. She too was ill, but not as seriously as her husband, who was 'all black' and still. Cendrars rushed to get a doctor, who said it was too late to help Apollinaire. The following evening, 9 November, he died.

The burial was held on the 13th, two days after Armistice Day. Cendrars has left an unforgettable account of it. After final absolution, a military guard of honour escorted the coffin out of the church of St Thomas Aquinas. Following it were the poet's widow, family members, artists and hangers-on, in effect,

> all of literary Paris, Paris of the arts, the press. But as it reached the corner of Saint-Germain, the cortege was besieged by a crowd of noisy celebrants of the Armistice, men and women with arms waving singing, dancing, kissing, shouting deliriously the famous refrain of the end of the war:
>
> > *No, you don't have to go, Guillaume*
> > *No you don't have to go...*
>
> That was too much. And behind me, I heard the old glories of the end of symbolism, all the 'immortal' poets forgotten today, chattering, discussing the future of poetry, what young poets will do after the death of Apollinaire and rejoicing, as if they had come to celebrate victory in the battle of the Ancients and the Moderns. That was awful and I felt anger, indignation come over me.

Cendrars left the cortege with his lover and future wife Raymone and the soldier-artist Fernand Léger. They had a warm drink to protect themselves against the flu. Then they took a taxi to the cemetery of Père Lachaise in north-east Paris, only to find that the cortege had travelled faster than they had expected. The ceremony was over, and Apollinaire's friends were leaving. The late-comers asked directions to the grave, and started searching among the headstones. To the annoyance of the gravediggers, they stumbled into two fresh graves. At times

they seemed to be in Elsinore, not Paris. They asked the way, but though the gravediggers were decent men, they were of little help:

> 'You understand, with the flu, with the war, they don't tell us the names of the dead we put in the ground. There are too many'.... But I said, he was a Lieutenant, Lieutenant Guillaume Apollinaire or Kostrowitsky. We have to fire a salvo over his tomb! – 'My dear sir', the head of the gravedigging team answered me, 'there were two salvoes. There were two lieutenants. We don't know which one you are looking for. Look for yourselves.'

They saw a grave with a bit of frozen earth nearby exactly in the shape of Apollinaire's head, with grass for hair around the scar where he had been trepanned. The psychic forces were 'so intense, that one did not believe one's eyes....

The Roman historian Tacitus had written two millennia before, 'They made a desert and called it peace.' In 1918 the desert was full of dead men, dead animals, annihilated villages, stinking trenches and decapitated forests.

We were stunned . . . We left the cemetery, where already a thick glacial mist was enveloping the tombs . . . and said: "It was he. We saw him. Apollinaire isn't dead. Soon he will appear. Don't forget what I tell you." '

This surrealistic scene took place just across from the grave of Alain Kardec, the founder of French spiritualism. Cendrars and the other mourners passed the motto on Kardec's grave. It reads: 'To be born, to die, to be born again and to progress without end. That is the law.' 'It was fantastic,' Cendrars said. 'Paris celebrating. Apollinaire lost. I was full of melancholy. It was absurd.' He returned to the question which obsessed him: 'Under what mask will Guillaume return to the great celebration in Paris?'

The incident surrounding the burial of Guillaume Apollinaire captures the bitter-sweet moment when, at least formally, the Great War came to an end. The mix of delirium and despair in the celebration of victory suggests something of the manic, melancholic nature of the Armistice of 1918. Cendrars' sense that a fresh grave somehow resembled Apollinaire's profile, that he wasn't really dead, indicates the power of denial, the retention of hope in a loved one's survival.

By 1918 9 million soldiers had died in the war. So many had no known grave that the possibility did indeed exist that some of them were still alive. But for most people such hope faded rapidly, and all that was left was finding and honouring the grave of a loved one. Here too Cendrars' difficulty in finding Apollinaire in Père Lachaise paralleled the problems of millions in locating their dead and making the pilgrimage to their graves. It took years for military cemeteries to be constructed in the devastated theatres of military operations. Until then, mourning for most of those who had died in the war was literally disembodied. Millions of survivors were denied the rite of passage so important for their expression of grief and its transcendence.

In a poem of October 1916, 'The War in the Luxembourg Gardens', Cendrars had imagined that on Victory Day

> *The sun will open up early like a candy store on Valentine's Day*
> *It'll be springtime in the Bois de Boulogne or out toward Meudon*
> *All the cars will be perfumed and the poor horses will wear flowers*
> *. . .*
> *Then*
> *That evening*
> *The place de l'Etoile will rise up into the sky*
> *The Dome of the Invalides will sing out over Paris like an immense golden bell*
> *And the voices of a thousand newspapers will acclaim* 'la Marseillaise'
> *Woman of France.*

How far that vision was from the mixed, strange ambiance of the first days after the shooting stopped and the war was won and lost. Exhaustion and epidemic muted the sounds of victory. There were celebrations mixing high spirits and a sense of relief, but as Cendrars saw, for many the war had ended on 11 November 1918 on a sombre, elegiac note, full of sadness for the 'Lost Generation'.

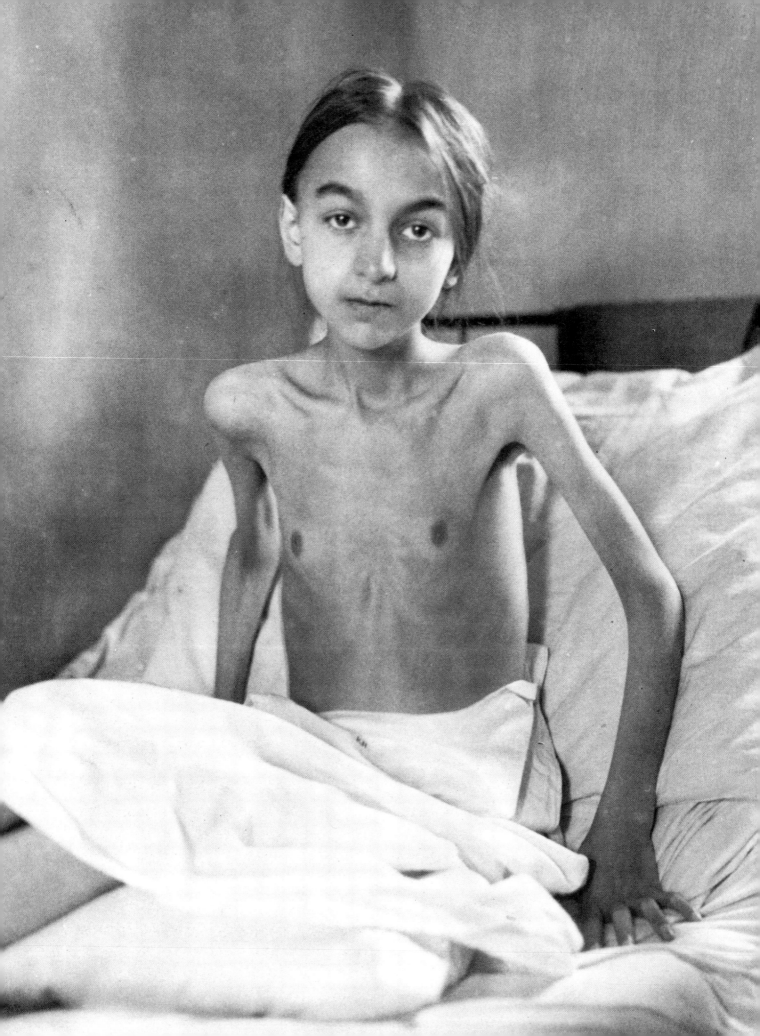

7

HATRED AND HUNGER

In 1919 the major combatants of the Great War demobilized their armies. But they all came to realize that creating a stable peace was at least as difficult as warmaking. The end of formal hostilities did little to relieve the misery of millions. Hunger, disease, revolution and civil war continued to take their toll on the population of Europe.

'Blessed are the peacemakers' is the last thing that anyone should say about the Peace Treaty of Versailles. 'For they shall inherit the earth' is more to the point as a description of the motives and outcome of the conference, for very little was resolved. Peacemaking was warmaking by other, and still vengeful, means. The central disputes were simply rearranged for an even more catastrophic war a generation later. Yet it was not greed which dominated the deliberations at Versailles. It was hatred and fear: hatred based on four and a half years of blood-letting and embitterment; fear based on the spread of violence and revolution in eastern Europe and Russia.

RED TERROR IN RUSSIA

Russia provided the first indication of what awaited the post-war world. In 1917, it stepped out of the Great War and into the cauldron of civil war, famine and chaos. The Bolshevik Revolution was contested internally by a motley group of counter-revolutionary or 'White' armies. It was clear that the Allies were on the side of the Whites: they supported the anti-Bolshevik forces, even to the point of sending troops to Russia.

To the Allies, the Bolsheviks had the blood of Allied soldiers on their hands. The Bolsheviks had taken Russia out of the war just before the last massive German offensive in March 1918. From then until the Armistice, the Western powers justified the stationing of their troops on Russian soil in terms of preventing Western arms from reaching the German Army and convincing a post-Bolshevik Russia to re-enter the war. After November 1918 Western troops, though relatively few in number, were there to help supply the regime's enemies.

Famine followed war in Russia. The new regime was unable to feed its population while engaged in a civil war against a medley of Western-backed armies. As always, the victims were the vulnerable ones: the old, the infirm, the children.

Such material aid was patchy, and supported the more moderate aim of President Wilson who wanted to find a way to broker a peace between Red and White forces.

The rest of the victorious coalition was nakedly hostile to the Bolsheviks. This international conflict placed the deposed Tsar and his family in a vulnerable position. They were symbols of the old order, and could not be allowed to escape to the West or to appear at the head of an anti-Bolshevik political bloc in Russia itself. Their freedom was out of the question. Soon, so was their survival.

The murder of the Tsar

In August 1917 the Tsar and his family were transported, first by train and then by boat, to Siberia. Their home for eight months was the town of Tobolsk, 200 miles north of the Trans-Siberian Railway. Some peasants still removed their caps and crossed themselves in the Tsar's presence, though peasant support for the monarchy vanished quickly after February 1917. In captivity the imperial family tried to simulate normality. They produced a play: the Tsar was Smirnov in Chekhov's *The Bear*. The Tsar's uniform at a family party annoyed some soldiers as he had continued to wear the epaulettes of the Army he had once commanded. This emblem of the old regime, the guards demanded, had to go. The Tsar at first resisted, but, fearing reprisals against his family, he agreed to hide his epaulettes under a cloak while in public. On 1 March 1918, the family's privileges were further reduced. From now on they had to live on soldier's rations and a small stipend. The Tsar drew up a budget.

Elsewhere, friends tried to organize their rescue. One supposed loyalist was Boris Soloviev, a mystic and son-in-law of Rasputin. He came from Petrograd to Tobolsk, plotted and planned, but never took a single active step. Much money for the Tsar entered his pocket; what happened to it is a mystery. Whether or not he was a Bolshevik agent may never be known. Instead of escape, the family now faced a medical emergency. The haemophiliac Tsarevich Alexei injured himself while playing, resulting in his worst haemorrhage in years. He suffered greatly and said: 'Mama, I would like to die. I am not afraid of death, but I am so afraid of what they will do to us here.'

His fears were well-founded, but they would not be realized in Tobolsk. A new commissar brought orders from the Central Committee of the Communist Party to send the Tsar to Moscow. The Tsar, his wife and one daughter left, but they never got there. Instead, while the imperial prisoners were on their way to Moscow, Bolsheviks in Ekaterinburg, a mining and smelting town in the Urals, demanded the right to hold the Tsar. They were strong enough to take him, possibly with Moscow's (and Lenin's) approval.

By mid-May the Tsar and his whole family were housed in a two-storey building in the centre of the town. The British consul in Ekaterinburg, T. H. Preston, mulled over the chances of rescue. But with thousands of Red Guards in the town, escape was impossible. The imperial family now had new guards, among them Austrian prisoners of war who had stayed on to work for the Cheka, the secret police.

The local soviet had already determined to kill the Tsar, but cabled Moscow

The deposed Emperor of all the Russias, now only a symbol of a vanished world, sawing wood in captivity at Tsarskoe Selo. He did what he could to provide his family with a semblance of normality.

for confirmation. There the Party leadership was undecided. Trotsky thought of holding a public trial, with himself as prosecutor. Lenin may have personally ordered the Tsar's execution, though his role in the affair is still unclear.

The way the Bolsheviks self-servingly presented the matter was simple: what sealed the imperial family's fate was not the hand of the new regime, but the hand of counter-revolution in the form of a force of forty thousand Czech soldiers fighting their way west. They had been prisoners of war, captured by the Russian Army before 1917, then freed and re-equipped by Kerensky to fight on the Eastern Front. After the peace treaty the Bolsheviks tried to disarm them, but failed to do so. Their presence in Siberia meant they controlled a long stretch of the Trans-Siberian Railway. The Czechs were useful in another way: they could conceivably capture the Tsar and his family.

In July 1918, these Czechs approached Ekaterinburg. On the 12th, upon learning that the town might fall within three days, the Ural soviet decided to shoot the Tsar and his family. The executioners received their orders the following day. At midnight on 16–17 July, they roused the captives and told them to dress immediately: the proximity of the Czechs, they were told, meant that they had to be moved. They were led to a basement, where they were told to await transport. A

truck revved its engines to reassure the victims that they were about to be driven away. Then a group of trusted soldiers, armed with revolvers rather than rifles, entered the room and killed the entire family. The bodies were removed to a pit, dismembered, burned and partially dissolved in acid. Later the remains were buried in a nearby forest. On 25 July 1918 the Czechs took Ekaterinburg, and monarchist officers raced to free the Tsar. But no one found the family or even their bodies. The house itself remained standing, scarred by bullet marks and a destination for pilgrims. In 1977 Boris Yeltsin, First Secretary of the region, ordered the house to be destroyed. The remains of the imperial family were found later and positively identified only in 1994.

The murder of the Tsar was part of one of the most vicious chapters in Russian history, but the Red Terror had begun before the executions at Ekaterinburg. Leon Trotsky, himself a future assassination victim, justified the killings in these words: 'The execution of the Tsar's family was needed not only to frighten, horrify and dishearten the enemy, but also to shake up our own ranks, to show them that there was no turning back, that ahead lay either complete victory or complete ruin. *This* Lenin sensed very well.'

ABOVE This room is where the 300-year-old Romanoff dynasty was snuffed out. The imperial family was killed because it was too dangerous for them to remain alive, and because the Bolsheviks wanted no one to doubt their determination to hold on to power.

RIGHT Fania Kaplan: her attempt on Lenin's life in August 1918 failed, but it still changed the course of history. Lenin never recovered, went into decline, and died in 1924.

Boris Savinkov and the Social Revolutionaries

Instability, confusion and bloodshed were everywhere. The Bolsheviks' enemies even included Russian groups who had also opposed the Tsar. Members of another radical group – the Social Revolutionary Party – had suffered in the Tsar's prisons, yet they strenuously opposed Bolshevik dictatorship and the Treaty of Brest-Litovsk, which they believed had betrayed Russia. Some of these radicals struck back in the hope of winning back a revolution they believed the Bolsheviks were betraying. They arrested the head of the Cheka, Felix Dzerzhinsky, known as the 'Jesuit of Terror', and captured the Lubyanka prison. But Latvian troops loyal to the Bolsheviks suppressed the rebellion and released Dzerzhinsky. Thirteen of the rebels were executed that day.

Other groups struck at the same time. On 6 July 1918 anti-Bolshevik forces under the banner of the Union for the Defence of the Motherland and Liberty struck in the Volga region north-east of Moscow. They took the industrial town of Yaroslavl, midway between Moscow and Archangel. The attack was the brainchild of one of the most extraordinary men in the anti-Bolshevik camp. Boris Savinkov was a consummate terrorist, a man who thrived in this murky atmosphere. Although he was ostensibly a Social Revolutionary, his real loves were intrigue and killing. Son of a tsarist official and prosecutor, friend of Apollinaire and Modigliani in pre-war Paris, a volunteer in the French Army from 1914 to 1917, he returned to Russia and served as deputy War Minister under Kerensky. He then fought with the Cossacks against the Bolsheviks, and was involved in virtually every plot launched against the new regime. In the town's cemetery, dressed as a French officer, he planned the taking of Yaroslavl.

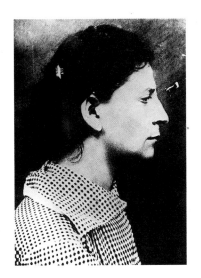

OVERLEAF The town of Yaroslavl was reduced to rubble in fighting between Red and White armies.

In Yaroslavl Savinkov's forces occupied key buildings, executed three senior Bolsheviks, placed two hundred hostages in a 'death barge' on the Volga, and abolished all Soviet laws and decrees. They held out for seventeen days. Savinkov was in nearby Rybinsk, where a large store of arms was the target. He put all his hope in Allied reinforcements, but none was promised and none was ever likely to appear. The revolt was doomed. On 23 July the Bolsheviks retook the town and reduced it to rubble. Somehow Savinkov managed to evade arrest, but his men in Yaroslavl were not so lucky. In the following forty-eight hours, four hundred prisoners were executed. 'Here there is a dance of life and death,' wrote Dzerzhinsky to his wife. It was 'a moment of truly bloody battle'. It was also the moment when the Tsar and his family were shot. This is when the Red Terror began.

On 30 August the head of the Cheka in Petrograd, Uritsky, was shot dead. The same day, after addressing factory workers in Moscow, Lenin was shot twice, once in the chest and once in the neck, but survived. His would-be assassin was a twenty-eight-year-old Social Revolutionary named Fania Kaplan, whose parents had emigrated to America in 1911. She was executed on 4 September. 'Red Terror is not an empty phrase,' her executioner intoned after she was shot.

One newspaper, the *Krasneia Gazeta*, echoed this remark: 'For the blood of Lenin and Uritsky ... let there be floods of blood of the bourgeoisie – more blood, as much as possible.' 'From now on', wrote *Pravda*, 'the hymn of the

working class will be a hymn of hate and revenge.' And so it was. In early September, five hundred prisoners were shot in Petrograd. The sailors of Kronstadt killed four hundred hostages in a single night. The same fate awaited prisoners in other parts of Russia. 'The Revolution suffered an inward change,' Trotsky observed. 'Its "good nature" gave way. The party steel received its last tempering.... In the autumn [of 1918] the great revolution really occurred. Of the pallid weakness that the spring months had shown there was no longer a trace. Something had taken place, it had grown stronger.'

Alexis Babine

One witness of this change was Alexis Babine. Russian-born, but educated at Cornell University, he had written a two-volume history of the United States in Russian, and out of boredom with America had returned to his homeland in 1912. There he found a teaching post at the university in Saratov, on the lower Volga. This provincial backwater lacked the cosmopolitan character of St Petersburg or the political turmoil of Moscow. The story of Saratov in the civil war was repeated hundreds of times in other towns and cities.

Babine's diary is a window on to the chaos and cruelty of the time when the Revolution hardened. No friend of the Bolsheviks or of any other revolutionary force, he told of daily indignities and rough justice. Black marketeers were whipped; prisoners shot; property taken by soldiers at random. Babine found the local Bolsheviks as corrupt as any tsarist government, staying the execution of condemned men for a bribe of alcohol, and then killing the prisoners anyway.

En route from Saratov to Moscow, Babine encountered many people who were fed up with the Bolsheviks and their 'despotism, cruelty, restrictions on commerce, and the constantly growing scarcity of food supplies'. On his return home, he found that twenty hostages had been shot after the attempt on Lenin's life.

The passport of Alexis Babine, an historian of America who taught at Saratov University during the Russian civil war, and survived to tell the tale. An enemy of the new order, he grumbled and criticized, but was left alone. He eventually escaped to the United States to a job in the Library of Congress.

Much of the skirmishing in the civil war took place around the rail networks, the vital arteries of both sides. Armoured trains were means of political control in a conflict between forces both lacking clear popular support.

Another 150 'conservatives' had been imprisoned. 'Since the beginning of Bolshevik rule, about 350 corpses have been brought to the university morgue,' Babine noted laconically in October 1918. Shops were ordered to remain open on Russian Orthodox holidays. Icons were banned from hospital wards. Homes were requisitioned at twenty-four hours' notice. Wealthy landowners were shot out of hand. For him and his friends, 'the pervading problem is to keep alive and to outlast the Bolsheviks'. How long would that take? Nobody knew. On the anniversary of the Bolshevik seizure of power Babine brooded about:

> the ease with which everybody endowed with intelligence and foolhardy enough to show the courage of his convictions is swept out of existence by order of a small but cleverly organized band of degenerates and by the hand of its pervert hirelings and blind tools, and the pitiless, bloody cruelty of the band, begin more and more to convince the intelligent surviving unwilling thralls of the regime that all liberal declarations and slogans of the Bolsheviks are a humbug; ... the real object of the Communist party is to sweep out of its way everybody to whom the undeceived and awakened people might turn for guidance in this active protest against oppression, and thus to perpetuate its rule.

After the Armistice on the Western Front, there arose wild and totally unfounded rumours of the collapse of Bolshevik power. On 25 November, Babine remarked that the Allies had demanded total surrender from the 'Bolshevik misrulers'; the next day, the 'news' was that Petrograd had been 'occupied'. Such illusions did not fill their stomachs: shortages were everywhere. '"Only the Jews have all they want", was the general refrain,' Babine wrote on 28 December.

The year 1919 dawned on a cold, hungry population. In Saratov, trapped near the front lines between the Bolsheviks and the White armies, Babine noted that everyone was praying 'to heaven for the Allies' and was desperate for liberation from 'the stiffest and the most brutal monarchy imaginable'. He welcomed news

Murder was justified by political expediency on both sides of the Russian civil war. These Bolshevik workers in the Ukraine were strung up by White militias, supported by Western troops.

of anti-Bolshevik uprisings, and bemoaned shortages – no kindling wood, no eyeglasses, pitifully little bread. He was forced to deal with a 'Jewish bread profiteer' in order to stay alive.

These reduced circumstances deepened Babine's hatred of the Bolsheviks and opened his mind to other visions, probably as fanciful as his political and military information. He noted on 29 April:

> A few days ago sentries at the Bolshevik monument on Theater Square heard cries and groans, as of one weeping, from the little chapel nearby. They threw down their muskets and ran to the Bolshevik authorities to report the fact. Two Bolsheviks were sent to investigate the matter. When they entered the chapel, they saw tears running from the eyes of the wooden icon of Our Lady. One of the emissaries dropped on the floor in a dead faint; the other ran away in terror.... Incessant services have been held for the ebbing and flowing crowds of worshippers. I was unable to elbow my way into the chapel this afternoon.

The implausible and impossible scenes described in Babine's diaries capture the fluid, dangerous and totally uncertain world of civil war. The fact remained, though, that Babine was on the losing side. Whatever the supernatural was up to, the mundane forces of the old order were blunted and by late 1919 the tide had turned in favour of the Bolsheviks. The White armies were as cruel and corrupt as the Bolsheviks; the only difference was that the Whites were more incompetent. Peasants had little confidence that, in the event of a restoration of the monarchy, they would keep the lands they had confiscated in the revolution of 1917. The new regime slowly consolidated its hold on the south and east of Russia, and held its own against Polish forces in the west. Bolshevism was there to stay, and the Red Terror had helped to keep it alive.

RIGHT Bolshevik prisoners. Prisoners-of-war stranded in Siberia by the Revolution and the Armistice joined both sides in the civil war. Some became prisoners again; many changed sides; others simply vanished.

It was a time of contradictions. The fact that Babine had remained free, and had kept his job, testifies to the limits of the terror; had he been in Saratov a decade later, during Stalin's time, he would not have lasted a day. The same regime that committed crimes and exonerated criminals on their own side also permitted a flowering of cultural life. Women's rights were recognized. Painting, sculpture, music and poetry all flourished. The artist Marc Chagall was appointed Commissar of Fine Arts in the town of Vitebsk in Byelorussia in 1919, and took seriously Bolshevik statements recognizing the Jewish people as a nation among others within the Soviet state. In May 1920, he left for Moscow where he painted the murals for the State Jewish Theatre. Then came a series of terrible pogroms – attacks on Jews and their property – led by White forces and Ukrainian nationalists. Thousands were killed in violence which grew out of the general anti-semitism of which Alexis Babine's was typical. Pogroms continued throughout the civil war. By 1922 Chagall decided he had to leave for Paris; the cultural and political climate in Russia had changed. The days of artistic freedom were over.

The same year Babine fled to the West. In London, he heard a young zealot using Trotsky's slogan about the bourgeoisie: 'It is easier to shoot them than to argue with them.' Babine had indeed been lucky. Settling in Washington, he became assistant head of the Slavic Section of the Library of Congress. He died in that city in 1930, at the age of sixty-four, a survivor of both the Red Terror and the Russian civil war.

WHITE TERROR IN GERMANY

In post-war Europe terror took many forms, including the brutal suppression of the revolutionary Left in Germany. This turbulent phase of German history followed the collapse of the old order. By late 1918, it was common knowledge in that country that the Allies would not make peace with Kaiser Wilhelm II: the price of surrender was political change. The Kaiser was therefore unceremoniously deposed on 8 November.

Into the power vacuum he had left behind came a new ruling group of socialists in a six-man provisional government. Three were right-wingers who had supported the war from the outset, and three were left-wingers who had come to oppose it. The chairman of the new ruling bloc was Friedrich Ebert. A deeply cautious man, Ebert saw himself as the German equivalent of Kerensky and had no intention of following the Russian precedent and being swallowed up by a second Bolshevik Revolution. To pre-empt this unwelcome prospect he immediately entered into a secret pact with the man who had replaced Ludendorff as effective head of the German Army, General Wilhelm Groener.

A commitment to containing or destroying the revolutionary Left of the socialist movement was part of the price that Ebert paid for the support of the Army. On 8 November, just before the provisional government was formed, he spoke on the telephone with General Groener. It was evident that the Imperial Army was about to become the Army of a new order. Groener's interest was to ensure that the Army survived the transition and more.

Here was a man with whom Ebert could work. Groener was not in the mould of the old guard, who, like the Kaiser, had contemplated turning machine guns on strikers. Groener was a conservative, but an enlightened one. He had organized the German mobilization in 1914. In 1916 he had been appointed to head the new *Kriegsamt* or War Office for munitions production. Too friendly to the trade unions, Groener had been dismissed by Ludendorff in 1917. Ebert was a socialist supporter of the war effort, and had worked with Groener. On the extreme right wing of the German Socialist Party, Ebert thought a constitutional monarchy would be a good idea for post-war Germany. He hated disorder and revolution. So did Groener. Out of this common outlook, a fateful partnership emerged.

It was an alliance formed in the dark. Ebert never told his socialist colleagues of the content of the fateful telephone conversation of 8 November:

> EBERT: What do you expect from us?
> GROENER: The Field Marshal [Hindenburg] expects that the government will support the Officers' Corps, maintain discipline, and preserve the punishment regulations of the Army. He expects that satisfactory provision will be made for the complete maintenance of the Army.
> EBERT: What else?
> GROENER: The Officers' Corps expects that the government will fight against Bolshevism, and places itself at the disposal of the government for such a purpose.
> EBERT [*after a slight pause*]: Convey the thanks of the government to the Field Marshal.

The new German Republic turned to the old army to consolidate its power. The price for military cooperation was the suppression of revolutionary workers. Here Friedrich Ebert (third from the left), chairman of the provisional government, consults with their military allies.

Groener knew very well that a provisional government was coming and that it would be composed of both left-wingers and right-wingers. For the government to fight against Bolshevism required the isolation and removal of anyone who was sympathetic to the revolutionary cause. This was precisely what both Groener and Ebert had in mind.

At the time of the Armistice, Ebert, with the Army's support, headed an uneasy coalition of moderate and radical socialists. The radicals were progressively alienated, and left the provisional government after a stormy six-week period of cohabitation. This enabled Ebert and his colleagues to get on with their tasks: to prevent a Bolshevik uprising in Germany, to return the country to peacetime conditions, to demobilize 10 million men and get them back to work, to negotiate a peace treaty and to establish the institutions of a stable democracy.

Ebert certainly faced a desperately difficult situation, and used his own predicament to justify moderate policies. In effect, in their first weeks in power the moderate socialists ensured that a post-war democratic Germany would be very similar to the pre-war *Kaiserreich*. After all, he brooded, who knew if the Allies would tolerate a more radical regime in Berlin? This, however, was just bluff. The victors did threaten military intervention, but by early 1919 they had more rhetoric than regiments. Everyone wanted to go home, especially in defeated Germany. Military demobilization accompanied a kind of political demobilization of the socialist programme.

Universal suffrage and the establishment of the institutions of representative democracy, with an executive answerable to the legislature, were no mean achievements. But the higher civil service was the same as under the old regime; the courts were run by the same men, and by and large, so was the Army. An effort to replace the Kaiser by a Western-style democracy was needed to end the war. And so these changes occurred. But the new provisional government was led by men determined to prevent the transformation of Germany into a socialist state. The old order had survived the shock of defeat and the arrival of the socialists in power.

Spartacus

The conservatism of the new regime triggered an attempted seizure of power by a small group of revolutionaries in January 1919. They were led by the Spartacus League, reborn as the German Communist Party on New Year's Day that year. But the revolt was doomed before it had begun. Rosa Luxemburg, who with Karl Liebknecht led Spartacus, thought the time for action was in the future. Liebknecht, more of a rabble-rouser, wanted to move then and there. Liebknecht won the argument, and, against her better judgement, Luxemburg went along with what she saw was a premature move to seize power.

Gambling that the workers of Berlin would join them, on 11 January their supporters seized a number of buildings in the capital and announced the overthrow of the provisional government. After four days of street fighting, the insurrection was totally crushed. Over a thousand people had been killed or wounded. Most Berlin workers had stayed behind closed doors.

On 15 January Liebknecht and Luxemburg were arrested and taken to the Hotel Eden in the centre of Berlin. This was the temporary headquarters of the Division of Cavalry and Riflemen, and housed one of the Freikorps or paramilitary police units that had crushed Spartacus. These groups were made up of ex-soldiers, thugs, drop-outs and adventurers who did the dirty work of the new regime. There is no evidence that the provisional government ordered the killings of Liebknecht and Luxemburg, but they did nothing to rein in the Freikorps, who meted out their own form of rough justice.

First Liebknecht was led out of the hotel and clubbed to the ground by a

The birth of the German Republic was proclaimed by the moderate leaders of the Social Democratic Party on the steps of the Reichstag in Berlin on 9 November 1918.

soldier named Runge. The prisoner was driven to a deserted part of Berlin where he was thrown out of the car. His body was riddled with bullets. Next it was Rosa's turn. An officer, Lieutenant Vogel, was ordered to take her to Moabit prison, where she had served time during the war. But before she had left the hotel, Runge clubbed her to the floor. Others restrained him from finishing the job in front of so many witnesses. She was dragged to a car, bleeding from her nose and mouth. As soon as the car had driven off, a shot was heard by those still in the hotel. In all likelihood it was Lieutenant Vogel, riding on the running board, who had fired it. Her body was dumped in the Landwehr Canal. 'The old slut is swimming now,' one of her killers scoffed. Her decomposed body was dredged out of the canal at the end of May, and she was buried alongside Liebknecht and others who had been killed in the January uprising.

The investigation into the killings was derisory. Dozens of witnesses saw Liebknecht and Luxemburg in the Hotel Eden; they watched the clubbings, then saw them being dragged out and driven off. The government was embarrassed; some accounting was necessary. The military closed ranks. A court-martial was held in May 1919. Charges were laid against Lieutenant Vogel for failing to report

RIGHT Photographs of the bodies of Luxemburg and Liebknecht, murdered on 15 January 1919. Her body was dredged out of the Landwehr Canal four months after she had been shot.

Freikorps volunteers in the Hotel Eden in Berlin on 15 January 1919, the day that Rosa Luxemburg and Karl Liebknecht were brought there, beaten, and dispatched to their deaths.

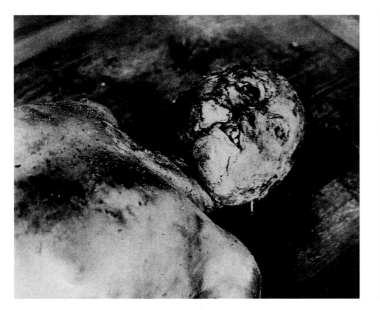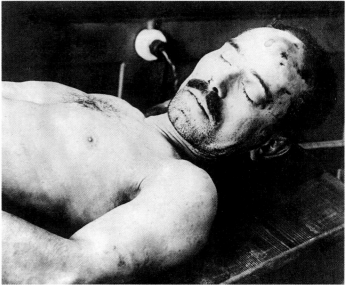

a death and for illegally disposing of a body. Sentenced to two years and four months' imprisonment, he was spirited away to Holland before he could be taken into custody. Runge was charged with attempted manslaughter for clubbing the prisoners; he got a two-year sentence and served it, but in 1933 he received a gratuity of 6000 Deutschmarks from the newly victorious Nazis for 'paying for his ideals in prison'.

Polarization

Other political murders followed. In conservative Bavaria a left-wing socialist, Kurt Eisner, was a marked man after he declared that Germany was indeed responsible for the outbreak of the war. Eisner was chairman of the Council of Workers, Soldiers and Peasants that had seized power in Bavaria in the turbulent days at the end of the war. On 21 February 1919 he was shot dead on his way to the parliament building in Munich by a Bavarian aristocrat, Count Arco-Valley. The delegates were told of the crime by Erhard Auer, who opened the session in place of Eisner. Then a demented butcher tried to assassinate Auer, firing wildly into the hall. Two other delegates were killed, though Auer, badly wounded, survived.

In March 1919 it was the turn of Rosa Luxemburg's former lover and fellow Communist, Leo Jögiches. He had made it his business to expose the cover-up of Rosa's death, and stayed in Berlin even though it was obviously very dangerous to do so. When he visited Rosa's apartment he remarked, 'It is beautiful here. I feel as though Rosa could walk in any moment.' Jögiches was arrested, severely beaten and shot.

Of these victims of assassination, Eisner and Luxemburg were Jews. This was no secret, and fitted in well with the stab-in-the-back legend concocted by Ludendorff and others to show that they had not lost the war but had been betrayed by revolutionaries and Jews. The transformation of Germany into a democratic country had not reduced anti-semitism; on the contrary, hatred of the enemy without passed easily to hatred of the enemy within. On the Russian Front, German soldiers had their first extended contact with eastern European Jews. Anti-semitism flourished among many of these men. Here was another example of the continuity of pre-war German political culture after 1918; the difference was that after the defeat, hatred grew.

The provisional government was only intended to hold power until a constituent assembly could be elected to frame a new constitution for a democratic order. The smashing of the revolutionary Left in 1919 helped legitimize the new order among middle-class people and conservative workers. It also destabilized Germany, with lasting results. The brutal repression permanently divided the socialist movement: the left wing never forgave the moderates their responsibility for the murders of Luxemburg and Liebknecht. Communists and socialists were to remain at each other's throats, even when they faced common enemies.

Public support for radical change had foundered on the rock of the innate conservatism of the bulk of the working population and its exhaustion after four years of war. Having survived one crusade, they were not interested in embarking on another. Perhaps what Oscar Wilde had said of socialism was truer in Germany than anywhere else in Europe in 1919. He wasn't a socialist, Wilde said, because it took too many evenings. There were plenty of other things to do. One was to restore ordinary life – to rebuild marriages and hopes, to raise children, to get back to work, to forget the smell of the trenches or the munitions factories.

This inner migration to the significant events of everyday life may help to explain the results of the election to the Constituent Assembly in 1919. Four days after the Spartacist uprising had been crushed, the electorate of 30 million people – for the first time including women – delivered its verdict on revolution: 36 per cent voted for the moderate socialists; 8 per cent for radical candidates; and the rest voted for conservative parties. The new Weimar Republic would not even have a socialist majority. The new capital of Germany, Weimar, was chosen both as the city of Goethe and as an alternative to revolutionary Berlin. The old order had survived the shock of defeat and the overthrow of the monarchy. The German revolution of 1918–19 had come to an end virtually as soon as it had started.

Kurt Eisner, who led the socialist revolution in Bavaria, declaring it a Republic on 7 November 1918. He was assassinated on 21 February 1919.

THE FAILED PEACE

Hatred and diplomacy went hand in hand in 1919. The Peace Conference which ended the Great War was more about punishment than about peace. Perhaps inevitably, anger and retribution followed four years of bloodshed, ensuring the instability and ultimate collapse of the accords signed in the Hall of Mirrors at Versailles on 28 June 1919. The road to World War II started here.

To understand what went wrong at Versailles it is necessary to consider the character of the men who made the Peace of 1919. In effect, four men dominated the proceedings. Clemenceau, the Premier of France, Lloyd George, the British Prime Minister, and US President Wilson were there, very much in the flesh. Lenin remained in Russia but was present at Versailles in spirit, a ghostly figure whose existence made everyone uncomfortable around the negotiating table.

Clemenceau hosted the conference, and imprinted his conservative vision on it. He had little choice: France had to reduce German power so as to preclude a repetition of the bloodbath of 1914, a nightmare that the smaller French population could not afford to face again. His strategy was to restore the old balance of power, with Germany as a much weaker element in international affairs. In other words, he aimed to re-create the pre-war world, with France dominant in Europe. In this effort he was supported by Lloyd George, whose vision was more imperial than European. His aim was to protect Britain's worldwide trading and political interests, while genuflecting to new notions such as the right to self-determination of subject peoples. Such rhetoric, he reasoned, would fade; national interests would remain.

Wilson's ideas were different. He stood for a new kind of international order, one based on 'reason' and 'right'. This is why he championed an international forum, the League of Nations, as a meeting-place where troubled neighbours could come to settle their disputes without the shedding of blood. There was a kind of American condescension in his thinking – the notion that Europe was a sink of iniquity, and that the Americans had had to come to Europe to help them sort out a mess that they were unable to sort out themselves.

It was evident from the start of the negotiations that these men were looking towards entirely different futures. Lloyd George, a master of diplomatic duplicity, could work with Clemenceau; they spoke the same worldly, untrustworthy language. But Wilson seemed to be from another planet. Lloyd George recalled: 'I really think that at first the idealistic President regarded himself as a missionary whose function it was to rescue the poor European heathen from their age-long worship of false and fiery gods. He was apt to address us in that vein, beginning with a few simple and elementary truths about right being more important than might, and justice being more eternal than force.'

Treating Americans as children in a world of grown men is an old European conceit, nicely complementing American disdain for European decadence. Wilson was no child, and American power was too important to be simply brushed aside. At home people listened to what he had to say. But no one in 1919, however cunning or spell-binding, could convert European leaders to the notion that the old way of doing things was over. The conservative impulse was too strong. After all, numbers counted. Roughly fifty thousand Americans had died in the war: fifteen times that number died among the British forces; thirty times in French uniforms. Why should Europeans pay heed to lofty arguments about principles for which Americans had sacrificed relatively little?

Still, Wilson tried. The Fourteen Points he had proclaimed in January 1918 echoed throughout the world, providing the background to German capitulation and to the negotiations at Versailles. And they formed a counter-force to the revolutionary aspirations unleashed by the Bolshevik Revolution. Wilson's position was not reducible to anti-Bolshevism, though his opposition to the new regime in Russia was evident. The problem was, though, that Wilson's outlook was too generous in spirit, too optimistic to suit the dark mood of peacemaking in 1919. The harsher creeds of Clemenceau and Lenin better reflected the bitterness of the day.

Wilson was the first American President to leave the continental United States for Europe while in office. Going to Paris was politically risky; but not going was, to him, unthinkable. As a child of four Wilson had stood at the gate of his home in Augusta, Georgia, when he heard 'someone pass and say that Mr Lincoln was elected and there was to be war. Catching the intense tones of his excited voice, I remember running in to ask my father what it meant.' He soon found out, as did everyone in Georgia.

In 1916, he was re-elected President on a promise to keep his country out of the war. Two years later, when he sailed for Europe on the *George Washington*, Wilson aimed to transform the international order which had led to the war of 1914–18. He was well aware of the difficulties he faced, telling one adviser: 'There must be no delay. It has been so always. People will endure their tyrants for years, but they tear their deliverers to pieces if a millennium is not created immediately. What I seem to see – with all my heart I hope that I am wrong – is a tragedy of disappointment.' A sense of foreboding continued to haunt Wilson. His royal welcome in London had been proper, but no more. George V judged him a cold and cerebral professor: 'I could not bear him,' was the royal comment to a friend. The public welcome in Paris was warmer, but still the President was uneasy. 'In six months,' he quipped, 'they may be dragging me in the dirt.'

The main order of business was what to do with Germany. The precedent was straightforward: in 1871, after the Franco-Prussian War, France had had to pay a huge indemnity of 5 billion francs; now it was time for Germany to pay. Alsace and Lorraine had been ripped from France; now they would be returned. And the question of responsibility for the outbreak of war was to be answered in a very simple way: Germany was guilty.

The centrepiece of the treaty was Article 231, in which Germany accepted sole responsibility for the war and the damage it had brought about. The Kaiser was arraigned for crimes 'against international morality and the sanctity of treaties'; the convening of a war crimes trial was specifically designated in article 227. The five judges were to come from Britain, France, Italy, the United States and Japan. The trial never took place, but served as a precedent for the Nuremberg trials twenty-seven years later.

The second punitive feature of the peace treaty was embodied in the reparations clauses, requiring Germany to pay over thirty years from 1921 the expenses of the Allied army of occupation, the costs of restoration of the physical damage to Allied property, the losses in ships, and other penalties. The Allies gained control of German waterways, especially the Rhine, and exercised a lien on basic industrial output such as coal and steel. Effectively, the German economy was to bear both the direct and indirect costs of the war. It was a crippling burden, and intended as such. While Germany never fully paid off this debt, the effort ensured the economic instability of Europe in the first post-war decade.

The third punishment was the loss of German colonies, all renounced to the Allies. The fourth was a strict limitation on the size of the German Army. It was to be no larger than a hundred thousand men and four thousand officers; forbidden were conscription, traffic in arms, military schools, submarines and an air force. This edict released into the German body politic hundreds of thousands of

A meeting of heads of state, but not a meeting of minds, took place in London in 1918 when President Wilson paid a formal visit to King George v at Buckingham Palace.

disgruntled career officers with nowhere to go but the radical Right. In *Mein Kampf*, written in 1924–5, Hitler made it clear what the settlement meant to him: 'What a use could be made of the Treaty of Versailles.... How each one of the points of that Treaty could be branded in the minds and hearts of the German people until sixty million men and women find their souls aflame with a feeling of rage and shame; and a torrent of fire bursts forth as from a furnace, and a will of steel is forged from it, with the common cry: "We will have arms again!"'

The League of Nations

Wilson was not naïve about the nature of the settlement. To him it was a starting point, not a set of principles fixed in stone. To secure the peace, he aimed first and foremost at the construction of his League of Nations. Wilson himself chaired the detailed work on planning the League. Most of the preliminaries had been completed in the United States; consequently, Wilson was able to present the finished covenant of the League after only ten days, on 13 February 1919. It was adopted by the leading Allied nations, the Council of Ten, the following day.

Wilson's heart and soul were in this new instrument of international order and the principles it embodied. His colleagues had their eyes on other matters: European boundaries, colonial possessions and the vexed question of economic reconstruction, inextricably bound up with German reparations. They knew too that Wilson faced a very difficult battle to convince the United States Senate to accept the new League. Still, Wilson was adamant: on this issue he would not hear of compromise, either with his American enemies or his European Allies. Already during his return to Washington in February 1919 the President knew that the going was bound to be rough. On questions of foreign policy, many influential members of Congress were not of his persuasion.

Winston Churchill watching the march past of the 47th Division in Lille shortly before the Armistice. He personally led the charge against the Bolsheviks at the Paris negotiations, going far beyond his own government's position.

Soon the strain began to tell on Wilson. His confidant Colonel Edward House recorded this glimpse of the American President during the Peace Conference: 'March 22, 1919: The President looked worn and tired. . . . Rumblings of discontent every day. The people want peace. Bolshevism is gaining ground everywhere. . . . We are sitting upon an open powder magazine and some day a spark may ignite it.' Wilson gave ground on many issues. He let Clemenceau have his way on reparations and boundaries, but on the League he remained immovable. When the Peace Treaty was signed on 28 June 1919, at least on this issue he could rest content.

Russia

One matter on which President Wilson believed a solution was beyond his powers was the future of Russia. All the leaders at Versailles were hostile to the Bolshevik regime; they differed, though, over the question of how to contain or overthrow it. Wilson was very sceptical about the effect that Western forces could have on the situation in Russia. In contrast the British Minister of Munitions, Winston Churchill, was adamant on the need for military intervention.

Churchill the arch-opponent of Communism, the man who in Fulton, Missouri after World War II warned of an 'iron curtain' descending from Stettin in the Baltic to Trieste in the Adriatic, Churchill the Cold Warrior of the 1950s, is plainly visible in these deliberations. He had made his position clear time and again. After the Bolsheviks had sacked the British Embassy in Petrograd and killed a British naval attaché, Churchill called for the prosecution of the leaders of the regime. On the day before the Armistice, Churchill remarked: 'We might have to build up the German army, as it was important to get Germany on her legs again for fear of the spread of Bolshevism.' On 13 November, Churchill was part of a working party which renewed the Allied commitment to supporting anti-Bolshevik forces and to keeping Allied troops in Murmansk and Archangel. To his political constituents he was more lurid. 'Russia', he told them, 'is being rapidly reduced to an animal form of Barbarism. . . . The Bolsheviks maintain themselves by bloody and wholesale butcheries and murders carried out to a large extent by Chinese executioners and armoured cars. . . . Civilisation is being completely extinguished over gigantic areas, while Bolsheviks hop and caper like troops of ferocious baboons amid the ruins of cities and the corpses of their victims.'

Lloyd George, like Wilson, was sceptical about the use of Western troops in Russia. Churchill was their tireless champion. He told the Imperial War Cabinet on 31 December that, if they ignored the need to intervene in Russia, 'we should come away from the Peace Conference rejoicing in a victory which was no victory, and a peace which was no peace; and in a few months we should find ourselves compelled to gather our armies again. . . .' His friend Mary Borden heard Churchill and Lloyd George arguing about Bolshevism: 'Winston told LG one might as well legalize sodomy as recognize the Bolsheviks.'

The same division of opinion surfaced during the Peace Conference itself. Churchill was the champion of an anti-Bolshevik crusade versus the more cautious

Wilson, with Lloyd George on Wilson's side. On 14 February 1919, the Council of Ten tried to formulate a policy on Russia. The problem was timing: Wilson had to return to America that day to open the 66th Congress. When Wilson rose to leave at 6.30 in the evening, Churchill asked whether they might try to formulate a consensus while he was still in Europe. Wilson looked at his watch, and said that he had precisely twenty minutes to spare before proceeding by car to Cherbourg, where his ship was docked. He stood behind his chair, then sat down, and under these extraordinary conditions the leaders of the world addressed the Russian problem.

Churchill insisted that his government had to know then and there if the Allied Supreme Council had decided on its policy towards Russia. This was nonsense: Churchill simply wanted to force the issue to a head. Clemenceau, perhaps the most fervent anti-Bolshevik of them all, objected that this matter required considered discussion, not a *coup de théâtre*. Wilson was in favour of informal contacts with the Bolsheviks; he would not support continued military intervention. Allied troops still in Russia 'did not know for whom or for what they were fighting'; their presence was not helping to establish order. Indeed they were too small a force to act decisively, and sooner or later they would have to go. Why not now?

Churchill thought that such a step would be like 'pulling out the linch-pin from the whole machine', and would result in the execution of tens of thousands of opponents of the new regime. Would the Allied Council support the sending of volunteers and experts to Russia? Wilson replied that he didn't think such volunteers could be found, and that sending arms to the White armies would only 'support reaction', meaning a return to the monarchy. Still, he had no settled views on the matter, and would go along with the majority. The problem was that there was no clear majority view.

There the meeting ended and Wilson's voyage back to Washington began. Despite the absence of a decision, this was also the beginning of concerted efforts by the Allies to overthrow the Bolshevik regime. Churchill urged an ultimatum to the Bolsheviks: withdraw your forces deployed in western Russia and Poland, or face military action from the Allies. Clemenceau said that military plans should be prepared, but that he preferred to isolate the Bolsheviks behind a *cordon sanitaire*.

Over the next few days the discussion grew much more acrimonious. Lloyd George wired Churchill to say that his plan was not at all the policy of the British government, which aimed at military assistance for the Whites in terms of arms and money, but not in manpower. If the Russians wanted to overthrow the Bolsheviks, they would have to do it themselves. On 17 February, the shouting match which ensued among Allied delegates was so fractious that they decided to delete their deliberations from the official minutes. Churchill stuck to his guns; the American representative, Colonel House, said that the United States would never support military intervention in a country with which they were not at war. The result was an impasse.

The whole issue was sidetracked when, on 19 February, Clemenceau was wounded by an assassin's bullet. Rumour had it that the Bolsheviks were behind

Japanese, American, British and French sailors at Vladivostok were part of a larger Allied intervention force operating in Russia against the Bolsheviks during the Civil War.

the attack; nothing of the sort was true, but the incident kept the Russian question in the shadows of the Peace Conference.

Wilson too was struck down later in the spring, not by a bullet but by influenza. This debilitating breakdown was a premonition of a much more severe attack which incapacitated him six months later in October 1919. The downward spiral of his health and political fortunes had begun. He had a continuous twitch; he grew thinner and greyer, more short-tempered and tired. His aides urged him to take a break. He shook his head: 'We are running a race with Bolshevism and the world is on fire.' In April he had a fever and suffered headaches, coughing fits and diarrhoea. While he was recuperating, his staff urged him not to strain his constitution. 'Constitution?' he replied. 'I'm already living on my by-laws.'

Even when the health crisis had passed, many of his aides said he was a changed man. He thought the French servants around him were spies, and feared that his furniture was being stolen. He hectored the other delegates and ignored his own

Lloyd George, Georges Clemenceau and Woodrow Wilson a few days before they signed the peace treaty at Versailles on 28 June 1919. Striding into a very uncertain future, these men made a peace which was doomed from the start.

advisers. 'I never knew anyone to talk more like Jesus Christ and act more like Lloyd George,' said Clemenceau.

On 24 May the Allies agreed to approach one of the White leaders, Admiral Kolchak, with an offer of support should he agree to repay the huge debts owed by the old regime to Western (and in particular French) creditors. Lloyd George and Wilson had now swung around to the view that individual volunteers should go to Russia, and that the Allies should offer material assistance to the White armies. In the interests of discretion, however, these points were to be left out of the official communiqué. Hardly a policy, these measures were holding actions pending what the Allies mistakenly believed was the imminent collapse of the Bolshevik regime.

Instead, the Red armies managed to hold their own against all their adversaries. This led to an Allied reconsideration. On 17 June, this exchange took place in the Council of Four – the meetings of the major Allied heads of state – Clemenceau, Lloyd George, Wilson and Orlando of Italy:

> MR LLOYD GEORGE: If I believed we could crush the Bolsheviks this year, I would favor making a great effort in which the English and French fleets would participate. But Admiral Kolchak has just been pushed back 300 kilometres. One of his armies is destroyed. In this strange war taking place in Russia, each time one of the two adversaries is defeated, part of his troops go over to the other side.
> PRESIDENT WILSON: Undoubtedly, the people don't have much faith either in one party or in the other....
> MR LLOYD GEORGE: It seems that the military affairs of the Bolsheviks are well managed. But the observers who keep us informed say that pure Bolshevik doctrine is being increasingly abandoned, and that what is being established over there is a state that doesn't differ noticeably from a bourgeois state.
> M. CLEMENCEAU: Are you sure of the fact?
> PRESIDENT WILSON: It is perhaps too early to believe it, but that is bound to happen.

Wilson was wrong by precisely seventy years. But he was right in his uneasiness about Western military intervention in Russia. Its sole achievements were to deepen the paranoid strain in Russian foreign policy and to convince its leaders that Western military intervention was always just around the corner.

The aftermath

The Peace Conference ended on 28 June 1919 with the signing of the Treaty by German and Allied representatives. The tenor of the occasion was captured by a British diplomat, Sir James Headlam-Morley, who played a large part in the drafting of the Treaty and saw through the legal and diplomatic language to the hatred underlying it. He was struck by the way the Germans were treated. When the representatives of the victorious powers were all seated, he told a colleague in the Foreign Office,

> the German Delegates were brought in; they passed close to me; they looked like prisoners being brought in for sentence, but on the whole bore it very

well.... When the signing was finished, the session was closed, and the Germans were escorted out again like prisoners who had received their sentence.

Looking back, the whole impression seems to me, from a political point of view, to be disastrous. The one thing which was forced on one by the whole scene was that it was the revenge of France for 1871. It took place in a building which was really erected on the ruin and humiliation of Germany; it was also the room in which Germany, having won a victory, inflicted a great humiliation upon France; France now once more having got the upper hand was having her revenge for the injury done to her, and in every detail complied with the utmost insult to Germany, and it was merely an episode in the secular rivalry of two nations which has been the curse of Europe.... Just the necessary note of reconciliation, of hope, of a change of view, was entirely wanting.

This view was shared by many observers. The economist John Maynard Keynes resigned from the British delegation in protest against the harsh and unrealistic economic terms imposed on Germany. The Oxford historian R. G. Collingwood had worked in Admiralty Intelligence during the war. He noted that

the intensity of the struggle seemed to have undermined, as if by the sheer force of the explosive it consumed, the moral energies of all the combatants; so that (I write as one who during the latter part of the war was employed in preparations for the peace conference) a war of unprecedented ferocity closed in a peace-settlement of unprecedented folly, in which statesmanship, even purely selfish statesmanship, was overwhelmed by the meanest and most idiotic of passions.... Whether it was deliberately plotted by a ring of German war-lords, as some believed, or by a ring of English trade-lords, as others believed, nobody has ever supposed that any except at most the tiniest fraction of the combatants wanted it. It happened because a situation got out of hand. As it went on, the situation got more out of hand. When the peace treaty was signed, it was more out of hand than ever. ... I knew that for sheer ineptitude the Versailles treaty surpassed previous treaties as much as for sheer technical excellence the equipment of twentieth-century armies surpassed those of previous armies.

The new international system erected at Versailles was hopelessly flawed. The war had killed too many men and too many dreams. Whatever the rhetoric, magnanimity was out of place at Versailles. The politics of hatred prevailed.

The absence of any relationship between the enormity of the slaughter and the political settlement which followed it was recognized and captured at the time in an unusual way. William Orpen, an Irish-born artist, was officially designated by the British to paint the peacemakers. First he depicted a formal version of events. In *Signing of the Peace in the Hall of Mirrors, Versailles* we see the dignity of the victors in their official rococo splendour. Then he painted another picture encapsulating its mood and anticipating its consequences. In *To the Unknown British Soldier in France* we see the same scene stripped of the politicians and generals. All that is left is the Hall of Mirrors with the tomb of the Unknown Soldier, guarded by two odd sets of figures: a pair of British soldiers wearing only helmets, and a pair of putti above them.

The Irish-born British war artist William Orpen's painting *Signing of the Peace in the Hall of Mirrors, Versailles*. The German delegates are on one side of the table, the Allies are on the other. The American delegates are to the left of Wilson; the British, to the right of Lloyd George. Presiding is Clemenceau, finally able to expunge the humiliation of the capitulation of France to Germany in the same room in 1871.

That was the design; but Orpen had gone too far. He was forced to paint out the odd figures surrounding the casket. The result is a stately palimpsest, which today forms part of the collection of the Imperial War Museum in London.

Orpen had touched on a profound and unavoidable point. The men who divided the spoils bore no resemblance to the men who had won the war in the field. The politicians – called 'frocks' because of the capes that men like Lloyd George wore – were like vain vultures, circling slowly over the devastated landscape of post-war Europe. This is how Orpen put it:

> I admit that all these little 'frocks' seemed to me very small personalities, in comparison with the fighting men I came into contact with during the war. They appeared to think so much – too much – of their own personal importance, searching all the time for popularity, each little one for himself – strange little things. The fighting man alive, and those who fought and died – all the people who made the Peace Conference possible, were being forgotten, the 'frocks' reigned supreme. One was almost forced to think that the 'frocks' had won the war. 'I did this', 'I did that', they all screamed, but the silent soldier man never said a word, yet he must have thought a lot.

At the signing of the Peace Treaty itself on 28 June, Orpen noticed the caricatured postures of the men in power:

> All the 'frocks' did all their tricks to perfection. President Wilson showed his back teeth; Lloyd George waved his Asquithian mane; Clemenceau whirled his grey-gloved hands about like windmills; Lansing drew … pictures and

LEFT William Orpen, *To the Unknown British Soldier in France* (original version), 1922.
RIGHT William Orpen, *To the Unknown British Soldier* (altered version).

In 1919 Orpen was commissioned to paint a canvas to honour the burial of the unknown soldier in Westminster Abbey. He chose the same triumphal arch setting as in the *Signing of the Peace*, but destroyed its conventional aspect by adding two naked British soldiers and two putti behind the casket. Outrage ensued. Orpen painted them out, but they still are there, ghostlike presences, under the official varnish.

> Mr Balfour slept. The 'frocks' had won the war. The 'frocks' had signed the Peace. The Army was forgotten. Some dead and forgotten, others maimed and forgotten, others alive and well – but equally forgotten. Yet the sun shone outside my window and the fountains played, and the German Army – what was left of it – was a long, long way from Paris.

Orpen was right. The peace of Paris was no peace at all. None of the major issues out of which the war had come was resolved. Wilson, though, still had faith in the power of the new League of Nations to help strengthen and defend the peace. He left Paris the day after the signatures had dried on the peace treaty. In his diary one of Wilson's trusted advisers, Colonel House, mused:

> June 29, 1919: An effort was made to enact a peace upon the usual lines. This should never have been attempted.... It may be that Wilson might have had the power and influence if he had remained in Washington and kept clear of the Conference. When he stepped from his lofty pedestal and wrangled with representatives of other states upon equal terms, he became as common clay....
>
> To those who are saying that the Treaty is bad and should never have been made and that it will involve Europe in infinite difficulties in its enforcement, I feel like admitting it. But I would also say in reply that empires cannot be shattered and new states raised upon their ruins without disturbance.... And yet I wish we had taken the other road, even if it were less smooth, both now and afterward, than the one we took. We should at least have gone in the right direction, and if those who follow us had made it impossible to go the full length of the journey planned, the responsibility would have rested with them and not with us.

Wilson was more laconic. He told his wife, 'Well, it is finished and, as no one is satisfied, it makes me hope we have made a just peace; but it is all in the lap of the gods.'

To come into effect, the Treaty required the advice and consent of the Senate. However, the Treaty worried many senators, since it seemed to curtail their country's sovereignty. Isolationism was a strategy to protect US sovereignty over what a broad coalition of Americans saw as their vital interests, especially in the Americas. It was not just blindness, but a point of view integral to American history. In addition, many Americans had left Europe behind, both physically and politically, and in the ethnic patchwork of American politics their desire to break with the past could not be ignored.

There were other, more unsavoury, strands to the opposition to the Treaty. The campaign against was headed by a dozen isolationist senators who came to be known as the 'Battalion of Death'. Senator James A. Reed of Missouri objected to the League's multi-racial composition. 'This colored league of nations,' he said, was to be composed of fifteen white nations and seventeen of 'black, brown, yellow and red races, low in civilization and steeped in barbarism.' Senator Lawrence Y. Sherman of Illinois described the Treaty as 'a revolutionary document', since it was launching an institution whose members included seventeen Catholic nations but only eleven Protestant countries. How powerful a Pope did the world need?

But by far the most important problem for Wilson was convincing the Senate that he was not engaged in a compromise on long-standing principles of US foreign policy, such as the Monroe Doctrine, the nineteenth-century affirmation of American pre-eminence in the Western hemisphere. Some feared a superstate of League of Nations members. Wilson's attempts at persuasion fell flat. Senator Brandegee left Wilson one day, feeling 'as if I had been wandering with Alice in Wonderland and had tea with the Mad Hatter'.

The most dangerous opponent of the President was Henry Cabot Lodge of Massachusetts, chairman of the Senate Foreign Relations Committee. He forced the issue by insisting on amendments or reservations to the Treaty which would have effectively crippled it. Wilson took the issue to the people. He tried to bypass the Senate and mobilize popular opinion on behalf of the Treaty through a whirlwind speaking tour, covering 8000 miles in twenty-two days. Following him were two Republican opponents. But Wilson no longer had the stamina for such barnstorming. He cut short the tour and returned to Washington, a sick and broken man. On 2 October 1919 his wife found him on the bathroom floor; he had suffered a stroke and was paralysed on his left side.

It took the President six months to recover sufficient strength to attend a Cabinet meeting. Then he was even more unbending than before, instructing his supporters to vote against the Treaty if Lodge's reservations were the price. Duly, the Senate voted the Treaty down. When he was told by his physician of this monumental defeat, he replied, 'Doctor, the devil is a busy man.'

Henry Cabot Lodge, Senator from Massachusetts, like Wilson, a scholarly statesman. He was the man who led the opposition to Woodrow Wilson's campaign for ratification of the Treaty of Paris.

HUNGER

The Treaty of Versailles transformed the boundaries of central and western Europe. In the west, Alsace and Lorraine reverted to France. In the east, the creation of an independent state of Poland divided Germany and the Soviet Union. East Prussia was reduced to a small German enclave, surrounded by Poland on the west and south, and by the Baltic states of Lithuania, Latvia and Estonia to the north. The Austro-Hungarian Empire had given way to the independent states of Austria, Czechoslovakia, Hungary and a Serb-dominated Yugoslavia.

In southern Africa, the former German colonies of what are now Tanzania and Namibia reverted to Britain; the Cameroons in west Africa became French. In the Middle East, under League of Nations mandates, Britain controlled the newly-formed entities of Palestine, from the Mediterranean to the River Jordan, Trans-Jordan, all of what is now Jordan to the east of the River Jordan, and present-day Iraq. To the south-east of Iraq, the entirely artificial entity of Kuwait was set up on extensive oil deposits at the mouth of the Persian gulf, separate from those of Saudi Arabia to the south and Persia to the east.

These boundary changes did not diminish international conflict; on the contrary. Ethnic Germans were now Austrians, Czechs, Poles, and German nationalists wanted them back. That would come within twenty years. It took longer for the Middle East to explode, but the powder keg was set up in 1919–20 through the Treaty of Versailles. The map of political identities in the Balkans, now torn to shreds by the fragmentation of Yugoslavia, was also a product of the deliberations at Paris at the end of the 1914–18 war. What Versailles accomplished was to set the international political agenda for the century, not to change its bloody character.

Versailles didn't even stop the shooting in large parts of eastern Europe. And a natural concomitant of such profound instability was hunger.

Famine followed the war as night follows day. The victims were primarily in Russia. Given the chaos of the post-1917 period, it was not at all surprising that the new regime could not feed its population. What is more surprising is that, while American visions of a new post-war international order fell apart, the capacity of American power and wealth to help heal the wounds of war was demonstrated in a new and significant way – through famine relief.

The New Europe and the Middle East Mandates

- Lost by Russia 1918
- Lost by Germany 1919
- Former Austro-Hungarian Empire
- British Mandate 1920
- French Mandate 1920

The first food aid programme

The man who ran the relief effort was Herbert Hoover, American Food Administrator and entrepreneur *par excellence*. Hoover was no friend of the Bolshevik regime, but he took a subtler view of how to handle the situation than did Churchill. If the Allies could not bomb the Bolsheviks into submission, they could – in Hoover's view – be fed into a state of political moderation. Hoover's prime belief was that Bolshevism came out of hunger: remove that hunger and Bolshevism would shrivel and die. But even if this happy outcome were unattainable, at least the Allies could prevent millions from starving. Tendentious humanitarianism is one way to characterize his plan. This is how he put it to Wilson on 28 March 1919:

> Dear Mr President:
>
> As the result of Bolshevik economic concepts, the people of Russia are dying of hunger and disease at the rate of some hundreds of thousands monthly in a country that formerly supplied food to a large part of the world....
>
> It simply cannot be denied that this swinging of the social pendulum from the tyranny of the extreme right to the tyranny of the extreme left is based on a foundation of real social grievance.... Their courses represent the not unnatural violence of a mass of ignorant humanity, who themselves have learned in grief of tyranny and violence over generations....

Herbert Hoover, a decade before he became one of America's most vilified presidents. The firmness of his jaw, the clarity of his eye, showed a man who knew what he wanted and what to do to get it. The business-man's businessman, he epitomized American drive and go in the food relief effort of 1914–21.

Yes, said Hoover, the Bolsheviks could export their revolution. But what could the Allies do? Act as policemen for decades, and appear to work for the restoration of the old order? Recognition of the Bolshevik regime – 'this murderous tyranny' – was out; far better to feed the people.

And that is precisely what he did. Among those who benefited were the children of the western Ukrainian town of Pinsk, who spoke variously Polish, Russian, Ukrainian, Yiddish and even Hebrew. Together, they sent Hoover a book of thanks. Each page consisted of a class photograph, surrounded by drawings and the signatures of the children. The pupils of a Jewish school sent this Yiddish poem, written in the summer of 1921:

> *We Jewish children from Pinsk*
> *To you American brothers*
> *Let us all be happy.*
>
> *We are drinking your milk*
> *In our school kitchen*
> *Instead of alcohol and wine*
> *You should be healthy*
>
> *We thank you unceasingly*
> *For your help until now.*
> *And ask from the depths of our hearts*
> *Help us in our pain and suffering.*
>
> *Send us as much as possible*
> *From today onwards and beyond*
> *As quickly as possible*
> *Money to buy books*
>
> *For clothes, rice*
> *And other kinds of spice*
> *So that we should be able*
> *To learn Torah without fear.*

The children of another school in Pinsk – this one a Zionist school – stare out from their photograph, pioneer hats on their heads, preparing for a desert life. Their letter, written by their teachers in literary Hebrew, recalled the bloody pogroms which had broken out in Pinsk in 1919:

> *We, among thousands of children in a Europe soaked with blood,*
> *Children who were miserable orphans*
> *During a war in which all of Europe became a killing field,*
> *When everyone waited for death,*
> *Only through your help,*
> *Were we saved from death.*
>
> *We offer you, even in our sadness and despair,*
> *Our profound gratitude towards your great generosity.*
> *The American people, both Christians and Jews,*
> *Were among the only people ready to aid the needy and the desperate.*
>
> *History will not forget your deeds,*
> *And until the last generations,*
> *Your name will be blessed in prayer.*

The children of the Hebrew Technical School of Pinsk, Summer 1921

What became of these children is a mystery. Some emigrated to Palestine; others perished in the purges and persecution to come; some may still be alive today.

The story of their survival during the post-war famine in revolutionary Russia reveals another side of the aftermath of war, the side of compassion rather than embitterment, of helping hands rather than clenched fists. In effect, Herbert Hoover was the prime mover behind the first foreign-aid package in history. Its origins can be traced to the beginning of the war.

Before Russia came Belgium. There, thousands of starving children were trapped during the early days of the German occupation in 1914. Hoover – an orphan himself – broke through the bureaucratic tangle and, as a neutral, got food through the lines to the non-combatant population.

Over the next four years Hoover cajoled, bullied and charmed his way through the Allied blockade of Germany and the German occupation of Belgium to provide food for civilians. Operating as an industrial magnate with absolute authority, he bought ships, organized consignments and concluded agreements with governments as if he headed a state himself. The frequently irritated British Foreign Office agreed: Hoover, they said, was the head of a 'piratical state organized for benevolence'. He was given over $700 million in subsidies from Britain and France, and a further $50 million from private sources. Those too poor to pay received food free; those with means were supplied through their retailers, who paid slightly over cost price for American goods. In this way, and through sales to neutrals, the operation actually made a profit. The Committee

These schoolchildren from Pinsk in the Ukraine sent their photographs and signatures to Herbert Hoover to express their gratitude to him for providing them with food in the famine of 1921.

for the Relief of Belgium dispersed food worth over $880 million – a larger sum than the pre-war United States budget.

The food made a difference: how much is impossible to say, but there is no doubt that hunger, though a fact of life in wartime Belgium, did not turn into famine. Most of the credit belongs to Hoover. Belgian children showed their gratitude in ingenious ways. Some sent Hoover dolls; others embroidered bucolic scenes or flowers and stars on the food sacks that had been sent to them from the United States.

Three years later, Hoover's private initiative turned public. When the United States entered the war he was appointed Food Administrator, with the same latitude of action and sole authority as he had exercised in the Belgian mission. After the Armistice he assumed responsibility for US relief aid. He brushed aside Allied objections to his authority, and in 1919 alone organized the delivery of about 4 million tons of relief supplies to twenty-two nations in Europe.

One of Hoover's first tasks was to do something about 3 million forgotten men: Russian prisoners of war stranded in Germany and Austria after the Armistice. Many were starving and, according to Marshal Foch, the French commander of Allied forces on the Western Front, ripe recruits for the Red Army. Something had to be done. Hoover was again the man for the job, and succeeded in imposing some order on to the chaotic world of provisioning Russian prisoners before their repatriation.

Two years later famine returned to Russia. By 1921, drought had hit the Volga region. Hunger and mass flight ensued. Reports of cannibalism surfaced. A population of about 25 million was affected; perhaps 2 – 3 million died of hunger or disease. Lenin appealed for help from the working class of the West. 'The Soviet republic of workers and peasants expects that help from laboring people, from the industrial workers, and from small farmers.' Instead he got it from the

Belgian relief preceded Russian relief. These sacks of flour came from all over the United States and were shipped by Hoover's American Relief Administration to Antwerp during the German occupation of Belgium. Children decorated these sacks and sent them back as presents to Hoover.

man of drive and go, the capitalist's capitalist, Herbert Hoover. The intermediary between Lenin and Hoover was the Russian writer Maxim Gorky. Widely known in the West, Gorky enjoyed the confidence of Lenin without sharing his beliefs. On 13 July 1921 Gorky launched an appeal on behalf of the All-Russian Famine Relief Committee; it was Hoover who answered his call.

Hoover's organization was already feeding over a million children in Poland and western Russia; and by mid-1921 he was no longer a private citizen, but Secretary of Commerce in the Harding administration. This position enabled him to persuade doubters that food relief would help reduce American crop surpluses and thereby help American farmers: egotism and altruism combined. Hoover indicated to Gorky that American help was on the way. On 26 July Gorky told Hoover that the Soviet government had approved the plan. His brief was to feed a million Russian children a day. This food relief effort started in the late summer of 1921 in a kitchen in Petrograd, spread to a Moscow restaurant four days later, then reached out to the Volga region and even beyond the Urals. At its peak, the relief mission fed over 500 000 people a day in 3000 kitchens in 191 towns and villages.

'The finest palace in the world being put to its finest possible use,' was the way the American relief mission described its work in Tsarskoe Selo, the Tsars' palace just outside Petrograd. 'More than 2000 children receive a hot meal in the palace every day from gift money of the American people. American charity provides only the food. All of the necessary kitchens, warehouses, offices etc. are provided by the Soviet government.' These children were in better shape than those in more remote regions. Photographs taken by members of the American mission offer evidence of the appalling effects of the famine on them. Their gaunt faces and haunting eyes tell us much about the aftermath of the war, and their survival

LEFT Russian children wearing American shoes, photographed to demonstrate the effectiveness of American relief during the famine of 1921.

The Tsars' Summer Palace at Tsarskoe Selo was converted into an American Relief Administration feeding station for hungry children during the 1921 famine. Over 2000 children received a hot meal there each day.

attests to the success of an unlikely alliance between Lenin and the Bolsheviks on the one hand, and Herbert Hoover, the apostle of capitalism, on the other. Yes, Hoover wanted to end the Bolshevik hold on power, but he believed in the intrinsic value of the relief operation whatever the future of Soviet power. Lenin was aware of both the dangers and the benefits of the operation. It was more than worth the risks. Together with Hoover, he found a way to supersede suspicion and manipulation and to create the means through which millions avoided starvation. Perhaps the best way to summarize the American relief effort is to see it as calculation mixed with compassion. The compassion was real: this too was a legacy of the Great War.

8

WAR WITHOUT END

The Great War, a leap into the modern age, unleashed an avalanche of the unmodern. This paradox has given the twentieth century its characteristic form. The war accelerated the ascent to a world dominated by machines of unparalleled power, and at the same time precipitated the descent into a world of unparalleled brutality. The trajectory of human progress was fractured: technical change leaped forward yet political life moved backward into a new age of cruelty, made worse than the past by the new and more efficient machinery of degradation and death.

The recognition that something terrible, something overwhelming, something irreversible had happened in the Great War explains its enduring significance for those born after the Armistice. For this war was not only the most important and far-reaching political and military event of the century; it was also the most important imaginative event.

New identities emerged during the war: new nations, new commitments, new solidarities. The United States emerged as an economic world power, although for a generation it withdrew from the political responsibilities that followed industrial pre-eminence. The ideological conflict between Communism and capitalism came out of this war; so did the European state system, the boundaries of which were set at Versailles in 1919. Seventy years later, Communism as a political system collapsed. Germany was reunified, without threatening the peace of Europe. In the 1990s the national boundaries created after 1918 began to disintegrate, either through the centripetal pressures of the European Community or through the centrifugal pressures of ethnicity and nationalist movements.

The Great War established not only the political framework of our time, but also many of the fundamental assumptions to which we turn in trying to understand it. Above all it normalized collective violence, the signature of our century.

At some time between 1914 and 1918, virtually the whole world put on the clothes of war. In terms of outlook, of pessimism, of fear, few have completely shed them since. For war has entered our imaginations, our mental landscape, as a permanent feature of the world we inhabit, both the world we see, and the world of dreams and nightmares our desolate century has created.

RECKONINGS

The face of war was transformed during the Great War. Nineteenth-century frontal assaults by massed infantry made no sense against the twentieth-century weaponry, yet more than a million men died in the first year of the war before generals began understanding the new nature of war.

Even then the lesson was not entirely learned: not at Verdun, not at the Somme, not at Passchendaele, or not even in the last year of the war when a desperate German Army launched its final offensive in an effort to win the war before Germany collapsed. All these hideous failures help to account for the fact that the successful Allied offensive in the last months of the war has largely been forgotten. It was a remarkable achievement, but this military feat has been obscured by the shock of earlier offensive failures.

Those who had seen war for what it was knew that older romantic illusions about war were inadequate, absurd or obscene. In order to absorb the shock, language itself changed, taking a more terse and realistic tone.

It is not surprising, then, to know that the men who endured combat were no longer the happy warriors of nineteenth-century romanticism. In 1927 Philippe Pétain, the hero of Verdun, inaugurated the giant ossuary at Douaumont. It was, as Antoine Prost has put it, 'a kind of cemetery of cemeteries'. Pétain spoke of the common soldier of the Great War: 'We who have known him know that he is simply a man, with his virtues and his vices, a man of the people, to whom he remained attached ... to the circle of his family, to his workshop, his office, his village, to the farm where he grew up.' Doing his duty, 'he went up the line without enthusiasm but without weakness'.

This war democratized suffering. In most combatant countries, roughly 50 per cent of the male population between the ages of eighteen and forty-nine were in uniform. Nothing like this had ever happened before. France and Germany mobilized the highest proportion: about 80 per cent of men of military age were conscripted. Austria-Hungary mobilized 75 per cent of its adult male population; Britain, Serbia and Turkey called up between 50 and 60 per cent. In Russia, about 16 million men or 40 per cent of the male population between fifteen and forty-nine served during the war. In the United States, in the brief space of eighteen months about 4 million men, or roughly 16 per cent of the same age group, were in uniform.

Total casualties and losses as a proportion of those who served passed a threshold beyond previous experience: the total of roughly 9 million dead soldiers (according to varying estimates) constitutes one in eight of the men who served. Adding statistics on other casualties, roughly 50 per cent of the men who served were captured, wounded or killed.

Overall, the Western Front was the most murderous theatre of operations. But a higher proportion of those who fought on the Eastern Front died. There, disease and enemy action killed combatants with equal force. This was a nineteenth-century war waged with twentieth-century weapons. Of the Serbs who served in the war, 37 per cent were killed; roughly one in four Romanians, Turks and Bulgarians also perished. On the Western Front, where the war was won and lost, combat was perhaps only half as lethal: German and French losses were about one in six of those who served; British losses one in eight.

Another feature of total war may be more surprising. Initially, casualties among social élites were higher than among the rest of the population. The reason is casualties of officers who led from the front were significantly higher than those in the ranks – about 10 per cent of men in the ranks were killed; between 12 and 20 per cent of all officers perished. And who were the officers? Men from the upper and upper middle class, since social selection of the officer corps mirrored the inequalities in pre-war life. Consequently in the early stages of the war, the higher up the social scale a man was, the greater were his chances of serving as an officer and of becoming a casualty of war. But by 1917 these strata of society had been sufficiently reduced to require the armies to draw junior officers from wider social groups, still mostly middle-class but now from commercial or shop-keeping families. These groups in their turn suffered disproportionately higher casualties in the last two years of the war.

Homecoming, Australia, 1919. These women knew not what awaited them when their soldiers stepped off the troop ship bringing them home. Six thousand miles and many hardships separated them from their loved ones; bridging that gap would take years.

Among the poor and the underprivileged, the story is different. Pre-war deprivation saved the lives of millions of working-class men, whose stunted stature and diseases made it impossible for them to pass even the rudimentary standards of medical fitness for military service. In Britain, roughly 35 per cent of men examined for military service were either unfit for combat or unfit to wear a uniform at all. They were the lucky ones. Inequality was their salvation.

Broken faces, missing limbs

During and after the war the wounded were there – on street corners, in public squares, in churches. No village or town in Europe was without them. The French textile worker Mémé Santerre described her village in the north of the country:

> The agricultural laborers came back as amputees, blind, gassed, or as 'scar throats', as some were called because of their disfigured, crudely healed faces. We began to see more and more returning. What a crowd! What a rude shock at the railway station, where the wives went to meet their husbands, to find them like that – crippled, sick, despairing that they would be of no use anymore. At first, we had the impression that all those returning had been injured. It wasn't until later that those who had escaped without a scratch returned. But, like their comrades, they were serious, sad, unsmiling; they spoke little. They had lived in hell for four years and wouldn't forget it.

The wounded came in many forms: psychologically damaged men, men who suffered from illness contracted during the war, men literally torn apart. Among them were thousands of ordinary men afflicted with extraordinary wounds. These were the *gueules cassées*, men with broken faces. Estimates vary, but at least 12 per cent of all men wounded suffered from facial injuries, and perhaps one third of these were permanently disfigured. Since in Britain, France and Germany alone roughly 7 million men were wounded, about 280 000 disfigured men in these three countries returned home after the 1914–18 war. Not all were severely disfigured, but those who were could no longer look in the mirror: they had literally lost their identities. For these men, the road back to some semblance of ordinary life was tortuous.

Henriette Rémi was a French nurse who knew first-hand of their fate. In the spring of 1918 she visited a friend, an officer who had in his care a man with no face: 'He has only one leg; his right arm is covered by bandages. His mouth is completely distorted by an ugly scar which descends below his chin. All that is left of his nose are two enormous nostrils, two black holes which trap our gaze, and make us wonder for what this man has suffered? ... All that is left of his face are his eyes, covered by a veil; his eyes seem to see. ...'

The wounded man talked of home, where his mother and sister lived: '"I cannot see them, it is true, but they will see me. Yes, they will see me! And they will care for me. They will help me pass the time. You know, time passes terribly slowly in hospital. My sister is a teacher, she will read to me. My mother's eyes are weak; she can hardly read; she sewed too much when we were kids; she had to provide for us; my father died when we were little."'

The authorities at the hospital did not encourage family visits, which were

Two mutilated veterans. Compassion was not a casualty of the Great War. Much of the help and support amputees of the Great War received came from their fellow victims. They formed associations, pressure groups, mutual-aid societies, and through solidarity, brought back a sense of dignity to men on occasion shunned by polite society.

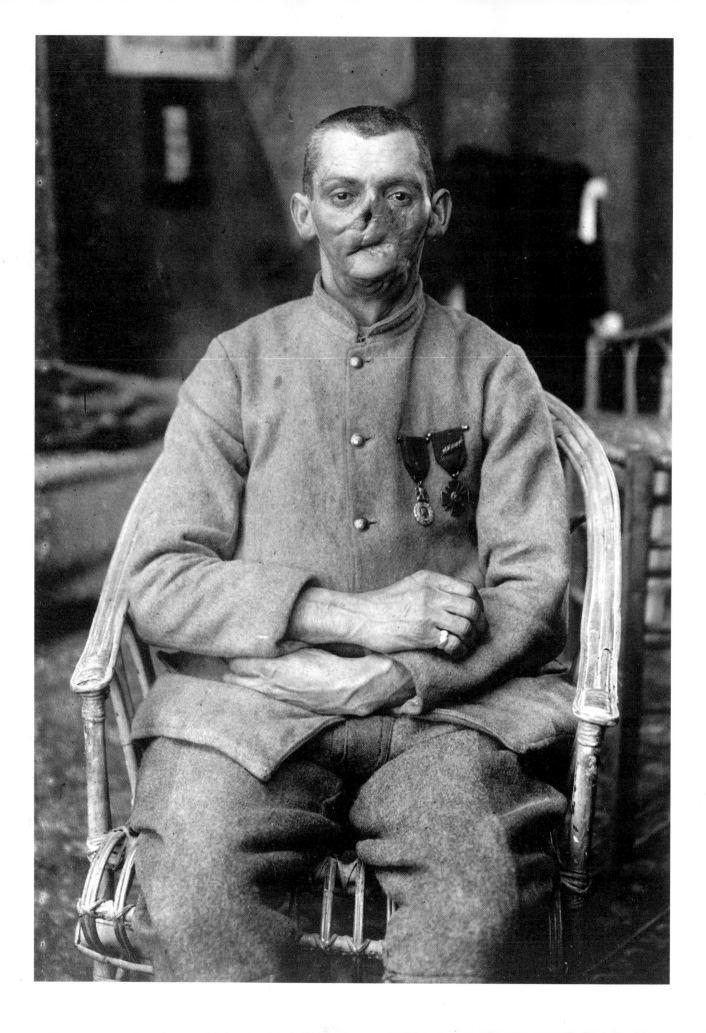

LEFT AND ABOVE The French called them 'the men with
the broken faces'. Some were rehabilitated slowly and painfully through
a series of plastic surgery operations. Others turned to prosthetic art.
This soldier jauntily smoking a cigarette had half his face restored
not through surgery, but through a skilfully sculpted mask.

potentially traumatic. But the time had come when this veteran would return to his family. He asked Rémi if they would recognize him. 'Certainly,' was her hesitant answer, hoping that if their eyes did not find the man, their hearts would. Then the sister came:

> A young woman, fresh, pretty, approaches quickly; she searches in the crowd for her brother. All at once, her face pales, an expression of terror forms; her eyes grow in fright, she raises her arms as if pushing away a vision of horror, and murmurs, 'My God . . . it's he.' A little further away, a woman in black, a bit bent, advances timidly, searching with an expectant smile. And in an instant, those poor tired eyes grow terrified, those tired hands raised in fear, and from this mother's heart comes the cry: 'My God . . . it's he.'

For this family, after the first shock of recognition the long journey towards recovery began. But others were not so fortunate. One man whom Henriette Rémi cared for was a Monsieur Lazé, a former teacher who was now blind. While recuperating, he was looking forward to a visit from his wife and small son Gérard, who had followed his father around on his last leave before being wounded. On Gérard's first visit to the hospital he asked the nurse if he could see his father, but was told it was not possible that day; the next day his father would come on a home visit. Sister Henriette agreed to accompany him. On the train, a child saw Lazé and asked his mother, 'What's wrong with that man?' Lazé replied: 'Have a good look, little one, and don't ever forget that this is war, this and nothing else.' From the station, he took his usual route home. His wife welcomed him at the door and called their son.

> Then the boy uttered a piercing cry: the boy shook. His father was shaken too, and stared at the floor. And Gérard turned and ran, much faster than he had come, crying in a loud voice: 'That's not Papa.' Lazé was desolate. His wife said: 'You've gone too fast; one must take precautions.'

At the other end of the garden, Gérard continued to say, 'That's not Papa.' Henriette tried to help.

> I approached him slowly, but Gérard didn't want to see me. He was shaking; better to leave him to his mother. He hid in her skirts. Lazé was rooted to the spot. He took his head in his hands and said: 'Imbecile, imbecile!' But how could I have known how horrible I am. Someone should have told me!'

Henriette agreed: 'Despair, shame, impotence shook me. Yes, he was right. At the hospital we had but one desire: to make them believe that they were not terrifying, and now look at the result.'

She took Lazé back to the hospital. Everyone told him that the child would forget, but he refused to believe them. He told Henriette:

> 'Having once been a man, having once understood the meaning of this word and wanting nothing more than just to be a man, I am now an object of terror to my own son, a daily burden to my wife, a shameful thing to all humanity.'

Another attempt to return home; another failure: again his son cries, 'That's

Max Beckmann, *The way home*, 1919. This lithograph is part of a searing cycle by Beckmann entitled '*Hell*'. Here Beckmann himself is asking a mutilated soldier the way home, as if there were no answer. Behind him under the street light stand the proverbial prostitute and two crippled soldiers. Hell indeed.

not Papa.' Lazé recoiled. 'It's finished. It's too late. I terrify him.' That night, back in hospital, Lazé committed suicide. He opened the veins in his wrist with his penknife.'

Other disfigured men and their companions succeeded in forming a new, collective identity. The Union of Disfigured Men (later the National Federation of Trepanned and Disfigured Men) was just one of a host of veterans' associations in post-war France, but it remained separate from the larger organizations – the disfigured had special problems of sociability which only their own association could address.

The idea was hatched by two disfigured men who had met at the Val-de-Grâce military hospital in Paris, and who invited all those whom they had known there to band together. Their first meeting was held on 21 June 1921, four years after other, inclusive groups of veterans began to create their own associations. Their leader, Colonel Picot, then aged fifty-nine, was a towering figure in the veterans' movement as a whole, but he always affirmed the special character of this association. Its members met at a banquet twice a year, and drew on each other's strength to face their terrible problems. In 1927 the association turned a country house with parkland at Moussy-le-Vieux, 25 miles from Paris, into a place where disfigured men could rest away from a still uncomfortable public. As Colonel Picot put it, it would be 'a place worthy of them, a château like those acquired by the men who got rich when we lost our faces'. Some men came for short stays; others for good. Their families were welcome too. All were invited to join in farming activities; even those who thought they were unemployable found work.

The presence of these victims was commonplace in the post-war generation. In Paris on Bastille Day, 14 July 1919, the crippled, the blind and the disfigured led the victory parade, creating an ambiance which converted celebration into sombre meditation. An entire industry grew to service the needs of men without limbs. In Britain, the money collected on 11 November each year in exchange for an artificial poppy went to the families of ex-soldiers in need. Some 80 per cent of the unemployed in the mid-1920s were ex-veterans; they were all in need. How much greater, then, the plight of those whose injuries would not go away.

Otto Dix

The German painter Otto Dix found such men everywhere in post-war Dresden. For four years he had served on the Western Front as an artilleryman and machine gunner, and at the end of the war he was training for the Air Force. He knew how a shell could tear a man apart.

Back in Dresden in 1920, he began painting grotesque images of the new German society. His *Match-seller* shows a blind and legless veteran, from whom all passers-by flee, trying to earn a living. In *Pragerstrasse* of 1920 (see p. 360), which Dix dedicated 'to my contemporaries', he showed a gloved hand depositing a postage stamp in the artificial hand of a paraplegic, while another disabled man rolls along on a board covering an anti-semitic pamphlet with the headline '*Juden raus!*' (Jews out!). One of his most celebrated collages, *Skat Players*, is a vicious satire of Cézanne's celebrated painting *The Card Players*. A man with no jaw, no legs and one arm, is dressed in the paper used for German clothes during and after the war. Another veteran plays a card with his toes; a third holds his card with his teeth.

In 1924, the German pacifist Ernst Friedrich opened an anti-war museum in Berlin, whose exhibits included photographs of horribly mutilated veterans. The caption under one of them read: 'In Germany alone there are still thousands of hospital inmates who are totally cut off from the world and drag on their existences far from their families and friends and relatives, in the hope that they may perhaps after years again acquire the appearance of human beings.'

Not surprisingly, the Nazis closed the museum down when they came to power in 1933. One of Dix's paintings caused a similar stir. *The War Cripples (with Self-portrait)* of 1920 showed all kinds of disability and deformity among ex-soldiers.

OPPOSITE Corporal Walter Briggs (RIGHT) of the Accrington Pals was killed on the first day of the Battle of the Somme. Among the effects returned to his family was a postcard (LEFT) sent to him by his fiancée Amelia. On the back of the postcard she had written a verse which begins:
'I'll never love another boy but you . . .'

In 1937, this painting was displayed prominently in the exhibition of 'Degenerate Art', a collection of those works which 'degraded' the notion of Germanness. The painting was destroyed, but the painter survived.

And so did the men whom Dix had depicted. The luckier ones carried on, and were paid pensions which varied according to the degree of disability and the generosity of the state. In France, the responsibility for proving that a disability was not war-related rested on the state; the men were initially given the benefit of the doubt. Not in Britain. There the burden of proof rested on the disabled man, and, if he died, on his widow.

Broken families

For some, the retrieval of family life was easy; for others, infinitely difficult. Throughout western Europe the divorce rate increased at the end of the war. Too many experiences had separated couples, some of whom had rushed to the altar in 1914 in an understandable wish to affirm life and imagine a future at a time of immense uncertainty. After 1918, when some saw the choices they had made and the people they had become, they parted ways. Coming home for

Tho' Far Apart To-Day We Be,
This Dainty Card I Send To Thee.

A.01.3

soldiers, maimed or whole, was a time first of relief, then of questioning. German and Austrian soldiers came home as defeated men, but even in Allied countries the tasks of demobilization and reintegration were formidable.

Everyone had lost someone, but the bodies weren't there; the wait for official notification of death was long and arduous. What did the army of widows do? After a period of mourning, the vast majority remarried and resumed ordinary life. This mundane reality contradicts one of the myths of the war: that it created a population of women who remained spinsters for life. Yes, the war killed millions of potential husbands, but it also stopped millions of others from leaving Europe, as they would have done given pre-war emigration trends. In addition, women started to marry men of their own age or younger, or from different towns and social classes. Adaptation meant that there was no long-term increase in celibacy on account of the war.

The resilience of the institution of marriage should not be surprising, since the fate of women who remained unmarried or widows was extremely difficult. In Germany at the time of the Armistice inflation soared and unemployment hit; in Britain and France, within two years there was mass unemployment in areas with industries such as textiles, which traditionally employed a large number of women. Staying single meant poverty or subordination to parents.

The First Man

Marriage was a means of survival. But for those who remained widowed, and who tried to raise children alone, the path ahead was difficult. The shattering effects of the Great War are well illustrated by the family life of the Algerian-born writer Albert Camus. Camus' father Lucien worked for a wine merchant, and the family was in an inland town in Algeria when his wife Catherine gave birth to their second child on 7 November 1913. The father was twenty-eight, the mother thirty-one. On the outbreak of war, Lucien sent his family back to the working-class quarter of Belcourt in Algiers and joined his unit of Zouaves, an Arab word for military recruits from North Africa. They wore baggy trousers and floppy berets in the North African style, and were considered fierce soldiers. The Zouaves were sent directly to Paris to stem the German advance on the capital. There, during the Battle of the Marne, Lucien Camus was hit by shell fragments. He was evacuated to a hospital at Saint-Brieuc in Brittany, from which he wrote reassuringly to his wife that he was recovering. Four weeks later he was dead. Catherine Camus received the official notification, followed by shell fragments removed from her husband's body. For the family, these relics were all that remained of Lucien Camus.

Catherine, who was deaf, took her two small children and moved in with her mother, a harsh Spanish-born domestic tyrant. Although she was able to lip-read, Catherine's speech became distorted and more limited. She worked in a cartridge factory during the war, and afterwards lived a passive existence of laundry work and obedience to her mother. A full four years after her husband's death she began to receive a widow's pension. No one at home could write to fill out the form, so the claim was made only when a neighbour helped.

Catherine Camus' young son Albert grew up in this household, with the

Lucien Camus (RIGHT) and Catherine Camus (BELOW) were poor French colonists in Algeria. Ten months after the birth of their son Albert in 1913, Lucien was conscripted and died of wounds suffered during the Battle of the Marne.

shadow of the absent father a constant, yet unknown, companion. There were no household documents, since no one could read; there were very few family stories, and only one or two pictures of the father, a postcard or two and the bits of metal that had killed him.

Throughout his life, Albert Camus searched to discover who his father had been. In 1953, at the age of forty, he made a pilgrimage to Saint-Brieuc in Brittany where his father lay. He found the grave in the military section of the St Michel Cemetery. In his last work, Camus tells the story through the voice of the hero, Albert Cormery, who reads the date:

> '1885–1914', and automatically did the arithmetic: twenty-nine years. Suddenly he was struck by an idea that shook his very being. He was forty years old. The man buried under that slab, who had been his father, was younger than he.
>
> And the wave of tenderness and pity that at once filled his heart was not the stirring of the soul that leads the son to the memory of the vanished father, but the overwhelming compassion that a grown man feels for an unjustly murdered child – something here was not in the natural order, and, in truth, there was no order but only madness and chaos when the son was older than the father.

Wandering around the cemetery, he saw other graves and 'realized from the dates that this soil was strewn with children who had been the fathers of greying men. . . .' He puzzled over who this missing father was, this 'younger father'. 'In a family where they spoke little, where no one read or wrote, with an unhappy and listless mother, who would have informed him about his young and pitiable father? No one had known him but his mother and she had forgotten him. Of that he was sure. And he died unknown on this earth where he had fleetingly passed, like a stranger'.

Could the son still discover the secret of this 'stranger's' life? All the son saw was the shadow of his father, like the 'light ash of a butterfly wing incinerated in a forest fire'. But even at the age of forty this orphan of the war 'needed someone to show him the way'. Without a father, he lacked a sense of heritage, of a past. He had 'never known those moments when a father would call his son, after waiting for him to reach the age of listening, to tell him the family's secret, or a sorrow of long ago, or the experience of his life....' Consequently, he – the son – had had to become 'the first man', and 'without memories and without faith' enter 'the world of the men of his time and its dreadful and exalted history'.

The 'dead stranger of Saint-Brieuc', the fallen soldier and father 'consumed in

Albert Camus (left) at the newspaper *L'Express*. A war orphan, Camus spoke out time and again on the moral issues of war.

374

a cosmic fire', was like millions of others. The war had created hundreds of 'new orphans each day, Arab and French', who 'awakened in every corner of Algeria, sons and daughters without fathers who would now have to learn to live without guidance and without heritage'. This is why 'war was the incubator of our era'. The war was everywhere: it was 'part of their universe and they heard about it all the time, it had influenced so many things around them that they had no difficulty understanding that you could lose an arm or a leg to it, and even that it could be defined as a time of life when legs and arms were lost'.

The mother of one of Camus' childhood friends worked in the laundry of a home for disabled men. The two boys would go there often, and to them 'the world of cripples was in no way sad'.

> Some of the men were closemouthed and somber, it is true, but most were young, smiling, and even joked about their disability. 'I have only one leg', one of them would say – he was blond, with a strong square face, and radiantly healthy; they often saw him prowling around the laundry – 'but I can still give you a kick in the ass', he would tell the children. And, leaning on the cane in his right hand, with his left hand on the parapet of the arcade, he would pull himself erect and swing his one foot in their direction. The children laughed with him, and then fled as fast as they could.

Some were lucky enough to come back unscathed. One, Camus' teacher when the boy was aged nine, was the most formative influence in the writer's life. Louis Germain was able to give children the sense that what they thought and felt mattered and that the world was there to be discovered. He also felt a special responsibility for war orphans like Camus. At the end of each term the teacher took up his copy of a war memoir, *The Wooden Cross* by Roland Dorgelès. There he read of the war and 'of a special kind of men, dressed in heavy cloth stiff with mud, who spoke a strange language and lived in holes under a ceiling of shells and flares and bullets'. Camus 'just listened with all his heart to a story that his teacher read with all *his* heart', a story of the war 'that cast its shadow over everything in the children's world'.

Germain helped to persuade Camus' mother and grandmother to let him stay at school, rather than leave and go to work, so that he could study for a scholarship enabling him to go to the *lycée*. They remained lifelong friends. Years later, Germain gave his gnarled copy of Dorgelès' war memoir to Camus, who, the teacher said, had earned it by the tears he had shed while the book was read aloud in a class in Algiers in 1922.

Camus was fortunate. He had had a surrogate father, a man who had suffered in the trenches and had retained the view that the 'generation of fire', the men of 1914, had a duty to raise the sons of their fallen comrades. He gave his pupil the belief that he could be more than a stranger, that he could find his way in a world disfigured by violence. Out of this war-torn environment Albert Camus created towering monuments to humanism, in prose which merited the Nobel Prize for literature in 1957. Camus died three years later, in a car crash. In the wreckage, the police found a large handwritten manuscript. It was the story of his search for his soldier-father, whose death in the Battle of the Marne had turned him, Albert Camus, into 'The First Man'.

Broken lives

After the Armistice, many spoke of a 'lost generation'. Some took it as a measure of the human costs of war, the vast loss of life, and the sense that the surviving generation was reduced not only numerically but qualitatively too. Others used the phrase to describe a group of writers on both sides of the Atlantic who sensed that in the shadow of the war they had lost their way, their moral bearings, and never fully found them again. But there was a third meaning too, more mundane but none the less important. Many served in the war and never put their lives together after it. This was due not to physical wounds, but to some sense of disintegration, of fragmentation. Such people were found in all combatant nations after the 1914–18 war, and some of them remained in the wilderness until the day they died.

One was T. E. Lawrence, known to posterity as Lawrence of Arabia, the leader of the Arab revolt of 1916–18 (see Chapter 3). After the war Lawrence spent his life in search of a name, an identity which could bring him peace. He never found it. Perhaps this would have been his fate, war or no war, but his story is not unique. For many, war was so indelible an experience that it could not be integrated into a post-war life. For such people war memories were crushing burdens, never losing their grip. Lawrence never escaped from his war experience, however hard or fast a life he led afterwards. In the aftermath of the war he was a man without a compass, a wanderer without a destination.

Part of the sense of alienation with which Lawrence had to live was directly related to his war service; part derived from his sense of betrayal by the British delegation at Versailles in 1919 of promises made to the Arabs during the war. In November 1917 Lawrence was liaison officer between the British forces in Egypt and Palestine and the Arab tribes in revolt against Turkey. Lawrence was arrested while in disguise, scouting out the defences of the Syrian town of Deraa. He tried to pass himself off as a Circassian, but the ruse failed: fluent Arabic couldn't hide his European features. He was then severely beaten and raped. Like many victims of rape, Lawrence felt the violation of his integrity for years afterwards. Some writers account for his aversion to physical contact of any kind by reference to this sexual assault. Marriage was unthinkable; loneliness unavoidable.

Severe bouts of depression dogged Lawrence for the rest of his life. Some occurred before the incident at Deraa, but many more seemed related to the shame, guilt and pain of the rape. But such shadows were but a specific form of a more general inability to forget. This is what he had in mind when he wrote to Robert Graves about their failure to get away from the terrors of the war. They could never say *Goodbye to All That*, the title of Graves' later war memoir; already in 1922 Lawrence wrote to Graves: 'What's the cause that you, and Siegfried Sassoon, and I . . . can't get away from the war? Here are you riddled with thought like any old table-leg with worms; [Sassoon] yawing about like a ship aback; me . . . finding squalor and maltreatment the only permitted existence; what's the matter with us all? It's like the malarial bugs in the blood, coming out months and years after in recurrent attacks.'

The second source of Lawrence's alienation from whom he had been and what he had done in the war may be traced to the Peace Conference of 1919. Lawrence

T. E. Lawrence crashed while riding this motorbike in 1935. He suffered brain damage and never recovered. The desert rider of the Arab revolt in the Great War had perished in a traffic accident after two decades searching for obscurity and peace. He found neither.

had accompanied Emir Feisal to France to take part in the deliberations. But from the beginning, it was apparent that allies in war were now to be reordered as either dominant or subordinate peoples. So much for Wilson's principle of self-determination. The Arabs were pawns again, and were to remain so. As Lawrence put it, the early months of 1919 were 'the worst I have lived through; and they were worse for Feisal'. Humiliation followed diplomatic slights: Feisal was to be an observer, not a representative, at the Peace Conference. As a French diplomat told him, 'You are being laughed at: the British have let you down.' The implication was that the French would be better allies. Feisal knew better. He replied: 'I have not come here to make bargains, but to impress on the world that we have not escaped from Turkey to enter a new servitude, or to be divided up. I beg to inform you that I revolted to be free and sovereign, and we will die for that principle.' Proud words, but such rhetoric carried little force. The Middle East had already been divided by a secret agreement in 1916 between France and Britain: the Sykes-Picot Pact. Arab freedom would have to wait.

Lawrence was disgusted. His words of comradeship and dedication were spoken in good faith, but they floated away when tested against the iron will of Lloyd George and Clemenceau. Lawrence had been used again; his integrity was once more broken. Even after a spell in 1921 as adviser on Arab affairs to Winston Churchill, then Colonial Secretary, he never lost sight of the promises broken, the faith not kept.

By then Lawrence's exploits in Arabia, as a British officer in flowing Arab robes sabotaging the Turkish war effort, had made him a celebrity. The terms of the peace settlement and British colonial policy embittered him and turned him into a man with a pathological hatred of publicity. It reminded him of who he had been and what he had endured. His aim was anonymity.

Here his war experience and his early life came together. He had learnt in his teens that he was illegitimate, as indeed was his mother. Having 'no name', in the Victorian sense of the term, he was free to shed the one by which the public knew him. He built a new life, in the Royal Air Force, as Aircraftsman First Class John Hume Ross. It didn't take long for the press to find out who he was, and the leak put the RAF in a difficult position. Lawrence was a decorated colonel: what the devil was he doing taking orders from junior officers on the RAF base at Farnborough? The solution was simple: Lawrence was discharged.

But his search for anonymity was far from over. This time he enlisted in the Tank Corps as a private soldier, under the name T. E. Shaw, found at random in the official list of those serving in the Army. Once more he went through the humiliations and rigours of basic training. Once more he tried to bury himself alive. To one Oxford friend, he mused that 'reason proves there is no hope'; anyone who hopes does so 'so to speak, on one leg of our minds'; 'perhaps', he wondered, 'there's a solution to be found in multiple personality'.

Another solution was in speed. He loved danger, and sought it out in many ways. One was on his motor-bike. He told a friend: 'When my mood gets too hot and I find myself wandering beyond control I pull out my motor-bike and hurl it at top-speed through these unfit roads for hour after hour. My nerves are jaded and gone near dead, so that nothing less than hours of voluntary danger will prick them into life. . . .' This was written by the author of *Seven Pillars of Wisdom*, the classic account of the revolt in the desert during the war. Written during 1920 – 2, it was revised and published in 1926 to become a best-seller in both Britain and America.

The greater the celebrity status, the greater the wish to fade into the background. Every time someone praised him to the skies, Lawrence shrank further into self-loathing. Why? Because 'I know the reverse of that medal, and hate its false face so utterly that I struggle like a trapped rabbit to be it no longer. . . .', or at least to 'shun pleasures', a partial 'alleviation of the necessary penalty of living on' – living on after the war; living on after his rape.

After the Tank Corps came more writing, followed by re-entry into the Royal Air Force. This time he tested speedboats, and found some quiet in the service. He even went so far as legally to change his name to Shaw. After twelve years in the RAF in Britain and India he tried to find solace in Devon, in a country house built to his specifications. But journalists still dogged his steps and stripped him of the tranquillity he so desperately sought. Lawrence still overshadowed Shaw. On 11 May 1935 he got on his motor-bike to send a telegram to another World War I veteran and writer, Henry Williamson, but never sent it. He swerved off the road and crashed to avoid hitting two cyclists on a country road. They were uninjured, but Lawrence suffered brain damage, went into a coma, and died on 19 May 1935, aged forty-six.

His was a broken life, undoubtedly, but one which said much about the profound difficulties of living as a survivor of World War 1. Lawrence, the artist who had created his own persona, constantly sought to escape the life he had lived and the romantic legend he embodied. That is why the RAF and its technical demands finally provided him with some degree of rest. As he told Robert Graves in February 1935, 'I went into the RAF to serve a mechanical purpose, not as a leader but as a cog of the machine. The key-word, I think, is machine. I have been mechanical since, and a good mechanic, for my self-training to become an artist has greatly widened my field of view. I leave it to others to say whether I chose well or not: one of the benefits of being part of the machine is that one doesn't matter!' The idealist, the crusader, the loner, the Victorian romantic hero, had finally found a home – one which enabled him to merge with machines of twentieth-century war. The Great War had finally claimed him, nineteen years after the Armistice, as one of its own.

Pilgrims

When T. E. Lawrence died, a monument was carved for his tomb by one of his friends, Eric Kennington, who had been an official war artist. The stone showed a crusader knight, recumbent. This medieval memorial captured much about Lawrence and even more about the aftermath of the Great War. A man who had embraced speed, machines and an anonymous career in the armed services was remembered as a solitary individual, a soldier of the truth, who in his own way had made his pilgrimage to the holy land. The old and the new, the archaic and the modern, merged in this work of art, as it did in the war as a whole.

Memorial card for an Australian soldier killed at Gallipoli and (OVERLEAF) bones at Gallipoli.

Gallipoli was sacred ground to Australians and New Zealanders, and soon after the Armistice, the bones of Allied soldiers were gathered and cemeteries built. But for most families in the Antipodes, visiting the cemetery of men killed in the war was out of the question. Instead they could apply for a photograph of the grave, providing a photographic homecoming to those buried half-way around the world from their homes.

There was nothing sacred about asphyxiating after a gas attack at Ypres, or being buried alive at Verdun, or being riddled with machine gun bullets on the Somme. Soldiers knew that; so did their families, and yet after the war virtually everyone tried to make sense of the carnage and the suffering in terms of older images of sacrifice. This was Christianity without the churches, an attempt to find some semblance of the sacred by travelling to the places where millions had died.

Pilgrimage is hard; it entails sacrifice, financial or physical. Pilgrims seek a goal, and offer their effort – even their lives, if need be – to reach it. After 1918, thousands of pilgrims engaged in an act of symbolic exchange. The dead had given everything, but what could the living offer? Pilgrimage was therefore an attempt to repay in part a debt that could never be discharged. The British journalist Stephen Graham went back to the battlefields in 1921. First he saw the effort to gather the dead in cemeteries. The exhumers did their job in a work-manlike fashion, remarking on oddities: the British dead kept longer than the Germans; those buried in oilskins remained intact. Then, like Hamlet, Graham picked up some remains in a field near Ypres: 'Lying in an old trench behold a skull! It is clear and polished – a soldier's head, low and broad at the brows, high at the back. There is a frayed hole in an otherwise perfect cranium.... The more you look at the skull the more angry does it seem – it has an intense eternal grievance. This one does not grin, for the mouth has been destroyed. It is just blind and senseless for ever and ever.' The dead challenged the living there, where the killing took place. 'There is a pull from the other world, a drag on the heart and spirit. One is ashamed to be alive.'

By 1922, the war cemeteries were completed. The Americans repatriated most of their dead, but for the British, French, Germans, Italians, Austrians, Australians, Russians, New Zealanders and many others the dead remained near where they had fallen. To this day pilgrims go to these sites of memory, and recall how and with what carnage the twentieth century began.

Visitation

The guilt of the survivors was palpable. Among the ways in which it was reduced or resolved was another kind of pilgrimage – from the dead to the living. Seances were conducted in every combatant nation. One of those who spoke out about the ways in which the dead returned to comfort the living, to help them let go and continue their lives, was the writer Sir Arthur Conan Doyle.

The creator of Sherlock Holmes, the ultimate rationalist, Conan Doyle was hit hard by the war. He was too old to fight, but he lost his son, Kingsley, his brother and his brother-in-law. The first to fall was his wife's brother, killed at Mons in 1914. Conan Doyle's son, a medical officer, was wounded while serving on the Somme and died of pneumonia in London in 1918. His brother, a staff officer in the 24th Division, also died in the last months of the war. In addition a bridesmaid at Conan Doyle's wedding, who had been a nanny to the family, lost three brothers in 1915. She claimed to be able to bring back messages from her dead brothers. Apparently her voice was fundamental in finally dispelling the lingering scepticism that Conan Doyle had had since his days at medical school about the possibility of communication with the dead.

French tourists visiting a battlefield of the Western Front. Pilgrimages
to battlefield sites took place while the war was still going on.
Visits were restricted, since bodies were scattered everywhere,
and unexploded bombs were a menace. After 1922, cemeteries
were delineated, and families could retrace the steps of their
loved ones. For many these sites were all that remained of them.

The Conan Doyle family attended seances during which he was able to reach his son. Through a 'Mrs B', Kingsley asked his parents for forgiveness and offered them consolation. Whatever had happened in the war, 'in any case he would not have stayed in England, as he had intended to go abroad in the medical services'.

Conan Doyle and his wife attended a more unusual seance at Portsmouth in September 1919. On this occasion the medium Evan Powell, a Welsh spiritualist from Merthyr Tydfil, spoke through his 'control', a Red Indian spirit named Black Hawk. The message was the same: Kingsley asked for forgiveness and said he was happy. Conan Doyle's brother also appeared to the couple in a seance: the spirit regretted not the fact of his death, but rather that he had died before seeing the Allied victory at the end of the war.

This was the characteristic form of the seance: the dead appeared to comfort the living. These were necessary acts to expiate the guilt of survival through the

Sir Arthur Conan Doyle in 1921 at the grave of his brother Innes, at Hals in Belgium. Innes had died of pneumonia on 19 February 1919.

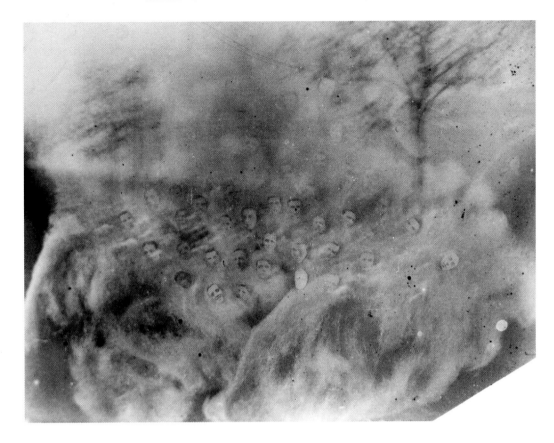

Mrs Ada Emma Deane took this photograph of a miasma of the spirits of dead soldiers coming to join the living during the two-minute silence on 11 November 1923. They are near the Cenotaph in the heart of London. Spirit photography flowered among the millions looking for solace during and after the war.

voices and presence of those who had died. Such rituals of separation were unavailable in the established Churches, most of which found Spiritualism repugnant and regarded it as either witchcraft or blasphemy.

Some Spiritualists were unbalanced; others were charlatans. Most were honest true believers. Their activities were controversial and occasionally bizarre, but the social and intellectual prominence of leading Spiritualists, as well as the widespread belief in the paranormal among soldiers, made it difficult to brush them aside simply as crackpots.

To be sure, some were out for the money. The business of psychic photography had started before the war, but had a special market during and after it. Mrs Ada Emma Deane was a charwoman from Islington, then one of London's poorer districts, whose brother, a chemist, set her up in a lucrative profession. She offered the credulous visions of the dead on Armistice Day, hovering above the living. One such photograph was taken from the wall of Richmond Terrace in Whitehall during Armistice Day in 1923. The photographic plate was given to her by Mrs E. W. Stead, whose late husband had been a well-known journalist and radical Spiritualist who had gone down with the *Titanic* in 1912. The plate was exposed throughout the two-minute silence, then developed in a dark room at 5 Smith Square, a half-mile away, in the presence of Mrs Stead. The inchoate mass floating above the heads of the mourners was flecked by faces, presumably of the dead. Similar photographs taken by Mrs Deane show other extraterrestrial presentations on Armistice Day. One was at the town hall in Woolwich, a London suburb with strong Army connections, where the dead, oddly, are at right angles

to the living. The tricks of her trade were never exposed, and she swore to the truth of her craft. A profitable business ensued.

Before we sneer at these and other photographs as hoaxes to dupe the gullible, it is important to note how widespread was the interest in psychic photography, and how many people of different social positions, levels of education and political beliefs were prepared, at least for a moment or two, to suspend disbelief about it. In this way the dead momentarily 'visited' the living and 'helped' them cope with the emptiness of loss.

Commemoration

In the decades after the war both nations and communities erected war memorials. At national monuments and at crossroads and in market squares, on 11 November each year the survivors gathered, their thoughts drifting back to another time and another place. Like the tombs of unknown warriors, under the Arc de Triomphe in Paris, in Westminster Abbey in London and Arlington National Cemetery in Virginia, these places are symbolic graveyards, for most of the dead are miles away, buried – as Stephen Graham had seen – not far from where they had fallen.

Some pilgrims were lucky enough to go further, to the place where their sons, husbands, fathers, lovers, friends, companions or workmates lay. The story of the pilgrimage of one mother and father to their son's grave stands for millions of others.

In August 1932 a war memorial was unveiled at the Roggevelde German war cemetery, near Vladslo in Flemish Belgium: a sculpture of two parents mourning their son, killed in October 1914. It is the work of Käthe Kollwitz (see p. 8). There is no more moving monument to the grief of those who lost their sons in the war than this simple stone sculpture of two parents, on their knees, before their son's grave.

There is no artist's signature, no location in time or space – only the universal sadness of two aged people, surrounded by the dead 'like a flock' of lost children. The phrase is Käthe Kollwitz's own. The story of her struggle to commemorate her son's death testifies both to her humanity and to her achievement in creating a timeless memorial, a work of art of extraordinary power and feeling.

Kollwitz was only able to complete the memorial eighteen years after her son's death, which alone should tell us something about the process of bereavement described so movingly in her diary and in her work. That process was in no sense unique. Kollwitz was haunted by dreams of her son, and felt his presence in the same way that other bereaved parents did throughout the world. She spent hours sitting in his room. In October 1916, she wrote in her diary that 'I can feel Peter's being. He consoles me, he helps me in my work.' She rejected the idea of spirits returning, but was drawn to the 'possibility of establishing a connection here, in this life of the senses, between the physically alive person and the essence of someone physically dead'. Call it 'theosophy or spiritism or mysticism' if you will, she noted, but the presence was there none the less. 'I have felt you, my boy – oh, many many times.' Even after the pain of loss began to fade she still spoke to her dead son, especially when working on his memorial.

What gives Kollwitz's mourning an added dimension was her sense of guilt,

of remorse over the responsibility of the older generation for the slaughter of the young. This feeling arose from her initial apprehensive but positive reaction to Peter's decision to volunteer. Her vision was internationalist, and hostile to the philistine arrogance of official Germany. But, as she said time and again, she believed in a higher duty than mere self-interest, and had felt before 1914 that 'in the back of the individual life ... stood the Fatherland'. She knew that her son had volunteered with a 'pure heart', filled with patriotism, 'love for an idea, a commandment', but still she had wept bitterly at his departure.

To find, as she did later in the war, that his idealism was misplaced, that his sacrifice was for nothing, was difficult for many reasons. First, it created a distance between her and her son. 'Is it a break of faith with you, Peter,' she wrote in October 1916, 'if I can now see only madness in the war?' He had died believing; how could his mother not honour that belief? But to feel that the war was an exercise in futility led to an even more damaging admission − that her son and

The Berlin artist Käthe Kollwitz (LEFT) spent eighteen years creating a war memorial for her son Peter, who died in Belgium in 1914. The sculptures (illustrated on p. 8) were unveiled in the cemetery where he lay in 1932. Twelve years later, Käthe Kollwitz's grandson, also named Peter (RIGHT), died on active service in Russia. The shadow of war accompanied her to her death in 1945.

his whole generation had been 'betrayed'. This recognition was painful, but when she reached it in 1918 she did not flinch from giving it artistic form. This is one reason why it took so long for her to complete the monument, and why she and her husband are on their knees before their son's grave. They are there to beg his forgiveness, to ask him to accept their failure to find a better way, their failure to prevent the madness of war from cutting his life short.

At Roggevelde, on their knees, Käthe and Karl Kollwitz suggest a family which includes us all. And that may be precisely what she had in mind: the most intimate here is also the most universal. In a powerful sense, this memorial in a German war cemetery is a family reunion, a foretaste of what her broad religious faith suggested would happen at some future date. The sense of completeness, of healing, of transcendence is transparently present in her moving account of her last visit to the memorial. She was alone with her husband: 'we went from the figures to Peter's grave, and everything was alive *and wholly* felt. I stood before the woman, looked at her – my own face – and I wept and stroked her cheeks. Karl stood close behind me – I did not even realize it. I heard him whisper, "Yes, yes." How close we were to one another then!'

This pilgrimage helped to heal one set of wounds just as another cruel period was about to begin. We shall turn to the Nazis, true children of the Great War, in a moment. For Käthe Kollwitz, the war they unleashed brought still more suffering to her life. Her work was derided, but she was left alone by the Nazis. Her husband died in 1940. Her grandson Peter, named after his uncle who had died in Belgium in 1914, was killed on the Russian Front in 1942. The next year, she had to leave Berlin due to Allied bombing: her house and much of her work was destroyed on 23 November 1943. If World War I had blurred the distinction between civilian and military targets, World War II erased it. 'Carpet bombing' of cities became an ordinary event. 'It is almost incomprehensible to me', Käthe Kollwitz wrote, 'what degrees of endurance people can manifest. In days to come people will hardly understand this age. What a difference between now and 1914. . . . People have been transformed so that they have this capacity for endurance. . . . Worst of all is that every war already carries within the war which will answer it. Every war is answered by a new war, until everything, everything is smashed.'

In the spring of 1945, Kollwitz knew she was dying. 'War', she wrote in her last letter, 'accompanies me to the end.' She died on 22 April 1945, two weeks before the end of World War II.

DESCENT INTO DARKNESS

The Age of Iron

One of the tragedies of the Great War is that, despite all the suffering it had entailed, war simply begat another war. The descent to an even more murderous conflict had begun shortly after the Armistice. The fusion of war and revolution in Russia was repeated in Germany, only in reverse: this time war and counter-revolution were joined in a murderous embrace.

In Germany, virtually all political parties objected to the harsh terms of the Versailles settlement with which the new Weimar regime had been saddled. The economic instabilities of the post-war period made many seek extreme solutions. The Communist Party fought the National Socialist (Nazi) Party on the streets as well as in the political forum. When the world economic crisis hit in 1930, the centre of German politics could not hold.

Five months after Käthe Kollwitz made her final visit to the memorial to her son at Roggevelde, the Nazis came to power. Eleven million people had voted for them in the general election of November 1932. And while the Nazi share of the vote had dropped from its July 1932 peak of 37 per cent to 33 per cent in November, they had received more votes than any other party. Conservative politicians gave Hitler a chance to rule. In an entirely legal manner, on 30 January 1933, the leader of the Nazi Party, Adolf Hitler, was named Chancellor by another old soldier, Paul von Hindenburg, President of the Weimar Republic.

Two old soldiers, a general Ludendorff (left) and a corporal Hitler (right), were among millions of Germans convinced that their country did not lose the war, but was betrayed by its own civilians. When, in 1933, the former commander, Paul von Hindenburg, then President of the Republic, appointed Hitler Chancellor of Germany, the party of revenge had won.

The Nazi takeover was democratic. Hitler took office by the book and then tore it up. There were many sources of his support, but one in particular relates to the Great War. It was the appeal of Hitler and the Nazi Party to men whose lives were defined by war – who were, in a sense, war incarnate.

One was Rudolf Höss. Born to a devout Catholic family in the west of Germany in 1900, Höss was a lonely child who developed a lifelong fascination with and love for natural landscape. He had a special fondness for farm animals, and pined for them when his family moved to the city of Mannheim in 1906. His parents gave him a pony: 'I had a comrade at last.' Höss recalled: 'My father had taken a vow that I should be a priest, and my future profession was therefore already firmly laid down. I was educated entirely with this end in view. My father brought me up on strict military principles.' Höss's father fascinated his son with stories of earlier military service in German East Africa, and the prospect of missionary work there sprang to young Höss's mind. But above all, he was taught respect for authority: 'It was constantly impressed upon me in forceful terms that I must obey promptly the wishes and commands of my parents, teachers and priests, and indeed of all grown-up people, including servants, and that nothing must distract me from this duty. Whatever they said was always right. . . . These basic principles on which I was brought up became part of my flesh and blood.' Duty seemed a substitute for ordinary affection, which his parents never displayed to him or to each other, and which he was never able to express to his two younger sisters. His sense of isolation was increased when details of his bad behaviour, revealed to his priest in the confessional, went straight back to his father, who punished his son for not telling him in the first place. Höss stopped going to confession, but feared taking Communion without first confessing his sins. When nothing happened at Communion, his religious faith was 'shattered'. In 1914, his father died.

When the war came, Höss, still a schoolboy, became a Red Cross auxiliary. It wasn't the suffering which made the deepest impression on him, but the camaraderie of the lightly wounded men. 'I never tired of listening to their tales of the front and of their first-hand experiences. The soldier's blood that ran in my veins responded. . . . I wanted to be a soldier. I was determined at all costs not to miss this war.' His mother insisted that he finish school, but to no avail. 'I often hid in troop trains, but I was always discovered. . . .' In 1916, he got his wish and joined the 21st (Baden) Regiment of Dragoons. 'After a short period of training I was sent to the front, without my mother's knowledge.' He never saw her again, for she died in 1917.

Still under sixteen, he was sent to Turkey and then to the Mesopotamian desert where he received his baptism of fire. When a British force attacked, the Germans' Turkish allies panicked and ran, leaving Höss and a few men isolated. He felt horror at the sight of a dead comrade, but had his will strengthened by the example of his captain standing firm and returning enemy fire. 'At that a strange calm descended on me too, such as I had never before known.' He killed his first enemy soldier, an Indian. But such blood-letting was not what mattered: it was bonding with his officer, his 'soldier-father'. At seventeen Höss became the youngest non-commissioned officer in the German Army.

War service was the formative moment of Höss's life. He had become, in his own words, 'a tough and hardened soldier'. He had taken on dangerous missions – sabotage behind enemy lines – and at the Armistice decided to return home with 'undefeated' men. From Damascus he led a group of older men through Anatolia, then across the Black Sea on a tramp steamer, through Romania to the Transylvanian Alps *en route* to Hungary, Austria and eventually back to the regimental depot in Baden-Baden. Their arrival was greeted with bewildered amazement.

Not only did the German empire for which Höss had fought no longer exist: with his mother dead and his sisters now at convent school, his home had been divided among relatives. In anger he told his uncle that now he had no intention of becoming a priest. Instead he set out to join the Freikorps or auxiliary troops being formed in central and eastern Germany, ostensibly to help restore order during the uprisings of 1919. Höss was there because the Army was the only home he knew.

The unit he joined, the Freikorps Rossbach, named after his leader, saw action in the Baltic, in parts of Silesia (now in Poland), around Berlin and in the Ruhr

Rudolf Höss (extreme right) showing his boss, Heinrich Himmler (second from left), around construction at the complex of Auschwitz-Birkenau. Part munitions factory, part death camp, Auschwitz was built for an Aryan future. After the extermination of Jews and Poles, Auschwitz was to be the centre of a new, German industrial region.

valley. This military unit was composed of a motley collection of veterans, students and others who simply liked the smell of blood. Emile Rossbach himself recalled nostalgically the days of

> the beautiful old Freebooter class of war and post-war times … organizing masses and losing them just as quickly, tossed this way and that way just for the sake of our daily bread; gathering men about us and playing soldiers with them; brawling and drinking, roaring and smashing windows − destroying and shattering what needs to be destroyed. Ruthless and inexorably hard. The abscess on the sick body of the nation must be cut open and squeezed until the clear red blood flows. And it must be left to flow for a good long time till the body is purified.

This was the man whom Höss followed, and who later became a central figure in the early Nazi movement.

Like many other volunteers, Höss had found his calling. Another volunteer, Heinz Oskar Hauenstein, also a non-commissioned officer, caught the mood well. 'Fighting was the whole content and meaning of their lives,' he wrote. 'Nothing else made any sense. … It was battle alone that they loved … the battle that was hard, brutal, pitiless.'

The face of the Freikorps, or auxiliary soldiers of the early Weimar Republic, was the face of the German radical right, proud, defiant, contemptuous of those too weak to stand up for their country and trample on its enemies.

Solidarity was everything, and betrayal was punishable by death. In May 1922, a former schoolteacher named Kadow was accused – without the slightest evidence – of having been a Communist spy in the Rossbach group. A few days before, one of their comrades had been arrested by the occupying French Army and condemned to death; Höss and his friends smelled a rat. They seized Kadow and beat him with clubs, slit his throat, and then finished him off with two bullets. At their trial, Höss kept silent. While he hadn't pulled the trigger, he still approved of the deed. He shielded the real killer, who got off scot-free. On 15 March 1924, Höss was sentenced to ten years' imprisonment for the murder.

Höss was shocked: he had thought his comrades would rescue him, or that the trial would never take place. But his trial opened after Adolf Hitler had attempted to seize power in a bungled *putsch* on 9 November 1923. The result was a sentence of hard labour that Höss initially had to serve in solitary confinement. He then became a model prisoner, and served as clerk in the prison stores. Following an amnesty of political prisoners on 14 July 1928, Höss was released. He had served four years.

Höss then went to Berlin, but was bewildered by the metropolis. Although, through his Freikorps associates, he had joined the Nazi Party in November 1922, he did not immediately seek a life in the party. He agreed with its ideas, but not with its vulgar 'tone'. Instead, he wanted to be a farmer. He joined the *Artamanen*, an association of nationalist pioneers on the land, spouting phrases about the purity of German soil and making life impossible for Polish migrant workers.

Then the Nazis came to power. A year later, in 1934, Höss was invited to join the *Schutzstaffel* (ss), the highly disciplined security police. 'The temptation of being a soldier again was … too strong.' The land had to wait. The leader of the ss, Heinrich Himmler, was also a member of the *Artamanen* and singled out Höss for special work. This led him to concentration camp administration, first as a corporal in the camp at Dachau, outside Munich, in November 1934. Höss was squeamish about seeing prisoners whipped. Despite his participation in the Kadow murder, Höss was no sadist: he was addicted to obedience, not bloodshed.

Pity for the enemies of the regime behind bars was also not in his nature. 'Any show of sympathy would be regarded … as weakness which they would immediately exploit.' On the other hand, he was concerned to provide one central activity to break the monotony of prison life: work, manual labour, the kind that to Höss gave each day its meaning. After all, he had been a prisoner himself and knew the pressure of time on a man's mind. This is why in later years, as commandant of Auschwitz, he placed over the entrance to the camp the banner 'Work Brings Freedom'. Freedom from emptiness, madness or total despair is what he really meant.

Transferred to the concentration camp of Sachsenhausen near Berlin in August 1938, he was able to see old friends from the Freikorps. They were all over the state apparatus: one in the Nazi youth organization, another in public relations for Alfred Rosenberg, the party's race 'theorist', a third in the Reich Chamber of Medicine, a fourth on the liaison staff of Rudolf Hess, third in line of succession in the party after Hitler and Hermann Goering, a World War 1 Luftwaffe ace.

All these old soldiers provided Höss with the camaraderie that gave his life form and meaning.

On the outbreak of war in 1939 Höss was in Sachsenhausen, and as head of the commandant's staff he was responsible for executing a Communist prisoner who had refused to carry out air-raid precautionary work in a factory in Dessau. Höss himself delivered the *coup de grâce*. This was the first of many executions which he carried out.

Among the prisoners supervised by Höss in Sachsenhausen was another Freikorps veteran, the former U-boat commander Martin Niemöller (see p. 134). He too had had a religious upbringing. He too had joined the paramilitary to fight Communism in 1919. He too had worked on the land, but had then decided – as Höss had not – to study for the Church. Niemöller had voted Nazi three times, but in 1936 he broke with his old comrades and their new leader. Niemöller had incurred Hitler's wrath by objecting to the Führer's face to the imposition on the Prussian Lutheran Church of a Nazi-appointed bishop. Niemöller had said that the Church belonged to God, not to the party. He was arrested, and given special prisoner status at Sachsenhausen. On the outbreak of war he asked for permission to volunteer for naval service, but was refused. Höss 'had many and searching discussions with Niemöller' before the pastor was transferred to Dachau in 1941. Like Höss, Niemöller survived the war.

Höss's next assignment was his most important. He was to head a newly built camp at Auschwitz. Recent research has shown that Auschwitz was never intended to be only a death camp. It was the embryo of a future German industrial centre, the factory-base of an area which the Nazis intended to resettle with Germans after not only the Jews but also the Poles would be exterminated. First came the killing, then the Aryan future. A maze of factories was set up, most of which used slave labour for munitions production.

But at the heart of Auschwitz, the assembly line also led to the gas chambers. There emerged one of the icons of the twentieth century: a factory of death on a scale and in a manner never before known. And over it all presided Höss, the bureaucrat *par excellence*, the party loyalist whose dedication to duty was iron-clad. He was the perfect agent of total war: an industrial killing machine requiring remarkable powers of organization and the deadening of any human feelings for the 'inputs', millions of men, women and children, who turned into 'outputs', stripped, gassed and turned into smoke and ashes. The British novelist Martin Amis has captured this project succinctly. The Nazis, he has written, found the reptilian heart of man and built an autobahn to get there. The man who helped build and maintain the autobahn, the man who ran what he called 'the Jewish Action' in Auschwitz, was Rudolf Höss.

Höss was an anti-semite, dedicated to the elimination of 'Jewish supremacy'. But he found the more vulgar forms of Nazi propaganda distasteful. Hatred was not part of his nature or his task, but systematic killing was. So was the conversion of Jewish possessions – including gold teeth and hair – into wealth after the Jews were killed. The order to Höss to prepare the killing machine came directly from Heinrich Himmler, head of the ss. As Höss had learnt from his father in childhood, from his commanders in World War 1, and from his Freikorps and

'Arbeit macht frei' ('Work brings freedom') is the message that greeted the millions of people brought to the gates of Auschwitz. Höss knew what prison meant: boredom, fear, despair. He used this phrase not cynically, but as a symbol of the religion of obedience he clung to throughout his life.

Nazi colleagues, life had only one meaning: obedience to authority. And obedient he was.

From February 1942, first in Auschwitz (until September 1943) and then in the office of the Inspectorate of Concentration Camps, Höss oversaw the murder of approximately 6 million people. After his capture in 1945, Höss himself provided an estimate of the total: 2 million in his time in Auschwitz alone. The numbers meant nothing to him, but by then his inhuman approach to killing had inured him from feeling anything about the individual murders he witnessed.

At the end of the war, he followed Himmler's order to drop out of sight, taking on a false identity and becoming a farmer. But on 11 March 1946 he was arrested, and according to his own account his interrogators got him to admit his identity by flogging him with his own whip. Eventually he was handed over to the Poles to go on trial for war crimes in Cracow. The verdict was death.

Millions of men had served in the German Army in both world wars without committing crimes against humanity. What the 1914–18 war did was to make those crimes possible. The war opened a doorway to brutality through which men like Höss willingly passed. To them, the war and the revolutionary upheaval that followed it were a training course in mass violence and male comradeship.

Women and children arriving at Auschwitz in 1944. One million Jewish children perished in the Nazi extermination camps. Most were killed quickly with their mothers and old women, directed to the gas chambers almost as soon as they had left the cattle cars that had brought them to Auschwitz and other death camps. Other children somehow survived in the camps. Their drawings and toys are all that remain of the light that was snuffed out in this age of darkness.

One of the icons of the twentieth century, the gas chambers at Auschwitz, brings us to the limits of language, perhaps to the limits of human reason itself. Hell came to the surface in Auschwitz and left a taste as of ashes for all of us who live in its shadow.

Höss was the perfect functionary of the time of total war, a man of mechanized discipline whose thirst for approval placed the principle of obedience above human life itself. The son of a devout Catholic, the soldier of World War I who had followed pilgrims to Jerusalem during his active service in the Middle East, had wound up presiding over a new kind of hell. He was hanged at Auschwitz on 16 April 1947.

The Age of Ice

War and revolution left a lasting legacy of brutality and violence in Russia as well. No observer of the Bolshevik revolution and its aftermath has captured its tragedy better than the poet and novelist Boris Pasternak. Born in a Jewish family in 1890, of artistic parents, Pasternak, like many other assimilated Jews, was both an outsider and an insider in his society. The name Pasternak means 'parsnip', echoing the humiliations of generations of Jews whose names were given them by their Christian overlords. In fact, the Pasternaks were only allowed to live in Moscow after 1891 because they had had higher education; uneducated Jews were evicted. For good measure, his nanny had him baptized. But instead of reacting to the anti-semitism endemic in tsarist Russia by flirting with Zionism or Marxism, Pasternak threw himself into music, philosophy and, above all, poetry.

Like many successful middle-class families, the Pasternaks had a *dacha* or summer home south-east of Moscow. There in 1903 Boris had a riding accident and broke his thigh bone, which never healed properly. The result was a lifelong limp, which probably saved his life: he was rejected for military service not only before the war, but during both the 1914–18 and 1941–5 conflicts.

A true European, Pasternak studied philosophy at Marburg in Germany and was as much at home in *Hamlet* as in the verse of his idol, the poet

Rainer Maria Rilke. The family was on a visit to Berlin in 1914 when the war broke out, 'in the last summer when life still appeared to heed individuals, and when to love anything in the world was easier and more natural than to hate'. A stunned Pasternak returned to Russia and placed the blame on the Germans and their 'inhuman act of banditry' unique in history. Banditry was contagious, as Pasternak soon learned. Anti-German riots led to a fire in which he lost most of his books and papers.

Although unfit for the Army, Pasternak still found a way to serve. He took a job in a chemical plant near the Urals, where his responsibility was to process exemption forms for workers in the district. He saw the disintegration of the last years of the tsarist empire, the 'abyss which is opening up between the cheap politics of the day and what is just around the corner'. A 'new era', he told his parents on 9 December 1916, was on the way. 'God grant it be so. One can already feel its spirit.' The old order was an 'absurdity', which 'will just break off at one of its absurd links when no one expects it to'. The times were dark, but the new day was dawning: 'it is seeking *us* out and tomorrow or the next day it will flood us with light'.

It was in this spirit that Boris Pasternak greeted the downfall of the Tsar two months later. 'Just imagine', Pasternak remarked, 'when an ocean of blood and filth begins to give out light.' This mood was similar to the early period of the French Revolution, which Pasternak thought of using as the setting of a never-completed novel. Only much later, in his masterpiece *Doctor Zhivago*, published in 1957, did he convey fully the effervescence of the spring and summer of 1917, the moment of hope before the Age of Ice set in.

Initially, he viewed the Bolshevik seizure of power not as a break with the earlier phase of the revolution, but as its continuation. The October revolution, he wrote, was an act of 'genius', 'splendid surgery' to 'cut away all the old stinking ulcers!' This is not the conviction of a party activist, but of a Russian moralist who saw the revolution as an expression of national character. 'This fearlessness, this way of seeing the thing through to the end, has a familiar national look about it', is the way Zhivago put it in the novel.

If only time had stopped, the white heat of the revolutionary moment would have fulfilled many of Pasternak's hopes. But as soon as revolution turned into civil war, and as soon as the brutality of the time turned into a way of life, the revolution turned cold, with 'its pitiless remedies invented in the name of pity'. It is this transformation to which Pasternak gave timeless formulation in *Doctor Zhivago*, a work of art about the opening of the Age of Ice presided over first by Lenin, then by Stalin, and extending even to our own times.

The horrors of Stalinism were partly due to the war and civil war, and partly due to the deformation of the state under the dictatorship of the Communist Party. First came the war, and its continuation after the Armistice. Pasternak gives voice to this argument through his heroine Lara, reflecting on a life of unhappiness:

> I believe now that the war is to blame for everything, for all the misfortunes that followed and that dog our generation to this day. I remember quite well how it was in my childhood. I can still remember a time when we all accepted

the peaceful outlook of the last century. It was taken for granted that you listened to reason, that it was right and natural to do what your conscience told you. For a man to die by the hand of another was a rare, an exceptional event, something quite out of the ordinary run. Murders happened in plays, newspapers and detective stories, not in everyday life.

And then there was the jump from this calm, innocent, measured way of living to blood and tears, to mass insanity and to the savagery of daily, hourly, legalized, rewarded slaughter.

Then came hardships. 'In the days of the triumph of materialism, matter had become an abstract concept. Food and firewood were replaced by the problem of food and fuel supplies.' Pasternak knew this well: he suffered from Spanish flu in 1918 and from deficiency diseases later. '*Nowadays*', one of Pasternak's poems has it, '*the very air breathes death: / Why, opening windows is like slitting veins.*' Typhus was everywhere, with sleighs bringing the dying into Moscow. In the novel, Yuri Zhivago treats its victims.

Then came the civil war, and more shortages. By late 1918 there was 'less and less revolutionary intoxication', but there was 'so much severity that people seem to age from week to week'. Shootings, arrests and requisitioning all reduced daily life to rudimentary proportions. 'We were the music in the ice,' Pasternak bitterly observed of the intellectuals and artists, those whose hopes were trodden on by the new regime and its interminable proclamations, so remote from reality. On 6 April 1920, Pasternak wrote to a friend: 'Here Soviet rule has gradually degenerated in a sort of philistine, atheistic almshouse with pensions, rations and subsidies . . . it is a perfect asylum for orphans. They keep people starving and make them profess their lack of faith as they pray for salvation from lice. . . . There it is. Was this worth all the fuss and bother?' His fate was to live through 'an epoch of shades', as he wrote in his poem 'Malady Sublime'. Bureaucrats, informers and police spies proliferated. All of them shouted:

> *Wake up poet, and show your permit.*
> *This is not the place for yawning.*

Trotsky himself quizzed Pasternak on why his verse had so little social content. The true answer – that he was a free spirit and his very freedom had precious social content – was unutterable at the time. Instead, he lived under the dictatorship of officially sanctioned greyness, under the gaze of what his fellow poet Osip Mandelstam called 'the age's sickly eyelids'. In 1925 Pasternak poured out his heart to Mandelstam about their fate. They lived at a time when 'Everything is corroded, broken, dismantled; everything is covered with hardened layers of insensitivity, deafness, entrenched routine. It is disgusting. . . . The premise of the extraordinariness of the age has been dispelled.'

By then Stalin had come to power, two years after Lenin's death in 1924. Lenin had warned his colleagues of Stalin's darker side, but his chief rival, Trotsky, failed to strike against him. The result was the isolation and expulsion of Trotsky, the man who had created the Red Army in 1918 and ensured the survival of the revolution. Trotsky became a non-person, a demon, the repository of unlimited hatred to Stalin and his thugs. To ensure the continuation of the dictatorship

The poet Osip Mandelstam defied Stalin to arrest him for denouncing the inhuman nature of the regime. Stalin obliged. Mandelstam died half mad near Vladivostok in 1938.

Stalin visiting Lenin in 1920. Lenin never recovered from the attempt on his life in 1918 by Fania Kaplan. In his declining years, he began to fear what his regime would become under men like Stalin. No stranger to terror, Lenin still placed the revolution first. To Stalin, who came to power two years after Lenin's death in 1924, terror was everything.

Stalin invented all kinds of internal conspiracies, aided by external enemies. He used the precedent of Allied intervention to show that it could happen again. Killing led to killing, and the orgy of murder itself re-created the lie that purges were needed to stabilize the regime. 'I kill therefore I am' was the summary of Stalin's rule, a time showing the terrible meaning of the normalization of violence after World War I.

What could poets do? Mandelstam, in an attempt to save some bank clerks falsely charged with sabotage, sent a volume of his poetry to the Kremlin with a note: 'Every line in this book argues against what you are planning to do.' He had the mad audacity to take a public stand. Pasternak was equally distraught, but expressed his views privately. He wrote to his cousin Olya, 'As you know, the terror has started again.' What had occurred under the cover of civil war in the early 1920s was now resumed under the cover of extirpating internal sabotage. Now Stalin turned the instruments of terror within, and waged a war against his own people.

No one who has lived outside such a world of terror can judge the compromises and silences of those who did. The charismatic poet Vladimir Mayakovsky began to preach the virtues of ideologically sound (that is, Stalinist) poetry. Pasternak never endorsed such nonsense. He had met Stalin, who left an indelible impression on him. To him the dictator was a kind of Georgian version of Richard III, 'the most terrible creature he had ever seen, a crab-like dwarf with a yellow, pockmarked face and a bristling moustache'. When Mayakovsky committed

Boris Pasternak's life and art bridged the years between the Great War and the Terror of the 1930s and beyond. His poetry and prose described the astonishing capacity of the human spirit to dream and to love, even in the midst of a political nightmare seemingly without end.

suicide in 1930, Pasternak was in an exposed position: the most celebrated poet in Russia on a collision course with the regime.

The first struggle was over Mandelstam. He had had the nerve to declaim to friends a short satirical poem on Stalin:

> *His fingers are as fat as grubs,*
> *And the words, final as lead weights, fall from his lips,*
>
> *His cockroach whiskers leer,*
> *And his boot tops gleam.*
>
> *Around him a rabble of thin-necked leaders –*
> *Fawning half-men for him to play with.*
>
> *They whinny, purr or whine*
> *As he prates and points a finger,*
>
> *One by one forging his laws, to be flung*
> *Like horseshoes at the head, the eye or the groin.*
>
> *And every killing is a treat*
> *For the broad-chested Ossete.*

No one could miss the last reference to Stalin as a man with origins in the southern Russian regions of Ossetia and Georgia. When Mandelstam recited this lethal ditty on the street, Pasternak said he hadn't heard it and Mandelstam hadn't said it. Stalin, though, had heard it, through informers, and phoned Pasternak to ask his opinion of Mandelstam's poetry. Pasternak didn't know what to say, and remained tongue-tied. Stalin hung up, and Pasternak for years regretted his silence. Mandelstam was sentenced to three years in exile. On his return he got in touch with Pasternak, who saw him not at home – too dangerous a venue for them all – but at the railway station. There they talked of poetry. In May 1938 Mandelstam was arrested again and sentenced to five years in a labour camp. He died within six months, starving and half-mad. Pasternak also begged Stalin for clemency – this time successfully – for an art historian who was living with the poetess Anna Akhmatova. Throughout, he had to contend with barbed threats from the conformists, the time-servers and informers who sniped at him and other poets. As he told his cousin Olga Freidenberg in 1936, these 'miserable and completely cowed nonentities' couldn't bear hearing 'someone asserting that the greatness of the Revolution lies precisely in a person's being able at a time of revolution – *especially* at a time of revolution – to speak out freely and think daringly'. Instead the hacks cried 'counter-revolutionary', which under the circumstances of Stalin's rule could and did lead to a bullet in the neck.

By the late 1930s the torrent of killings and disappearances had reached its peak. The official organization of Soviet authors, the Writers' Union, did its bit for Stalin by writing to him demanding the death sentences for old Bolsheviks, who were framed in ludicrous show trials. Pasternak's name appeared on the appeals, but probably against his will. 'Everything snapped inside me in 1936 when all those terrible trials began, instead of the cruelty season ending as I had expected it would in 1935.' The 'cruelty season' had begun much earlier, and was to last another twenty years. It went on despite the terrible sacrifices made to defeat the German Army after its invasion in 1941. It went on after the war was over, and continued in the last years of Stalin's mad rule until his death in 1953.

In those terrible years, Pasternak saw human life reduced to mere pebbles, to be picked up by the dictator and crushed at will in his hands. In 1956, when Stalin had been dead three years, he placed his grief in a poem offered to the dead:

> *In an age of ice*
> *like a conscience it stands,*
> *a wall where ashes end*
> *and the dead rest in peace.*
>
> *It bows to the ground*
> *under their agony,*
> *smells of dust and decay,*
> *the morgue and the grave mound.*
>
> *My soul full of pain*
> *heard all and saw all*
> *and remembered well*
> *and ground all into grain.*
>
> *Pound, compound and smash*
> *all I witnessed in tears*
> *for nearly forty years,*
> *to compost and to ash.*

In the small village of Sailly-Saillisel, near the front lines of the battlefields of the Somme, there is a war memorial: a statue of a woman, holding her husband's empty greatcoat, at his grave. That is all that he left behind. In later years the names of those who died in the Second World War, civilians and soldiers alike, were added to the monument. The loneliness, the cruelty, the sadness of thirty years of war, is frozen here in stone.

He pounded these thoughts too into *Doctor Zhivago*, the epic story of war without end. Begun in July 1946, and published only in November 1957, this novel brought Pasternak the opprobrium of the Soviet regime and the award of the Nobel Prize for literature in 1958, a year after Camus had been similarly honoured. Both men were children of the war, in the sense that their adult lives were shaped by the conflict and its aftermath. There are hundreds of references in the novel to the deforming effects of war and civil war on Russian life, but one metaphor stands out. On the very first page of the novel, when the ten-year-old child Yuri Zhivago is standing by the grave at his mother's funeral, 'He raised his head and, from his vantage point, absently surveyed the bare autumn landscape and the domes of the monastery. His snub-nosed face was contorted. He stretched out his neck. If a wolf cub had done this it would have been obvious that it was about to howl. The boy covered his face with his hands and burst into sobs.' The novel is the story of this boy's life, his maturation through the revolution, his work as a doctor in the civil war, his being taken hostage by partisans, and then freed to live for a brief period with the woman he loves in a house in Siberia. There he pens some of the finest poetry in Russian or any other language, the 'Lara poems' named after his doomed lover – doomed because her husband, Strelnikov, a Red Army commander, is on the run and his enemies are using Lara as bait to catch him, so she can't stay long with her lover Zhivago. For a short while they create an island of humanity in the midst of the forest, surrounded by wolves.

What better metaphor for the challenges of this war-torn century? How do we survive and love in a world with wolves everywhere? Zhivago found an answer in art, in the poems he wrote to Lara and for them both. Millions of others, perhaps less gifted and less courageous, faced the same separations and sacrifices. Once war had been transformed from a limited clash of arms to an entire way of life, the decencies of civil society, of art and its healing power, became vulnerable indeed. Pasternak died in 1960 – the same year as Camus' fatal car crash. They had much in common; victims of war and violence, they cried out against them both. They are among those who stood by art, who asserted human values even in the face of extinction, and in so doing stood by us all.

NOTES ON SOURCES

Introduction

P. 9   'Your pretty shawl . . .' Hans Kollwitz (ed.), *The Diary and Letters of Kaethe Kollwitz*, trans. by R. and C. Winston (Evanston, Ill., Northwestern University Press, 1955), p. 146 (hereafter *Kollwitz Diary*)

P. 9   'There is in our lives . . .' *Kollwitz Diary*, entry for 11 Oct. 1916, p. 74

P. 9   'I will come back . . .' *Kollwitz Diary*, entry for 25 June 1919, p. 92

P. 9   'In the fall . . .' *Kollwitz Diary*, entry for 22 April 1931, p. 119

P. 9   'Her work was exhibited . . .' *Kollwitz Diary*, entries for 1 June, 4 June, 23 July and 14 Aug. 1932, pp. 120–2

P. 10   'This earthquake ended . . .' Eric Hobsbawm, *The Age of Extremes, The Short Twentieth Century 1914–1991* (London, Michael Joseph, 1995)

1 EXPLOSION

P. 15   'Of the 70 million men . . .' J. M. Winter, *The Great War and the British People* (London, Macmillan, 1986), ch. 3

P. 15   'When he received . . .' See Pierre-Jakez Hélias, *The Horse of Pride. Life in a Breton Village*, trans. and abridged by June Guicharnaud (New Haven, Yale University Press, 1978), p. 56 (Paris, Plon, 1975), pp. 8–9, and Jean Giono, *Le grand troupeau* (Paris, Gallimard, 1931), p. 41

P. 15   'held up . . .' Jean Giono, *To the Slaughterhouse*, trans. by N. Glass (London, Peter Owen Publishers, 1969), pp. 61–3

P. 16   'The war has spared me . . .' Erich Ludendorff, *My War Memoirs, 1914–1918*, 2 vols (London, Heinemann, 1929), vol. 11, pp. 483, 602

P. 16   'On Sunday . . .' Roy Jenkins, *Asquith* (Oxford, Oxford University Press, 1960), pp. 414, 415

P. 17   'We are simply . . .' Philipp Witkop (ed.) *German Students' War Letters*, trans. by A. F. Wedd (London, Methuen, 1929), pp. 7–9

P. 17   'This is the day . . .' Joseph Cohen, *Journey to the Trenches. The Life of Isaac Rosenberg. 1890–1918* (London, Allen & Unwin, 1976), p. 174

P. 18   'We were lying . . .' Harold Owen, *Journey from Obscurity. 111. War* (Oxford, Oxford University Press, 1968), pp. 198–201

P. 19   'They had received . . .' Ibid.

P. 19   'Berlin turned from . . .' J. M. Winter and J.-L. Robert, *Paris, London, Berlin. Capital Cities at War, 1914–1919* (Cambridge, Cambridge University Press, 1996), ch. 2

P. 22   'The Wright brothers . . .' Stuart Hughes, *Consciousness and Society* (Cambridge, Mass., Harvard University Press, 1964)

P. 22   'He first served . . .' Ester Coen, *Umberto Boccioni* (New York, Metropolitan Museum of Art, 1988)

P. 22   'We intend to sing . . .' J. C. Taylor, *Futurism* (New York, Museum of Modern Art, 1961), pp. 124–5

P. 23   'The auditorium erupted . . .' Modris Eksteins, *Rites of Spring. The Modern in Cultural History* (New York, Bantam Books, 1990), p. 38

PP. 23–5   Ludwig Meidner. On Meidner, see Richard Cork, *A Bitter Truth. Avant-garde Art and the Great War* (New Haven, Yale University Press, 1994), pp. 12–15; Carol S. Eliel, *The Apocalyptic Landscapes of Ludwig Meidner* (Munich, Prestel, 1991), and Eliel, 'Les paysages apocalyptiques de Ludwig Meidner', in *Figures du moderne. L'expressionnisme en Allemagne, 1905–1914* (Paris, Musée de l'art moderne de la ville de Paris, 1991). All citations of Meidner's writing and that of his circle are from Eliel, *The Apocalyptic Landscapes*

P. 25   'The people . . .' and 'End of the World' Both Heym's and Hoddis' poems are in M. Hamburger and C. Middleton (eds), *Modern German Poetry* (New York, Grove Press, 1964)

P. 25   'The apocalypse was . . .' J. M. Winter, *Sites of Memory, Sites of Mourning. The Great War in European Cultural History* (Cambridge, Cambridge University Press, 1995), ch. 6

P. 25   'A great destruction . . .' See Sixten Ringbom, *The Sounding Cosmos. A Study of the Spiritualism of Kandinsky and the Genesis of Abstract Painting*. Acta academiae Aboensis, Ser. A., Humaniora, vol. 38, no. 2 (Abo, Abo Akademi, 1970)

P. 27   'Today art . . .' W. Kandinsky and F. Marc (eds), *The Blaue Reiter Almanac*, trans. by H. Falkenstein (New York, The Viking Press, 1974), p. 252

P. 27   'Then a week later . . .' Jeff Verhey, 'The spirit of 1914: the myth of enthusiasm and the rhetoric of unity in World War 1 Germany', PhD thesis, University of California at Berkeley, 1992

P. 27   'They responded . . .' Francis Haskell, 'Art and the

Apocalypse', *New York Review of Books* (15 July 1993), pp. 5–9

P. 29 'There awoke in me . . .' As cited in Robert K. Massie, *Dreadnought. Britain, Germany and the Coming of the Great War* (London, Jonathan Cape, 1992), p. 151

P. 29 '*Quelle famille* . . .' J. C. G. Röhl and N. Sombard (eds), *Kaiser Wilhelm II. New Interpretations* (Cambridge, Cambridge University Press, 1954), p. 53

P. 29 'I was worried . . .' As cited in Massie, *Dreadnought*

P. 29 'I really found . . .' Citations in this paragraph are from Massie, *Dreadnought*, p. 33 and chs 2–3

P. 30 'Under the Reich Constitution . . .' For a brilliant account of this political system, see Volker Berghahn, *Imperial Germany 1871–1914. Economy, Society, Culture and Politics* (Oxford, Berghahn Books, 1994), ch. 13

P. 31 'One of the best . . .' Röhl and Sombard (eds), *Kaiser Wilhelm II*, p. 123

P. 31 'I expect that . . .' Citations in this paragraph are from Röhl and Sombard (eds), *Kaiser Wilhelm II*

P. 31–2 'Although, like others . . .' J. C. G. Röhl, *The Kaiser and his Court. Wilhelm II and the Government of Germany*, trans. by Terence F. Cole (Cambridge, Cambridge University Press, 1994), ch. 8

P. 32 '. . . he declaimed violently . . .' Röhl and Sombard (eds), *Kaiser Wilhelm II*, p. 129

P. 32 'The German Emperor . . .' Ibid. p. 121

P. 32 'This was the source . . .' Röhl, *The Kaiser and his Court*, chs 2–3

P. 32 'The Kaiser insists . . .' Röhl and Sombard (eds), *Kaiser Wilhelm II*, p. 30

P. 32 'All of you . . .' As cited in Röhl, *The Kaiser and his Court*, p. 12

P. 32 'By then Bunsen . . .' Röhl and Sombard (eds), *Kaiser Wilhelm II*, p. 139

P. 32 'An arms race . . .' Jonathan Steinberg, *Yesterday's Deterrent. Tirpitz and the Birth of the German Battlefleet* (London, Macdonald, 1965)

P. 32 'The bayonets of . . .' *The Intimate Papers of Colonel House Vol. 1. Behind the Political Curtain* (London, Ernest Benn, 1926), p. 261.

P. 36 'Eighteen months . . .' Volker Berghahn, *Germany and the Approach of War in 1914* (London, Macmillan, 1984)

P. 36 'What Germany has . . .' Röhl and Sombard (eds), *Kaiser Wilhelm II*, p. 53

P. 36 'Turn-of-the-century German . . .' See Röhl, *The Kaiser and his Court*, p. 25

P. 42 'There she quickly emerged . . .' Elzbieta Ettinger, *Rosa Luxemburg. A Life* (Boston, Beacon Press, 1986), chs 6–7

PP. 42–3 'I feel so much . . .' J. P. Nettl, *Rosa Luxemburg*, 2 vols (Oxford, Oxford University Press, 1966), vol. 11, p. 666

P. 43 'An international proletarian . . .' Nettl, *Rosa*, p. 502

P. 45 'Sir, if you had . . .' Ibid. vol. 11, pp. 490–1

P. 46 'but two days later . . .' J.-J. Becker, 'Jouhaux, le 4 août, devant la tombe de Jaurès', in J.-J. Becker *et*

al. (eds), *14–18. La très grande guerre* (Paris, Le Monde, 1994), pp. 35–40

P. 47 'Slowly, in a silence . . .' Harvey Goldberg, *The Life of Jean Jaurès* (Madison, Wisconsin, University of Wisconsin Press, 1962), p. 3

P. 47 'The day was . . .' On the assassination, see J.-J. Becker, 'Le 28 juin de Gavrilo Princip' in Becker, *14–18. La très grande guerre*, pp. 3–5

P. 50 'The bloody deed . . .' Massie, *Dreadnought*, p. 861

P. 50 'But in 1914 . . .' See the definitive discussion in the final chapter of Berghahn, *Imperial Germany*

P. 52 'This war is fine . . .' Alain-Fournier
'The German soul . . .' Thomas Mann
See Ronald Stromberg, *Redemption by War* (Lawrence, Kansas, University of Kansas Press, 1970); see also R. Wohl, *The Generation of 1914* (New York, Knopf, 1975)

PP. 52–6 '"The tocsin!" cried someone . . .' Serge Grafteaux, *Mémé Santerre: a French Woman of The People*, trans. by L. A. and K. L. Tilly (New York, Schocken, 1985), p. 74

P. 56 'At five . . .' Pierre-Jakez Hélias, *The Horse of Pride. Life in a Breton Village*, trans. by June Guicharnaud (New Haven, Yale University Press, 1978), pp. 30–1

2 STALEMATE

P. 59 'It took five hundred trains . . .' Martin van Creveld, *Supplying War* (Cambridge, Cambridge University Press, 1977), pp. 112–24

PP. 59–60 'In the offensive . . .' Alistair Horne, *The Price of Glory: Verdun 1916* (Harmondsworth, Penguin Books, 1962), p. 19

P. 60 'Success . . .' Field Regulations of 1918. Drafted by committee, General Pau chairman, pp. 445–7

P. 60 'It's every man . . .' Henri Desagneaux, *A French Soldier's War Diary 1914–1918* (London, Elmfield Press, 1975), p. 3

P. 61 'The women are . . .' Ibid., p. 3

P. 61 '*Incroyable!*' Philip Gibbs, *The War Dispatches* (London, Times Press, 1964), pp. 13–15

P. 61 'She was very . . .' Maurice Paléologue, *La Russie des Tsars pendant la Grande Guerre* (Paris, Plon, 1921), p. 58

P. 64 'At last I . . .' Ernst Toller, *I was a German* (London, John Lane, 1934), p. 51

P. 64 'They made no . . .' *Times History of the War I*, p. 336. Quoted in Barbara Tuchman, *Guns of August* (London, Macmillan, 1962), p. 200

P. 65 'I was taken . . .' Gabriel Hanotaux, *Histoire illustrée de la guerre de 1914* (Paris, Gounouilhou, 1916), vol. III, p. 254

P. 65 'Our advance in . . .' Franz Conrad von Hotzendorff, *Aus Meiner Dienstzeit, 1907–18*, 5 vols (Vienna, Rikola Verlag, 1923), vol. IV, p. 193

P. 66 'The invading forces . . .' Alan Kramer, 'Les atrocités allemandes: mythologies populaires, propagande et manipulations dans l'armée allemande', in J.-J. Becker *et al.* (eds), *Guerre et cultures 1914–1918* (Paris, Armand Colin, 1994), pp. 147–64

P. 66 'We shall wipe ...' Martin Gilbert, *The First World War* (New York, Henry Holt & Co, 1994), p. 43

P. 66 'When one sees ...' Rudolf Binding, *A Fatalist at War* (Boston, Houghton Mifflin, 1929), p. 19

P. 68 'Thank God ...' Vincent Monteil, *Les Officiers* (Paris, Editions du Seuil, 1959), p. 34

P. 69 'They took into account ...' J.-J. Becker, 'Lorraine sanglante', in J.-J. Becker *et al.* (eds), *14–18. La très grande guerre* (Paris, Le Monde, 1994), pp. 69–71

P. 70 'by which God ...' Fernand Engerand, *Le Secret de la Frontière. 1815–1871–1914. Charleroi* (Paris, Brossard, 1918), p. 471

P. 70 'There was a ...' Gibbs, p. 55

P. 70 'At first ...' Serge Grafteaux, *Mémé Santerre: a French Woman of the People*, trans. by L. A. and K. L. Tilly (New York, Schocken, 1985), p. 78

P. 71 'Afterwards ...' Gibbs, p. 32

P. 73 'If the Germans ...' Gerd Krumeich, 'Tannenberg, la revanche et le mythe', in J.-J. Becker *et al.* (eds), *14–18. La très grande guerre*, pp. 49–56

P. 77 'The Austro-Hungarian ...' Erich Ludendorff, *My War Memories, 1914–1918* (London, Hutchinson, 1919), p. 71

P. 77 'A single soldier ...' C. E. Callwell, *Field Marshal Sir Henry Wilson: His Life and Diaries* (London, Cassell, 1927), vol. 1, p. 78

P. 78 'I don't know ...' Peter Simkins, *Kitchener's Army* (Manchester, Manchester University Press, 1988), p. 34

P. 79 'Going to war ...' For an excellent profile of John Lucy see Trevor Wilson, *The Myriad Faces of War* (Cambridge, Polity Press, 1986). Lucy quotes are taken from *There's a Devil in the Drum* by John F. Lucy (London, Faber & Faber, 1938)

P. 79 'Our rapid fire ...' Lucy, pp. 73–4

P. 79 'The retirement ...' Malcolm Brown, *The Imperial War Museum Book of the Western Front* (London, Sidgwick & Jackson, 1993), p. 14

P. 79 'For God's sake ...' Lucy, p. 142

P. 79 'Our minds ...' Ibid. pp. 145, 147

P. 80 'It seemed that ...' P. J. Flood, *France 1914–18* (London, Macmillan, 1990)

P. 80 'We have only ...' Max Hoffmann, *War Diaries and Other Papers*, trans. by Eric Sutton (London, Martin Secker, 1929), vol. 1, p. 41

P. 80 'This ghastly battle ...' Philipp Witkop (ed.), *German Students' War Letters*, Munich, 1928; trans. by A. F. Wedd (London, Methuen, 1929)

P. 81 'I have been having ...' F. H. Keeling, *Keeling Letters and Recollections* (London, Allen & Unwin, 1918)

P. 81 'This time only ...' Lucy

P. 81 'On Christmas Eve ...' Cited in Malcolm Brown and Shirley Seaton, *Christmas Truce: The Western Front December 1914* (London, Leo Cooper, 1984), p. 56

P. 85 'I have been ...' Gibbs, pp. 64–5

P. 88 'Lord, how ...' Wilson, pp. 55–6

P. 89 'There they are ...' Lucy, p. 166

P. 89 'We had all thought ...' Ibid. pp. 190, 283

P. 90 'I fell and ...' Jean Lacouture, *De Gaulle. The Rebel 1890–1944*, trans. by P. O'Brian (London, Collins, 1990), p. 18

P. 92 'What would happen ...' Martin Gilbert, p. 112

P. 92 'Neutrals never ...' Ibid. p. 89

P. 93 'His decision ...' Martin van Creveld, *Command in War* (Cambridge, Mass., Harvard University Press, 1985), ch. 5. On the impossibility of the Schlieffen Plan, see van Creveld, *Supplying War*, ch. 4

P. 94 'the *Materialschlacht* ...' Ernst Jünger, *Storm of Steel* (New York, Howard Fertig, 1992), p. 32

P. 96 'As early as ...' J.-J. Becker, *The Great War and the French People* (Leamington Spa, Berg, 1988), ch. 1

P. 96 'Our chief enemy ...' As cited in Modris Eksteins, *Rites of Spring* (New York, Bantam Books, 1990), p. 105

P. 96 'We were all ...' Herbert Sulzbach, *With the German Guns* (London, Leo Cooper, 1973), p. 115

P. 96 'a Frenchman singing ...' As cited in Malcolm Brown and Shirley Seaton, *Christmas Truce: The Western Front December 1914* (London, Macmillan, 1994), p. 73

P. 96 'English soldiers ...' Cited in ibid. p. 64. Original source: O. F. Bailey and H. M. Hollier, *The Kensingtons* (London, Regimental Old Comrades Association, 1930), p. 27

P. 97 'They finished ...' Ibid. pp. 58–9. Original sources: 'Saturday afternoon soldiers' (unpublished memoir); interview for *Peace in No Man's Land*, BBC TV, 1981

P. 97 'Throughout ...' Cited in ibid, p. 73. Original source: L. Rimbault, *Journal de campagne d'un officier de la ligne* (Paris, Librairie Militaire Berger-Lenrolt, 1916)

P. 98 'It was freezing ...' Cited in ibid. p. 72. Original source: Robert de Wilde, *Mon journal de campagne* (Paris, 1918)

P. 99 'They protested ...' Cited in ibid.

PP. 99–101 'Lice, rats, barbed wire ...' E. Karcher, *Otto Dix, 1891–1964. Leben und Werke* (Cologne, Benedikt Taschen, 1988), p. 38

P. 101 'One can joke ...' Robert Graves, *Good-bye to All That* (London, Penguin, 1988), p. 98

P. 104 'were few and ...' Stephen Westman, *Surgeon with the Kaiser's Army* (London, William Kimber, 1968), pp. 151, 78, 106

P. 104 'I got through ...' Harry Lauder, *A Minstrel in France* (New York, Hearst, 1918), pp. 170–1

3 TOTAL WAR

P. 109 'Churchill was convinced ...' Robert K. Massie, *Dreadnought* (London, Jonathan Cape, 1992), p. 750

P. 110 'fills me ...' Sir Ian Hamilton, *Gallipoli Diary* (London, Edward Arnold, 1930), p. 245

P. 110 'I talked to the Turks ...' Aubrey Herbert, *Mons, Anzac and KVT* (London, Hutchinson, 1919), p. 189

P. 112   'The anniversary of the first landing...' Ken Inglis, 'Le 25 avril en Australie et en Nouvelle-Zealand', in J.-J. Becker *et al.* (eds), *Guerre et cultures* (Paris, Armand Colin, 1994), pp. 397–410

P. 113   'Why are you running...' *Atatürk* (Ankara, Turkish National Commission for Unesco, 1963), p. 21

P. 114   'I visited most parts...' For the full text of Murdoch's letter see Desmond Zwar, *In Search of Keith Murdoch* (Melbourne, Macmillan, 1980), ch. 4

P. 118   'On 22 April...' S. Audoin-Rouzeau, 'Le gas, nouvelle frontière de l'horreur', in J.-J. Becker *et al.* (eds), *14–18. La très grande guerre* (Paris, Le Monde, 1994), pp. 87–8

P. 118   'Midnight. The frogs...' Jean Giraudoux, *Adorable Clio* (Paris, Grasset, 1939), p. 208

P. 118   'Sinking of the...' Evelyn, Princess Blücher, *An English Wife in Berlin* (London, Constable, 1920), p. 51

P. 119   'The summer of...' Konstantin Paustovsky, *Slow Approach of Thunder*, trans. by M. Harari and M. Duncan (London, The Harvill Press, 1965), p. 87

P. 119   'Sir, I have the...' Leslie A. Davis, *The Slaughterhouse Province. An American Diplomat's Report on the Armenian Genocide, 1915–1917* (New Rochelle, New York, Aristide D. Caratzas, 1989), pp. 143–7

P. 120   'the war would spread...' Chaim Weizmann, *Trial and Error* (London, East and West Library, 1950), p. 189

P. 122   'Well, Dr Weizmann...' Ibid. p. 220

P. 122   'the biggest thing...' M. R. Lawrence (ed.), *The Home Letters of T. E. Lawrence and his Brothers* (Oxford, Basil Blackwell, 1954), p. 327

P. 122   'Is this man God?' Richard Aldington, *Lawrence of Arabia* (London, Collins, 1959), p. 159

PP. 127–8   The quotations of the Goodyear family are taken from David Macfarlane, *The Danger Tree: Memory, War and the Search for a Family's Past* (Toronto, MacFarlane, Walter & Ross, 1991)

P. 130   'What the war did...' J. M. Winter and R. Wall (eds), *The Upheaval of War: Family, Work and Welfare in Europe, 1914–1918* (Cambridge, Cambridge University Press, 1988)

P. 131   'the sound of...' Stanley Weintraub, *Journey to Heartbreak* (London, Macmillan, 1989), p. 179

P. 132   'The commander of the Zeppelins...' See Douglas Robinson, *The Zeppelin in Combat* (Seattle, University of Washington Press, 1988)

P. 134   'The Allies deemed...' Alan Kramer, 'Les atrocités allemandes: mythologies populaires, propagande et manipulations dans l'armée allemande', in *Guerre et cultures*, pp. 147–64

PP. 135–8   The quotations of Niemöller are taken from Martin Niemöller, *From U-Boat to Concentration Camp* (London, William Hodge & Co, 1939)

P. 139   'The moon shines...' Kevin Brownlow, *The War, the West and the Wilderness* (New York, Knopf, 1979), p. 39

P. 139   'I really thought...' Ibid. p. 39

P. 140   'A slender finger...' H. M. Tomlinson, *Waiting for Daylight* (Cassell & Co, London, 1922), pp. 16–24

P. 140   'Last night Mr Gahar...' Hugh Gibson, *A Journal from our Legation in Belgium* (London, Hodder & Stoughton, 1917), p. 9

P. 141   'The days are...' Jean Broussac, *Lettres de guerre inédites* (Paris, O.E.I.L., 1986)

P. 141   'It is impossible...' *Story of the Scottish Women's Hospitals* (London, Hodder & Stoughton, 1919), pp. 157–8

P. 142   'No wonder one British...' Ibid. pp. 40–1

P. 142   'A doctor serving...' Ibid. p. 41

P. 142   'the idea being...' *Kinematograph Weekly*, 20 April 1917, p. 61, as cited in *The War, the West and the Wilderness*, p. 41

P. 142   'On 8 April...' Denis Gifford, *Chaplin* (New York, Doubleday, 1974), p. 91

PP. 142–3   'This very minute...' Charles T. Maland, *Chaplin and American Culture. The Evolution of an Image* (Princeton, Princeton University Press, 1989), p. 38

P. 143   'grabbed Marie Dressler...' Charles Chaplin, *My Autobiography* (New York, Simon & Schuster, 1964), p. 215

P. 143   'There were over...' Jerzy Toeplitz, 'The cinema in Eastern and Central Europe before the guns of August', in Karel Dibbets and Bert Hogenkamp (eds), *Film and the First World War* (Amsterdam, Amsterdam University Press, 1994), p. 21

P. 143   'This national total...' Nicholas Hiley, 'The British cinema auditorium', in *Film and the First World War*, p. 160

P. 143   'Initially, the film industry...' Maurice Bardèche and Robert Brasillach, *The History of Motion Pictures*, trans. by Iris Barry (New York, W. W. Norton, 1938), p. 134

P. 143   'The legacy of...' Ramona Curry, 'How early German film stars helped sell the war(es)', in *Film and the First World War*, pp. 141–2

P. 144   'consists in the first...' Moritz Busch, *Bismarck. Some Secret Pages of his History* (New York, Macmillan, 1898), vol. I, p. 128

PP. 145–8   'This "uprising"...' R. G. Hovannisian (ed.), *The Armenian Genocide. History, Politics, Ethics* (London, Macmillan, 1992) and Tribunal permanent des Peuples, *Le Crime de Silence. Le génocide des Arméniens 1915–17* (Paris, Flammarion, 1984)

P. 149   'He prepared a detailed...' Johannes Lepsius, *Rapport secret sur les massacres d'Arménie (1915–1916)* (Paris, Payot, 1987)

P. 152   'The American consul...' Leslie A. Davis, *The Slaughterhouse Province*

4 SLAUGHTER

P. 157   'This document...' Stéphane Audoin-Rouzeau, 'Driant au bois des Caures', in J.-J. Becker *et al.* (eds), *14–18. La très grande guerre* (Paris, Le Monde, 1994), p. 122

P. 157   'There remains only...' Alistair Horne, *The Price of Glory: Verdun 1916* (Harmondsworth, Penguin Books, 1962), pp. 42–5

P. 159   'I say good-bye . . .' Philipp Witkop (ed.), *German Students' War Letters*, trans. by A. F. Wedd (London, Methuen, 1929), pp. 242–3

P. 159   'Ironically, eight years . . .' Audoin-Rouzeau, p. 121

P. 159   'I await the cyclone . . .' Ibid. p. 123

P. 160   'Mr Jas. Caldwell . . .' A. Clark, *Echoes of the Great War: The Diary of the Reverend Andrew Clark*, ed. J. Munson (Oxford, Oxford University Press, 1985), p. 105

P. 160   'Over the whole . . .' Jules Romain, *Verdun*, trans. by Gerald Hopkins (London, Peter Davies, 1938), pp. 265–6

P. 160   'The first man . . .' Max Caulfield, *The Easter Rebellion* (Dublin, Gill & Macmillan, 1995), p. 80

P. 161   'One fears to . . .' Michael Moynihan (ed.), *God on Our Side* (London, Secker & Warburg, 1983), p. 35

P. 161   'On 2 June . . .' Herbert Sulzbach, *With the German Guns*, trans. by R. Thonger (London, Leo Cooper, 1917)

P. 161   'I do not propose . . .' A. A. Brusilov, *A Soldier's Notebook* (London, Macmillan, 1930)

P. 163   'I could feel . . .' Stephen Westman, *Surgeon with the Kaiser's Army* (London, William Kimber, 1968), pp. 92–3

P. 165   'We are lost . . .' Horne, p. 135

P. 165   'entered a lunatic . . .' Ibid. p. 156

P. 165   'One eats, one drinks . . .' Ibid. p. 199

P. 166   'Over the course . . .' S. L. A. Marshall, *World War One* (Boston, Houghton Mifflin Co., 1964), pp. 248–9

PP. 167–9   'When one heard . . .' Horne, pp. 189–90

P. 169   'Having despaired . . .' Ibid. p. 198. Dubrulle got his wish. He survived Verdun only to die in the Nivelle Offensive in the spring of 1917

P. 169   'Dear Parents . . .' Witkop, p. 207

PP. 169–70   'Numb and dazed . . .' Henri Desagneaux, *A French Soldier's War Diary 1914–1918* (London, Elmfield Press, 1975), pp. 29–30

P. 171   'Legend had it . . .' Antoine Prost, 'Verdun', in P. Nora (ed.), *Les Lieux de mémoire. 2. La nation* (Paris, Gallimard, 1984), pp. 188–233

P. 171   'We saw a handful . . .' Wilhelm Hermanns, *The Holocaust: From A Survivor of Verdun* (New York, Harper & Row, 1972), p. 63

P. 174   'By November . . .' Paul Fussell, *The Great War and Modern Memory* (Oxford, Oxford University Press, 1975), p. 9

P. 174   'Just two months . . .' Trevor Wilson, *The Myriad Faces of War* (Cambridge, Polity Press, 1986), p. 9

PP. 174–5   'I sit and stare . . .' Helen Thomas, *World Without End* (London, William Heinemann, 1931), quoted in *The Penguin Book of First World War Prose*, John Glover and John Silkin (eds) (London, Penguin Books, 1984), p. 84

P. 180   'I feel that . . .' Douglas Haig, *The Private Papers of Douglas Haig 1914–1918* (London, Eyre & Spottiswoode, 1952), p. 151

P. 180   'You will be able . . .' Martin Middlebrook, *The First Day on the Somme* (London, Penguin Books, 1984), p. 97

P. 180   'A few soldiers . . .' John Keegan, *The Face of Battle* (London, Penguin Books, 1976), p. 241

P. 183   'For some reason . . .' Middlebrook, p. 125

P. 183   'I can't remember . . .' Vera Brittain, *Testament of Youth* (London, Gollancz, 1933), p. 284

P. 183   'Good God . . .' Wilson, p. 323

P. 183   'Of the 752 men . . .' J. M. Winter, 'L'hécatombe de la Somme', in J.-J. Becker *et al.* (eds) *14–18. La très grande guerre*, pp. 129–35

P. 186   'The poetry of the . . .' Witkop, p. 325

P. 186   'We were two years . . .' Middlebrook, p. 270

P. 186   'You seem to forget . . .' Ibid. p. 201

P. 187   'I should like to . . .' Lyn MacDonald, *1914–1918: Voices and Images of the Great War* (London, Penguin Books, 1988), p. 189

P. 188   'In the autumn . . .' Nicholas Hiley 'La bataille de la Somme et les médias de Londres', in *Guerre et cultures*, J.-J. Becker *et al.* (eds) (Paris, Armand Colin, 1994), p. 203

P. 188   'In another six . . .' Haig, Private Papers

P. 191   'Deafness deadens terror . . .' August Stramm, 'Granaten', trans. by Jeremy Adler, originally published in R. Radrizzani (ed.), *August Stramm. Das Werk* (Wiesbaden, Limes Verlag, 1963)

P. 192   'The result was . . .' Robin Prior and Trevor Wilson, *Command on the Western Front* (Oxford, Blackwell, 1992), p. 168

P. 193   'The English attack . . .' Witkop, pp. 372, 374

P. 194   'One keeps cherishing . . .' Ibid. pp. 229–30

P. 195   'all those grand . . .' Middlebrook, p. 315

P. 195   'Chivalry here . . .' Ernst Jünger, *Storm of Steel* (New York, Howard Fertig, 1975), p. 110

P. 196   'First day . . .' Emile-Marie Fayolle, *Cahiers secrets de la grande guerre* (Paris, Plon, 1964), p. 91

P. 196   'Dear parents . . .' Jacques Lovie (ed.), *Poilus Savoyards (1913–918)* (Chambéry, Jacques Claudes et Jean-Francois Lovie, 1981), p. 179

P. 196   'He, Marschall . . .' Gerald Feldman, *Army, Industry and Labor in Germany 1914–1918* (Oxford, Berg, 1992), pp. 141–2

P. 197   'Hoppy and I . . .' Cecil Lewis, *Sagittarius Rising* (London, Greenhill Books, 1993), pp. 142–3

P. 197   'I profoundly . . .' Austen Chamberlain Papers 15/3/10 (Birmingham University Library)

P. 197   'The campaign . . .' Prince Max von Baden, cited in Alistair Horne, *The Price of Glory. Verdun 1916* (London, Penguin, 1978), p. 231

P. 199   'They were all . . .' Thomas, p. 53

P. 199   'In Lille . . .' Jackson Hughes, 'The Monstrous Anger of the Guns. The Development of British Artillery Tactics 1914–1918', PhD thesis, University of Adelaide, 1992, p. 175

P. 199   'Scientific warfare . . .' Malcolm Brown, *The Imperial War Museum Book of the Western Front* (London, Sidgwick & Jackson, 1993), p. 175

P. 202   'Nothing is so trying . . .' Witkop, pp. 362–3

PP. 202−6 'From the darkness . . .' Edward Campion Vaughan, *Some Desperate Glory: the Diary of A Young Officer 1917* (London, Frederick Warne, 1982), entry for 27 August 1917, p. 228

P. 206 'those men who are . . .' Witkop, p. 363

P. 206 'the enemy is tottering . . .' Haig Diary, 28 September 1917, p. 216

P. 207 'As I saw it . . .' Philip Gibbs, *The War Dispatches* (London, Times Press, 1964), p. 286

P. 207 'Haig had not even fought . . .' Wilson, p. 483

P. 207 'For the first time . . .' Philip Gibbs, *Realities of War* (London, Heinemann, 1920), p. 396

5 MUTINY

P. 209 'As a Commander . . .' G. S. Hutchinson, *Warrior* (1932), pp. 204−5, as cited in John Fuller, *Troop Morale and Popular Culture in the British and Dominion Armies 1914−18* (Oxford, Oxford University Press, 1991), p. 68

P. 212 '. . . neurasthenia' Martin Stone, 'Shellshock and the psychologist', in W. F. Bynum *et al.* (eds), *The Anatomy of Madness*, 3 vols (London, Macmillan, 1990), vol. 11, ch. 11; Eric Leed, *No Man's Land: Combat and Identity in World War I* (Cambridge, Cambridge University Press, 1979), ch. 5

PP. 212−16 The quotations of soldiers on these pages come from E. E. Southard, *Shell-shock and other Neuropsychiatric Problems* (Boston, W. M. Leonard, 1919) and are anonymous

P. 213 'In earlier wars . . .' Ernst Jünger, *Storm of Steel* (New York, Howard Fertig, 1993), p. 109

P. 217 'one enlisted man . . .' Marc Roudebush, 'A battle of nerves: hysteria and its treatment in France during World War I', PhD thesis, University of California at Berkeley, 1995

P. 217 'some soldiers resisted . . .' Paul Lerner, 'Rationalizing the therapeutic arsenal: German neuropsychiatry in the First World War', in G. Cocks and M. Berg (eds), *Medicine in Germany: Politics, Ethics, Law* (Cambridge, Cambridge University Press, 1995)

P. 217 W. H. R. Rivers. For more biographical detail, see F. C. Bartlett's obituary in *Man*, 61 (July, 1922), pp. 97−104

P. 219 '*My spirit longs . . .*' From 'The church of St Ouen', in *The War Poems of Siegfried Sassoon* (London, Faber & Faber, 1983)

P. 219 'Luckily it didn't . . .' R. Hart-Davis (ed.), *Siegfried Sassoon Diaries 1915−1918* (London, Faber & Faber, 1983), p. 155 (hereafter *Diaries*)

P. 219 'At present . . .' Ibid. p. 156

P. 219 '*I'm back again . . .*' From 'To the Warmongers', in *The War Poems of Siegfried Sassoon*

P. 219 'My brain is . . .' *Diaries*, p. 161

P. 219 '. . . just as he . . .' Ibid. p. 162

PP. 219−22 'Things must take . . .' Ibid. p. 162

P. 220 'This was a . . .' Gerd Krumeich, 'L'hiver des navets outre-Rhin', in J.-J. Becker *et al.* (eds), *14−18. La très grande guerre* (Paris, Le Monde, 1994)

P. 220 '975th day of . . .' E. C. C. Genet, *An American for Lafayette*, ed. W. Brown (Charlottesville, University Press of Virginia, 1981), p. 180

P. 221 'The waves of . . .' J. W. Bishop, *Winged Warfare* (London, Bailey Brothers, 1932), p. 210

P. 221 'I don't think . . .' André Kahn, *Journal de guerre d'un Juif patriote, 1914−1918* (Paris, Jean-Claude Simoën, 1978)

P. 221 'I went over . . .' General Sir Charles Harington, *Plumer of Messines* (London, John Murray, 1935), p. 104

P. 222 'For a while . . .' *Diaries*, p. 167

P. 222 'blundering about . . .' Ibid. p. 170

P. 222 'began to think . . .' Siegfried Sassoon, *Memoirs of an Infantry Officer* (London, Folio Society, 1974), pp. 184−5

P. 222 'I am making . . .' *Diaries*, pp. 173−4

P. 222 'would speak out . . .' Ibid. p. 175

PP. 222−3 'I am writing . . .' Ibid. p. 177

P. 223 'In that Mecca . . .' Siegfried Sassoon, *Sherston's Progress* (London, Folio Society, 1974), pp. 13 and 18

P. 223 'father-confessor' Ibid. p. 36

P. 223 'reinforced by his reading . . .' *Diaries*, p. 184. Sassoon to Lady Ottoline Morrell, 19 August 1917

P. 224 'the only way . . .' Ibid. p. 190. Sassoon to Lady Ottoline Morrell, 17 October 1917

P. 224 'As Sassoon himself . . .' *Sherston's Progress*, p. 150

P. 224 'It would be a . . .' *Diaries*, p. 192. Sassoon to Robert Graves, 19 October 1917

P. 224 'Petulantly he said . . .' *Sherston's Progress*, p. 48

P. 224 'This time he had a ditty . . .' Ibid. p. 50

P. 224 'obtained, previously . . .' *Diaries*, p. 196, Sassoon to Robert Graves, 7 December 1917

P. 225 'I can see no excuse . . .' H. Owen and J. Bell (eds), *Wilfred Owen Collected Letters* (London, Oxford University Press, 1967), p. 427

P. 226 'I certainly was . . .' Ibid. p. 456. Wilfred Owen to Mary Owen, 8 May 1917

P. 226 'you have *fixed* . . .' Quoted in J. Johnston, *English Poetry of the First World War; a study in the evolution of lyric and narrative form* (Oxford, Oxford University Press, 1964), p. 157

P. 226 'which set him . . .' Siegfried Sassoon, *Siegfried's Journey* (London, Faber & Faber, 1945), p. 161

PP. 226−8 All quotations from the poetry of Siegfried Sassoon come from *The War Poems of Siegfried Sassoon*

PP. 228−9 All quotations from the poetry of Wilfred Owen come from *The Collected Poems of Wilfred Owen*, ed. C. Day Lewis (London, Chatto & Windus, 1963)

PP. 232−3 'We fought because . . .' *Le Tord-boyau*, Aug. 1917, as cited in Stéphane Audoin-Rouzeau, *Men at War. Trench Journalism and National Sentiment in France 1914−1918*, trans. by H. McPhail (Oxford, Berg, 1992), p. 181

P. 233 'I am ready . . .' Len Smith, *Between Mutiny and Obedience. The Case of the French Fifth Infantry Division during World War I* (Princeton, Princeton University Press, 1994), p. 192

P. 233 'to generate . . . "chickenshit" . . .' Paul Fussell, *Wartime* (Oxford, Oxford University Press, 1985)

P. 234 'I understand . . .' Cited in Audoin-Rouzeau, p. 65

PP. 234–9 Details of Louis Barthas' story and quotations from his writings are taken from Louis Barthas, *Les carnets de guerre de Louis Barthas, tennelier 1914–1918* (Paris, Maspéro, 1978)

P. 234 'The *poilu* is a man . . .' *Le Périscope*, 1916, cited in Audoin-Rouzeau, p. 156

P. 238 'Poor happy stay-at-home . . .' *Le Crapouillot*, August 1917, as cited in Audoin-Rouzeau, p. 39

P. 241 'He suffers from . . .' *Le Périscope*, as cited in Audoin-Rouzeau, p. 156

P. 241 'We want peace . . .' *Between Mutiny and Obedience*, p. 192

P. 241 'In the 1917 . . .' Ibid. passim

P. 242 'His first posting . . .' This irony is noted by Jean Lacouture in *De Gaulle. The Rebel 1890–1944*, trans. by P. O'Brian (London, Collins, 1990), p. 16

PP. 242–6 Quotations of or about de Gaulle in this section are taken from *De Gaulle. The Rebel*

P. 244 *La Grande Illusion.* Marcel Diamand-Berger, 'De Gaulle en captivité', *Espoir*, 14 (March 1976), pp. 4–5 and Jean Renoir, *Renoir on Renoir*, trans. by C. Volk (Cambridge, Cambridge University Press, 1989), pp. 90–1

P. 244 'De Gaulle was transferred . . .' A. J. Evans, *The Escaping Club* (London, Bodley Head, 1921)

P. 244 'This is the castle . . .' 'De Gaulle en captivité', p. 5

P. 246 'just a common spy . . .' J. P. Nettl, *Rosa Luxemburg*, 2 vols (Oxford, Oxford University Press, 1966), vol. II, p. 651

PP. 248–9 Quotations of Rosa Luxemburg are taken from S. Bronner (ed.), *The Letters of Rosa Luxemburg* (New Brunswick, New Jersey, Humanities Press, 1993)

P. 249 'Retrieved by his father . . .' J. Stern, *Ernst Jünger* (New Haven, Yale University Press, 1953), pp. 8–9

P. 250 'All night long . . .' Florence Farmborough, *Nurse at the Russian Front* (London, Constable, 1974), pp. 269–70

P. 250 'The battle opened . . .' Guy Chapman, *A Passionate Prodigality* (New York, Holt, Reinhart & Winston, 1966)

P. 250 'The fortified knobs . . .' Erwin Rommel, *Infantry Attacks* (London, Greenhill Books, 1990), pp. 186–7

P. 251 'I tried to . . .' Morgan Philips Price, *My Reminiscences of the Russian Revolution* (London, Allen & Unwin, 1921), p. 147

P. 251 'But the *pièce* . . .' George Coppard, *With a Machine Gun to Cambrai* (London, Imperial War Museum, 1980), pp. 122–3

PP. 252–7 The quotations from the writings of Jünger come from Ernst Jünger, *Storm of Steel: From the Diary of a German Storm-troop Officer on the Western Front* (New York, Howard Fertig, 1933)

PP. 252–3 'Instead of crowding . . .' Timothy T. Lupfer, *The Dynamics of Doctrine: the changes of German tactical doctrine during the First World War*, Leavenworth Papers No. 4 (Fort Leavenworth, Kansas, US Army Command and General Staff College, 1981), p. 13

P. 257 'Lice, rats, barbed wire . . .' E. Karcher, *Otto Dix, 1891–1964. Leben und Werk* (Cologne, Benedikt Taschen, 1988), p. 38

P. 258 'the proletariat . . .' Marc Ferro, *The Russian Revolution of February 1917*, trans. by J. L. Richards (Englewood Cliffs, New Jersey, Prentice Hall, 1972), p. 32

P. 259 'While the Palace . . .' Ibid. p. 43

P. 259 'drive the Germans . . .' Maria Botchkareva, *Yashka. My life as peasant, exile and soldier* (London, Constable, 1919), p. 136. These memoirs were told to an American journalist, Isaac Don Levine, and though anti-Bolshevik in character, have a clear documentary value, if used critically

P. 262 'You have heard . . .' Ibid. p. 154

P. 263 'Yashka was knocked . . .' Ibid. p. 46

P. 264 'He loved the . . .' Isaac Deutscher, *The Prophet Armed. Trotsky: 1879–1921* (Oxford, Oxford University Press, 1954), p. 35

P. 264 'In all the . . .' Leon Trotsky, *Our Revolution. Essays on Working-class and International Revolution, 1904–1917*, trans. by M. J. Olgin (New York, Henry Holt, 1918), pp. 181ff

P. 265 'The soldiers sang . . .' Leon Trotsky, *My Life. An attempt at an autobiography* (New York, Pathfinder, 1970), p. 288

P. 268 'The soldiers were . . .' Leon Trotsky, *The History of the Russian Revolution*, trans. by Max Eastman (New York, Simon & Schuster, 1932), p. 389

P. 269 'Should they defend . . .?' Trotsky, *My Life*, p. 317

P. 269 'Every soldier . . .' Trotsky, *Revolution*, p. 427

P. 269 'October 24 . . .' Trotsky, *My Life*, p. 321

P. 272 'A telephone call . . .' Ibid. p. 324

P. 272 '"Give me a . . ."' Ibid. p. 325

P. 273 'in tense silence . . .' Ibid. p. 327

P. 272 'Later that evening . . .' Ibid. p. 327

6 COLLAPSE

P. 277 'single soldiers . . .' Erwin Rommel, *Infantry Attacks* (London, Greenhill Books, 1990), p. 202

P. 278 'I came to . . .' Ibid. p. 21

P. 278 'It was a staggering . . .' Martin Gilbert, *First World War* (London, Weidenfeld & Nicolson, 1994), p. 369

PP. 279–87 'Seaman Richard Stumpf . . .' D. Horn (ed.), *War, Mutiny and Revolution in the German Navy. The World War I Diary of Seaman Richard Stumpf* (New Brunswick, Rutgers University Press, 1967). All the citations from Stumpf's diaries in the following pages come from this source

P. 280 'I note the words . . .' Jean-Baptiste Duroselle, *Clemenceau* (Paris, Fayard, 1990), p. 754

P. 280 'I am expecting . . .' Max Hoffmann, *War Diaries and Other Papers*, trans. by Eric Sutton (London, Martin Secker, 1929), vol. I, p. 302

P. 280 'During the night . . .' Interview cited in Martin

Middlebrook, *The Kaiser's Battle* (Harmondsworth, Penguin, 1983), p. 146

P. 281 'Anzac Day was ...' F. M. Cutlack (ed.), *War Letters of General Monash* (Sydney, Angus & Robertson, 1935), p. 236

P. 281 'I was equipped ...' J. E. Redinell, *One Man's War: the Diary of a Leatherneck*, ed. G. Patullo (New York, Sears, 1928), pp. 111–12

P. 281 'I have lived ...' Rudolf Binding, *A Fatalist at War*, trans. by I. Morrow (London, Allen & Unwin, 1929), pp. 234–7

P. 289 'A tremendous roll ...' Ernst Jünger, *Storm of Steel* (London, Chatto & Windus, 1929), p. 149

P. 292 'Most of the brigade ...' Martin Middlebrook, *The Kaiser's Battle*, p. 306

P. 292 'His Majesty returned ...' W. Görlitz (ed.), *The Kaiser and his Court* (London, Macdonald, 1961), p. 344

P. 295 'Their task had ...' Robin Prior and Trevor Wilson, *Command on the Western Front* (Oxford, Blackwell, 1992), ch. 33; Robin Prior and Trevor Wilson, 'What manner of victory?', *Revue internationale d'histoire militaire* (1990)

P. 295 'General Budworth described ...' The citations here and in the following discussion are based on Jackson Hughes, 'The Monstrous Anger of the Guns' (PhD, Adelaide, 1992), ch. 8, a new discussion of the subject based on the Fourth Army Papers, Australian War Memorial, Canberra, and especially on the report by General Budworth, 'Fourth Army artillery in the attack on the Hindenburg Line, Sept. 29 1918'

P. 298 'Everyone seemed ...' Ed Cray, *General of the Army* (New York, W. W. Norton, 1990), p. 53

P. 303 'We stood and talked ...' D. Clayton James, *The Years of MacArthur* (London, Leo Cooper, 1970), p. 211

P. 303 'We had the Americans ...' Pierre Teilhard de Chardin, *Genèse d'une Pensée* (Paris, Bernard Grasset, 1961), p. 284

P. 304 'We had expected ...' Gerd Krumeich, 'La journée noire de l'armée allemande', in J.-J. Becker *et al.* (eds), *14–18. La très grande guerre*, p. 218

P. 304 'Graincourt being ...' Deneys Reitz, *Trekking On* (London, Faber & Faber, 1932), pp. 264–5

P. 305 'Striking news ...' André Kahn, *Journal de guerre d'un Juif patriote, 1914–1918* (Paris, Jean-Claude Simoën, 1978), p. 325

P. 305 'What has the war ...' Mary-Alice Waters (ed.), *Rosa Luxemburg Speaks* (New York, Pathfinder Press, 1970), p. 412

P. 305 'Twenty-five minutes ...' Anne Oliver Bell (ed.), *The Diary of Virginia Woolf*, vol. 1 (New York, Harcourt Brace Jovanovich, 1977), p. 216

P. 306 'But what made it ...' Thierry Bonzon and Belinda Davis, 'Feeding the cities', in J. M. Winter and J.-L. Robert, *Paris, London, Berlin. Capital Cities at War* (Cambridge, Cambridge University Press, 1996)

P. 306 'During the war ...' *Vorwaerts*, 5 May 1916, cited in Bonzon and Davis, 'Feeding the cities'

PP. 306–7 'In effect ...' Avner Offer, *The First World War. An Agrarian Interpretation* (Oxford, Oxford University Press, 1989)

P. 307 'now eat the soup ...' Volker Berghahn, *Modern Germany* (Cambridge, Cambridge University Press, 1988), pp. 57–9

PP. 309–10 'I should like ...' R. H. Lutz (ed.), *The Fall of the German Empire* (Oxford, Oxford University Press, 1932), p. 478

P. 314 'Here is the coffin ...' Oliver Bernard (ed. and trans.), *Apollinaire. Selected Poems* (London, Anvil Press Poetry, 1986), p. 145

P. 317 'all of literary Paris ...' Blaise Cendrars, *Oeuvres complètes*, 8 vols (Paris, Denoël, 1964), vol. VI, pp. 662–3 (trans. by J. M. Winter)

P. 318 'You understand ...' Ibid. pp. 663–4

PP. 318–19 'The psychic ...' Ibid. p. 664

P. 319 'It was fantastic ...' Ibid. pp. 664–5

P. 319 '*The sun will ...*' Blaise Cendrars, *Collected poems*, trans. by Ron Padgett (Berkeley, University of California Press, 1992), pp. 85–6

7 HATRED AND HUNGER

P. 321 'It was clear ...' John Bradley, *Allied Intervention in Russia* (London, Weidenfeld and Nicolson, 1968)

P. 322 'Some peasants still ...' Thanks are due to Orlando Figes for advice on this and other points

P. 322 'The Tsar at ...' See W. Bruce Lincoln, *Red Victory. A History of the Russian Civil War* (New York, Simon & Schuster, 1986), pp. 150–4, and Robert K. Massie, *Nicholas and Alexandra* (New York, Atheneum, 1967), p. 458

P. 322 'Mama, I would ...' Massie, *Nicholas*, p. 468

P. 322 'But with thousands of ...' Ibid. p. 486

P. 324 'The remains ...' For further details, see Marc Ferro, *Nicholas II. Last of the Tsars*, trans. by Brian Pearce (New York, Oxford University Press, 1993) and Robert K. Massie, 'The last Romanov mystery', *New Yorker* (21–8 Aug. 1995), pp. 72–95

P. 324 'The execution ...' Leon Trotsky, *Diary in Exile*, trans. by E. Zarudnaia (New York, Columbia University Press, 1963), p. 81

P. 325 'They too had suffered ...' George Katkov, 'The assassination of Count Mirbach', *St Antony's Papers*, 12 (1962), pp. 53–93

P. 325 'Jesuit of Terror ...' Richard B. Spence, *Boris Savinkov: Renegade on the Left* (New York, Columbia University Press, 1991), p. 202

P. 325 'In the town's cemetery ...' Ibid. pp. 208*ff*

P. 325 'Here there is ...' Lincoln, *Red Victory*, p. 146

P. 325 'Red Terror is not ...' Ibid. p. 158

P. 325 'From now on ...' George Legett, *The Cheka: Lenin's political police* (Oxford, Oxford University Press, 1981), p. 108

P. 328 'The Revolution suffered ...' Leon Trotsky, *Lenin. Notes for a Biographer*, trans. by Tamara Deutscher (New York, Unwin, 1971), pp. 160–1

P. 328 'The story of Saratov ...' Donald J. Raleigh (ed.),

A Russian Civil War Diary. Alexis Babine in Saratov, 1917–1922 (Durham, N. C. Duke University Press, 1988), introduction (hereafter 'Babine diary'). Reprinted with permission

P. 328 'Black marketeers ...' Ibid. 12 Aug. 1918

P. 328 'property taken by ...' Ibid. 3 Sept. 1918

P. 328 'killing the prisoners anyway ...' Ibid. 10 Sept. 1918

P. 328 '*En route* from Saratov ...' Ibid. 23 Sept. 1918

P. 329 'Another 150 ...' Ibid. 2 Oct. 1918

P. 329 'Since the beginning ...' Ibid. 2 Oct. 1918

P. 329 'Shops were ordered ...' Ibid. 14 Oct. 1918

P. 329 'Icons were banned ...' Ibid. 25 Oct. 1918

P. 329 'Wealthy landowners ...' Ibid. 22 Oct. 1918

P. 329 'the pervading problem ...' Ibid. 21 Oct. 1918

P. 329 'the ease with which ...' Ibid. 7 Nov. 1918

P. 330 'On 25 November ...' Ibid. 25, 26 Nov. 1918

P. 330 'the stiffest and ...' Ibid. 12 March 1919

P. 331 'He was forced ...' Ibid. 10 April 1919

P. 331 'A few days ago ...' Ibid. 29 April 1919

P. 331 'Whatever the supernatural ...' Lincoln, *Red Victory*, p. 424. See also, Richard H. Ullman, *Intervention and the War* (Princeton, Princeton University Press, 1961), epilogue; and John Silverlight, *The Victors' Dilemma: Allied Intervention in the Russian Civil War* (London, Barrie & Jenkins, 1970), ch. 7

P. 331 'Peasants had little ...' Orlando Figes, *Peasant Russia, Civil War: The Volga Countryside in Revolution (1917–1921)* (Oxford, Clarendon Press, 1989)

P. 332 'The days of freedom ...' *Marc Chagall. Les années russes, 1907–1922* (Paris, Musée d'art moderne de la ville de Paris, 1995), p. 246ff

P. 332 'It is easier ...' Babine diary, 15 Oct. 1922

P. 333 'What do you expect ...' As cited in R. G. L. Waite, *Vanguard of Nazism. The Free Corps Movement in Postwar Germany 1918–1923* (Cambridge, Harvard University Press, 1970), p. 5

P. 335 'After all, he brooded ...' C. B. Burdick and R. H. Lutz (eds), *The Political Institutions of the German Revolution 1918–1919* (New York, Frederick A. Praeger, 1966), pp. 70–1

P. 336 'The old slut ...' Elisabeth Hannover-Drück and Heinrich Hannover (eds), *Die Mord an Rosa Luxemburg und Karl Liebknecht* (Frankfurt, Suhrkamp Verlag, 1967), pp. 72, 29, 39

P. 336 'Her decomposed ...' J. P. Nettl, *Rosa Luxemburg* (London, Oxford University Press, 1969), pp. 488–94

P. 336 'The government ...' Burdick and Lutz (eds), *The Political Institutions of the German Revolution*, pp. 248–9, 291

P. 337 'paying for his ...' Elzbieta Ettinger, *Rosa Luxemburg. A Life* (Boston, Beacon Press, 1986), pp. 249–50

P. 337 'Two other delegates ...' Egon Larsen, *Weimar Eyewitness* (London, Bachman & Turner, 1977), pp. 11–13

P. 337 'It is beautiful ...' Ettinger, *Rosa Luxemburg*, p. 248

P. 337 'Jögiches was arrested ...' Ibid. pp. 248–9

P. 337 'hatred of the ...' Peter Paret, Beth Irwin Lewis

P. 338 and Paul Paret, *Persuasive Images: Posters of war and Revolution from the Hoover Institution Archives* (Princeton, Princeton University Press, 1992)

P. 338 'Public support ...' Barrington Moore, *Injustice* (London, Macmillan, 1980)

P. 338 'The new Weimar ...' A. J. Ryder, *The German Revolution of 1918. A Study of German Socialism in War and Revolt* (Cambridge, Cambridge University Press, 1967), p. 208

P. 339 'I really think ...' David Lloyd George, *Memoirs of the Peace Conference* (New Haven, Yale University Press, 1939), p. 141

P. 339 'And they formed ...' Paul Kennedy, *The Realities behind Diplomacy* (London, Fontana, 1981), p. 212

P. 339 'The harsher creeds ...' We are grateful to David Kennedy for advice on this point. See George Kennan, *American Diplomacy* (Chicago, University of Chicago Press, 1984), and David Kennedy, *Over Here. The First World War and American Society* (Oxford, Oxford University Press, 1980), ch. 5

P. 340 'He soon found ...' Arthur S. Link (ed.), *The Papers of Woodrow Wilson* (Princeton, Princeton University Press, 1966), vol. xix, p. 63

P. 340 'There must be ...' George Creel, *The War, the World and Wilson* (New York, Harper & Row, 1920), p. 122

P. 340 'In six months ...' Ibid. p. 125

P. 340 'And the question ...' A. Lentin, *Guilt at Versailles. Lloyd George and the Pre-history of Appeasement* (London, Methuen, 1985)

P. 340 'While Germany never ...' In general, see Charles S. Maier, *Recasting Bourgeois Europe. Stabilization in France, Germany, and Italy in the decade after World War I* (Princeton, Princeton University Press, 1975)

P. 341 'What a use ...' Adolf Hitler, *Mein Kampf* (London, Benn, 1938), p. 87

P. 342 'It was adopted ...' Charles Seymour (ed.), *The Intimate Papers of Colonel House. Volume IV. The ending of the war, June 1918–November 1919* (London, Benn, 1928), p. 329 (hereafter 'House papers')

P. 342 'On questions of ...' Kennedy, *Over Here*, p. 358

P. 343 'The President looked ...' House papers, p. 405

P. 343 'After the Bolsheviks ...' Martin Gilbert, *Winston S. Churchill, Volume IV 1916–1922* (London, Heinemann, 1975), pp. 224–5

P. 343 'We might have ...' Ibid. p. 226

P. 343 'Russia is being rapidly ...' Ibid. p. 227

P. 343 'we should come ...' Ibid. p. 229

P. 343 'Winston told LG ...' Ibid. p. 235

P. 344 'When Wilson rose ...' Churchill's biographer has the meeting at 7 p.m. in Pichon's room in the Quai d'Orsay. See Gilbert, *Winston S. Churchill, Volume IV 1916–1922*, p. 243

P. 344 'Churchill insisted that ...' John M. Thompson, *Russia, Bolshevism and the Versailles Peace* (Princeton, Princeton University Press, 1966), p. 135

P. 344 'Still, he had ...' Ibid. pp. 136–7

P. 344 'Despite the absence ...' Arno J. Mayer, *Politics*

and Diplomacy of Peacemaking. Containment and Counterrevolution at Versailles 1918–1919 (New York, Vintage, 1967), chs. 10, 13, 22

PP. 344–5   'Rumour had it . . .' Thompson, *Russia*, p. 138; see also B. M. Unterberger, 'Woodrow Wilson and the Russian Revolution', in Arthur S. Link (ed.), *Woodrow Wilson and a Revolutionary World* (Chapel Hill, University of North Carolina Press, 1982), pp. 82–3

P. 345   'Wilson too was . . .' Herbert Hoover, *The Ordeal of Woodrow Wilson* (Baltimore, Johns Hopkins University Press, 1992), ch. 19

P. 347   'I never knew . . .' Gene Smith, *When the Cheering Stopped* (New York, William Morrow, 1964), pp. 49–50

P. 347   'Hardly a policy . . .' Arthur S. Link (ed.), *The Deliberations of the Council of Four (March 24 – June 28 1919). Notes of the official interpreter, Paul Mantoux* (Princeton, Princeton University Press, 1992), ii, pp. 200–5

P. 347   'If I believed . . .' Ibid. pp. 483–4

PP. 347–8   'the German Delegates . . .' Sir James Headlam-Morley, *Memoir of the Paris Peace Conference, 1919* (London, Oxford University Press, 1972), pp. 178–9

P. 348   'the intensity of . . .' R. G. Collingwood, *An Autobiography* (London, Oxford University Press, 1939), pp. 89–90

P. 350   'The result is . . .' We owe this point to Professor Samuel Hynes

P. 350   'I admit that . . .' Samuel Hynes, *A War Imagined* (London, Bodley Head, 1990)

P. 351   'June 29, 1919 . . .' House papers, pp. 503–4

P. 351   'Well, it is finished . . .' Gregor Dallas, *At the Heart of a Tiger. Clemenceau and his World 1841–1929* (London, Macmillan, 1993), p. 561

P. 351   'To come into . . .' On the history of the Treaty and its rejection by the United States Senate, see Thomas A. Bailey, *Woodrow Wilson and the Great Betrayal* (New York, Knopf, 1963)

P. 354   'But even if . . .' Eugene F. Trani, 'Herbert Hoover and the Russian Revolution, 1917–1920', in L. E. Gelfand (ed.), *Herbert Hoover, the Great War and its Aftermath, 1914–23* (Iowa City, University of Iowa Press, 1979), pp. 111–42

P. 355   'Recognition of the . . .' Hoover, *The Ordeal*, p. 118

P. 355   '*We Jewish children* . . .' Hoover Institution, Palo Alto, California, ARA Papers, Book of thanks of children from Pinsk to Herbert Hoover, 1921. Thanks are due to Gillian Davidson, who translated the poem

P. 355   '*We, among thousands* . . .' Book of thanks. Thanks are due to Nicole Hochner, who translated the poem

P. 356   'There, thousands of . . .' Pete Scholliers and Ralph Daelemans, 'Belgium during the First World War', in J. M. Winter and R. Wall (eds), *The Upheaval of War: Family, Work and Welfare in Europe, 1914–1918* (Cambridge, Cambridge University Press, 1988), pp. 102–31

P. 356   'Hoover – an orphan . . .' George I. Gay and Harold

H. Fisher (eds), *Public Relations of the Committee for Relief in Belgium: Documents* (Stanford, Stanford University Press, 1929), vol. 1, pp. 21–2; Herbert Hoover, *Years of Adventure: 1874–1920* (New York, Macmillan, 1961), pp. 157–8

P. 356   'The frequently irritated . . .' Benjamin M. Weissman, *Herbert Hoover and Famine Relief to Soviet Russia 1921–1923* (Stanford, Hoover Institution Press, 1974), p. 24

PP. 356–7   'The Committee for . . .' Hoover, *Years of Adventure*, pp. 228–9

P. 357   'Some sent Hoover . . .' Many of these sacks are held at the Hoover Institution, Palo Alto, California. We are grateful to Elena Danielson for drawing them to our attention

P. 357   'He brushed aside . . .' Frank M. Surface and Raymond L. Bland, *American Food in the World War and Reconstruction Period: Operations of the Organizations under the direction of Herbert Hoover 1914–1924* (Stanford, Stanford University Press, 1931), p. 36

P. 357   'One of Hoover's . . .' Edward F. Willis, *Herbert Hoover and the Russian Prisoners of World War I* (Stanford, Stanford University Press, 1951), pp. 22–3

P. 357   'A population of . . .' Weissman, *Herbert Hoover and Famine Relief*, pp. 4–5

P. 357   'The Soviet republic . . .' Ibid. p. 10

P. 358   'On 26 July . . .' Ibid. pp. 47–8

P. 358   'At its peak . . .' Herbert H. Fisher, *The Famine in Soviet Russia, 1919–1923* (New York, Macmillan, 1927), p. 528

P. 358   'The finest palace . . .' Hoover Institution Archives, Palo Alto, Hoover ARA papers, photographs and commentary

8 WAR WITHOUT END

P. 361   'it was also the most important . . .' A point made eloquently by Samuel Hynes in *A War Imagined* (London, Bodley Head, 1990), p. 1

P. 362   'language itself changed . . .' The locus classicus of this argument is Paul Fussell, *The Great War and Modern Memory* (Oxford, Oxford University Press, 1975)

P. 362   'We who have known him . . .' Philippe Pétain, *Le Temps*, 19 Sept. 1927, as cited in Prost, '*Les représentations*', p. 18

P. 362   'This war democratized suffering.' J. M. Winter, 'Morale and Total War', in J. M. Winter, M. Haybeck and G. Parker (eds), *The First World War: 80 Years After* (New Haven, Yale University Press, 1996)

P. 364   'Among the poor . . .' For a fuller discussion of the social distribution of war losses, see J. M. Winter, *The Great War and the British People* (London, Macmillan, 1986), ch. 3

P. 364   'The agricultural laborers . . .' Serge Grafteaux, *Mémé Santerre: a French Woman of the People*, trans. by L. A. and K. L. Tilly (New York, Schocken, 1985), p. 83

P. 364 'The wounded came in many forms ...' Sophie Delaporte, 'Les Blessés de la face de la grande guerre', *Mémoire de maîtrise*, Université de Picardie Jules Verne, 1991–2, introduction (hereafter 'Les Blessés'); and Delaporte, 'Les défigurés de la grande guerre', *Guerres mondiales et conflits contemporains*, no. 175 (1994), pp. 103–21

P. 364 'He has only ...' Henriette Rémi, *Hommes sans visage* (Lausanne, s.p.e.s., 1942), pp. 21–3. I am grateful to Sophie Delaporte for providing me with a photocopy of this remarkable memoir

P. 368 'Then the boy ...' Ibid. pp. 89–109

P. 369 'Other disfigured men ...' Antoine Prost, *Les Anciens combattants et la société française 1914–39* (Paris, Presses de la Fondation Nationale des Sciences Politiques, 1977), ii, 52

PP. 369–70 'The idea was hatched ...' J. M. Winter, *Sites of Memory, Sites of Mourning* (Cambridge, Cambridge University Press, 1995), p. 36 (hereafter *Sites*)

P. 370 'In 1927 the association ...' Delaporte, 'Les Blessés', ch. 2

P. 370 'As Colonel Picot put it ...' Ibid. pp. 200–13

P. 370 'In Germany alone ...' Ernst Friedrich, *War against War!* (Seattle, The Real Comet Press, 1987), p. 225

PP. 370–1 'Not surprisingly, the Nazis ...' *Otto Dix 1891–1969* (London, Tate Gallery, 1992), pp. 99–101, 54. We are grateful for the advice of Sarah O'Brien-Twohig on this and other points

P. 371 'And so did the men ...' Winter, *The Great War and the British People*, p. 265

P. 372 'Everyone had lost someone ...' Ibid. ch. 8

P. 372 'Catherine, who was deaf ...' Herbert R. Lottman, *Albert Camus. A Biography* (London, Weidenfeld & Nicolson, 1979), chs 1–2

P. 373 '1885–1914, and ...' Albert Camus, *The First Man*, trans. by David Hapgood (New York, Alfred A. Knopf, 1995), pp. 25–8

P. 374 'light ash ...' Ibid. p. 314

P. 374 'needed someone ...' Ibid. p. 297

P. 374 'the first man ...' Ibid. pp. 195, 197

P. 374 'dead stranger ...' Ibid. p. 82

PP. 374–5 'consumed in a cosmic fire ...' Ibid. pp. 73, 70

P. 375 'war was the incubator ...' Ibid. p. 312

P. 375 'part of their universe ...' Ibid. p. 239

P. 375 'Some of the men ...' Ibid. p. 239

P. 375 'of a special kind ...' Ibid. pp. 147, 148

P. 375 'Germain helped to persuade ...' Ibid. p. 149

P. 376 'After the Armistice ...' J. M. Winter, 'Britain's "lost generation" of the First World War', *Population Studies*, xxxi (1977), pp. 482–504

P. 376 'Others used the phrase ...' Noel Riley Fitch, *Sylvia Beach and the Lost Generation: a History of Literary Paris in the Twenties and Thirties* (Harmondsworth, Penguin, 1985); Martin Green, *Children of the Sun: a Narrative of 'Decadence' in England* (London, Pimlico, 1992); Samuel Putnam, *Paris Was Our Mistress: Memoirs of a Lost and Found Generation* (New York, Viking Press, 1947)

P. 376 'Part of the sense ...' Jeremy Wilson, *Lawrence of Arabia* (London, Heinemann, 1989), p. 460 (hereafter *Lawrence*)

P. 376 'Some writers account ...' *Lawrence*, p. 666

P. 376 'What's the cause ...' Ibid. p. 668

P. 377 'As Lawrence put it ...' Ibid. p. 598

P. 377 'I have not come here ...' Ibid. p. 599

P. 378 'Here his war experience ...' Ibid. p. 696

P. 378 'But his search ...' Ibid. p. 710

P. 378 'reason proves ...' Lawrence to Lionel Curtis, 19 March 1923, in D. Garnett (ed.), *The Letters of T. E. Lawrence* (London, Jonathan Cape, 1938), p. 412. (hereafter *Lawrence Letters*)

P. 378 'When my mood ...' Lawrence to Curtis, 14 May 1923, *Lawrence Letters*, pp. 416–17

P. 378 'I know the reverse ...' *Lawrence*, p. 739

P. 378 'He even went ...' Ibid. p. 789

P. 379 'I went into ...' Lawrence to Graves, 4 Feb. 1935, *Lawrence Letters*, p. 853

P. 379 'When T. E. Lawrence died ...' Winter, *Sites*, pp. 97–8

P. 382 'Soldiers knew that ...' The artists who gathered in Zurich from 1916 to form Dada, the art of nonsense, are the exception that proves the rule. See Hans Bolliger, Guido Magnaguagno, Raimund Meyer, *Dada in Zürich* (Zurich, Arche/Kunsthaus, 1985); Marc Dachy, *Journal du mouvement Dada* (Geneva, Skira, 1990); Tristan Tzara, *Lampisteries, précédées des Sept manifestes Dada* (Paris, J. J. Pauvert, 1963)

P. 382 'This was Christianity ...' See David Lloyd, 'Tourism, pilgrimage and the commemoration of the Great War in Great Britain, Australia and Canada, 1919–1939', PhD thesis, Cambridge, 1995

P. 382 'Lying in an old trench ...' Stephen Graham, *The Challenge of the Dead* (London, Cassell, 1921), p. 28 (hereafter *Challenge*)

P. 382 'There is a pull ...' Graham, *Challenge*, p. 36

P. 382 'To this day ...' Winter, *Sites*, ch. 1; Romy Golan, *Modernity and Nostalgia. Art and Politics in France between the Wars* (New Haven, Yale University Press, 1995), ch. 1

P. 382 'His brother ...' Kevin I. Jones, *Conan Doyle and the Spirits. The Spiritualist Career of Sir Arthur Conan Doyle* (Wellingborough, Aquarian, 1989), pp. 109, 129, 131 (hereafter *Conan Doyle*)

P. 382 'Apparently her voice ...' Jones, *Conan Doyle*, p. 111

P. 384 'in any case ...' Ibid. p. 131

P. 384 'Conan Doyle's brother ...' Ibid. p. 131

P. 385 'Such rituals ...' Winter, *Sites*, ch. 3

P. 385 'Some Spiritualists ...' See Nicole Edelman, 'L'histoire du spiritisme en France 1850–1914', Thèse d'état, Université de Paris-VII (1992); and Alex Owen, *The Darkened Room, Women, Power and Spiritualism in Late Nineteenth Century England* (Cambridge, Cambridge University Press, 1989)

P. 385 'The business of psychic ...' See 'The ghost in the machine', *Observer*, 6 Feb. 1989

P. 385 'The inchoate mass ...' British Library, Barlow Collection, Cup.407.a.1, E. J. Dingwall, 'Psychic Photography', introduction, p. 6; and E. Stead, 'Faces of the Living Dead'. We are grateful to Dr

Joanna Bourke for referring us to this valuable collection

P. 387 'Like the tombs...' Winter, *Sites*, ch. 4

P. 387 'The phrase...' Hans Kollwitz (ed.), *The Diary and Letters of Kaethe Kollwitz*, trans. by R. and C. Winston (Evanston, Ill., Northwestern University Press, 1955), diary entry of 23 July 1932 (hereafter *Kollwitz Diary*)

P. 387 'I have felt you...' *Kollwitz Diary*, 13 Oct. 1916, p. 76; letter to Hans Kollwitz, 16 Jan. 1916, ibid. p. 147

P. 387 'Even after the pain...' Ibid. 22 April 1931, p. 119

P. 390 'in the back of the individual...' Letter to Hans Kollwitz, 21 Feb. 1915, ibid. p. 146

P. 390 'pure heart...' Ibid. 11 Oct. 1916, p. 74

P. 390 'love for an idea...' Ibid. 1 Feb. 1917, p. 78

P. 390 'but still she had wept...' Ibid. 1 Aug. 1919, p. 93

P. 390 'Is it a break...' Ibid. 11 Oct. 1916, p. 74

P. 391 'This recognition...' Ibid. 19 March 1918, pp. 87–8

PP. 391–2 'we went from...' Ibid. 14 Aug. 1932, p. 122

P. 392 'It is almost incomprehensible...' Letter to Hans Kollwitz, 16 April 1945, ibid. p. 196

P. 392 'the Nazis came to power...' For some recent accounts, see Ian Kershaw, *Hitler* (Harlow, Longman, 1991); Karl Dietrich Bracher, *Die deutsche Diktatur: Entstehung, Struktur, Folgen des Nationalsozialismus* (Frankfurt, Ullstein, 1979); Martin Broszat, *Hitler and the Collapse of Weimar Germany*, trans. by V. Berghahn (Leamington Spa, Berg, 1987); William Sheridan Allen, *The Nazi Seizure of Power: The Experience of a single German town, 1922–45* (Harmondsworth, Penguin, 1989)

P. 394 'Born to a devout...' Rudolf Hoess, *Commandant of Auschwitz*, trans. by Constantine Fitzgibbon (London, Weidenfeld & Nicolson, 1959), p. 29 (hereafter *Commandant*)

P. 394 'My father had...' Ibid. p. 31

P. 394 'It was constantly...' Ibid. p. 32

P. 394 'His sense of...' Ibid. pp. 34–5

P. 394 'I never tired...' Ibid. pp. 35–6

P. 394 'He killed his first...' Joachim C. Fest, *The Face of the Third Reich* (London, Weidenfeld & Nicolson, 1970), p. 28

P. 395 'From Damascus...' *Commandant*, p. 41

P. 396 'the beautiful...' As cited in R. G. L. Waite, *Vanguard of Nazism. The Free Corps Movement in Postwar Germany 1918–1923* (Cambridge, Harvard University Press, 1952), pp. 51–2

P. 396 'Fighting was the...' As cited in ibid. p. 52

P. 397 'He shielded...' *Commandant*, pp. 44–5

P. 397 'He had served...' Ibid. p. 61

P. 397 'He agreed...' Ibid. p. 62

P. 397 'He joined...' Klaus Theweleit, *Male Fantasies, 1. Women, floods, bodies, history*, trans. by S. Conway (Cambridge, Polity Press, 1987), p. 19

P. 397 'The temptation of...' *Commandant*, p. 64

P. 397 'This led him...' Ibid. p. 64n

P. 397 'Any show of...' Ibid. p. 68

P. 397 'he placed over...' Ibid. p. 77

P. 397 'Transferred to the...' Ibid. p. 82

P. 398 'Höss himself...' Ibid. p. 85

P. 398 'had many and...' Ibid. p. 98

P. 398 'Like Höss...' Martin Niemöller, *From U-Boat to Concentration Camp* (London, William Hodge & Co, 1939)

P. 398 'Recent research...' Deborah Dwork and Robert van Pelt, *Auschwitz* (New Haven, Yale University Press, 1996)

P. 398 'A maze of...' Primo Levi, *Survival in Auschwitz*, and *The reawakening: two memoirs*, trans. by Stuart Woolf (New York, Summit Books, 1986)

P. 398 'The Nazis...' Martin Amis, *Time's Arrow* (Harmondsworth, Penguin, 1991), p. 176

P. 398 'the Jewish Action' *Commandant*, p. 117

P. 398 'But he found...' Ibid. pp. 130–1

P. 398 'So was the...' Ibid. p. 139

P. 399 'But on 11 March...' Ibid. p. 173

P. 399 'male comradeship' For Höss's views on women, see Theweleit, *Male Fantasies*, 8–9, 18, 101, 134–8, 154, 196

P. 402 'But instead of reacting...' The best study of this phase of Pasternak's life is Christopher Barnes, *Boris Pasternak. A Literary Biography, Volume 1, 1890–1928* (Cambridge, Cambridge University Press, 1989). See page 13 for Jewish evictions from Moscow and Pasternak's baptism

P. 402 'There in 1903...' Ibid. pp. 48–9

PP. 402–3 'A True European...' Ibid. p. 111

P. 403 'in the last summer...' Ibid. p. 175

P. 403 'inhuman act...' Ibid. p. 178

P. 403 'Anti-German riots...' p. 186

P. 403 'abyss which is...' Ibid. p. 214

P. 403 'Just imagine...' As cited in Barnes, *Pasternak*, p. 224

P. 403 'This fearlessness...' Boris Pasternak, *Doctor Zhivago*, trans. by Max Hayward and Manya Harari (London, The Harvill Press, 1988), p. 177 (hereafter *Zhivago*)

P. 403 'its pitiless remedies...' Ibid. p. 451

PP. 403–4 'I believe now...' Ibid. pp. 395–6

P. 404 'In the days...' Ibid. p. 111

P. 404 'Nowadays the very air...' As cited in Barnes, *Pasternak*, p. 249

P. 404 'Typhus was everywhere...' Ibid. p. 247

P. 404 'less and less revolutionary...' Ibid. p. 251

P. 404 'Here Soviet rule...' As cited in ibid. p. 253

P. 404 'an epoch of shades...' As cited in ibid. p. 315

P. 404 'Wake up, poet...' As cited in ibid. p. 322

P. 404 'The age's sickly eyelids...' As cited in ibid. p. 326

P. 404 'Everything is corroded...' As cited in Elliott Mossman (ed.), *The Correspondence of Boris Pasternak and Olga Freidenberg 1910–1954* (New York, Harcourt Brace Jovanovich, 1981), p. xix (hereafter *Freidenberg Correspondence*)

P. 405 'Every line...' As cited in Barnes, *Pasternak*, p. 399

P. 405 'He had the mad...' On Mandelstam, see Nadezhda Mandelstam, *Hope against Hope*, trans. by Max Hayward (London, Collins, 1971), and Nadezhda Mandelstam, *Hope Abandoned*, trans. by Max Hayward (New York, Athenaeum, 1974)

P. 405 'As you know, the terror...' *Freidenberg*

P. 405   *Correspondence*, Letter to Olga, 10 May 1928

'The charismatic poet ...' On Mayakovsky, see Herbert Marshall (ed.), *Mayakovsky and His Poetry* (London, Pilot Press, 1942); and Barnes, *Pasternak*, pp. 412–13

P. 405   'Pasternak never endorsed ...' Peter Levi, *Boris Pasternak* (London, Hutchinson, 1990), p. 165 (hereafter Levi, *Pasternak*)

P. 406   'The first struggle ...' Mandelstam, *Hope against Hope*, p. 13

PP. 406–7   'When Mandelstam recited ...' Levi, *Pasternak*, p. 183

P. 407   'Stalin hung up ...' Mandelstam, *Hope against Hope*, pp. 143–7

P. 407   'He died within ...' Mandelstam, *Hope Abandoned*, pp. 433–7

P. 407   'Pasternak also begged ...' Levi, *Pasternak*, p. 187

P. 407   'miserable and completely ...' *Freidenberg Correspondence*, p. 223

P. 407   'Pasternak's name appeared ...' Levi, *Pasternak*, p. 191

P. 407   'Everything snapped ...' As cited in Levi, *Pasternak*, p. 191

P. 407   '*In an age of* ...' Ibid. pp. 192–3

P. 409   'He raised his head ...' *Zhivago*, p. 11

P. 409   'For a short while they create ...' *Zhivago*, p. 430

FURTHER READING

Readers can find on pages 410–22 sources for the direct citations or scholarly support for the interpretations offered in this book. For those who wish to pursue particular subjects more deeply, or to follow up suggestions made in the text, we offer the following brief reader's guide to recent historical literature on the First World War.

1 EXPLOSION

The best account of the war crisis of 1914 is the final chapter of Volker Berghahn's magisterial *Imperial Germany* (Oxford, Berghahn Books, 1994). On the explosive growth of pre-1914 Europe, see Eric Hobsbawm's *The Age of Empire 1865–1914* (London, Weidenfeld & Nicolson, 1987). *Rites of Spring* (New York, Bantam Books, 1990) by Modris Eksteins is full of insights on cultural ferment. On the socialist movement. J. P. Nettl's masterly life of *Rosa Luxemburg* (Oxford, Oxford University Press, 1966) is still the best introduction. Harvey Goldberg's *Life of Jean Jaurès* (Oxford, Oxford University Press, 1966) is definitive.

2 STALEMATE

On the Schlieffen Plan, Martin van Creveld's two studies *Supplying War* (Cambridge, Cambridge University Press, 1977) and *Command in Wartime* (Cambridge, Mass., Harvard University Press, 1985) are still the most persuasive. On the Christmas truce, Eksteins is stimulating, as is Malcolm Brown and Shirley Seaton's *Christmas Truce: The Western Front December 1914* (London, Macmillan, 1994). Tony Ashworth's *Trench Warfare* (London, Macmillan, 1980) carries the story into 1915. On the humanization of trench warfare by soldiers themselves, the best studies are Stéphane Audoin-Rouzeau's *Men at War National sentiment and Trench Journalism in France during the First World War* (Oxford, Berg, 1992) and John Fuller's *Troop Morale and Popular Culture in the British and Dominion Armies 1914–18* (Oxford, Oxford University Press, 1991).

3 TOTAL WAR

On Gallipoli, the best work is Bill Gammage, *The Broken Years* (Cairns, University of Queensland Press, 1975). On the Armenian genocide, see Richard G. Hovannisian (ed.), *The Armenian Genocide in Perspective* (London, Allen & Unwin, 1985). On women's work and war industry, see the essays in two recent collections of essays, M. Higonnet *et al.* (eds), *Behind the Lines* (New Haven, Yale University Press, 1990) and J. M. Winter and R. Wall (eds), *The Upheaval of War* (Cambridge, Cambridge University Press, 1988). On propaganda and the general cultural history of the war, see J.-J. Becker *et al.* (eds), *La très grande guerre* (Paris, Le Monde, 1994). On war industry, see Gerald Feldman, *Army, Industry and Labor in Germany* (Oxford, Berg, 1992), P. Fridenson (ed.), *The French Home Front* (Oxford, Berg, 1992), and Gerd Hardach, *The First World War* (London, Penguin, 1980).

4 SLAUGHTER

On morale and the nature of combat, see J. Keegan, *The Face of Battle* (London, Penguin, 1976); E. Leed, *No Man's Land* (Cambridge, Cambridge University Press, 1979), Len Smith, *Between Mutiny and Obedience* (Princeton, Princeton University Press, 1994), and Denis Winter, *Death's Men* (London, Penguin, 1980). On Verdun, the Somme and Passchendaele, the best introductions are Alistair Horne, *Verdun 1916. The Price of Glory* (London, Penguin, 1962); Trevor Wilson, *The Myriad Faces of War* (Cambridge, Polity Press, 1986), and two books by Robin Pryor and Trevor Wilson, *Command on the Western Front* (Oxford, Blackwell, 1992) and *Passchendaele. The Untold Story* (New Haven, Yale University Press, 1996). On the Eastern front, Norman Stone's *The Eastern Front* (London, Weidenfeld & Nicolson, 1974) should be read alongside John Reed's *Eastern Europe at War* (London, Pluto, 1994). On soldiers' journals, see S. Audoin-Rouzeau, *Men at War 1914–1918;* and John Fuller, *Troop Morale and Popular Culture*. We still await a scholarly account of German soldiers' journals.

5 MUTINY

On shell shock, see Eric Leed, *No Man's Land* (Cambridge, Cambridge University Press, 1979); E. Showalter, *The Female Malady* (Princeton, Princeton University Press, 1990), and the splendid fictional trilogy of Pat Barker, *Regeneration*, *The Eye in the Door* and *The Ghost Road* (all London, Penguin, 1992, 1994, 1995). On mutiny, Len Smith, *Between Mutiny and Obedience* (Princeton, Princeton University Press, 1994), Daniel Horn, *German Naval Mutinies of the First World War* (New Brunswick, Rutgers University Press, 1970), and A. Wildman, *The End of the Imperial Army* (Princeton, Princeton University Press, 1979). On German dissent and repression, see C. Schorske, *The Great Schism* (Princeton, Princeton University Press, 1970), and Barrington Moore, *Injustice* (London, Macmillan, 1980). On the Russian Revolution, contrasting interpretations include Richard Pipes, *The Russian Revolution 1899 – 1919* (London, Fontana, 1992), and Rex Wade, *Red Guards and Workers' Militias in the Russian Revolution* (Stanford, Calif., Stanford University Press, 1984).

6 COLLAPSE

On the rule of Hindenburg and Ludendorff in 1918, see Martin Kitchen, *The Silent Dictatorship* (London, Batsford, 1976), and the classic work of Arthur Rosenberg, *Imperial Germany: the Birth of the German Republic 1871 – 1918*, trans. by I. F. D. Morrow (Boston, Beacon Press, 1964). On the greater ability of the Allies to feed their people, see L. Borchardt, 'The impact of the war economy on the civilian population', in W. Deist (ed.), *The German Military in the Age of Total War* (Leamington Spa, Berg, 1987); A. Offer, *The First World War. An Agrarian Interpretation* (Oxford, Oxford University Press, 1989), and J. M. Winter, *The Great War and the British People* (London, Macmillan, 1986). On America in the war, the best guides are David Kennedy, *Over Here* (New York, Random House, 1985) and Ron Schaeffer, *America and the Great War*. See also David McCulloch, *Truman* (New York, Simon & Schuster, 1992), and August Heckscher, *Woodrow Wilson. A Biography* (New York, Scribners, 1991).

7 HATRED AND HUNGER

On the assassinations of the Tsar and Rosa Luxemburg, see Robert Massie, 'The last Romanov mystery', *New Yorker* (8 Aug. 1995) and Elzbieta Ettinger, *Rosa Luxemburg. A Life* (Boston, Beacon Press, 1986). On the German revolution, see A. J. Ryder, *The German Revolution of 1918* (Cambridge, Cambridge University Press, 1967) and the fictional account in L. Doblin, *Karl and Rosa*, trans. by R. Manheim (London, Allen & Unwin, 1967). On peacemaking, see Arno Mayer's two volumes, *Wilson versus Lenin* (Princeton, Princeton University Press, 1970) and *The Politics and Diplomacy of Peacemaking* (New York, Random House, 1973). On the Hoover mission, we still await a comprehensive study. For other voices, see Harvey Pitcher, *Witnesses of the Russian Revolution* (London, John Murray, 1994).

8 WAR WITHOUT END

On casualties, see J. M. Winter, *The Great War and the British People* (London, Macmillan, 1986). On the cultural history of the war and its aftermath, see Paul Fussell, *The Great War and Modern Memory* (Oxford, Oxford University Press, 1975); Samuel Hynes, *A War Imagined* (London, Bodley Head, 1990); George Mosse, *Fallen Soldiers* (New York, Oxford University Press, 1990); J. M. Winter, *Sites of Memory, Sites of Mourning* (Cambridge, Cambridge University Press, 1995); and the two volumes edited by J.-J. Becker *et al.*, *Guerre et cultures* (Paris, Armand Colin, 1994) and *14 – 18. La très grande guerre* (Paris, Le Monde, 1994). On the political, social and economic aftermath, see Adrian Gregory, *The Silence of Memory: Armistice Day, 1919 – 1946* (Oxford, Berg, 1994); Antoine Prost, *In the Wake of War, 'Les anciens combattants' and French society 1914 – 1939*, trans. by Helen McPhail (Providence, Berg, 1992), and, more generally, Eric Hobsbawm, *The Age of Extremes* (London, Michael Joseph, 1995).

PERMISSIONS

The authors and publishers are grateful to the following for permission to quote from the copyright material listed below. Although every effort has been made to acknowledge all copyright holders either here or in the Notes, we apologize if there are any errors or omissions, and invite copyright holders to contact us for correction in future editions if they have been omitted.

Anvil Press Poetry: 'Here is the Coffin' is taken from *Apollinaire Selected Poems*, trans. by Oliver Bernard published by Anvil Press Poetry in 1986.

Professor Stephen Bronner: *The Letters of Rosa Luxemburg*, ed. by Stephen Bronner.

Cambridge University: Christopher Barnes, *Boris Pasternak: A Literary Biography* and J. C. G. Rohl and N. Sombard (eds.), *Kaiser Wilhelm I*.

Chatto & Windus: Fritz Fisher, *Germany's Aims in the First World*.

Chatto & Windus, Harcourt Brace & Co. and the Estate of Virginia Woolf: *The Diary of Virginia Woolf*, ed. by Anne Olivier Bell.

Chatto & Windus, New Directions Publishing Corp. and the Estate of Cecil Day-Lewis: *Wilfred Owen: The Collected Poems of Wilfred Owen*. Copyright © 1964 by Chatto & Windus.

Constable & Co Ltd: Evelyn, Princess Blucher, *An English Wife in Berlin*.

Editions Denoël, Paris: Henri Desagneux, *Journal de guerre 1914–18*.

Duke University Press: *A Russian Civil War Diary: Alexis Babine in Saratov 1917–1922*, ed. by Donald J. Raleigh. Copyright 1988, Duke University Press, Durham, N.C. Reprinted with permission.

Martin Gibbs and Mrs Frances McElwaine: Philip Gibbs, *War Despatches*.

Gill & Macmillan Publishers: Max Caulfield, *The Easter Rebellion*.

Greenhill Books: Cecil Lewis, *Sagittarius Rising* and Erwin Rommel, *Infantry Attacks*.

George Alexander Eujene Douglas, The Earl Haig: *The Private Papers of Douglas Haig, 1914–1919*.

Harcourt Brace & Company: Elliott Mossman (ed), *The Correspondence of Boris Pasternak and Olga Freidenberg*.

Harvard University Press: Robert G. L. Waite, *Vanguard of Nazism: The Free Corps Movement in Postwar Germany 1918–1923*. Copyright © 1952 by the President and Fellows of Harvard College. Reprinted by permission of Harvard University Press.

The Harvill Press: Boris Pasternak: *Doctor Zhivago*, first published in Great Britain by Collins and Harvill 1958. © Giangiacomo Feltrinelli Editore 1958. © in the English translation by Manya Harari and Max Hayward.

Henry Holt and Company, Inc.: Martin Gilbert, *The First World War*. Copyright © 1994 by Martin Gilbert. Reprinted by permission.

John Johnson Ltd: Peter Levi, *Boris Pasternak*.

Jonathan Cape: Robert K. Massie, *Dreadnought* and D. Garnett (ed.), *The Letters of T. E. Lawrence*.

David Macfarlane, Little Brown and Simon & Schuster: *The Danger Tree: Memory, War & the Search for a Family's Past* (published in the USA and UK as *Come from Away*).

Macmillan Press Ltd and St Martin's Press Inc: P. J. Flood, *France: 1914–18*.

Methuen & Co: Sir James Healam-Morlay, *Memoir of the Paris Peace Conference*.

Martin Middlebrook and A. P. Watt Ltd.: *The First Day on the Somme* and *The Kaiser's Battle*.

Christopher Middleton and Grove Press: Georg Heym's poem 'Umra Vitae' in a translation by C. Middleton from *Modern German Poets*.

Dr Jan Niemöller: Martin Niemöller, *From U-Boat to Concentration Camp*.

Pathfinder Press: Leon Trotsky, *My Life: An Attempt at an Autobiography*. Reprinted by permission of Pathfinder Press. Copyright © 1970 by Pathfinder Press.

Librarie Plon: Maréchal Fayolle, *Les cahiers secrets de la Grande Guerre*.

Librarie Plon and Yale University Press: Pierre-Jakez Helias, *The Horse of Pride: Life in a Breton Village*.

Peter Owen Publishers: Jean Giono, *To the Slaughterhouse*.

Oxford University Press: Andrew Clark, *Echoes of the Great War: the Diary of the Reverend Andrew Clark*, R. G. Collingwood, *An Autobiography* and J. P. Nettl, *Rosa Luxemburg*.

Oxford University Press and New Directions Publishing Corp.: Harold Owen, *Journey from Obscurity* and Wilfred Owen: *Collected Letters*.

Princeton University Press: Charles Maland, *Chaplin and American Culture*; Len Smith, *Between Mutiny and Obedience*; John M. Thompson, *Russia, Bolshevism and the Versailles Peace*; Arthur S. Link (ed.), *The Deliberations of the Council of Four*; J. Johnston, *English Poetry of the First World War: A Study of the Evolution of Lyric and Narrative Form*.

Random House UK Ltd: Samuel Hynes, *A War Imagined* and Ernst Jünger, *Storm of Steel*.

Reed Books: Michael Moynihan (ed.), *God on Our Side* and Jeremy Wilson, *Lawrence of Arabia*.

Rutgers University Press: *War, Mutiny and Revolution in the German Navy: The World War I Diary of Seaman Richard Stumpf*, edited, translated and with an introduction by Daniel Horn, copyright © 1967 by Rutgers, The State University. Reprinted by permission of Rutgers University Press.

George T. Sassoon: *The War Poems of Siegfried Sassoon*.

George T. Sassoon and Faber & Faber: Siegfried Sassoon, *Memoirs of an Infantry Officer, Sherston's Progress, Siegfried Sassoon Diaries 1915–18* (ed. by Rupert Hart-Davis) and *Siegfried's Journey 1916–20*.

Stanford University Press: R. H. Lutz (ed.), *The Fall of the German Empire*.

Myfanwy Thomas and Carcanet Press Ltd: Helen Thomas, *World Without End* (now published with *As It Was* under the title *Under Storm's Wing*).

Professor L. Tilley and Schocken Books: Serge Grafteaux, *Madame Santerre: A French Woman of the People* trans. by L. A. and K. L. Tilly.

Transworld Publishers: Modris Eksteins, *Rites of Spring*, © Modris Eksteins 1989. Published by Bantam Press, an imprint of Transworld Publishers Ltd. All rights reserved.

University of California Press and Editions Denoël: 'The War in Luxembourg Gardens' from Blaise Cendrars, *Complete Poems*, trans. and edited by Ron Padgett. Copyright © Ron Padgett, © 1947 Editions Denoël.

University of Washington Press: Douglas Robinson, *The Zeppelin in Combat*.

University of Wisconsin Press, Madison: Harvey Goldberg, *The Life of Jean Jaurès* © 1962. Reprinted by permission of The University of Wisconsin Press.

Frederick Warne & Co: Edmund Campion, *Some Desperate Glory*.

Weidenfeld & Nicolson: Rudolf Hoess, *Commandant of Auschwitz*.

Anne Westman: Stephen Westman, *Surgeon with the Kaiser's Army*.

PICTURE CREDITS

INDEX

Page numbers in *italic* refer to the illustrations and their captions